Religious Traditions in Modern South Asia

F   RSTT

This book offers a fresh approach to the study of religion in modern South Asia. It uses a series of case studies to explore the development of religious ideas and practices, giving students an understanding of the social, political and historical context. It looks at some familiar themes in the study of religion, such as deity, authoritative texts, myth, worship, teacher traditions and caste, and some of the key ways in which Buddhism, Hinduism, Islam and Sikhism in South Asia have been shaped in the modern period. The book points to the diversity of ways of looking at religious traditions and considers the impact of gender and politics, and the way religion itself is variously understood.

Jacqueline Suthren Hirst is Senior Lecturer in South Asian Studies at the University of Manchester, UK. Her publications include *Sita's Story* and *Śaṃkara's Advaita Vedānta: A Way of Teaching*.

John Zavos is Senior Lecturer in South Asian Studies at the University of Manchester, UK. He is the author of *The Emergence of Hindu Nationalism in India*.

Religious Traditions in Modern South Asia

Jacqueline Suthren Hirst
and John Zavos

Routledge
Taylor & Francis Group

LONDON AND NEW YORK

First published 2011
by Routledge
2 Park Square, Milton Park, Abingdon, Oxon OX14 4RN

Simultaneously published in the USA and Canada
by Routledge
711 Third Avenue, New York, NY 10017

*Routledge is an imprint of the Taylor & Francis Group, an informa
business*

British Library Cataloguing in Publication Data
A catalogue record for this book is available from the British Library

Library of Congress Cataloging in Publication Data
A catalog record for this book has been requested

ISBN: 978–0–415–44787–4 (hbk)
ISBN: 978–0–415–44788–1 (pbk)
ISBN: 978–0–203–80242–7 (ebk)

Typeset in Sabon
by Prepress Projects Ltd, Perth, UK

MIX
Paper from
responsible sources
FSC
www.fsc.org   FSC® C004839   Printed and bound in Great Britain by the MPG Books Group

Contents

vi *Contents*

Figures

Boxes

Preface

This book began life in a series of conversations amongst colleagues at the University of Manchester in the early and mid-2000s. At that time, we were fortunate to have the input of a range of scholars whose research work focused on religious traditions in South Asia. Along with ourselves, Roger Ballard, Jeanne Openshaw, Mary Searle-Chatterjee, Alan Williams and, later, Nile Green and Atreyee Sen were all engaged in research work that explored elements of the dynamic, developing histories and contemporary practices associated with these traditions. As we have all at various times been part of the Department of Religions and Theology (with colleagues in South Asian Studies in other departments across the university), we have all also been engaged in teaching about these traditions, confronting the challenges thrown up by the postcolonial twins that are 'South Asian Studies' and 'Religious Studies'. Our book is an attempt to come to terms with these challenges, bringing together our own research interests and our joint interest in opening up new ways of teaching and learning about the field of study that we love.

Being able to identify these two 'postcolonial twins' is very much the result of stimulating research work in these two areas of study over the past thirty years or so. Both 'South Asia' and 'Religion' have been subjected to some rigorous and vigorous critique by scholars such as Dipesh Chakrabarty, Sudipto Kaviraj, Gayatri Spivak, Peter van der Veer, Richard King and Timothy Fitzgerald. In particular, such scholars as these have challenged established structures of knowledge, by considering how the encounters and entanglements of colonialism have contributed to the development of modern social and political relations, and modern cultural practices. In the light of such work, research on religious traditions in and of South Asia has taken a critical and reflexive turn, exploring the categories through which we understand everyday life in an attempt to get closer to understandings of just how such life has been and is experienced.

This is challenging enough in a research context. In a teaching context, we have found that the challenge is often amplified. This is partly because many students in our experience have entered university with quite fixed ideas of what religion is. Within this framework, they then have further fixed ideas about what South Asian religion should constitute. Often, these ideas are fashioned through the experience of Religious Education at school. In the UK at least, the study of Christianity often continues to dominate while the study of other traditions is very much configured by what we have come to know as the 'World Religions' model. Such a model is also encouraged by Ethics syllabuses, which require students to respond to particular issues from the point of view of different religions. This World Religions model is the model through which religion is understood as a universal, generic category, within which a range of sub-categories articulate the experience of billions of people around the world in terms of six or seven discrete 'systems' (Buddhism, Christianity, Hinduism, Islam, Judaism, Sikhism – and sometimes Bahai and/or Jainism and/or Zoroastrianism as well). As you will come to see as you read our book, we recognize the significance of this model as a real force in the shaping of people's lives. At the same time, we are keen to introduce other ways of looking, because we believe that it is only through such multiple perspectives that it is possible to encompass the very diverse ways in which people have experienced in the past, and continue to experience in the present, what is referred to by the umbrella term 'religion'.[1] Teaching and learning about South Asian religious traditions in particular demands this multiplex approach, because it enables us to de-centre [or, to borrow a term from Chakrabarty (2000), provincialize] the World Religions model, to explore the possibility of other ways of experiencing and understanding the world, and to unpack the relations of power through which dominant ways of looking are established.

In addressing these issues, we have often been struck by the way in which texts designed for students seem to re-instantiate these relations of power, by presenting 'the religions of South Asia' as discrete, self-evident forms. Many of the texts we have used in a teaching context do this implicitly by presenting students with an introduction to Hinduism, Sikhism and so on. Even those that seek to encompass a broader range of traditions often present these traditions separately in different chapters. A recent work edited by the US-based scholars Sushil Mittal and Gene Thursby (2006) takes this approach, presenting nine well-informed chapters that deal with Hinduism, Jainism, Buddhism, Sikhism, Zoroastrianism, Judaism, Christianity, Islam and Bahai in turn. In their introduction, Mittal and Thursby do acknowledge theoretical work that interrogates such categories, and have included a concluding chapter that addresses these issues. At the same time, they argue that the introductory nature of the book means that such issues should be dealt with after students have been acquainted with 'good to think with' prototypes or first models of traditions, unburdened by 'on-going problems and alternative perspectives that are debated at scholarly conferences and in academic journals' (Mittal and Thursby 2006: 9). Our approach is different. We believe that it is important for students to engage with these problems and perspectives in the first instance, in order to encourage them to develop a critical approach to their material. Engendering a critical approach, in which the idea of religion is approached contextually, will help students to come to their material without presuppositions about what Hinduism, Sikhism, Islam and so on 'are'.

Our approach has been developed through close discussion with colleagues at Manchester and at two international seminars in 2001 and 2003 focused on 'teaching across South Asian religious traditions'. This work then led us to guest edit a special issue of the journal *Contemporary South Asia* on this topic in 2005 (Volume 14, Number 1), showcasing a range of articles with different ways of approaching the diverse religious traditions of the region. Since then we have engaged in research and teaching projects that have helped us to develop our ideas further. In particular, the broader Religions and Theology research cluster at Manchester held a series of internal seminars in 2004 and 2005 that looked to interrogate the category of religion across the diverse range of our collective research interests. This project led to a collective publication (Green and Searle-Chatterjee 2008) in which both of us published essays that extended our thinking about alternative ways of looking at our field. As you can see, then, the ideas that inform this book have been germinating for some time, and we are very grateful to all our colleagues at Manchester for their encouragement, and for helping to engender a stimulating environment in which research and teaching are persistently held to be in dialogue.

On this basis, of course, we also owe a great deal to our students over the years. We have both been inspired and challenged by students who have shown an enormous enthusiasm both for new material and for new ways of approaching that material. In particular we have been helped in the writing of this book by the following, who have read sections of it for us – Harry Bonnell, Jenni Jackson, Francesca Robinson, Priya Thakrar and her father Vijay Thakrar – and by others who have gone out of their way to help us find illustrations to bring this book to life, including Deepa Ganesh and James Madaio. We would also like to thank Dan Wand for his technical help in turning transparencies into digital images for us.

We are also grateful to a range of international colleagues who have replied to queries large and small with a generosity and speed that has been very much appreciated. Their work is credited in the book. To two of them our special thanks. Mary Searle-Chatterjee read parts of this book, often at short notice, and made her usual sharply perceptive comments. Nile Green, now at the University of California Los Angeles, generously made available to us the ethnographic material in Chapter 5, and has replied tirelessly to our numerous emails. The faults of the book remain, of course, our own.

Finally, we both wish to thank our families, Guy, Sara and Rebecca Hirst, and Christina, Niki, Callum and Isla Macrae. They have been so supportive, bringing us measured perspectives, material refreshments, hands to hold and, of course, love, to the very end!

A note on orthography (how words are written)

In this book, you will come across a range of terms drawn from various South Asian languages. These include Sanskrit, Tamil and Persian, as well as a range of languages that developed particular modern forms in our period, for example Bengali, Hindi and Urdu. These, with many others, are all languages that have been important in South Asia for various reasons in the past and present. They are written in a range of different scripts. They also include sounds that are not all the same as those in English. It is therefore not always straightforward representing their sounds in the roman letters in which English is written (the kind we are using here!). Scholars for each of these languages have developed internationally agreed ways of transliterating them, that is, representing their sounds in roman letters. This involves writing some letters with what are called diacritical marks to distinguish them as different from one another in the original language. So, for example, Sanskrit includes four different 'n' sounds that are represented in roman as ñ, ṅ, ṇ and n, and two slightly different 'sh' sounds: ṣ and ś. In particular, when writing many of these languages in roman script, long vowels (e.g. 'ā' as in c*a*r, rather than short 'a' as in southern English 'b*u*t') are marked by a macron (the bar over the roman letter). We asked our students whether they thought we should include these diacriticals to help you learn how to pronounce the words correctly, or whether this would just make it too confusing. They all had different views! In the end, we have dispensed with most diacriticals but have retained them in quotations and the bibliography. This tends to follow the convention of anthropologists, and fly in the face of textual scholars. As we include both amongst our range of approaches we hope you will bear with us.

What you will notice also is that some words have variant spellings in this book. There are two main reasons for this. '*Shaykh*', '*sheikh*' and '*shaikh*' are all different ways of representing the same Perso-Arabic word for an authoritative teacher or person of status. We use one standard form ('*shaykh*') but other authors we quote may use different ones. Somewhat differently, 'Ramayana', 'Rama' and 'Lakshmana' all represent the pronunciation of these names in Sanskrit, whereas 'Ramayan', 'Ram' and 'Lakshman' represent their pronunciation in Hindi and some other modern Indian languages. We have used the spellings for these appropriate to the particular context.

To help with this and to help you keep track of the other Indian language terms we use, we have provided an extensive glossary at the end of the book. As well as sounding different and being written differently, words from other languages do not always have a straightforward translation into English – their meanings may vary in different contexts, or they may represent ideas that are very different from those that are expressed in English. It is of course our responsibility to provide translations that will help you get to grips with such ideas. We hope, though, that you will find that becoming familiar with such terms helps you in understanding some of the many varying ways – some overlapping, some taking radically different directions – in which people see our world.

1 Introducing South Asia, re-introducing 'religion'

'South Asia' is the name given to a region that includes the modern nation-states of Bangladesh, Bhutan, India, Nepal, Pakistan, Sri Lanka and the Maldives. Together, these countries constitute an enormous area of the world, home to a population of roughly 1.6 billion people, about 23 per cent of humanity. It is an area that has, for centuries, been strategically significant in global geo-political terms, the site of many empires, and a critical global trade arena since at least the first millennium BCE. In the contemporary era, it is distinctive as a region where you will find, in the Republic of India, one of the fastest-growing and most powerful economies in the world. At the same time, it is one of the world's poorest regions; World Bank figures indicate that in 2005 more than 40 per cent of the population across the region lived on less than $1.25 per day (World Bank 2011: 66). It also hosts two of the world's nuclear powers (India and Pakistan).

South Asia is, then, a region of great significance in the contemporary world. Our objective in this book is to provide some insights into one important feature of the region: its religious traditions. It is a commonplace to say that South Asia is a region of great religious diversity (see Box 1.1). In this book we want to investigate what this well-worn phrase actually means, by exploring the development of its religious traditions in a range of social and political contexts.

In the broadest sense, these contexts are configured by the region itself. Its seven independent nation-states define South Asia geographically by their position on or adjacent to the Indian subcontinent. South Asia has also been defined by its historical link to the British empire, dominant in this region during the nineteenth and first half of the twentieth centuries. On this view, we should include Burma (Myanmar) within South Asia, as it formed part of the administrative unit known as British India. We could, however, also exclude Sri Lanka, which was administered separately during the colonial period. Alternatively, if we included modern nation-states that have cultural continuities with an earlier Indian empire, the Mughal empire, we might look to the area of Persian influence and include modern Afghanistan and even Iran in our subject matter. Certainly Afghanistan has, in more recent years, been increasingly drawn into the region, as indicated by its membership since

Box 1.1 Enumerating religion in South Asia?

- Bangladesh (total population 154 million): 89.7 per cent Muslim; 9.2 per cent Hindu; 1.1 per cent other.
- Bhutan (700,000): 'Two thirds to three quarters' Buddhist; 'approximately one quarter' Hindu; 'less than one percent' Christian and non-religious.
- India (1.15 billion): 80.5 per cent Hindu; 13.4 per cent Muslim; 2.3 percent Christian; 1.9 per cent Sikh; 'Groups that constitute less than 1.1 percent of the population include Buddhists, Jains, Parsis (Zoroastrians), Jews and Baha'is'.
- Maldives (298,000): 'The vast majority of the Muslim population practices Sunni Islam'.
- Nepal (30 million): 'According to the government, Hindus constitute 80 percent of the population, Buddhists 9 percent, Muslims 4 percent, and Christians and others 1 to 3 percent. Members of minority religious groups believe their numbers were significantly undercounted.'
- Pakistan (174 million): 'Approximately 95 percent of the population is Muslim. Groups composing 5 percent of the population or less include Hindus, Christians, Parsis/Zoroastrians, Baha'is, Sikhs, Buddhists, Ahmadis, and others.'
- Sri Lanka (20.1 million): 'Approximately 70 percent of the population is Buddhist, 15 percent Hindu, 8 percent Christian, and 7 percent Muslim.'

These figures and quotations are drawn from the US Department of State's (2010) 'Annual Report to Congress on International Religious Freedom'. As you can see, the ability of the report to provide accurate figures is variable, as in some nation-states the exact religious identity of citizens or subjects has not been established. Where accurate figures are provided, they are generally based on 2001 census statistics gathered by the respective nation-states.

Even where census data has been gathered, the diversity that is hidden by labels such as 'Hindu' and 'Muslim' means that the language of accuracy and exactness can be misleading. As we shall see in this book, the way that religious identity is actually lived out can contradict the apparent order and stability that such figures seek to represent.

2007 of the South Asian Association for Regional Cooperation (SAARC). What these points demonstrate is that South Asia, rather than being a fixed entity, is a conceptual construct that changes according to the contexts in which it is located.[1]

As with the region, so with its religious traditions! They are also, we argue, constructed differently in different contexts. Under such circumstances, attempting comprehensive coverage of these traditions would appear a dubious enterprise; it is not one we will attempt in this book. Our intention, rather, is to supply you, the reader, with a range of perspectives and diverse examples and so, we hope, provide a critical and thought-provoking method for studying religious traditions in modern South Asia.

You may already have noted the play on 'tradition(s)' and 'modernity' in our title. This partly reflects our desire to trace the continuities as well as the changes that have shaped understandings of religion in the modern era. It is also a challenge, an initial encouragement to reflect on such categories. Religion is often presented as the traditional antithesis to the inexorable secularity of modernity. Our hope is that this book will question such neat assumptions, demonstrating, rather, that the categories through which we understand the world around us are continually and mutually constructed. 'Tradition' and 'modernity' are two such categories. 'Religion' is another.

So one of the tasks we have set ourselves in this first chapter is to 're-introduce' religion within such a critical framework, as a prerequisite for our exploration of South Asian religious traditions.[2] Before turning to this task, however, we want to provide some perspectives on the region itself, to situate it in space and time. As with our broader project in this book, we do not attempt to provide a sense of totality; rather, we give a series of specific 'snapshots', brief views of a vast, multi-dimensional (and indeed limitless) terrain.

Situating South Asia 1: landscapes of diversity

Fly then from the Himalaya mountains in the north down the west coast of India to the southern town of Kochi (Cochin) in the state of Kerala. Engaged in trade with the Mediterranean, Arabia and the Persian Gulf from Roman times onwards, and later used as a staging post for trade to China, this coast of southwest India has enjoyed cosmopolitan status for centuries. A swift look around the small district of Mattancheri in Kochi confirms this history and its impact upon religious traditions in South Asia. Just north of Jew Town Road stands the Paradesi Synagogue, founded in 1538 and rebuilt in the eighteenth century – the synagogue for 'foreigner' traders or White Jews as they were known. By contrast, the so-called Black Jews, long-time Indian Jews whose ancestors married Jewish traders from perhaps as early as the sixth century CE, were deemed in the Paradesi Synagogue to have lower status. This alerts us that issues of social status cross-cut religious allegiance here as elsewhere in the world. Since 1948, the majority of Cochin

Jews have emigrated to the modern state of Israel, having lost their political privileges when the Princely State of Cochin became part of Kerala in 1947 (Gerstenfeld 2005). They do not show by religion on the 2001 census. In the past, though, local Hindu rulers acted as patrons to Jews (as well as Christians and others), giving financial support and guaranteeing their right to practise their own traditions. The ability of different groups to 'slot' into local social relations has been an important factor in shaping religious traditions in South Asia.

Right next door to the synagogue is the Dutch Palace, first built by the Portuguese in 1555 for the Hindu Raja of Cochin. Now a museum, within its walls is the still-functioning Pazhayannur Bhagavati temple, to the Goddess of the rulers of Cochin, alerting us to the idea that state and religion may be closely connected. Another wall of the synagogue is shared with a temple to Krishna, a different deity. Later in the book, we shall ask about the relations between such temples and deities. Part of the answer may be to do with the places from which different groups have migrated. To the west and north of the synagogue is an area now largely inhabited by people from Gujarat and Kutch in northwest India, who have settled here again largely as the result of trade links. During the Navratri nine nights festival to the Goddess in September/October, the Dariyasthan temple is full of Gujaratis dancing the *dandiya*, a lively stick dance that they have brought with them and taught their children. They are probably mainly Lohana, belonging to a particular trading caste, temples (and deities) being sometimes linked with caste groups as well as regional leanings. This is the case with churches too. Following the road from there north, you will come across a Gujarati school, reminding us of the importance of retaining one's own language* when surrounded by neighbours who speak a different one, here, Malayalam. Perhaps 400 metres along the same road, you will see the Cutchi Memon Hanafi Mosque, its name aligning its community with an area spanning the India/Pakistan border (Kutch), a particular group of Muslims (Memons) and one of the four main branches of Islamic law (the Hanafi). They will share a language (if not the exact dialect) with those who dance at the Gujarati temples nearby, as

---

* The language diversity of the South Asian region is immense. There are no fewer than eighteen official state languages in India, in addition to the national official languages, Hindi and English. Overall there are twenty-nine languages in the country with over a million speakers. Over the rest of the region, the main languages are Bengali (the main language spoken in Bangladesh), Punjabi, Pashto, Sindhi, Seraiki, Urdu and Balochi (each with more than 6 million speakers at the very least), and Sinhala and Tamil (the main languages in Sri Lanka). Nepali is spoken by about 40 per cent of the population of Nepal, but there are recognized to be about 120 different languages spoken in this country. The three main languages spoken in Bhutan are Dzongkha, Tshangla and Nepali, and the main language in the Maldives is Dhivehi, although English is increasingly the language of commerce and education there.

well as with worshippers at the big Jain temple lying between the mosque and the Gujarati school. This Bhagwan Shri Dharmanath Jain temple, built in 1904, represents another migration from Gujarat, going back perhaps to the early nineteenth century. Now its website proclaims proudly its place in the pluralistic microcosm of Mattancheri, 'Mini-India'. We have started to see why.

The Ernakulam district in which Mattancheri lies is also diverse. It had as many Christians as Hindus according to the 2001 census. Although some churches in this area date back to the influence of Portuguese Catholics from the sixteenth century, there were Christian communities in this part of India from as early as the second century, as we know from Roman sources (even if there is no hard evidence for the story that St Thomas, one of Jesus' twelve disciples, himself came to south India). The history of Christianity in India therefore predates that in, say, Britain by at least a couple of centuries, that in America by over a millennium. When we look at religious traditions in modern South Asia, we need to keep this history of diversity and change in mind.

Now fly over a thousand miles northeast. You will come to a sprawling megacity. Not Kolkata (Calcutta), in West Bengal, the colonial capital of British India until 1911, and fifth largest city in the world (13,217,000 population in the 2001 census), but Dhaka, the capital of modern Bangladesh, East Bengal, with a current population of over 10 million. In this great 'City of Mosques', straddling the banks of the River Baraganga, just over 10 per cent of its population are Hindus. Sometimes, major Muslim and Hindu festivals coincide, leading to extended celebrations in the city.[3] In 2007, for example, Eid ul-Fitr fell in October. Each Eid, between 7:30 and 10:00 A.M., Dhaka's 360 specified Eidgahs (Eid grounds) and mosques are packed with Muslims saying their Eid prayers, with special provision made for women. Dressed in colourful new clothes, people visit family and friends, and share Eid delicacies and sweets. In 2007, in the days that followed, Hindu neighbours celebrated Durga Puja, the biggest festival of the Bengali Hindu year. Visit Shakari Bazar and women are walking in brightly coloured saris just like those of their Muslim counterparts at Eid, twenty temples packed into the sixty metres or so of this old Hindu street with buildings three or four storeys high going back deep from the narrow road. *Pandals* (pavilions) for the Goddess Durga are set up, neighbours visited, sweets enjoyed. A Muslim writer, Fakrul Alam, remembers Eids and Durga Pujas in the 1960s of his childhood, when Hindu and Muslim friends and families would exchange sweets and share one another's festivities in the Ramakrishna Mission area of Dhaka. Now his young nephew does not go inside *puja pandals*. 'We aren't supposed to', he says (Alam 2007). But the government takes measures to ensure both festivals pass off peacefully, stressing that Bangladesh protects the religious rights of all.

Northwest a further thousand miles lies the village of Dadyal, Hoshiarpur District, Punjab, India (Figure 1.1). Affected, like Bengal, by the partition of

Figure 1.1 Dadyal village across the tank. Reproduced courtesy of Roger Ballard.

India and Pakistan in 1947, the villages in this area are now Sikh and Hindu. Muslims fled over the border into Pakistani Punjab.[4] Yet on a Thursday evening in this area, women, men and children from the villages will gather at Sufi shrines to offer their respects to the *pir* or holy man in the place where he was united in 'marriage' with Allah at death. Then they will stay for the *langar* (meal), sitting in rows on the ground, sharing food offered to all who come. Just outside Dadyal village itself is the shrine of Baba Hasan Das. He bears a Muslim name (Hasan), is worshipped by Sikhs and Hindus, offers cures to any who come to the place under a tree where he used to meditate, and now has his picture in the *gurdwara*, alongside the Guru Granth Sahib (Figure 1.2). Nearby, the village temple to the Hindu deity Shiva lists donations from both Hindus and Sikhs, many from the UK, especially from Leicester, where a blogger notes a *langar* for Baba Hasan Das is held in one of the Sikh *gurdwara*s (Randip-Singh 2007).

Our final port of call, a mere hop of around 300 miles southwest, is in the heart of the 'cow-belt', the area of Uttar Pradesh in north India where Hindu identity is particularly strongly emphasized. Mathura, on the river Yamuna, is renowned as the birthplace of Lord Krishna. In the holy area of Vraj (Braj), where Krishna played with the *gopi*s (the girls who looked after the cows), he is believed to play still with those who have eyes to see. Yet in this area, different local traditions have jostled since the time of Gautama Buddha, who is supposed to have commented that Mathura was overrun with devotees of the Yakki (Yaksha) cult, semi-divine beings associated with the earth and trees. In Mahaban, for example, a village of largely low-caste people and Muslims, the cult of Jakhaiya is run by Sanadhya brahmins, but preserves some very non-brahmin Yaksha rituals, involving a rooster and

Figure 1.2 Inside the *gurdwara*: Baba Hasan Das (left of our picture) and Guru Gobind Singh (right) with Guru Granth Sahib and Dasam Granth on twin *palkhi*s. Reproduced courtesy of Roger Ballard.

a pig that in the past would have been sacrificed. Now the pig's blood is offered to the earth from a cut made in its ear.

Local stories also bear testimony to contestation and negotiation between particular groups of brahmins who moved into the area from the sixteenth century onwards, when Krishna devotion really started to flourish here. Different sites and forms of devotion were legitimated from the mouth of Shree Nathji himself (Krishna), devotees of the Vallabha Pushtimarg tradition and the Bengali Chaitanya tradition telling the same story very differently (Sanford 2002). As in the other places we have visited, you can find in Mathura an imposing mosque among the many temples and wayside shrines. Yet alongside manifestations of Hinduism and Islam, the paths of ancient ritual, multiple traditions and renegotiated pilgrimage routes run deep.

Situating South Asia 2: snapshots of history

We now turn from space to an exploration of South Asia in time. In the course of this book, we will be looking at particular historical moments in some depth, especially in Part II. Here, we offer a series of snapshots of South Asian history. These help us to map our landscapes of diversity further. For maps, of course, exist in time as well as space. Consider, for instance, the two maps shown in Figures 1.3 and 1.4. The latter is a contemporary political map of the region, showing the independent nation-states of South Asia (although not their contested boundaries). The former is a map of the region in 1795, showing British territories and others. As you can see, the largest

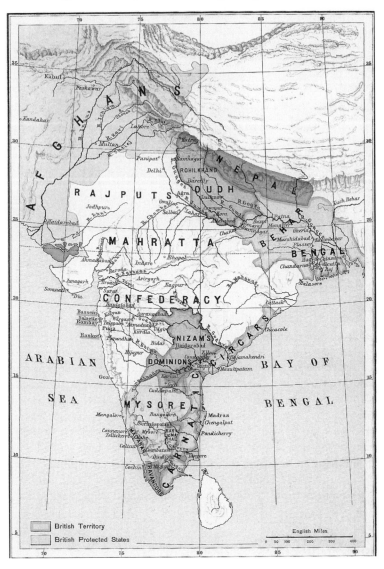

Figure 1.3 South Asia in the eighteenth century. Originally published in Charles
Joppen (ed.) (1907) *A Historical Atlas of India for the Use of High Schools,
Colleges and Private Students*, London: Longmans, Green and Co.

identifiable presence at this time was the 'Mahratta Confederacy', a network
of federated states that during the eighteenth century had superseded the
Mughal empire as the principal political authority in large areas of central
India. The change over this period of just over 200 years is demonstrably
dramatic. A map of India from a period in between – say, 1860 – would
again show a dramatically different picture.

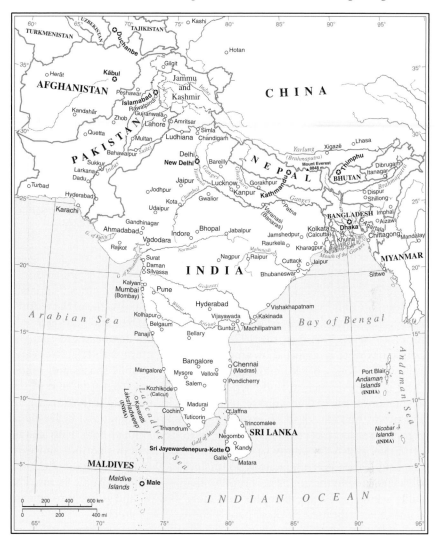

Figure 1.4 South Asia: modern nation-states (South Asia, UN Map No. 4140 Rev. 3, January 2004). Reproduced courtesy of the United Nations.

Examining these maps in time does not, then, provide us with a story of straightforward development. Rather, they seem to emphasize disjuncture and a multiplicity of narratives. This is a principle that we want to apply more widely. The temptation is always to bring order to history by demonstrating that one thing led to another, and that historical development has occurred in a series of eras. But there are always interests involved in such ordering. Most notoriously in South Asia, history has been seen as divided into Hindu, Muslim and British eras. This simplification springs originally from a nineteenth-century history of the region by the Scottish intellectual James Mill (1817). We can immediately see the political interest behind such a systematization, legitimizing the British era as 'rational' government by comparison with its predecessors. Our approach in this section aims to disrupt such narratives of development by presenting a series of snapshots from South Asian history. Each provides a different view, or narrative map, of this history. Continuities may or may not be apparent, but the snapshot form helps emphasize the need to be alert to the narrative processes that make such links. We also remind the reader that the snapshots themselves remain 'interested'. Just like Mill, we do have an agenda. Because of the subject of the book, each of our historical snapshots is linked with particular portrayals of religion in modern South Asia. As you engage with them, you should remain alert to this interest, and ask questions about what sort of history is missing.

Snapshot one

Located in the northwest of our region, modern Pakistan, cities flourished from roughly 2600 BCE to form the Indus Valley civilization, one of the world's oldest civilizations.[5] Traces of the cities of Mohenjo-Daro and Harappa only started to be excavated in the 1920s. The evidence demonstrates that the Indus cities were established on an orderly grid pattern with effective water and sewage works, brick buildings and a range of public spaces and roads. There is also evidence of trade across central and western Asia, and of the production of finely worked artefacts in gold, copper and lead. In terms of evidence of religious practice, seals showing a horned god, and figures with large breasts have been found. These have been linked both with claims for the unbroken continuity of Vedic Hinduism from this period, and with opposing claims that indigenous south Indian Dravidian religion (supposedly evidenced in the goddesses) is older than north Indian Vedic forms. The reality seems both more complex and more elusive, and is likely to remain so until the script used by these people can be deciphered.

Snapshot two

The Indus Valley civilization, the reasons for whose decline are still unclear,[6] was superseded in the northwest by the so-called Vedic civilization.[7] The theory that Vedic civilization spread as a result of invasion has now been refuted (see Chapter 3). The relation between the two civilizations has, however, been a subject of much (politically loaded) dispute, and remains important in understandings of religion in modern South Asia (for a range of views see Bryant and Patton 2005). On current knowledge, it seems likely that Vedic civilization emerged slowly through interactions and cultural fusions between some of the different peoples present and proximate to the remains of the Indus Valley culture after 1700 BCE. Largely nomadic rather than city dwelling, these pastoral people moved across the plains of northwest India, later moving down to graze cattle along the Gangetic plain, before settling to form a range of kingdoms (*mahajanapadas*) that dominated the northern part of the Indian subcontinent during the course of the first millennium BCE. Our knowledge of these people and their religious practices comes largely from the Vedic texts; unlike the Indus Valley, nothing in the way of objects and buildings has survived from this later period.

The orally transmitted Vedic texts (which have become seen as the sacred texts of Hinduism; see Chapter 3) give us a rather partial view of the structure of Vedic society through the eyes of its male brahmin transmitters. In particular, they introduce the idea of *varna* (ideal social group or class) and its relation to cosmic and ritual order (see Chapter 7A). The texts also portray links between the individual and the cosmos itself, links that can be manipulated in ritual chants or meditations. This key theme reappears in later Hindu epic and devotional traditions when these come under brahmin control (see Chapter 4). It also surfaces in Tantric traditions (Chapter 6) in different ways.

Snapshot three

In the latter half of the first millennium BCE, we may detect emerging forms of resistance to a 'Vedic view' of the world. Vardhamana Mahavira and Siddhartha Gautama are cast as agents of change in this respect.[8] The stories of their lives say they came from royal backgrounds in the *mahajanapadas* of northeast India, defied the conventions of their period by renouncing their position in the world and spoke out against the structures of society and cosmos established in Vedic texts. The anti-Vedic teachings of these two figures are better known today as Jainism and Buddhism. However, it is important to put this understanding in context. To present this just in terms of 'Vedic' and 'anti-Vedic'[9] worldviews oversimplifies. These were just two of many varying views of the world that were developing over this period, influenced by complex social, economic and political changes (Olivelle 1995). Both teachings did, however, emerge to gain varying degrees of influence over social relations and political structures. In particular, they were influential in the development of the enormous Mauryan empire, which grew during the late fourth century and by the mid-third century covered much of the subcontinent. Most famously, Siddhartha Gautama's teaching was promoted vigorously by the Emperor Ashoka (reigned 269–232 BCE), who has become an icon of just rule. His symbol, the *chakra* (the wheel of *dharma*, or order/justice), features on the flag of the modern nation-state of India.

Snapshot four

The Tamil country in the far south of the subcontinent around the first to fourth centuries CE was known as the country of the three kingdoms. It supported trade from the interior, along the coast, with southeast Asia and Rome, and sustained a thriving culture expressed in Tamil love and war poems, and in plays. These literary sources bear witness to the diversity of religious practices current at the time. In Maturai (Madurai), already the capital of the Pandiyan kings, temples to the deities Shiva, Vishnu, Murugan, Balarama and the goddess Pattini flourished, as did Jain temples. A Buddhist nunnery was an option for a woman who wished to renounce. Women became spokespeople for deities, ascetics of various kinds wandered, tribal hunters performed ceremonies, brahmins chanted the four Vedas; other brahmins turned from Vedic ritual and sang, perhaps to different deities, ornamented and worshipped with flowers. As Buddhists flourished with the growth of rice agriculture in the coming centuries, and Jains expanded and gained patronage through maritime trade, some brahmins sought to gain influence over devotional (*bhakti*) movements, drawing their poetic inspiration from early high-culture poems as a way to reassert and extend their power (see Chapters 4 and 5). As this suggests, devotional cults became engaged with the structures of established authority (kingly as well as brahminical).[10]

Snapshot five

After the decline of the Mauryan empire in the second century BCE, different regions of South Asia were ruled by successions of kingdoms, including the short-lived Greco-Bactrian in the northwest. Key dynasties included the Gupta dynasty, a major power linked with brahminical strengthening in central and eastern India around the fourth to sixth centuries CE, and the Chola dynasty, another long-established power in southern India (mentioned in inscriptions from the Mauryan period), one of the 'three kingdoms'. By the ninth century CE, this had expanded throughout the south and extended its influence up the eastern coast of the subcontinent into Bengal, as well as further south into Sri Lanka. This snapshot shows South Asia as a region of dynamic economic growth, trade links developing with many other parts of the world. The Indian Ocean trade had a significant impact on western India in particular, with different groups, including Christians, settling in coastal regions such as Kerala, establishing the kind of cosmopolitan culture we saw in Mattancheri. Part of this cosmopolitanism was generated by long-established trading links with Arab communities from across the Indian Ocean. These links provided the primary route for the spread of Islamic culture in southern and central India from as early as the eighth century.

Snapshot six

The northwest was also the site of emerging Islamic influence, both through a range of invading forces and through economic and religious integration associated with Sufi Muslim shrines. In the twelfth and thirteenth centuries, a range of Turk and Pathan armies pushed down through Punjab into northern India, establishing the Delhi Sultanate, a succession of unrelated dynasties that ruled over a fluctuating area of north and central India. Like contesting powers in other parts of the subcontinent, they used force and violence where necessary to establish their own superiority. Stories of these interactions, however, show huge variation in their attitude to and presentation of these encounters and subsequent social relations.[11]

The Delhi Sultanate was superseded by the Mughal dynasty, a major force that established paramountcy in much of the subcontinent from the sixteenth to the eighteenth century. Islam, although ever present in the culture and politics of the court, was by no means the defining factor in the governance of the empire. Largely, the Mughals ruled by the so-called 'segmentary system', whereby imperial authority was focused on the towns and cities of the Gangetic plain, Punjab and Bengal, whilst other areas were governed by client kingdoms of a range of different types. Many people in India became Muslims during this period, but for the most part their new practices were assumed through the influence of Sufi *pirs* and *shaykhs* (Eaton 2000), holy men who operated within the fabric of South Asian society, and whose influence we will refer to throughout this book.

Snapshot seven

Regional rulers remained a significant factor in the administration of South Asia throughout the Mughal period. As the empire began to decline in the mid-eighteenth century, some of these regional administrations assumed a greater degree of power. Amongst these were the Mahratta Confederacy, established by Shivaji Bhosle in the late seventeenth century, the Hyderabadi kingdom ruled over by the Nizams, and the East India Company, a British trading company established by Royal Charter of Elizabeth I of England in 1600. The Company gradually expanded its influence in South Asia, in the first instance through coastal trading posts at Surat, Madras and Calcutta. Of course, the British were not the only European power interested in the trade possibilities opened up in South Asia (we noted both Portuguese and Dutch influence in Mattancheri), but by a combination of political alliance and military conquest they expanded their influence, winning political control of Bengal and Bihar after the Battle of Plassey in 1757. From here, the Company expanded its influence dramatically across the subcontinent. By 1857, it had direct control over much of the region. The great rebellion of that year, however, demonstrated the limitations of this commercial company's ability to administer these vast territories, and in 1858 the Company was effectively nationalized, with the British Crown assuming administrative control. Hence began the period known as the British Raj, which ended in 1947 with the partition of the subcontinent into the independent nation-states of India and Pakistan.

The period of Company and direct Crown rule is one to which we will refer consistently during the course of this book, as it is a period that had a great deal of influence on the development of modern religious traditions. This influence, however, should be viewed in perspective; it was always an influence that developed in dialogue with myriad existing traditions in South Asia. For example, it is important to remember that throughout this period British India existed side by side with a large number of what became known as Princely States. These states, such as that of the Nizam of Hyderabad (see Chapter 5), were tributary states that officially recognized the paramountcy of British power in the region. Nevertheless, they represented a longer history, which was reflected in their critical position in the negotiations towards independence in the first half of the twentieth century. Most of these states were absorbed into Pakistan and India in 1947, but one in particular has retained a major, explosive influence over the geo-politics of the region: Kashmir.

Snapshot eight

The political problems in modern Kashmir are frequently presented as arising from friction between Hindus and Muslims in South Asia, the same friction that apparently led to partition in 1947. Although these identities are undoubtedly significant, it is important to take note of the complexities of political association and cultural development in this area. The Princely State of Kashmir was in fact formed only in the early nineteenth century, as a result of political negotiations resulting from the Anglo-Sikh Wars. The area covered is one of great diversity, with Hindu, Muslim and Buddhist traditions all being well established. More than this, the area is marked by influences of Sufi traditions and a Tantric form of the worship of Shiva, which take distinct Kashmiri forms. Such interactions show that the stark divisions between Hindu and Muslim invoked in the Kashmiri conflict emerge more through very modern social and political processes than through any ancient enmity.

In this way, our snapshot of Kashmir represents a broader point: notions of traditional enmity between monolithic religious identities need to be treated with caution, as even their projections of tradition are likely to have been fashioned in the context of modernity. Having said this, at the same time we should be wary of presenting the pre-modern period as a panacea of religious tolerance. Such a view would in itself be something of an a-historical representation, as the forms of religious identity that we associate with the idea of religious tolerance are, we argue, as much a part of our modern idea of religion as are those associated with religious antagonism.

Snapshot nine

However such faultlines have developed, it is undeniable that the partition which created India and Pakistan in 1947 was a defining moment in the history of modern South Asia. Millions of people were killed during this period. Many more millions were displaced. The antagonisms that have led to three outright wars and one proxy war between India and Pakistan since this date cannot be divorced from this history, recently described as 'a nightmare from which the subcontinent has never fully recovered' (Bose and Jalal 2004: 164). Bangladesh was also fashioned in this crucible, emerging out of the 1970 war as an independent nation-state, no longer tied to Pakistan under the pretext of religious commonality. (On the process, experience and ramifications of partition, see Hasan 1993; Khan 2007; Butalia 1998; Pandey 2001; a good summary is provided in Bose and Jalal 2004: chs 16 and 17.)

Snapshot ten

A final contemporary snapshot of the region has to take account of these threads of history, and also acknowledge again the diversity that we have emphasized throughout. The formal forms of government in the region, for example, range from secular republics (India, Nepal), through republics defined by religion in various ways (Pakistan, Bangladesh, Maldives, Sri Lanka), to religiously defined monarchy (Bhutan). As this suggests, democracy has been the dominant political principle in the region during the postcolonial period, although all the republics have had periods when democratic rule has been compromised in one way or another, and Nepal has only recently turned to this system, having been a monarchy before 2008.

Some of the most dramatic changes in the region in recent years can be attributed to various effects of globalization. In the 1990s, the Indian economy was radically opened up to world markets through a process known as liberalization, having previously been dominated by a form of protectionist state control under the aegis of the Congress Party.[12] The Indian economy has grown rapidly since this time, with multiple ramifications in Indian society. The Indian middle class has expanded enormously, now numbering hundreds of millions.[13] Some groups have undoubtedly been left behind, creating sharp divisions in social relations, a scenario graphically described in the recent novel *The White Tiger* by Aravind Adiga (2008). India's urban environments have changed rapidly, with discourses of consumerism and some strident forms of nationalist and religious identity becoming prominent features.

Another major impact of globalization has been the involvement of the region in the politics of militancy and counter-militancy associated with Islam. Since the attacks on the USA in 2001, Pakistan in particular has become a major launch pad for the propagation of what has become known as the 'war on terror' in Afghanistan. The growth of US influence in Pakistan has had its ramifications, with a strain of militant Islamic resistance flourishing on the basis of institutions and ideologies previously promoted during the 1980s, partly by the Islamizing Pakistani military dictator Zia ul-Haq, and partly, ironically, by the same US influence which was at that time geared towards combating the Russian invasion of Afghanistan. Militancy in the twenty-first century has had its effects over the whole region, with the Indian nation-state in particular demonstrating a sensitivity to the threat, and a tendency to relate it to its post-Independence antagonism towards Pakistan.

These snapshots of history and landscapes of diversity have provided us with some glimpses of our region. We hope they have indicated that the constantly adapting practices and ideas of South Asia's religious traditions are deeply embedded in the politics, social and economic relations, and cultural discourses of South Asian life. In the next section we turn to situating the concept of 'religion' more explicitly, and show how we intend to use that concept in relation to the 'religious traditions' of our title.

Situating religion: the growth of a concept

We began this book by noting the common assertion that South Asia is an area of the world that is marked by the presence of many different religious traditions. It is often presented as the 'home' of Hinduism, Sikhism, Jainism and Buddhism, and the 'host' to other religions – Zoroastrianism, Judaism, Bahai, Christianity and especially, of course, Islam. Indeed, this is a model used by one recent introduction to the religions of South Asia (Mittal and Thursby 2006). Using this model, we could say that different elements of our landscapes of diversity represent the presence of these different religions: that, for example, the different institutions we have referred to in Mattancheri represent the presence of Judaism, Hinduism, Christianity, Islam and Jainism in this small area. Although we see value in acknowledging this range of traditions, we want at the same time to signal a sense of caution about seeing the diversity apparent in a place like Mattancheri as the proximate presence of five different religions, two of them indigenous and three of them imported. Our caution relates to what we see as the sense of organizational coherence and organic growth implied in such a picture, attributes that need to be critically examined in the light of other evidence from our landscapes, which might challenge this picture.

But what do we mean by 'organizational coherence' and 'organic growth'? By the first we refer to the sense that different religions each have a kind of systematic, internal logic that entails a distinct mode of being and thinking. So:

- I will act in this or that way because I am a Muslim/Hindu/Sikh.
- Hinduism is a religion of spirituality and peace.
- Islam is a religion of the Book.

Such statements almost suggest that religions have their own personalities, and that adherence to them will 'naturally' lead one to act and think in coherent and predictable ways. 'Organic growth' invokes along with this the idea of singular development. So:

- Sikhism is a son of the soil that has grown and developed since its birth in the sixteenth century.
- Christianity first came to the Indian subcontinent in the second century CE. Since that time the religion has developed slowly, receiving a boost after the arrival of missionaries from the sixteenth century onwards.

Here, we get a sense of Sikhism and Christianity developing at slower or faster rates from 'birth' or 'importation' but always, as it were, following parallel paths towards their contemporary status. Both ideas imply that these religions have a distinct, objective existence of their own, and that together they make up 'the religions of South Asia'.

This book seeks to challenge this view of South Asian religious traditions *as a normative view*. That final phrase is important, as it signals that we are not trying to deny that this view has value; rather, we are trying to de-centre it, to encourage you to see it not as the only or 'natural' way to think about religion in South Asia, but rather as one of several valuable models for understanding the many practices that make up these landscapes of diversity.

Our reasons for doing this are several. First, as we intimated above, we are concerned that such a model does not adequately encompass the range of practices, ideas and objects operating in these landscapes. The residents of Dadyal, for example, seem to defy expectations, with practices that ride roughshod over the idea of religions as coherent, discrete entities. Various authors have commented on this apparent incongruity. For example, in the introduction to his book *The Construction of Religious Boundaries* (discussed in Chapter 9), Harjot Oberoi describes the process of researching religion in nineteenth-century Punjab, commenting:

> I was constantly struck by the brittleness of our textbook classifications. There simply wasn't any one-to-one correspondence between the cat-egories that were supposed to govern social and religious behaviour on the one hand, and the way people actually experienced their everyday lives on the other.
>
> (Oberoi 1994: 1–2)

For Oberoi, then, there is a kind of lack of fit between these 'textbook class-ifications' and the realities of his research data.

One way to explain this is to take a step backwards and think about the idea of religion itself. You may have come across the idea that there is no equivalent word to 'religion' in any of the languages that are prevalent in

South Asia. In particular, the classical Indian language, Sanskrit, has no such word, although the terms *dharma* and *parampara* are often adopted nowadays for this purpose.[14] Languages, of course, are critical components in the construction of social reality (Hall 1997). What this might suggest, then, is that the social realities of South Asia do not 'have' religion, and that consequently we should not use this term when talking about South Asian ideas and practices.

In one sense this is a ludicrous statement.[15] It certainly goes against the popular understanding of this region as uniquely spiritual and 'driven by religion'. The argument against the use of religion, however, is grounded in an objection to just such exoticization. 'Religion' (as we understand it today) is recognized in this line of argument specifically as a category that has developed in Europe (and to a certain extent America), and been brought to other areas of the world through European expansion and colonialism. Authors such as Tim Fitzgerald (2000) and Roger Ballard (1996) identify it as a kind of instrument of oppression that has functioned since the colonial era (and especially the nineteenth century) to discipline certain elements of South Asian culture and society. Subversive practices and ideas that defy classification or threaten particular types of social order have been pushed to the margins. In addition, the economic vitality of the region has been implicitly devalued by its identification as uniquely spiritual or religious. Such 'otherworldliness' provided a convenient justification for colonial rule, with its promise of 'material progress'. In an era in which the Indian economy is growing at a faster rate than that of any in the so-called First World, this seems particularly inappropriate. There is, then, a certain postcolonial logic to the rejection of the idea of religion in a South Asian context.

Various authors have, however, argued against this. Some argue that, despite its 'brittleness', it is a category which has to be deployed in order to construct valid comparative analyses (Fuller 1992; Sweetman 2003a). Others argue that denying religion to South Asia is little more than another Western power game, through which South Asian practices and ideas will be marginalized further as 'folk practices', not 'proper' religion (Viswanathan 2003). A related and interesting line of argument is that the 'Western imposition' model is a rather simplistic understanding of the dynamics of power relations. Complex social and political processes are erased in the invocation of 'Western power', ironically marginalizing oppressed people yet again by denying them any agency in the construction of their own social realities (Lorenzen 2005). In addition, there is a further danger that the Western imposition argument places too much emphasis on the changes of the nineteenth century. As we will demonstrate in this book, the traditions we are dealing with have long and intricate histories, informed by complex political and social relations developed over centuries, and the intervention of charismatic figures, movements of resistance and philosophical insights into the nature of the world in which we live. All these aspects should be acknowledged as critical factors in the development of modern South Asian religious traditions.

At the same time, there is a persuasive argument to suggest that the modern period has had a major influence on the way in which these traditions have come to be organized and understood. We acknowledge that the idea of 'the modern period' is contestable, just like the category of modernity itself. Nevertheless, the last 300 years or so have seen a period of rapid and dramatic change in the world. Enormous social mobility and conceptual exchange have been fuelled by economic integration and technological advances. For our purposes, we take such processes of mobility to represent the onset of modernity (a similar argument is made in Appadurai 1996: 28), and it seems undeniable that the concept of religion, as a facet of human practice and experience, has developed through them. Roughly from the Enlightenment (early and mid-eighteenth century), ideas about how to understand the concept of religion and its place in social and political life were transformed in many parts of Europe and North America. The emergence of self-consciously non-religious approaches towards science and reason was accompanied by the development of newly powerful social groups and opportunities for political association. Religion came to be considered *beside* science and reason, simply one aspect of social existence, rather than interwoven throughout (Asad 1993). This transition is sometimes known as 'objectification' – understanding religion as self-contained, having an objective reality, identifiable *as* religion.[16]

Geo-political expansion was also a feature of the transformation of these societies. European powers increasingly fought over and acquired control of territories across the globe. In this context, an objectivized Christianity-as-religion was brought into contact with other 'religions', perceived as similarly self-contained, objective realities. Increasingly, the notion of World Religions emerged through such processes.[17] Perhaps the clearest example of this is the modern idea of 'Hinduism'. Many scholars have noted the introduction of this specific term in the late eighteenth and early nineteenth centuries (see, for example, Oddie 2006), in missionary and other traveller accounts. The term derives from the older term 'Hindoo'. There is much debate between scholars as to whether (and when) this term itself had a religious meaning, or was used primarily to signify geographically located people (for a good account of these debates, see Pennington 2005). The suffix '-ism', however, is undeniably new in this period, and indicates the kind of shift in thinking about 'religion' to which we are referring. Hinduism is characterized at least paradigmatically as a 'system', comparable to others apparent in the South Asian landscape. A similar 'constructivist' history has also been told about Jainism (Flügel 2005) and Sikhism (Oberoi 1994). In the context of global historical developments, these categories began to emerge as discrete social realities, major or minor instances of the general phenomenon known as 'World Religion' or 'the World's Religions'.

In the book we will be referring to this idea of a 'World Religions model' as a significant factor in modern South Asia. But as we made clear earlier, it is not the only way of looking. By briefly historicizing its development, our intention here has been to demonstrate that this is just one intellectual history (albeit a very influential one). Others are also significant.

The problem arises, however, as to how to locate these alternative histories, without reference to the religion concept. One possibility is to deploy apparently indigenous categories. This has been the approach taken by the anthropologist Roger Ballard (1996), who has developed a four-dimensional approach to Punjabi religion based on the key concepts of *panth*, *kismet*, *dharm* and *qaum*.[18] These refer to commitment to a spiritual teacher (*panth*); ideas or practices designed to deal with adversity and the unexpected (*kismet*); divine norms variously understood, to which all should conform (*dharm*); and forms of community identity (*qaum*). Ballard's argument is that one can identify these different dimensions operating in Punjabi religious practice in a way that frequently contradicts the logics of the World Religions model. A person who might qaumically identify as a Hindu, for example, might have values (*dharm*) related to honour that are shared with his Sikh neighbour, and might turn for panthic and kismetic inspiration to the shrine of a Muslim *pir*, as we saw in Dadyal.

It is important to realize that what Ballard is suggesting is not a model of syncretism. Syncretism implies a merging or combination of elements of *existing* discrete traditions (an approach that, ironically, seems to reinforce the World Religions model).[19] Rather, he suggests that these dimensions enable a different way of understanding the organization of everyday religious practice, which has not been governed by, or organized on, the basis of religion as such. There are some problems with this somewhat schematic model (see Suthren Hirst and Zavos 2005), but it does help us to see that there are other ways of looking that can make sense of, and help us to understand more fully, the way religious traditions play out in South Asia.

Looking at religious traditions

We wish to take a lead from this general observation, and move from it to explore not so much an alternative way of looking at religion, but rather a whole range of ways of looking at religious traditions that may be deployed selectively and critically as a means of developing a multi-perspectival approach to our field. In presenting this approach, we aim to provide not only ways of looking that may be more appropriate to different ideas and practices, but also a range of ways of looking at the same sets of ideas and practices. This multiple approach is based on our understanding that the world of social actors (i.e. people) is always constituted through layers of discourse – what the anthropologist Peter Gottschalk (2000: 3–4) describes as 'temporal, spatial and social maps' through which people make sense of and understand the world around them.

To establish a sense of this multiplicity, our approach is heavily engaged with context, or rather with investigating the many *different* factors that effectively operate within and constitute those networks of contexts critical to the social construction of knowledge. The emphasis of this book is on placing religious phenomena within these networks. Responding to this dynamic social reality, we differentiate the terms 'religion', 'religions' and 'religious traditions' as follows. We use 'religion' to refer to that modern category whose development we have outlined above, and which different 'religions' – Christianity, Hinduism, Islam and so on – are held to exemplify. These terms will enter consistently into our analysis, deployed as one of the ways we address our subject matter. At the same time, we employ the term 'religious traditions' to denote something different. We use it in a pragmatic attempt to represent the panoply of ideas, practices and objects that today are commonly recognized as belonging to a religion, but which *we* wish to signify could be understood through a range of different ways of looking. These traditions may have old roots, but they may also be recently invented (Hobsbawm 1992). We are, then, emphatically not proposing 'religious traditions' as a pre-modern alternative to the modernity of 'religion'. Our intention is rather to demonstrate how continuities have come to form a significant feature of modern social formations, often alongside and indeed woven into, and becoming, modern articulations of religious identity. In pursuing this approach, we apply different ways of 'cutting across the available data', to use Will Sweetman's (2003a: 50) phrase. These include looking at teacher traditions as key social formations in South Asia, but 'religious traditions' are not to be reduced to this formal notion of *parampara* (teacher–pupil succession). Rather, the term indicates our open, multi-layered approach, based on different ways of looking. Distinguishing this from the idea of religion as one particular way of looking is critical, and we ask you, as our reader, to hold this distinction with us, to commit at least temporarily to our construction of reality, as you would if you were attending a play.

The shape of the book

In what we might then imagine as the prologue to this play, you may have noted a range of metaphors associated with looking. Snapshots, maps, glimpses have all helped us to explain our approach to our field. But there is a loaded history in such metaphors. In particular, the look or 'gaze' of colonialism has been implicated in the construction of colonized societies as exotic, other, ripe for political domination (Mitchell 1988, and also Chapter 8). Under such circumstances our use of such metaphors to explore religious traditions in a region of postcolonial nation-states may be considered rather risky. Our objective, however, is to subvert the power of dominant ways of looking by producing, as it were, new perspectives on the gaze. So our interest is always on many ways of looking, rather than on the acceptance of a single, authoritative view. As Gottschalk (2000: 4) says, 'If we find that only one map is enough, then we should suspect ourselves of oversimplification.' What we need instead is 'a set of maps that we shuffle occasionally according to the questions we ask'.

In this connection, we introduce one further metaphor that we will deploy throughout this book. It is suggested on the front cover. This is the metaphor of the kaleidoscope. We are indebted to the scholar Diana Eck, from whom we have drawn this idea. As you will see in Chapter 2, she has used it to describe the relative position of deities in Hindu traditions (Eck 1998: 26). We would like to move outwards from this to deploy the metaphor as a critical *method* of looking. Twisting the kaleidoscope delivers 'a constantly changing pattern of . . . reflections as the observer looks into the tube and rotates it' (SOED 1993: 1470). This twist of the kaleidoscope will be our way of referring to that multi-perspectival approach towards our subject matter described above, enabling, we hope, a range of such reflections, or understandings, to emerge. As with the kaleidoscope, so with these twists: the same data will be viewed in different ways, each a construction itself, yet allowing us to develop a more nuanced view of our subject than a single perspective could give.[20]

The book is divided into two parts. The chapters in Part I are structured around some fairly standard concepts associated with the study of religion. We begin with the idea of the divine in Chapter 2, before moving to explore texts, myths and ritual in the following chapters, and then turn to two issues that apparently relate more particularly to the religious traditions of South Asia, the teacher–pupil relationship and the concept of caste. With each of these chapters, however, our approach will move outwards from this ini- tial identification of a core concept to disrupt notions of how it should be approached. In particular, we want to disrupt the idea that the specificity of these concepts in a South Asian context is always best interpreted through the World Religions model. We will then explore continuities that appear to cross the boundaries between different religions in relation to notions of ritual practice. We will also problematize the idea that each religion is tied to one particular way of approaching these key concepts. Our approach to the divine, for example, explores the many ways of understanding the idea of divinity, which are apparently encompassed by that which we commonly recognize as Hinduism. These chapters inhabit landscapes of diversity; they demonstrate from modern examples, and, by drawing on the histori- cal development of diverse traditions, how our settled notions of religious identity, Oberoi's 'brittle categories', are transgressed by practices and ideas in context.

If Part I of the book is focused on disrupting these settled yet 'brittle' ideas of how religion is organized, Part II is focused more on understanding the ways in which the category 'religion' has come to be part of, and has influenced, the shaping of South Asian religious traditions. Our focus here is initially the nineteenth century, when the radical encounter between dif- ferent knowledge systems influenced ways of looking at and representing religious identities in profound ways. In Chapters 7–9, we will explore in particular the emergence of modern ideas about what constitutes Hinduism, Islam, Sikhism as South Asian religions. This is not necessarily to say that definite notions of religious identity were not apparent in the region before the nineteenth century. Rather, our argument is that it is not possible to understand the ways in which religion operates in contemporary South Asia without taking account of the complex historical processes that marked this period. In Chapters 10 and 11, we move from this focus to consider some further key factors in the broader modern period that have impacted on ways in which religions are understood and acted upon. In particular, notions of public and private space, and political activism at a variety of levels, have been very influential in the articulation of modern religious identities. In Chapter 11, we also return to the idea of different ways of looking, to show how the contrasting approaches in Parts I and II help develop a critical, multi-layered understanding of religious practices and ideas in modern South Asia.

As well as the contrast between the two parts of the book, we hope you will also see continuities. In particular, there is a continuity in the structure of each chapter. Each begins by focusing on a case study, a particular event or text intended to provoke questions to deepen understanding. We hope to encourage a questioning approach throughout the book. From questions raised, we work outwards from the case study to explore how different contexts provide us with new ways of looking and understanding, to develop answers to questions raised. This strategy is deployed in both parts, as our approach stresses the constant need to ground the phenomena studied in a range of interconnected contexts.

Sometimes these contexts are straightforwardly historical. It is necessary, for example, to understand something of the historical background of particular figures such as Anandamayi Ma and Rammohun Roy in order to understand the texts associated with them in Chapters 5 and 2. In addition, however, these contexts may be more discursive or theoretical. In Chapter 8, for example, we explore the issue of Orientalism and postcolonial theory as one context for understanding the work of Sayyid Ahmad Khan and others. This is because events and texts are always affected by a range of broader ideas, as well as more immediate elements of cultural, social, economic and political life. As Kim Knott (2005: 119) explains, religion operates as 'a dynamic and engaged part of a complex social environment or habitat, which is itself criss-crossed with wider communications and power relations'.

In each chapter in Part I of the book, this concern will be reflected not just in an examination of a range of broader contexts to the case study, but also by three consistent 'twists of the kaleidoscope', helpful for exploring the wider power relations associated with each chapter's conceptual theme. These three twists will focus respectively on issues of gender, politics and religion, in relation to the examples used in the chapter. The final one of these twists, religion, is similarly deployed in Part II of the book, where the focus is more clearly on the specific significance of this idea in shaping the modern realities of South Asian religious traditions. We hope that these continuities will enable you to make interesting connections across the material available in this book. Questions, tasks and suggested further reading are there to help you develop your own research beyond it.

Encouraging further research is an important objective for us. As we have emphasized, our treatment of the region, and religion within it, is not and cannot be comprehensive. At a pragmatic level, our main focus is on – even then necessarily limited – examples from the Indian subcontinent and the modern nation-states of Pakistan, India and Bangladesh. For Bhutan, the Maldives, Nepal and Sri Lanka, other sources will provide perspectives on their history and religious traditions, doing them more justice than we can here.[21] Carrying out research will enable you to follow up your own particular interests. At a methodological level, you will already realize that we are intent on encouraging you to develop a critical approach to the conceptual categories through which understandings of South Asian 'religion' have been constructed. There are no fixed boundaries to these traditions (as with the region itself) – they are negotiated, developed, contested in a range of historically grounded contexts, and so necessarily resist any idea of total coverage. Our hope, rather, is that the range of examples and different ways of looking explored in the following chapters will help you to develop your own critical and nuanced approach, both to the examples of the landscapes of diversity explored within, and to the far wider landscapes you will discover beyond.

Part I
Exploring landscapes of diversity

2 Deity

We are going to begin our exploration of South Asian religious traditions at a point that many people might see as the appropriate place – that is, with notions of the divine. The idea that religion emanates from the focal point of the divine figure of God is a common one, yet it is often skewed by presuppositions that do not fit the South Asian context. As a consequence, the nature of the divine in South Asian traditions can appear perplexingly complex and contested. This can be particularly the case with Hindu traditions. In 2006, for example, a UK Hindu group wrote to the *Times Educational Supplement* complaining about the representation of Hinduism in British schools as a 'naive paganistic religion happy to accept many all-mighty Gods' (*Times Educational Supplement* 2006). This group rather argues that Hindu gods are 'facets of the same Brahmm, the Supreme God' (Hindu Council UK n.d.), a very different view.

In this chapter, our first objective is to place depictions such as this into a broader context, seeing how they have developed and what forces have driven them to become embedded into different inflections of 'common sense' ideas about Hinduism. We shall see that these two classic modern depictions of Hindu notions of the divine are both to a certain extent underpinned by political, as well as theological, concerns. The idea of Hindu polytheism as symbolizing a somehow less developed ('naïve') form of religion is one that is articulated in Christian missionary accounts of Hinduism in the colonial period. The depiction of the many deities of Hindu tradition as manifestations of one supreme, essentially monotheistic God has become a major retort to this representation; it has also become a key theme in what is commonly understood today as modern Hinduism.

As this suggests, the issue of the divine in modern South Asia is partly influenced by the way religious traditions define themselves in relation to one another. If Hinduism is represented as a polytheistic religion, then, this is partly because of the strong articulation of other South Asian traditions – especially Islam, Christianity and Sikhism – as monotheistic. Of course, these traditions are often defined in a range of contexts by a reference to monotheism; what we are suggesting, however, is that the idea of a polarity between monotheism and polytheism has been one of the ways in which religious communities have asserted their difference in South Asia. It has become, in a sense, a way of expressing power in different situations, as we shall see below.

We hope to show that constructions such as 'monotheism' and 'polytheism', understood as polar *opposites*, are not the only way of thinking through questions about deity, beings and the world. There are many other ways of relating the One and the many; God and the gods; ultimate reality and the cosmos. We shall get you thinking about these by examining some of the philosophical and devotional trends of South Asian religion as they have developed through history. We emphasize the fluidity of South Asian notions of the divine and show how they flow through social, cultural and political relations, being constructed in different situations in different ways.

Case study: a dialogue between a missionary and three Chinese converts

Our focal case study for this chapter will be a piece of writing produced in the 1820s by a prominent cultural commentator of the time, Rammohun Roy (Figure 2.1). This piece of writing was published in Calcutta, which was at the time the capital of British India and the cultural and economic hub of the empire.

A dialogue between a missionary and three Chinese converts (extract)

Missionary:	How many Gods are there, my brethren?
1st Convert:	Three
2nd Convert:	Two
3rd Convert:	None
Missionary:	Horrid! The answers are from the Devil.
All:	We know not where you have got the religion which you have taught us, but thus you have taught us.
Missionary:	Blasphemers!
All:	We have heard you with patience nor ever thought of crying out against you, how much so ever you surprised us by your doctrine.
Missionary	*(Recovering himself and addressing the first convert):* Come, come, recollect: how can you imagine that there are three Gods?
1st Convert:	You told me there was God the Father, and God the Son, and God the Holy Ghost, and by my *Swanpan* I find that one and one and one are three.
Missionary:	O! I see your blunder. You remember but half the lesson. I told you also that these Three are One.

Figure 2.1 A statue of Rammohun Roy outside the Council House in Bristol. Rammohun died in Bristol during a visit to England in 1833. Reproduced courtesy of John Zavos.

1st Convert:	I know you did, but I thought you had forgotten yourself, and concluded that you spoke the truth at first.
Missionary:	O no! You must believe not only that there are Three persons, each God, and equal in power and glory, but also, that these Three are One.
1st Convert:	That is impossible. In China we do not believe contradictions.
Missionary:	Brother! It is a mystery.
1st Convert:	What is that, pray?
Missionary:	It is – it is – I know not what to say to you, except that it is something which you cannot possibly comprehend.
1st Convert	*(smiling):* And is it this that you have been sent 10,000 miles to teach?
Missionary:	O the power of carnal reason! Surely, some Socinian has been doing the Devil's work in China. But (*turning to the 2nd Convert*), how could you imagine, there are two Gods?
2nd Convert:	I thought there were many more till you came and lessened the number.

Missionary: Have I ever told you that there are two Gods? (*Aside*) The stupidity of this people makes me almost despair.

2nd Convert: True, you have not said in so many words that there are two Gods, but you have said what implies it.

Missionary: Then you have been tempted to reason upon this mystery.

2nd Convert: We Chinese are wont to put things together and to come at truth by comparison. Thus you said that there were three persons that were each perfect God, and then you said one of these persons died in one of the countries of the West, a long while ago; and I therefore concluded the present number to be two.

Missionary: Astonishing depravity! O the depths of Satan! It is in vain to reason with these poor benighted creatures. But (*addressing the 3rd convert*) perverse as your two brethren are, you appear worse than they; what can you possibly mean by answering that there are no Gods?

3rd Convert: I heard you talk of three, but I paid more particular attention to what you said on the point of there being only one. This I could understand; the other I could not; and as my belief never reaches above my understanding . . . I set it down in my mind that there was but one God, and that you take your name Christian from him.

Missionary: There is something in this; but I am more and more astonished at your answer – 'none'.

3rd Convert (*taking up the* Swanpan): Here is one. I remove it. There is none.

Missionary: How can this apply?

3rd Convert: Our minds are not like yours in the West, or you would not ask me. You told me again and again, that there never was but one God, that Christ was the true God, and that a nation of merchants living at the head of the Arabian gulf put him to death upon a tree, about eighteen hundred years ago. Believing you, what other answer could I give than 'none'?

Missionary: I must pray for you, for you all deny the true faith, and living and dying thus, you will without doubt perish everlastingly . . . .

(Rammohun Roy, 'A Dialogue between a Missionary and Three Chinese Converts', see Ghose 1982: 911–13)

Explaining terms

Socinian – a Christian sect active in sixteenth-century Europe, in which the doctrine of the Trinity, as well as the divinity of Christ, is rejected

Swanpan – a kind of Chinese abacus

Task

Before continuing, think about the kind of questions this piece might raise. Jot down the questions you would like to ask in order to understand the piece more, and also to understand notions of divinity in South Asia.

You may have picked up from reading this dialogue that Rammohun is not being entirely serious in his depiction of this scenario. The inexorable logic of the three Chinese 'converts' is juxtaposed with the reasoning of the missionary in a way that is explicitly designed to lampoon the position of the latter. In addition, you may have picked up that this piece is not really about China at all – it is more of a comment on missionaries and their practice in India.

You might have raised questions such as: Who was Rammohun and in what context did he write? What does his depiction of the dialogue tell us about his understanding of the divine, and how might this understanding compare with others, both contemporary and earlier? You might also have raised questions about the status and activity of missionaries in South Asia during the period that Rammohun was writing: What was their approach to Indian religious ideas and practices? In the following sections, we will address these questions, and also widen the context to address the whole issue of how divinity has been and is understood in South Asian contexts.

Rammohun Roy: cultural critic, colonial commentator

We will start our investigation by providing some context on Rammohun Roy. At the time that he produced the 'Dialogue', the early 1820s, Rammohun was already a well-known figure in intellectual circles in Calcutta. Having been employed by the East India Company (see Chapter 1) as a *munshi* (personal clerk), he had by 1815 given up his position and turned his attention to publishing, intellectual pursuits and social commentary. Rammohun was a member of the Bengali elite (the *bhadralok*, or 'gentle people'). Although he was born in a village in rural Bengal, his family were *kulin* brahmins, a very high caste,[1] and his father was relatively well off. In his earlier life Rammohun had acquired an eclectic education; he was conversant with Persian, Arabic, Sanskrit and English, as well as Bengali, and many of the forms of learning and major philosophical systems associated with these different languages. Importantly, he translated texts such as the Upanishads into Bengali, broadening access where this had hitherto been confined to those who were able to speak and/or read Vedic Sanskrit (see Chapter 3).

The breadth of Rammohun's education points us towards a common description of him that tells us much about the way he is perceived in mainstream histories of modern India. He is often described as a 'renaissance man'.[2] This powerful image immediately throws up allusions in Western culture to the Italian renaissance, to polymaths such as Leonardo da Vinci and to the beginnings of intellectual processes that have led to the dominance of humanism and rational learning in Western culture. The implication here is that Rammohun may be seen as a harbinger of this form of modernity in India. Although he is often associated with the early flourishing of Bengali intellectual culture sometimes called the Bengal Renaissance, we need to be wary of such characterizations, because of the way in which they tie the myriad processes of Indian history to a dominant narrative fashioned on the template of early modern Europe. We need to see Rammohun Roy in context, rather than relying on the powerful narratives that inform official histories.

So what exactly did Rammohun do, what attitudes did he take? In short, Rammohun Roy was primarily a publicist who, in a series of newspapers and journals in English and Bengali, commented on educational and social issues as well as issues related to religious tradition. He advocated education for women, and campaigned against practices such as child marriage and *suttee*, the burning of widows on the funeral pyres of their husbands.[3] In addition, Rammohun provided comment on and critique of British rule in India.

At this stage (the early nineteenth century), Calcutta was the centre of British government in India, providing a co-ordinating focus to the rapidly expanding bureaucratic machinery that administered Company rule across the subcontinent. It was also a bustling, cosmopolitan centre for an increasingly globalized trading network configured by British commercial and political interests. Rammohun provided comment on the developing character of British rule. In particular, he was critical of the Company's refusal to allow Indians to hold any high office in the administration, and of its tight control over press freedom. On the other hand, he was an advocate of Western learning and technological advance, seeing colonial rule as an opportunity for interaction and development rather than entirely in negative terms.

This nuanced position was also one he brought to his approach to Christianity and the influence of Christian missionaries in India. By the 1820s, missionaries were a prominent voice in colonial India, even though they had been allowed entry to Company territories only in 1813. This voice was often intensely critical of indigenous religious and social practices. Missionaries focused on issues such as the position of women, caste and untouchability, and of course the whole notion of polytheism and what they termed 'idolatry' as indicative of the degenerate character of native religion (see Oddie 2006; Pennington 2005). Such critiques were, of course, strategic, underpinned by the desire to gain converts to the true faith.[4] It is in this context that we can place the 'Dialogue'. It operates as a pointed response to the missionary critique. Significantly, Rammohun's strategy here is one of inversion. Where the 'Hindoo religion'[5] had so frequently been represented as superstitious and irrational, in thrall to the riotous will of many gods, the 'Dialogue' depicts the Christianity of the missionary in similar terms, by contrast with the inexorable, calm logic of the coolies, and their insistence on the indivisibility of the divine force.

Rammohun's position in the 'Dialogue' helps us to see that the representation of Hindu traditions as polytheistic in contrast to Christian monotheism is an overly simplistic model, one that demonstrates the dangers of what has been termed 'Orientalist' discourse, informed by straightforward binary oppositions between 'the West' and 'the East' (see Chapter 8 on this idea). The self-confidence of Rammohun's critique is predicated on the knowledge that Hindu traditions include notions of the divine that are strongly monotheistic. In another publication, *A Defence of Hindu Theism*, he stresses:

> I have urged in every work that I have hitherto published, that the doctrines of the unity of God are real Hindooism, as that religion was practised by our ancestors; and as it is well-known even at the present age to many learned Brahmins.
> (Rammohun, see Ghose and Bose 1906: 90, cited in Killingley 1993: 63)

It is an understanding he finds too in the poems of Guru Nanak (see Chapters 6 and 9) and Kabir (see below). Rammohun himself rejected image worship amongst Hindus, seeing it not only as absurd and not in the real spirit of the 'Hindoo scriptures', but also as a product of priestly self-interest and financial gain. Where the Upanishads speak in apparently polytheistic terms, he explains that they do so using allegory and figurative representation. Rammohun's preference is for the rational worship of the God of nature (see Killingley 1993: ch. 3), a truth he believes common to all religions before its distortion in particular doctrines and practices. This is a view he had already developed in his earlier work, 'A Gift to Monotheists' (*Tuhfat al-Muwaḥḥidīn*, see Ghose and Bose 1906), when he wrote in Persian, using the terminology of Islamic learning, to address the educated elite who still used the language of the Mughal and Mughal successor states. In our extract above, it is a truth he is prepared to turn against Christian missionaries in their 'own' terms to show the irrationality of Christian claims about a Three-in-One and dying God. Far from being the monotheists they claim to be by contrast with Hindu idolaters, the Christian missionary opponents are shown to be polytheists, distorting understanding of the one true and unchanging God. (As we shall see below, however, their preaching of a crucified God did appeal to some.)

Rammohun was what we may call a skilled cultural navigator, addressing different audiences in different languages and with different nuances. His views on divinity were crafted in a particular and complex context. In the next section we indicate the kind of resources he had to draw on, by exploring some of the different ways in which divinity is conceptualized in Indian traditions.

Notions of the divine in Hindu traditions

In his important text on popular Hinduism, based on ethnographic case studies, Christopher Fuller (1992: 30) notes that 'all Hindus sometimes, and some Hindus always, insist that there is in reality only one God, of whom all the distinct gods and goddesses are but forms'. He goes on to note that some deities can have multiple forms and names; sometimes these names and forms are recognized as such – that is, manifestations of a source divine figure – but sometimes they are recognized as deities in their own right, and even considered as the supreme being. The modern understanding of Krishna is one such. In one sense he is recognized as a manifestation of Vishnu; at the same time, however, some Hindus recognize Krishna as the Godhead, supreme lord, to be venerated through absolute devotion. For other Hindus, the supreme deity is Devi, the Goddess. Not only may she incorporate the powers of all the male deities, but also she may be seen as the source of all there is, as well the embodiment of the nation (see Chapter 3), or the commissioning power of local village goddesses, as we see below.

Fuller also points out that divinity is a quality that can be assumed by humans, either temporarily during particular ritual moments such as the marriage ceremony, or for the duration of their life, as with popular gurus and yogis such as Sai Baba and Anandamayi Ma (see Chapter 6). These individuals are treated as divine beings by their devotees. The notion of fluidity is a vital one here, as Fuller (1992: 30) notes. Here, it helps us to understand the shifting character of relationships between divine figures, and between human and divine figures, as well as between the divine and its images (see Chapter 5 on images). We can also use it as a way in to understanding diverse notions of the divine now considered to be Hindu. What follows is a range of examples of this diversity.

A village shrine

Yellamma is a popular goddess across parts of southern India, particularly amongst low-caste groups. She is perceived as the 'mother of the universe', and her attitude is one of benevolence and caring for the poor and those who are suffering. Her image is often worshipped in small shrines in villages and towns and she has a major shrine at Saundatti in Karnataka, south India, which we shall be exploring in Chapter 11. Figure 2.2 is a portable image of Yellama used in festival rituals. What attitude do you think Rammohun would have taken to such worship?

A contemporary image

Figure 2.3 is a modern depiction of Vishnu in his 'universal form', Vishvarupa. The image is associated with an incident in the *Bhagavad Gita,* when Krishna

Figure 2.2 The goddess Yellamma. Reproduced courtesy of Jackie Assayag.

reveals his universal form to Arjuna on the battlefield (see p. 36). The *Gita* describes the universal form as follows:

> It had many mouths and eyes, innumerable wonderful aspects, uncounted divine ornaments, countless divine weapons at the ready;
>
> It was wearing divine garlands and robes, divine perfumes and ointments; it was made up of every prodigious thing; divine, infinite, facing in every direction.
>
> If the light of a thousand suns should all at once rise into the sky, that might approach the brilliance of that great self.
>
> (*Bhagavad Gītā* 11: 10–12, see Johnson 1994)

Just as the *Gita* has often been projected in modern Hinduism as the key text of devotional Hinduism, so this passage and associated dramatic images are frequently deployed to legitimize the idea that polytheistic Hinduism is underpinned by monotheism. Despite the significance of many different divine forms, there is, as we have seen, a pressure to represent Hinduism in modern contexts as fundamentally monotheistic. The influence of that missionary critique to which Rammohun Roy responded so pointedly in the 1820s is still significant.[6]

Figure 2.3 Vishnu's universal form. Reproduced courtesy of http://www.harekrsna.de.

An Upanishadic story

Looking at the divine from a different point of view, we can see an expression of the one and the many as early as the *Brihadaranyaka Upanishad*, a brahminical text dating from about 900 BCE. In this famous text, brahmin ritual specialists are gathered at the court of King Janaka for a public competition. They are annoyed with Yajnavalkya (also a brahmin) who is claiming knowledge superior to the ritual. One of them asks him, 'How many gods are there, Yajnavalkya?' Yajnavalkya answers, very properly, with a ritual phrase calling on the All-gods: ' "Three and three hundred, and three and three thousand." '

> 'Yes, of course,' he said, 'but really, Yajnavalkya, how many gods are there?'
> 'Thirty-three.'
> 'Yes, of course,' he said, 'but really, Yajnavalkya, how many gods are there?'

'Six.'

'Yes, of course,' he said, 'but really, Yajnavalkya, how many gods are there?'

'Three.'

'Yes, of course,' he said, 'but really, Yajnavalkya, how many gods are there?'

'Two.'

'Yes, of course,' he said, 'but really, Yajnavalkya, how many gods are there?'

'One and a half.'

'Yes, of course,' he said, 'but really, Yajnavalkya, how many gods are there?'

'One.'

(*Brihadaranyaka Upanishad* 3.9.1, see Olivelle 1996: 46–7)

Yajnavalkya's replies lead him, and us, through a very different way of thinking about deity. His answers in the thousands refer to what he sees as the powers of the gods. His answer 'thirty-three' refers to aspects of the cosmos and the self in a way that signifies all there is, in terms of ritual and the way it constructs our world. His next answers give us a progressively simpler and different way of thinking about the whole and its parts, until we get to the one, which is 'Breath: that is *brahman*. They call it "the beyond"' (Roebuck 2003: 55). The one source of all there is, ultimate reality, *brahman*, breath within each and all, is both beyond all there is and its source, the One and the many. Is this monotheistic? Polytheistic? Or both? These are later and foreign terms for grappling with the problem. We need both to stay with the story and to understand how texts such as this could later be used as a resource to counter Christian and other criticisms of polytheism, by authors such as Rammohun.

Indian Islamic and other conceptions of the divine

A *dialogue between two talking birds*

The sharāk *bird said*: Please be kind enough to explain the manner of the coming into being of all creation and of everything which exists . . . *The parrot answered*: Know that the *Way of Eternity* (*Marsād ul-Abad*) gives an explanation of the beginning of created existences in the world and in heaven . . . . Now listen with your mind and from your heart to this other explanation. There is a difference between human souls and the pure soul of Muhammad the Prophet. . . . he was the first thing God created. They called him a light and a spirit and he himself was the existence of existences, the fruit and the tree of created beings . . . . Then God Most High, when He wished to create created beings, first brought forth the light of Muhammad's soul from the ray of light of His Unity as is reported in the Prophetic traditions, 'I am from God and the believers are from me.' In some traditions it is reported that God looked with a loving eye upon that light of Muhammad . . . and the tears dropped from Him. From those drops He created the souls of the prophets. From those lights He created the souls of the saints, from their souls, the souls of believers . . . [then, the disobedient, hypocrites, infidels, angels, jinns, devils, animals, vegetation, minerals, fire and water, seven heavens, constellations etc].

(Ibn 'Umar Mihrābī, *Hujjat ul-Hind*, see Embree 1992: 397–9)

The Indian Islamic tradition stresses that God is eternal, a 'Unity'. His attributes are also eternal, though they appear in limited form in humans as part of the created world. You can hear how Rammohun echoes such views. *Shirk*, or associating another with God, however, is a sign of *kufr* or infidelity and there are many Indian Islamic criticisms of idolatry. Yet this should not mislead us into thinking that Islamic writers inexorably opposed themselves to something called 'Hinduism' even in terms of understandings of the divine (see Ernst 2003). There is enormous diversity in Indian Islamic traditions as well as within the traditions they have encountered.

In 'The Indian Proof', from the reign of the Mughal emperor Jahangir (1605–27), the *sharak* bird asks questions to allow the parrot to give simple Muslim answers, designed to keep Indian Muslims from 'slipping' away from their (in most cases, relatively recent) acceptance of Islam. The text's simple Persian and setting within a popular love story was intended to draw 'ordinary' Hindavi-speaking people into the Persianate world of Mughal rulers and Hindu elite. It thus had a political element, creating people as subjects participating in a common culture, as well as removing doubt so that 'reality is distinguishable from error and truth from falsehood' (Ibn 'Umar Mihrābī in Embree 1992: 398).

Yet what constitutes truth is not unchallengeable. The text's view of Muhammad as Nur, Light, was shared across Sunni, Shia and Sufi Islamic traditions from around the ninth century (Embree 1992: 398). However, modern Sunni reformers of the north Indian Deoband school (see Chapter 8) categorized this 'Sufi view' as *shirk*. The rebuttal of such criticisms, using relevant Hadith, remains a contemporary subject of debate crucial to their Sunni Barelwi opponents (Alam 2008: 622). Each is likely to label their Muslim opposites as *kafir* on this point. By contrast, our author drew on Sufi sources, such as the thirteenth-century *Way of Eternity*, in presenting his orthodox understanding of the divine, as was common in medieval Indian Islam. The two were not then seen as incompatible.

A medieval poem

O servant, where dost thou seek Me?
Lo! I am beside thee.

I am neither in temple nor in mosque: I am neither in Kaaba nor in
  Kailash:
Neither am I in rites and ceremonies, nor in Yoga and renunciation.
If thou art a true seeker, thou shalt at once see Me: thou shalt meet Me
  in a moment of time.
Kabîr says, 'O Sadhu! God is the breath of all breath.'

(Kabir, 'O Servant', see Tagore 1915)

This poem is by the fifteenth-century poet Kabir, translated into English
by the famous Bengali poet of the late nineteenth/early twentieth century, Rabindranath Tagore. It is an example of a strong tradition that
developed in the medieval period in north India, known as the Sant (or
Saint) tradition. This tradition also encompasses a very significant figure
in modern South Asian religious traditions, Guru Nanak (see Chapter
9 on this cultural heritage). Kabir was a weaver by trade, probably a
Muslim. His work, along with that of other *sant*s, has become much loved,
recited and sung by Hindus, Muslims and Sikhs alike. Today the global
Kabirpanthi community has an institutional presence in Europe, America
and the Caribbean as well as India. A characteristic of Kabir's approach
was his declaration that the divine was not to be sought in institutional
settings ('the temple or the mosque') or ritual practices ('rites and ceremonies', 'yoga or renunciation') – but in the inner self, by contemplating the
name of God. Like the broader Sant tradition, Kabir understood the divine
as a Lord without attributes (*nirguna*). At the same time, this was and is
an intensely devotional (*bhakti*) tradition. Together these factors provide
a spiritual tension: devotion to a Lord who is unrealizable. Yet realization
will occur 'in a moment of time', as long as one continues to meditate on
the name of the Lord.

The examples above demonstrate that trying to establish a normative
approach to the divine, even in Hindu traditions, can be unproductive. In
images, sacred texts, devotional poetry, local sacred spaces, a diversity of
approaches is apparent. Understanding these approaches depends as much
on understanding diverse contexts as it does on theology (i.e. literally 'discourse on god'). The 'Dialogue' demonstrates this well. It is only possible
to understand the way Rammohun presents his ideas of the divine by reference to a network of contexts: some linked with past or currently recreated
traditions, others related to the socio-economic and cultural conditions in
which he was writing. Now we turn to our three regular 'twists of the
kaleidoscope' – gender, politics, religion – to explore his approach to the
divine in more depth, and gain a wider perspective on ideas of the divine in
South Asian contexts. Chapters 5 and 11 also explore how the divine may
be worshipped by people from diverse religious traditions in a single locale,
giving further examples of the fluidity of understandings of the divine in
South Asia.

The gender twist: the 'father' of modern Hinduism; the goddesses of Hindu traditions

Rammohun has become a major figure in the established history of modern South Asia. Indeed, he is often described as the 'father of modern Hinduism', giving an indication both of his significance and of the ways in which official history has frequently operated to foreground particular figures, over-emphasizing their role in complex historical processes. The idea that a religion, even a historicized one such as this, should have a 'father' is also indicative of the way in which official history, and official religion, is frequently gendered in ways that express particular relations of power. It would be very unlikely, for example, that such histories would identify a 'mother of modern Hinduism' in the form of an inspirational figure like this. The idea of Rammohun as a 'father figure' is indicative of the way in which modern Hinduism is projected as being 'reformed' by a series of inspirational male leaders. Rammohun is followed in this 'his-story' by Dayananda Saraswati, Swami Vivekananda, Sri Aurobindo Ghosh, Bal Gangadhar Tilak, M.K. Gandhi, Sarvepalli Radhakrishnan and others; a succession of men depicted as reforming and fashioning the shape of modern Hinduism and its representation in the world.

How far does this story reflect the actual character of modern Hinduism, the ways in which it is played out in countless houses, *mandirs* and other spaces both in India and across the world? This is an area in which you could pursue further research, comparing the ideas and organizations associated with the men listed with Hindu practice. Often, there is a mismatch between the public representation of religion and the more private and domestic practices that sustain communities constructed around a particular religious identity. This of course is as much true of other religious traditions as it is of Hinduism, and in Chapter 10 we will explore this issue in more detail. The role of the male is also questioned by examining the importance of the female in Hindu conceptions of the divine.

Many goddesses are worshipped within Hindu traditions. Indeed, the Goddess, or Devi, has a major role in the ideas and practices of millions of Hindus on a day-to-day basis (see Box 2.1). But immediately this raises a question. Singular Goddess (perhaps with a capital G in English – Indian scripts generally do not make a difference), or multiple goddesses? What is the relation between them? The points about monotheism and polytheism above should warn us both about the dangers of oversimplification and of power issues involved. That also applies to whom goddesses are 'for'. Figure 2.4 gives some examples of goddesses and their power, but you may want to follow these up with your own further research on other goddesses, practices or texts.

Hindu goddesses are sometimes nurturing, sometimes fierce, reflecting, in the views of some interpreters, male ambiguity about female power. Frequently, they are both (Erndl 1993). Sometimes they are worshipped in

Box 2.1 Caring for the deity

The importance of the relation between the worshipper and the Goddess is shown in the way a *murti* (image) of the deity must be cared for when taken into the worshipper's home.

Bhuvaneshwari arrives

Bhuvaneshwari arrived only this September. It was a major decision. She was first given to my mother's aunt (grandmother's elder sister) by Kanchi Sankaracharyar (the earlier pontiff who is now no more). This aunt was doing daily puja and adorned her with gold ornaments and an extensive wardrobe. However due to her generosity in helping anyone who used to come for help, for example, brahmins asking for financial assistance to marry off their daughters, Bhuvaneshwari's jewellery was gifted away. When this old aunt used to visit, she carried her Bhuvaneshwari everywhere as she has to be fed and decorated daily. So as a child when I used to stay in my granny's house, I remember her sister coming along with Bhuvaneshwari. In my mind (I was then around 8 years), here was Bhuvaneshwari, the invincible, all-powerful yet compassionate soul mate. Eventually when this aunt passed away, my mother's cousin (another aunt's daughter) took over responsibility. I was then asking my mother why she could not take the Bhuvaneshwari, nostalgically recounting how she was part of my childhood memories. My mom said that not only was she not in a position to take up that responsibility but more importantly her cousin was also better qualified as she was a more religious, orthodox person living in the village who follow 'norms' unlike my mother who was part of modern city life. Interestingly in August 2010 when we met my mom's cousin who had broken her hip, she was lamenting how it is now time to pass on the Bhuvaneshwari to the next caretaker. I immediately suggested my mother to take over (after 20 years when I first suggested). After much deliberation (it is more than adopting a baby!) and getting permission from my father, my mother went again to her sister's house in Nurani village, Kerala, and brought Bhuvaneshwari home to Chennai. I understand it was a very tearful parting for her cousin who was nevertheless confident that her baby would be well taken care of. (I understand that she even commented that later I might take her over!!) I am not sure if Bhuvaneswari's daily rituals have changed since she was passed on by the Kanchi pontiff. However as far as my mother is concerned, since that day, her routine has changed. She has stopped eating onion and garlic and has stopped eating food outside home (unless it is an emergency.) She implicitly follows what was prescribed by her cousin for Bhuvaneswari's daily routine. Come what may she spends that 20 minutes with the Goddess.

(Ganesh 2011)

rough stones at village boundaries, or offered cooling substances to ward off particular misfortunes, as with Shitaladevi, goddess of smallpox. Sometimes they are worshipped in groups (the 'seven mothers' occur in many ancient and more modern sets, with considerable variation). They may personify a mountain, tree (*yakshi*) or river (Ganga Ma being the clearest example), be the product of a film (Santoshi Mata, see Chapter 4), or the heroine of an epic or love story (Sita, Radha). They may be wife, consort or literally other half of a male deity (Lakshmi, Radha, Ardhanarishvari), an independent

Figure 2.4 A gallery of goddesses. (a) Durga riding on her lion, Pracin Nag temple, Anantnag, Kashmir. In 2011 the Indian army was occupying the temple. Durga is very widely worshipped. She is often associated with Devi, the Goddess in the *Devimahatmya*, a text of praise to Devi who destroys the demon threatening the world when the male gods cannot. She takes their weapons into battle. Durga is sometimes shown in eight- or ten-armed form, carrying the weapons each of the male gods gave. Reproduced courtesy of Christine Marrewa Karwoski. (b) Kali, Pracin Nag temple, Anantnag, Kashmir. Kali tramples on Shiva who lies beneath her feet to contain her great power so it does not destroy the whole world. It is important to realize that by her devotees Kali is often worshipped as a nurturing mother whose liberating power helps them overcome ignorance and gives blessings. Reproduced courtesy of Christine Marrewa Karwoski. (c) Kalika Mata and Durga, Kalika Mata temple, Chittorgarh, Rajasthan. Kalika Mata, a manifestation of Durga, is the presiding goddess of Chittorgarh. She was also the *ishtadeva* (chosen form of God) of Mohan Lal Sukhadia, Chief Minister of Rajasthan (1954–71). Reproduced courtesy of Jacqueline Suthren Hirst. (d) Mansha Devi, the snake goddess at the Nag Kuan (snake worship), Banaras, Uttar Pradesh. Manasha is also very important in Bengal and south India. Reproduced courtesy of Christine Marrewa Karwoski. (e) Kumari, living goddess of Patan, Nepal. In many parts of South Asia, young girls before puberty are honoured as manifestations of the goddess. This may be temporarily during a ceremony celebrating a stage in pregnancy (as in Gujarat, for example). In Nepal, a young Buddhist Newar girl will be chosen as a Kumari and as living goddess will be present at Hindu and Buddhist festivals

(a)

(b)

(c)

(d)

and give blessings until she retires at puberty. Reproduced courtesy of Aayushree Kharel and Sushant Tuladhar. (f) Bhuvaneshwari arrives at the Ramanathan's house in Chennai. Reproduced courtesy of Deepa Ganesh. (g) Swetkali ('white/black') is the main deity at the Nardevi temple in Kathmandu, Nepal. She is called Neta Ajima by Newars. She is believed

(e)

(f)

(g)

(h)

to have come to the aid of several local rulers and her cult includes tantric rituals. Reproduced courtesy of Aayushree Kharel and Sushant Tuladhar. (h) Madayil Chamundi Theyyam, a powerful Kali goddess from Kerala, south India. Chamundi got this name as she followed the *asura*s to hell to eliminate them. *Theyyam* are considered as God and give blessings to their devotees (see Vengara 2010; Freeman 2005). Reproduced courtesy of Santhosh Vengara (see http://www.vengara.com/theyyam/index.html).

village deity absorbed into a Sanskritic or pan-Indian picture, the combined power of all the gods (Durga), the commissioning deity of all. They may be worshipped across India in different ways (Lakshmi), associated with the culture of a specific region (Durga in Bengal became particularly important as nationalism rose; McDermott 2008, 2011), or linked with a particular lineage or caste (as their *kuldevi*). Women may worship them for the continuance of the patriline (Bennett 1983), men for the furtherance of their own power (Caldwell 1999), a low-caste group to challenge oppressive social structures in particular circumstances (Hardiman 1995).

Here are two examples. The Bhinmal Tragad Brahmin Sonis who come from Naniad, Gujarat, western India, explain their caste origins (as brahmins), current occupation (goldsmiths), worship patterns and status as Hindus who faced Muslim oppression in terms of the goddess Lakshmi – wife of Narayan (Vishnu), their *kuldevi* – Vagheshwari Mata, and Kalika Mata – the *kuldevi* of another caste group, the Kansaras (see Bhinmal Tragad Brahmin n.d.a). Their temple at Naniad enjoys the support of non-resident Indians (NRIs). Its home page has a picture of the shrine of the rudimentary *murti*s of Vagheshwari Mata on a lion next to Kalika Mata on an elephant, from which, through HTML animation, emerge Amba Mata, the most popular form of the goddess in Gujarat on a tiger, Lakshmi goddess of wealth, Sarasvati goddess of learning, Durga slaying the buffalo demon, Vagheshwari herself, and then Vagheshwari with Kalika (Bhinmal Tragad Brahmin n.d.b). The message is clear yet layered through the popular devotional oleographs: all forms of the Goddess emanate from one, Vagheshwari with Kalika being both source and end. Caste and family claims, regional claims, Hindu claims, all represented within a modern 'universal' style of 'photos of the god(desse)s'.[7]

As a second example, let us take the fierce goddess Kali, who is often adorned with symbols of motherhood such as house keys. In the eighteenth century, there was a major revival of Shakta worship in Bengal, one of the roots of the Bharat Mata image we will explore in Chapter 3. *Shakti* means 'power', the female power in the universe and in human beings. In Shakta traditions, Devi is supreme, whatever particular name she takes. Many poems about Kali are attributed to the eighteenth-century poet Ramprasad, who influenced key nineteenth-century contributors to modern Hinduism such as Ramakrishna and probably Rammohun before him. Ramprasad identifies Kali with the whole universe (she is *jagatmoyi*) and with the power that can be tapped within the meditating individual:

> O mind, you're still making the same mistake,
> Don't you know who Kali really is?
> My *Jagatmoyi* Mother, she has no equal in the world,
> Why do you want to make an earth image, and worship that as Mother?
> A person should have confidence in being her son, not in anything else,
> Do you think you can make her happy by killing a kid?

Prasad says, O stupid mind, worship only with devotion,
You show off to people your worship of Kali but she won't accept your
    bribe.

(Ramprasad, 'O Mind', see McLean 1998: 120)

Can you see how poems like this could be a resource for critiques like
Rammohun's? And for later nationalist uses? In addition to influences such
as these, Ramprasad's songs to Kali are still sung by poor itinerant singers on
trains in Bengal and blared from devotional cassettes today. Devi worship, in
a great variety of forms, is in many ways a key to modern Hinduism. Look
out for further examples in the rest of this book.

The politics twist: God of the Dalits

Divine figures, and the idea of divinity itself, can play a major role in developing politics in South Asia. We have already seen in our case study how the
monotheism/polytheism divide was deployed as a subtle act of resistance by
Rammohun Roy. In Chapter 4, we consider ways in which the divine figure
of Ram has been transformed into a strident, fierce warrior, symbolic of the
machismo associated with militant political Hinduism. Here, however, we
want to develop an example that takes us into a different arena of power:
that of caste relations.

Caste is a factor of South Asian societies we will be considering in some
depth in Chapter 7. Here, we note that one aspect of the functioning of caste
has been the oppression of certain groups as 'untouchable': that is, a recognition of such groups as ritually and socially impure. Over time there has
been a great deal of resistance to this idea; the Kabir Panth explored above
provides a good example from the fifteenth century. Kabir's attributeless
god approached through attitudes of personal devotion enabled the side-
stepping of dominant approaches to the divine, which were characterized by
a range of ritual and social constraints related to caste identity. As Kabir said
in another of his poems, 'It is foolish to ask a saint his caste . . . . The barber
has looked for God too, and so has the washerman and the carpenter' (see
Klostermaier 2007: 184).

A perhaps comparable politics of resistance is found in contemporary
Dalit theology. As we indicated above, despite Rammohun Roy's lampooning of Christian missionizing, it is nevertheless the case that missionaries in
colonial India did have some success, particularly amongst low-caste groups
who saw conversion as one means of escaping their predicament (Oddie
1991). Dalit, meaning 'oppressed', is a term that has come into use during
the twentieth century (but see Chapter 7B) as a self-identifier by those for-
merly known as 'untouchable'. Dalit theology refers to a movement amongst
low-caste Indian Christians to develop a theology of the oppressed, in a way
quite similar to the more widely known liberation theology developed in
Latin America.

The particularity of Dalit theology lies partly in the recognition that conversion to Christianity itself is not enough. Despite the aspiration to escape the oppressions associated with caste through conversion, many low-caste Christians found that the constraints of this institution were also apparent in Christian churches in India. This reflects the fact that caste is not an institution that operates only amongst Hindus; as we will see in Chapter 7A, it operates across the boundaries between different religious identities. Dalit theology envisages the Christian divine as a Dalit-god, one who identifies with the plight of servants and, as Jesus in particular, suffers the plight of the Dalit. As one Dalit theologian says: 'On the Cross, he was the broken, the crushed, the split, the torn, the driven-asunder man', and in this sense he revealed his Dalitness (Nirmal 1994: 39). The goal of Dalit theology has been described as 'the realisation of our full humanness or, conversely our full divinity, the ideal of the Imago Dei, the image of God in us' (Oomen 2010). Although in many ways this is a view underpinned by a classic Christian doctrine of incarnation, Dalit theology also seems to parallel the Kabir Panth in the context of an increasingly assertive political consciousness. An assertion of political consciousness may also be detected in the way that Rammohun draws on a much older philosophical tradition in his idea of the divine, which was fashioned in the context of missionary critique. In the next section we explore this idea in some depth.

The religion twist: Rammohun's Advaita Vedanta

It may seem unnecessary to look at religion as a contextual factor in understanding the idea of the divine, but, as indicated in the introduction, in this book we are precisely interested in how the category of religion has had an impact on developing ideas of what we recognize as the religious. Religion, re-capping, needs to be recognized as a category with a history and particular, shifting cultural locations. The ideas of Rammohun Roy about the divine provide us with a very good example of the colonial encounter as a critical cultural location for the development of the category 'religion'. In this section, we want to explore this further.

The response of the 'Chinese converts' to the missionary's attempts to get them to understand the mysteries of the Trinity was to produce an inexorably logical deconstruction, lampooning the idea that the divine force was both three and one. The 'Dialogue' and its message works because Rammohun himself propagated an idea of God that was uncompromisingly monotheistic. There was one true God, an Absolute Truth, which was supremely rational and free of contradiction (unlike the Trinity). Although this understanding had complex roots, Rammohun frequently represented his notion of the divine as the philosophy of Advaita Vedanta.

The Advaita tradition is often associated with the name of Shankara (c.700 CE). In much nineteenth-century European scholarship, it became seen as more or less equivalent to 'Indian philosophy' for reasons you might like to explore. In turn, it often became foundational in explanations of 'Hinduism', including in the works of Rammohun Roy and the great twentieth-century statesman and scholar Sarvepalli Radhakrishnan (1888–1975). It is nevertheless only one of several different Vedanta traditions that developed through the centuries (Ramanuja's was another), and these form only one set of schools among the many brahminical, Buddhist and Jain schools that debated with one another.[8]

As a Vedanta school, the Advaita tradition was based on the Upanishads, the brahminical texts that form the last layer of the Veda (see Chapter 3). It is called 'non-dualist' (*a-dvaita*) because it identifies the principle of consciousness within the person (*atman*) with ultimate reality, that which grounds the universe (*brahman*). Other Vedantins rejected this identity claim and spoke in different ways of the dependence of individual selves on Brahman, or the relation of the multiplicity of the world to the unity of its source. Each school tried to take into account the very varied views that are found in the Upanishads themselves and to show how the interpretation of their school was the most consistent, economical and logically defensible.

Rammohun himself was familiar with both the classical Upanishads and the *Brahma* or *Vedanta Sutras*, the enigmatic summary verses of the Vedanta school on which every Vedanta teacher had to write a commentary. He translated several of the Upanishads into English and Bengali and wrote his own Bengali commentary on the *Vedanta Sutras*, heavily influenced by Shankara's own commentary. It was for the worship of the one invisible God he found taught in these texts that in 1814 Rammohun began the Atmiya Sabha, an association of like-minded individuals that would develop later into an enduring organization propagating Rammohun's basic ideas, the Brahmo Samaj.

Rammohun's view was rather different from that of the classical Advaita Vedanta tradition. For Rammohun this one true God was the absolute, quintessential and supremely rational God attested to both in nature and in the scriptures of different religions prior to their distortion, including the Upanishads. To his English (Christian) audience, he says that the *Vedanta Sutras* explain the Supreme Being not in terms of its essence, but in terms of its effects and attributes, terms drawn more from discussions of natural religion in Europe than from the Upanishads. His Bengali translations of the Upanishads, addressed to Hindus, are more faithful to Shankara's own interpretations. However, Rammohun often ignores Shankara's vital distinction between ultimate and provisional truth, sees Brahman as a benevolent God showing favour to his worshippers, and emphasizes worship and good conduct rather than knowledge as the way to liberation, opening this path to all, unlike the elitist Shankara (Killingley 1993: 104).

So although Rammohun, at least in his later works, squarely located his idea of God in Hindu tradition, tracing it back to Shankara's view of Vedanta, his approach, like that of many differing figures of nineteenth- and twentieth-century Hinduism, is often described as 'neo-Vedantic'. Their 'new' interpretations of Vedanta are partly configured by the challenge from the West, the response to criticisms of Hinduism from missionaries and others. Rammohun's emphasis on rationality, and equation of Brahman with God, need to be understood in this context. It is this idea of neo-Vedanta that the scholar Timothy Fitzgerald (1990: 101, 112) describes as the basis for the projection of Hinduism as a World Religion (on neo-Vedanta, see also Halbfass 1988).

In conclusion: 'Twisting the wrist'

With Fitzgerald's argument about neo-Vedanta, we have come back to the idea with which we started: that religion is primarily associated with notions of God. A World Religions approach sees the comparative approach to God as a way of distinguishing different religious 'systems'. Our exploration of some of the many ways in which the divine is conceptualized in South Asia, however, demonstrates that sometimes this approach can be problematic, as the notion of the divine is not fixed – it is fluid, and it frequently undermines established modes of understanding such as the opposition of monotheism to polytheism; it even challenges the divisions that are perceived between different 'systems' such as 'Hindu', 'Christian', 'Muslim' and so on. The scholar Diana Eck has produced an interesting analogy in her discussion of Hindu deities, which, as you will know if you have read Chapter 1, we have developed as part of our general approach in this book. This is the idea of the kaleidoscope. Eck (1998: 26) comments that

> the frustration of students encountering the Hindu array of deities for the first time is, in part, the frustration of trying to get it all straight and to place the various deities and their spouses, children and manifestations in a fixed pattern in relation to one another. But the pattern of these imaged deities is like the pattern of the kaleidoscope: one twist of the wrist and the relational pattern of the pieces changes.

Rather than seeing this as frustration, however, we prefer to see this as the challenge for students of South Asian religions. The 'twist of the wrist', we would argue, represents the critical issue of contextualization. In order to understand notions of the divine, you must also understand some of the multiple contexts within which these notions are developed and expressed by particular individuals and groups. Our core example of Rammohun Roy is, we hope, an indication of this. Without the historical context of early colonial power relations, and a variety of other contexts that help to situate the idea of the divine, it is difficult to understand the meaning and significance of Rammohun's neo-Vedantic rational monotheism as a projection of 'real' or 'true' Hinduism. This contextual approach is one we will deploy in relation to other facets of modern South Asian religions. 'Twisting the wrist' provides perspective, enabling a developing, critically aware understanding of the dynamic nature of the ideas, practices and objects that we recognize as religion.

Questions for further discussion and research

- How far is Roy's monotheism continuous with older Indian traditions?
- Discuss the proposition that Hinduism is not polytheistic.
- What role does gender play in the development of modern notions of Hinduism?
- Is Dalit theology Hindu?
- Is Advaita Vedanta the theological heart of modern Hinduism?

Further reading

Killingley, Dermot (1993) *Rammohun Roy in Hindu and Christian Tradition: The Teape Lectures 1990*, Newcastle upon Tyne: Grevatt & Grevatt.
    A fascinating contextualization of Rammohun's work.

Fuller, Christopher (1992) *The Camphor Flame: Popular Hinduism and Society in India*, Princeton: Princeton University Press: 30–32.
    Chapter 2 explores gods and goddesses, including a discussion of the relationship between divine figures and humans.

Klostermaier, K. (2007) *A Survey of Hinduism*, 3rd edn, Albany: State University of New York Press.
    Chapter 26 in this or earlier editions gives an introduction to Vedanta and its sister school, and covers three very different key Vedantin thinkers: Shankara and his Advaita Vedanta, Ramanuja and Madhva.

Pennington, B. (2005) *Was Hinduism Invented? Britons, Indians and the Colonial Construction of Religion*, New York: Oxford University Press.
    Chapter 3 provides a useful account of the approaches and impact of missionary accounts of Hinduism in the late eighteenth and early nineteenth centuries.

Rajkumar, P. (2010) *Dalit Theology and Dalit Liberation: Problems, Paradigms and Possibilities*, Farnham: Ashgate.
    A recent comprehensive exploration of the phenomenon of Dalit theology.

3   Texts and their authority

In a World Religions model of religion, one of the most fundamental features to be identified is a core text or foundational set of scriptures. For some religions, this seems straightforward: the Hebrew Bible for Judaism; the Bible for Christians;[1] the Qur'an for Islam; the Guru Granth Sahib for Sikhs. In standard introductions, the equivalent in Hinduism is often taken to be the Veda.

In this chapter, as in Chapter 2, we are going to put this way of presenting religions and their texts into a broader context to help us understand both how such a view developed and how it can be related to the rich diversity of actual South Asian 'sacred texts'.[2] We argue that some of the factors that affected the shaping of this idea of 'one religion, one key scripture' developed in the nineteenth century and were intimately linked with the reshaping of religion in modern South Asia, which we examine in Part II of the book. These factors affected interpretations of the place and status of a wide variety of 'sacred texts' including the Qur'an and the Guru Granth Sahib, but the example we shall take as our case study here is the Veda. To understand the reshaping – and also what remains outside it – we need to explore the authority of particular texts, who they are authoritative for, who has the right to preserve and transmit them, and for what purposes this is done. Clearly such issues existed prior to the nineteenth century, as did numerous constructions of the significance of the Veda – and the Qur'an. However, it is important to realize that religion in pre-modern South Asia was often organized in local or regional as well as pan-continental teaching traditions, each of which might have its own particular (oral and written) texts and understanding of authority. And this continues to be the case today, despite the work of reformers such as Swami Dayanand Saraswati (1824–83), whose work we look at below. First, though, look at the photos in Figures 3.1 and 3.2, both of which show contemporary uses of the Veda.

Case study: the Veda in modern use

Figure 3.1 Young brahmins learning to chant the Veda at Nasik, Maharashtra. Reproduced courtesy of James Madaio.

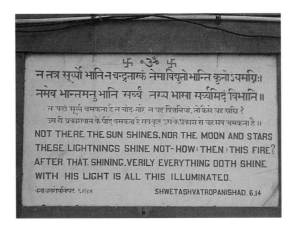

Figure 3.2 A verse from the Upanishads in Sanskrit, Hindi and English on the wall of the huge Birla temple, New Delhi. The Upanishads form the last of four layers of Vedic texts. Reproduced courtesy of the photographer, Nishanth Jois.

Task

- Thinking carefully about the two photos in Figures 3.1 and 3.2, how many differences can you find?
- Are there any similarities?
- Are there any questions you would like to ask to help you understand these uses of the Veda better?

Raising questions

The most obvious difference between the two photos is that the first shows the Veda being chanted orally in Vedic Sanskrit, whereas the second presents it in written form on a plaque in a huge modern temple in Delhi, sponsored by the business magnates, the Birla family. Another difference is that the first transmits the Veda in the way that it has been taught for centuries, to brahmins by brahmins (see below), hand gestures helping with the memorization process. The second represents a modern way of making a text known, through a kind of 'print' or written form. Third, this represents a different view on who should have access to the texts: just twice-born groups who alone were able to hear the Veda being recited, or anyone at all who can read the text, in translation if need be. The photos also suggest a difference between language as 'doing' something, primarily having a ritual function, and language as 'meaning' something, giving a teaching that is to be understood.

In what follows we shall explore these issues about orality, authority and access further. But you might also have asked: How important are the Vedic texts shown in these pictures? Who are they actually important for? What about the texts of the local and regional devotional traditions mentioned in the introduction to this chapter? What about texts such as the *Bhagavad Gita*, which we came across in Chapter 2? And are there particular texts used by Muslims in South Asia as well as the Qur'an and *ahadith*, for example (see Box 3.1)?

These are extremely important questions. They help us to realize that particular paradigms, or models for studying a religion, although very useful, can also blinker us or prevent us from looking at other material which might be of great importance but is simply excluded from that particular viewpoint. In this case, presenting the Veda as the scripture of Hinduism tends to blind us to a vast body of texts that are very much better known, either to Hindus across South Asia, or to Hindus who belong to particular devotional traditions. The former include the so-called Hindu epics, one of which will be the focus of Chapter 4. They also include the Puranic texts that contain the stories of many of the gods of popular Hinduism, texts that both Rammohun

Box 3.1 *Ahadith*

The *ahadith* are narratives of the words and actions of the Prophet Muhammad and his Companions. They provide the basis for *sunna*, the proper way of behaviour conforming to theirs. As such they are one of the four bases of Islamic law (see Chapter 8). They are collected in voluminous texts and strict criteria have been developed for judging the reliability of each *hadith*. Two of the most famous of the six authentic collections (*Sahih*) are known by the names of their collators: Bukhari (810–70 CE) and Muslim (817–74 CE).

and other Hindu elite writers in the nineteenth century criticized as linked with polytheism and idolatry. Nonetheless, these remain very important in temple art, comic books, devotional reading and worship, and Bollywood films, to name but a few examples. In this chapter, keep a careful eye out for other material linked with particular devotional traditions too, which helps you to see both why the stress on Veda is important and why it can be very misleading. First, though, we will see what the Veda contains and consider the nature of its authority.

Veda . . .

The Veda is primarily a body of ancient oral texts controlled by, and representing the viewpoint of, the brahmin specialists who were, and are, its custodians. Brahmins are brahmin by birth and so descend from brahmin families (although the vast majority of brahmins nowadays do not actually train as Vedic specialists).[3] The boys in Figure 3.1, however, are being taught by such specialists and will themselves become specialists in turn.

The standard classical view of what the Veda comprises is this. There are four Vedas, the *Rig*, *Sama*, *Yajur* and *Atharva Veda*. Brahmins may be trained to pass down one, two, three or even four Vedas. The last are known as Chaturvedi ('four-Veda' brahmins). Each Veda also contains four 'layers' of texts, which build in turn on the previous 'layers', sometimes even 'nestling' within them.[4] The core hymns are the earliest of all. The four layers are:

- *Samhita*s, collections of hymns used in the solemn sacrificial ritual;
- *Brahmana*s,[5] reflections on that ritual;
- *Aranyaka*s, developing the *Brahmana* material; and
- *Upanishad*s, texts often framed by ritual concerns but seeking the grounding of cosmos and person, on which the correspondences of the ritual might be seen to depend.

These Vedic texts are extremely difficult to date. The earliest hymns might have been composed around 1500–1200 BCE; the oldest Upanishad, from which our story in Chapter 2 came, perhaps around 900–800 BCE. But even the classical Upanishads were composed over maybe a millennium, and new Upanishads have been added right down to recent times. It is therefore important to note that the Veda is not a 'closed' canon in the sense of a body of texts that cannot be added to. We shall see the importance of this below.

The Vedic texts are often classed as *shruti*, literally 'hearing'. They were also said to have been 'seen' by the ancient *rishi*s or seers. From a theological view, this stresses their authority over their human transmitters. The *mantra*s (formulae for chanting) found in the hymn collections had to be passed on correctly. They were thought to be vital for structuring the cosmos – and society – via the ritual sacrifices. This may seem rather strange, but the basic idea was that there are a series of correspondences (*bandhu*s) between the microcosm, the 'little world' of the sacrificer, and the macrocosm, 'the large world' of the universe. Because the sounds of the *mantra*s were in a sense structured into the fabric of the universe, they could be used to order these connections and ensure a stable world. Very importantly, then, these texts were passed on orally, brahmin teacher to twice-born pupil, as continues today.

The twice-born were so-called because they were believed to have a 'second birth' through the sacred thread ritual that began their actual (or nowadays often nominal) period of Vedic study. The twice-born were defined in the brahminical texts as brahmins – those alone permitted to teach the Veda (note the way their own power is enshrined in this categorization); *kshatriya*s – warriors and rulers; and *vaishya*s – generally merchant groups. The vast majority of people, classified by this brahminical scheme as *shudra*s or servants, were thus excluded from even hearing these texts as they were not eligible for Vedic studentship. This immediately raises questions about the 'reach' of these texts and to what extent people excluded from them had, or developed, alternatives of their own. We shall see some answers to this below. You may now though be able to understand why these texts were not committed to writing until long after writing was used for secular purposes in India. Correct pronunciation and exclusivity were part of a fundamental worldview under brahminical control. Even when Vedic texts were written down with extensive commentaries, they were learned and discussed in brahmin teacher–pupil transmission lines to ensure correct interpretation (although the content varied from school to school). The notion that open access or individual reading of these texts would be appropriate was entirely alien. The plaque on the Birla temple therefore represents a massive modern change.

Lajpat Rai (1865–1928), a key member of the Arya Samaj reform movement in the early twentieth century, attributed this change to Dayanand Saraswati, the Samaj's founder, whom we shall meet below. Rai (1915: 54–5) wrote:

It may be difficult for us to visualize that in the second half of the 19th century the Vedas were a sealed book in India, and no one could even read them, much less quote them in open debate attended by all communities, Hindus and non-Hindus alike. At present the Vedas are being read, studied and commented upon by all classes and castes of Hindus. This is the greatest service rendered by Dayanand to the cause of religious and intellectual as well as social freedom in India, and this alone entitles him to be called the Saviour of Hindu India.

Notwithstanding Rai's enthusiasm, the extent to which the (now-printed) Vedic texts really are widely known and studied amongst Hindus remains questionable, although claims about their content as the source of all knowledge, including modern scientific inventions, are indeed widespread.[6] Other texts, as we have indicated, remain far better known and much more influential in people's everyday lives. Nonetheless, a very significant shift did take place in the modern period and we shall explore that further below. Here, though, we note that there was also an important sense in which the Veda had exercised authority for millennia, even while its contents were largely unknown. So we turn next to investigate its status as 'canon', that is, literally, as a 'measuring stick' for the authority of other texts.

. . . and 'Veda'

We have already mentioned that certain layers of the Veda, especially the Upanishadic layer, have been added to over the centuries. So the Veda cannot be a canon in the sense of a fixed text or body of texts. This immediately differentiates it from the Christian Bible, the Qur'an or the Guru Granth Sahib, for example.[7] To grasp how the Veda does nevertheless function as canon, the work of Jonathan Z. Smith and Julius Lipner is very helpful. Smith defines canon as both a 'process of limitation' and the ingenuity that seeks to overcome such limitation (Smith 1982: 52). Lipner (1994: 58–62) helps us to understand this in our context easily. He makes a distinction between Veda and 'Veda'. Veda (no inverted commas) is that set of texts with four layers referred to above. 'Veda' refers to any text that models its authoritative status on that of the Veda proper, by any one of a number of different strategies. These texts, if Sanskrit, usually fell into the broad brahminical category of *smriti* ('remembering'), a vast corpus of texts of varying kinds. They included the Epics and Puranas, as well as the many texts on *dharma*, which gave guidelines for custom and practice on how people of different statuses should behave (see Chapter 4). The *smriti* texts were open to all, not just the twice-born. So to that extent the claim to be 'Veda' was actually quite subversive (although this is not always recognized nowadays).

Here are two examples of very well-known 'Vedic' texts – the first one told throughout India, the second set also widely known but reflecting use within a particular devotional tradition. Look out for other uses of the term 'Veda' in the rest of the chapter too.

- The great epic of India, the Sanskrit *Mahabharata*, frequently calls itself 'the fifth Veda'. Its stories have been retold in plays, songs, regional and caste-based dramas and temple friezes, not to mention modern chapbooks, comics and the ninety-four part 'soap' on Indian TV (Chopra 1988–90), now available as DVD and You Tube episodes.
- The Gaudiya Vaishnava tradition of Chaitanya (1486–1534) bases itself chiefly on the well-known *Bhagavadgita* (part of Book 6 of the *Mahabharata*) and the *Bhagavata Purana*, a long devotional text about Krishna's childhood pranks and adult relationships with the *gopi*s. Both of these are important *smriti* texts. The Hare Krishna Movement (ISKCON), which see itself as a Gaudiya Vaishnava tradition, refers to these as Vedic texts – in inverts if you are looking at this from Lipner's point of view, but not if you are looking at it from ISKCON's.

We shall see more examples of the ways in which particular devotional traditions construct their own sets of texts later in the chapter. These form an important counterpoise to the notion of a single religion, Hinduism, with a single set of foundational texts, the Veda. First, though, we look at the shift to this latter position.

A crucial shift

The shift to identifying a religion's most ancient authoritative texts as its key defining feature is seen very clearly in the writings of Swami Dayanand Saraswati (1824–83), the founder of the Arya Samaj reform movement. The plan for his *Light of Truth* shows this plainly. For each chapter, Dayanand takes pains to identify the texts of the respective tradition that he criticizes, at length for the Jain tradition, more briefly for the Buddhist, Christian and Islamic (Dayanand Saraswati 1883). In addition, he mentions the Puranas, Tantras and 'like books' of the (Hindu) 'sectaries' whose teaching he rejects. His criticisms proceed by highlighting the inconsistencies and irrationalities of these texts, and the teaching and practices based on them. His apologetic context, defending (his view of Vedic) Hinduism as manifesting the 'light of truth' compared with other religions, is clear. In his approach if not his conclusions he shares much with Rammohun.

Dayanand, unlike Rammohun though, is known for rejecting even the Upanishads and other later layers of the Veda, to focus solely on the hymns as his authentic source. He said:

> I hold that the four *Vedas* – the repository of Knowledge and Religious Truths – are the Word of God. They comprise what is known as the

Sanhita-Mantra portion only. They are absolutely free from error, and are an authority unto themselves.

('A Statement of My Beliefs', see Bharadwaja 1984: 725)

A detailed look at the texts that Dayanand actually draws on shows that this is a considerable exaggeration (Llewellyn 1993), but it does seem that he increasingly rejected the Brahmanas and some of the book of Manu (a key Dharma Shastra text; see box on *dharma* in Chapter 4) in preference for the hymns. Given that the hymns are addressed to a host of different gods rather than the one God of whom he speaks, you might want to question why.

His general strategy of sorting out authentic from inauthentic texts was probably influenced by Swami Virjanand, his teacher from 1860–3. Virjanand distinguished between texts by genuine *rishi*s or sages, which were to be valued, and those that were by later teachers, and were to be disavowed. However, Dayanand's specific focus on the Vedic hymns may have resulted from European study. The first complete translation of the *Rig Veda* into a modern European language was produced by H.H. Wilson from 1850 onwards. It is not insignificant that a little later Dayanand requested books from Germany and employed a Bombay brahmin to teach him English and read Max Müller's translation of the *Rig Veda* to him (Jordens 1978: 56, based on Ghasiram's account). Scholars from Müller to A.B. Keith emphasized the superiority of the *Rig Veda* compared with the 'twaddle' of later Vedic texts (Tull 1991: 27). The high value that they placed on these 'originary' texts and their provision of new printed editions undoubtedly raised their status and made them more accessible to brahmin and other Indian scholars. Such attitudes may well have influenced Dayanand in his preference for the earliest Vedic layer. Below we shall examine the longer roots of processes of textualization in the construction of religion in modern South Asia. For now, we turn to a range of examples that suggest other continuing and developing patterns of practice.

The broader context: groups and their texts

So far we have suggested that a process of textualization focusing on the Veda as the 'scripture' for the religion of 'Hinduism' emerged in the work of Dayanand and others in the nineteenth century. In the second part of this chapter we want to look at a very different view of the way texts function in Indian contexts. Rather than stressing a unified religion, such as Hinduism, we shall indicate the enormous variation of authoritative texts that exists in India, linked with particular *sampradaya*s or devotional traditions. This will help us to understand the authority of the teacher's word (which we will look at again in Chapter 6), mechanisms of transmission and the importance of specific devotional traditions when trying to understand religion in modern South Asia. In addition, we want to stress the oral nature of many of these texts. It is not just that they are written down and then read or recited out loud. Many of them are oral compositions, songs, stories, poems or chants. They are passed on both orally and in written forms, by grandparents, teachers and interpreters, but the power of the text may be as much in its sound and in its performance as in its meaning and application, although this varies widely from case to case.

A hymn to Vishnu

> As he came and faced [God]
> there was a state of infinite bliss
> being with the servants [of God]
> in the great canopy of gems.
> Those who can [say] the thousand verses
> spoken by Caṭakōpaṇ from Kurukūr
> [city] abundant with gardens
> where bunches of blossoms grow
> are silent sages.
>   (Nammālvār, *Temple Tiruvāymoḻi* 10.9.11, see Narayanan 1994: 189)

Nammalvar (or Catakopan) (c. ninth century CE) was one of the Tamil Alvar poets from south India, ten men and one woman believed to have been 'drowned' in the love of Vishnu (Ramanujan 1981: ix). Nammalvar's *Tiruvaymoli*, 'Sacred Sayings' or 'Divine Word', was composed in Tamil. Its thousand verses are part of the *Divyaprabandham*, the main scriptural source of the Shrivaishnava community, to which the famous Vedanta commentator, Ramanuja, belonged. The verse above is part of a digest of songs from the *Tiruvaymoli*, which are still used in Shrivaishnava temples. During the major annual ritual procession enacting Nammalvar's own ascent to Vaikuntha, Vishnu's sacred abode, songs from this digest are sung (Narayanan 1994: 116–31). Vasudha Narayanan describes how, at the great temple of Srirangam, the reciters stop at 2.00 A.M. having read section 10.8, the one before the section given above. 'At 6.00 A.M. they resume with 10.9, and Nammalvar's liberation is enacted in front of a crowd of thousands, which has been gathering since 4.30 A.M.' (Narayanan 1994: 186). Imagine that verse sung then . . . .

In this tradition, the *Tiruvaymoli* is explicitly called the 'Tamil Veda' and is believed, like the Sanskrit Veda, to be eternal and faultless, yet more accessible because in the people's language. Nammalvar is called a *rishi*, a seer, or a *muni*, silent sage, who sees or hears this eternal Veda and manifests it in his singing. Note that the verse above suggests that *anyone* who recites the whole text is also a *muni*, hinting at the power of the recitation itself. The thirteenth-century work, *The Heart of the Teacher* (Purushothama Naidu 1965), already explains in detail how the *Tiruvaymoli* is equivalent to the Veda as the sacred text of this particular community (Narayanan 1994: 19). Such a view continues today as was affirmed on the 'Web Page for the Sri

Vaishnava tradition of Ramanuja, Alvars, and rishis of the Upanishads and Vedas' (Varadarajan 2010).

Two Lingayata vachanas (songs) to Shiva

In a brahmin house
where they feed the fire
as a god
when the fire goes wild
and burns the house
they splash on it
the water of the gutter
and the dust of the street,
beat their breasts
and call the crowd.
These men then forget their worship,
and scold their fire,
O lord of the meeting rivers!
[Basavanna (probably 1106–1167/8 CE), see Ramanujan 1973: 85]

Better than meeting
and mating at the time
is the pleasure of mating once
after being far apart.
When he's away
I cannot wait
to get a glimpse of him.
Friend, when will I have it
both ways,
be with Him
yet not with Him,
my lord white as jasmine?
[Mahadeviyakka (younger woman contemporary, twelfth century CE),
see Ramanujan 1973: 140]

The Lingayatas or Virashaivas, in contrast to the Alvars, give us an excellent example of a movement that has constructed its sacred texts almost without reference to the Vedas. Rejecting both brahminical ritual (including the maintenance of the household fire) and *puja* (see Chapter 5), along with caste constraints, Lingayatas seek their Lord Shiva within themselves, sometimes externalizing this by a small *lingam* worn around the neck. The movement's fundamental texts are the *vachana*s or songs written in Kannada, particularly in the twelfth century, by wandering saints, male and female, including Mahadeviyakka quoted above. The songs were given contexts in hagiographies written from the thirteenth century on. When the movement underwent a revival in the fifteenth century, the *Shunyasampadane* or *Attainment of the Void*, which became an authoritative Virashaiva text, selected key *vachana*s and wove them into a new narrative (Schouten 1991: 12–14). Virashaiva editors arranged the *vachana*s according to the six steps of devotion that were developed within the tradition. The texts then continue to construct the tradition as the tradition constructs its texts. This is a constant process of renegotiation. Nowadays, Basava's *samadhi* at Kudala-sangam, the place of the meeting rivers in his poem above, is marked by a temple and he is now worshipped (by once-rejected *puja*) in a *lingam*, showing his identity with Shiva at the sixth and final stage of devotion (see Rainbow Skills n.d.).

Guru Granth Sahib

Figure 3.3 shows a picture of the Guru Granth Sahib, the collection of *shabd*s (hymns) made by Guru Arjun, the fifth Sikh Guru (1563–1606). The tenth Guru, Guru Gobind Singh (1666–1708), declared that on his death it would function as the next and permanent Guru, instructing with its teachings the Sikh community he had instituted. Its *gurbani* (hymns – literally, 'words of the Guru = teacher = God') are then identified as the scripture or authoritative teaching of Sikhism. It is noteworthy that this is not how Dayanand (who spent much of his life in the Punjab, the region in which Sikh traditions developed) sees it. 'Sikhism' does not feature either in Dayanand's plan for his book mentioned above or in the later chapters of *Light of Truth* (1883),

Figure 3.3 Hand writing a copy of the Guru Granth Sahib. Each copy is written or printed with 1,430 pages. Credit: NARINDER NANU/AFP/Getty Images.

which Dayanand reserves for his critique of the religions mentioned there. Rather, he includes a criticism of both Guru Nanak (the first Guru) and Guru Gobind Singh in his Chapter 11. 'An Examination of the Various Religions Prevailing in Aryavarta', immediately after dismissing the Kabirpanthis, those who follow Kabir (see Chapter 2). He recognizes different teaching traditions among them, including the Udasis, the Nirmalas, the Akalis and so on, rather than a single 'Sikhism' (for the construction of which see Chapter 9). Criticizing the five Ks,[8] which he links with the need to fight off 'the Mohammedans', now anachronistic, he says that they 'have now come to be regarded as part and parcel of the *religions* of the Sikhs. It is true that they do not practise idolatry but they worship the *Grantha* even more than idols. Now is not this idolatry?' (Bharadwaja 1984: 445, our emphasis).

You might wish to consider how such a charge might be rebutted from different Sikh points of view (McLeod 1995) and from an understanding of popular religion in the Punjab (Ballard 1996). What Dayanand's discussion does point to, though, is an understanding of the Guru Granth Sahib as the authoritative text of a particular *panth* or devotional tradition, akin to the teachings of Kabir (Hess and Singh 1983). Although we do not support his critique, we do stress that an understanding of plural *panthic* traditions, based on the teachings of an inspired teacher (like Guru Nanak or Kabir) or set of poets (like the Alvars), may give us a better model for understanding the role that authoritative texts often have played and still do play in South Asian religious traditions.

The Qur'an in vernacular use

In Islamic traditions, the Qur'an and *ahadith* have, of course, always been recognized as authoritative, in South Asia as elsewhere, not least as part of the fourfold basis for Islamic law. The *'ulema* (scholars) were trained in at least one of the main schools of law and were expected to be proficient in its fourfold basis. From the late eighteenth century, major shifts took place as some Muslim scholars started to emphasize the Qur'an over the other three foundations (*ahadith*, analogy and consensus; see Chapter 8), while individuals without traditional training (such as the major twentieth-century Islamist thinker, Syed Abul Al'a Maududi; see Chapter 10) claimed the right to interpret the Qur'an themselves.

However, the Qur'an has played other roles in South Asian Islam, as elsewhere, while teaching belonging to particular Muslim Sufi lineages or *silsila*s has developed as a key text base alongside it (see Box 5.1 on *silsila*s in Chapter 5). A very good example of this is Amir Hasan's Persian *Fawa'id al Fu'ad*, or *Morals for the Heart* (Lawrence 1992), still in print nowadays in India and Pakistan in Urdu translation. It collects together a record of 188 occasions when Amir Hasan heard the great Chishti saint and teacher, Nizam ad-Din Awliya (1238–1325),[9] teach in Delhi. It covers many topics including the importance of one's *shaykh* or teacher as the one who brings you to God, a beautiful passage on ways of preparing the heart to recite the Qur'an, and compassionate understanding for those who find it hard to memorize, based on the example of Muhummad himself. As a generic model for other such *mulfuzat* (collections of saints' teachings), the *Fawa'id al Fu'ad* helped shape the reading practices of the Chishti *silsila* in particular, Chishtis tending to read Chishti works, Naqshbandis Naqshbandi ones and so on. As a consequence, these Sufi lineages operated in a not dissimilar way to Hindu devotional traditions based on particular texts of their own, though the Qur'an and *hadith* remained central to Sufi traditions as well (Green 2006: 23–7, 2010a).

In Figure 3.4 we see a very different use of the Qur'an in what the anthropologist, Joyce Flueckiger, calls vernacular Islam. In her healing room in Hyderabad, south India, Amma sees people from many different social and religious backgrounds, offering them teaching and prescriptions to address the troubles they face. These include childhood illnesses, failing business, infertility and marital infidelity amongst others. Here we see Amma writing

Figure 3.4 Amma writing a prescription for unfaithfulness. Reproduced courtesy of Joyce Flueckiger.

on a *chapati* to deal with unfaithfulness. She writes Qur'anic verses, the names of God and his *maukil* (messengers and deputies, including angels), number squares and then another name on each piece. That name is the name of the offending husband and the *chapati*s are to be fed to a dog. As the dog is faithful to the one who feeds it, so may the husband return to fidelity with his wife (Flueckiger 2006: 85–6).

You, like Muslim Deobandi reformers (see Chapter 8), might see this as superstition to be dismissed. This would be to reject a massive domain of religion in modern South Asia (Ballard's 'kismetic' dimension referred to in Chapter 1), perhaps on Dayanand's basis of 'rationality' or (highly selective) scriptural teaching. In Chapters 5 and 11 we return to related forms of popular practice and their complex underlying logics. Here, though, we note that Amma's unusual authority as a female healer in this community is grounded not only in her *shaykh* husband's sanction and in the messages she receives through her own relationship with God. Importantly, she stresses that everything she needs for healing is given in the Qur'an and is justified by it (*Suras* 113 and 114). Her act of writing takes its root in the teaching of God who 'taught man with the Pen' (*Sura* 96: 4, cited by Flueckiger 2006: 67).

The gender twist: women's voices and textual authority

The issue of the authority of particular texts, who has the opportunity to learn them, teach them and use them in ritual contexts, is, then, thrown sharply into relief when looked at it in terms of gender. Searching for a ('Hindu') Golden Age, scholars have looked back to an idyllic period when men and women had equal access to the Veda, both as students and as teachers. Gargi and Maitreyi, two women scholars mentioned in one of the oldest Upanishads, have largely borne the glory of this view. Not so Katyayani, Maitreyi's co-wife, for she was 'pre-occupied with women's matters' (*Brihadaranyaka Upanishad* 4.5.1, tr. J. Suthren Hirst), 'mere' domestic affairs or, perhaps rather, a grip on the food and robes needed by her husband for each ritual (Roebuck 2003: 404). Gargi and Maitreyi, however, by refusing to take no for an answer and engaging in debate, gained the highest teaching about ultimate reality.

This is a very partial picture, however. As Uma Chakravarti (1989) has pointed out, it edits out the majority of the female population, namely the low-caste *dasi*s or servant/slaves, as well as most other women. If we search the stories carefully, we gain further clues about their social background, but this remains relatively minimal in terms of gender spread (Black 2007). This alerts us to a very important issue in the whole of this book. What we may call the normative view of World Religions as -isms, which emerges during our period, is to a large extent an elite construction, particularly when it is grounded in Vedic textual foundations. Women often remain marginalized by this too.

In her study of contemporary women Vedic scholars in India, Laurie Patton (2009) is analysing the different ways in which Vedic access is being granted or still debarred to women in different geographical and social contexts. She has found that this varies from those allowed to study it in a university context but not to chant it, to those allowed to chant, particularly in Pune, Maharashtra. She suggests that it is significant that this region had a strong tradition of female education going back into the nineteenth century, perhaps most famously exemplified by Tarabai Shinde (see Chapter 10). The persisting context in which these women are forging new ways of engagement is nicely shown by a statement of Shankaracharya Kapileshwaranand Saraswati. Like many who opposed female education in the nineteenth century in Muslim and Hindu households, he announced in August 1994 that if women recited the Veda their health would be affected and they would be unable to bear healthy babies (*India Today*, 15 August 1994: 26, cited in Narayanan 2002: 122). Patton's examples show how issues of gender, power and sacred text continue to be intertwined.

This is not just a modern issue. Vasudha Narayanan has uncovered a thirteenth-century woman scholar who clearly had familiarity with at least parts of the Veda. Tirukkoneri Dasyai was a commentator on the part of the Tamil Veda from which Nammalvar's poem above came. In her *Garland of Words*, Tirukkoneri quotes the *Taittiriya Upanishad* and sections of the Saṃhitas in Sanskrit to support her understanding of the Tamil text she is interpreting (Narayanan 2002: 122). Yet her *Garland of Words* was only recently discovered; it had been marginalized for centuries by comparison with the five male-authored commentaries that her Shrivaishnava tradition recognizes – this despite the poems of a woman, Andal, being included in the Tamil Veda itself. As in other religious traditions, it seems that the sacred texts of this tradition and their authoritative commentaries have in the past too been constructed to prioritize the male voice and excise female scholarship from public view.

The politics twist: Vedic speech and nationalist politics

During the nationalist movement in the late colonial period, India became envisaged as the Mother Goddess, Bharat Mata. It is not incidental that one verse of 'Bande Mataram', Bankim Chandra Chatterjee's (1882) nationalist 'Hymn to the Mother' (see Lipner 2005: 297), praises the Goddess in three forms:

> *tvaṃ hi durgā daśapraharaṇadhāriṇī*
> *kamalā kamaladalavihāriṇī*
> *vāṇī vidyādāyinī namāmi tvām*
> We greet you Durga holding ten weapons, Lakshmi borne on the lotus petal, Speech giving knowledge.

In hailing the Mother in this trio, India's identity is firmly grounded not only in Hindu devotional traditions, but also implicitly in a Vedic foundation, since Speech (*Vac, Vani*) was already addressed as a goddess in an early hymn of the Veda. One of the Veda's oldest mantras, the Gayatri, was held to epitomize Vedic speech; it is still recited three times daily by brahmins. Nowadays, the numerous websites devoted to the Gayatri, and the multitudinous devotional posters of Gayatri pictured as goddess, testify to both the democratization of this Vedic mantra and the ineradicably Hindu nature of her modern form (e.g. Gayatri Mantra 2010; Gayatri Mantra: the Mother of all Mantras n.d.; Gayatri Mantra – Enigma n.d.). Gayatri Mata is shown in Figure 3.5; Bharat Mata, Mother India, in Figure 3.6. Riding a lion, she recalls the Goddess Durga, also mentioned in the poem above.

Bankim's verse shows that nineteenth-century constructions of the Veda as the sacred text of proper Hinduism, such as Dayanand's, ran parallel to nationalist constructions of India free from the British. From the Figures, we see how easily these lend themselves to a conflation of 'Indian' with 'Hindu'. It is therefore not surprising that the attempt in 2006 by the Hindu nationalist Bharatiya Janata Party to make the singing of 'Vande Mataram'[10] compulsory in government-funded schools aroused severe opposition from those who pointed out that it, in effect, excludes from the nation Muslims, Christians and others who do not recognize such Hindu goddesses.[11] 'Muslims cannot sing Vande Mataram as they worship only Khuda[12] and no one else', Muslim leader Kari Raise Ahmed said (Chaubey 2006).

Figure 3.5 The Gayatri Mantra as goddess. Reproduced courtesy of Jacqueline Suthren Hirst.

In 2009, the controversy was still bubbling. The national convention of the Jamiat-e-Ulema-e-Hind was held at Darul Uloom Deoband, one of the largest Muslim seminaries in South Asia, about 150 kilometres from Delhi. The Home Minister, a Congress Party politician, was present at the convention, which endorsed a 2006 *fatwa* (decree) against 'Vande Mataram' as 'against the religious principles of Islam'. In turn, the BJP declared the Congress Party was being 'anti-national' and that the Home Minister's presence showed Congress's willingness to 'appease' the Muslim minority.

Yet the song remains popular as a projection of Indian identity. Aurobindo's widely used translation: 'Thou art Durga, Lady and Queen, With her hands that strike and her swords of sheen, Thou art Lakshmi lotus-throned, And the Muse a hundred-toned' can be found, for example, on websites such as The Holiday Spot (n.d.) on its Indian Independence Day page.

The religion twist: textualization and its roots

The 'textualization' of Indian religion in the late eighteenth and nineteenth centuries was a highly complex process with many roots. Earlier we saw how European translations of, and attitudes to, the Vedic hymns may have contributed to Dayanand's own views. In this section, we are going to trace four of these roots back further to see how they fed into the general approach that characterizes a 'religion' by its ancient texts.

The first root is in Christian missionary activity. In 1800, Baptists set up a

Figure 3.6 Bharat Mata (Mother India). Reproduced courtesy of John Zavos.

printing press in the Danish enclave of Serampore in Bengal, to disseminate Bibles and other Christian texts in Indian languages. This consolidated the position of the authoritative text as the basis for dispute between religious traditions and led to authoritative texts becoming more widely available through print culture. As those such as Rammohun Roy started to define 'Hindooism' in dialogue with Christian critique (see Chapter 2), text-based doctrine became a major locus for the demonstration of 'rationality' on either side. The Bible had, in Protestant Christianity, long enjoyed the status of being the only infallible authority: the principle of *sola scriptura*, 'according to scripture alone', was developed during the Reformation by reformers such as the German Martin Luther (1483–1546) to reject what they saw as the degenerative tradition developed by the Roman Catholic church. A parallel search for originary scripture prior to later degeneration gave a basis for the search for a Golden Vedic Age that preceded the superstition, idolatry, polytheism and maltreatment of women, identified by Europeans – administrators as well as missionaries – and Indian reformers alike as evils to be removed.

A second root of textualization lay in the development of colonial legal systems. British administrators, familiar with the text-based canon law of the Church, assumed the same would be so of Indian religions. They asked *pandits* to make judgments based on 'Hindoo' Dharma texts (understood as law books), and *maulvis* on the basis of the Qur'an and *ahadith*. As well as marginalizing local custom and practice and the way legal decisions were made, this clearly contributed to the textualization of religion, issues such as *suttee* being decided through disputes about textual interpretation, rather than on social or ethical grounds (Mani 1998).

A third and older root also lay in the work of Orientalists such as Sir William Jones (1746–94). Scholars trained in Latin, Greek and Avestan, they sought their own Indo-European roots as they realized the linguistic parallels that Sanskrit provided. In this context, they developed the notion of the 'Aryan invasion' of northwest India, held to have taken place around 1500 BCE, by people who called themselves Aryas ('noble ones') and brought with them Vedic texts composed in a language descended from an earlier Indo-European source and a social structure based on a tripartite distinction between priests, warriors and producers that they imposed on the indigenous people made servants. Although the notion of an 'invasion' is now discredited and the development of 'caste' seen to be highly complex (see Chapter 7A), a fierce debate continues today over the way in which Vedic Sanskrit did spread in northern India (Bryant and Patton 2005; Doniger 2009). You might want to follow this up. Here we note that early scholars such as Jones had been keen to get hold of Vedic texts for a long time (the '*Beds*' were mentioned from the sixteenth century on by Portuguese sources), but brahmins were very reluctant to disclose them to European scholars, who were clearly not twice-born. Jones did, however, have sight of a Veda manuscript.

This was later deposited in the British Museum in 1789, initiating serious European study into the Veda.

It would be misleading, though, to suggest that European influence alone accounted for textualizing factors. European knowledge came through brahmin sources, themselves elite controllers of the Vedic tradition, an important fourth root. As far back as the seventh century CE, Kumarila, a prominent thinker of the ritualist school, and Shankara, the famous Advaitin, distinguished between more and less authoritative parts of the Veda (they differed over which were which), and criticized their opponents on grounds of the sources they employed. Although in a very different context, they were also engaged in establishing which schools and texts were 'properly' Vedic (Suthren Hirst 2008). What they did not do, however, was to employ a typology similar to the modern 'World Religions' one that Dayanand used. Shankara places the Buddha, the Jina (Jain teacher) and Kapila, the teacher of another brahminical school, all on a par as teachers of misleading teaching traditions with unreliable texts.

It is also worth noting that, in Islamic traditions, procedures for authenticating texts had been rigorously developed both for Qur'anic verses, and to classify the *ahadith*, the words and actions of Muhammad and his Companions that form one of the bases for Islamic law. In addition, Muslim writers in India had displayed an interest in the textual sources of others from Al-Biruni's eleventh-century CE account on (see Sachau 1910: ch. XII). Abul Fazl's sixteenth century *Ain-i-Akbari*, commissioned by the Mughal emperor Akbar, specifically identifies the brahmins with their respective Veda (Gladwin 1786: 84) and comments that the nine sects of Hindus all 'have many books . . . which contain sublime doctrines and valuable instructions' (pp. 96, 97). Such preoccupations identifying groups and texts belonged, however, primarily to brahmin and scholarly Muslim elites. Here, as with the British later, the motivation was to provide good governance. Power politics, textualization and the construction of religion went hand in hand. And one model that emerged as a result in the nineteenth century was that of the World Religion with its ancient scripture, vying for truth with other comparable religions, or claiming that its view of truth transcended particular forms.

Concluding thoughts

In this chapter, we have seen the continuing vibrancy of devotional traditions based on their own foundational texts that may or may not relate themselves to the authority of the Veda, whether positively or by rejecting it. The Tamil Veda of the Srivaishnava tradition adopts its name and the efficacy of the recited text, but differs fundamentally from the Veda in the type of devotional understanding it embodies; the systematized texts of the widespread Lingayat tradition stand apart from any Vedic claims; the poems of the various Kabir Panth branches (see Chapter 2) uncompromisingly criticize brahminic (and Islamic ritual) practice, even while being absorbed back into Hindu devotional use; and the hymns of the Guru Granth Sahib, many sung by Guru Nanak out of a similar tradition to Kabir, are now presented as the scripture of (Khalsa) Sikhism, which marginalizes other Sikh traditions in its wake. Alongside these we have seen how, in some senses, the different Sufi *silsila*s function rather like these *sampradaya*s, centring around the teachings of their own revered saints, transmitted in texts read particularly within each tradition itself. Now twist the wrist and look back in the kaleidoscope: the –ism and its scripture appears. Twist it again and you see the devotional traditions, and the glinting contexts of interaction and change. The picture remains dynamic and invites us to look again.

Questions for further discussion and research

- How many different examples of links between sacred texts and power can you find in this chapter? What does this suggest?
- Discuss the view that the stress on the ancient authority of the Veda is itself a modern phenomenon.
- Compare the authoritative texts of a number of South Asian traditions. Possible modern ones to consider are the Swaminarayan movement (Williams 2001); the Radhasoami movement (Babb 1987; Juergensmeyer 1996; Gold 1987); Ramanandis' use of Tulsidas's *Ramcharitmanas* (Lutgendorf 1991); and the Baul tradition of Bengal (Openshaw 2002).
- A constitutional principle:

> The Government of Pakistan will be a state . . . . Wherein the principles of democracy, freedom, equality, tolerance and social justice as enunciated by Islam shall be fully observed; Wherein the Muslims of Pakistan shall be enabled individually and collectively to order their lives in accordance with the teachings and requirements of Islam as set out in the Holy Quran and Sunnah.
> [Adapted from Government of Pakistan (GOP), Ministry of Justice and Parliamentary Affairs, the Constitution of the Islamic Republic of Pakistan as Modified up to 19 March 1985 (1985) (hereafter '1985 Constitution'), Art.2-A, cited in Kennedy 1992: 769]

What might be the implications of a state including mention of an authoritative text in its constitution?

Further reading

Flueckiger, J.B. (2006) *In Amma's Healing Room: Gender and Vernacular Islam in South India*, Bloomington: Indiana Press.
>   A sensitive ethnographic study of the way in which Amma draws people of many different backgrounds to her healing room, showing the many ways in which she and her husband rely on the Qur'an.

Jones, K.W. (1989) *Socio-Religious Reform Movements in British India*, Cambridge: Cambridge University Press.
>   Includes a summary on Dayanand and the Arya Samaj (pp. 95–103).

Lipner, J. (2010) *Hindus: Their Religious Beliefs and Practices*, 2nd revised edn, London: Routledge.
>   A comprehensively revised version of this detailed introductory text, which draws the distinction between Veda and 'Veda' with numerous examples.

Lawrence, B.B. (tr. and annotated) (1992) *Morals for the Heart: Conversations of Shaykh Nizam ad-din Awliya Recorded by Amir Hasan Sijzi*, introduction by K.A. Nizami, New York: Paulist Press.
>   A fascinating collection to dip into, to gain a flavour of Indo-Persian Sufi concerns in fourteenth-century South Asia in a form that has shaped this kind of literature ever since.

Narayanan, V. (2002) *The Vernacular Veda: Revelation, Recitation, and Ritual*, Columbia: University of South Carolina.
>   A detailed readable study of the historical and contemporary importance of the Tamil Veda, by an anthropologist and historian, with poetic translation and key comparisons to the Sanskrit Veda.

4 Myth

Having looked questioningly in Chapters 2 and 3 at two classic features of religion (deities and foundational texts), we now turn to a third, namely myth. We shall explore this using a very striking development in recent South Asian social history. This is the now famous 'TV *Ramayan*', produced and directed by Ramanand Sagar and broadcast in over ninety episodes on Doordarshan, the Indian state TV network, in the late 1980s (Sagar 1987–8). Through this media event, we shall consider how myths can become integral to ways of defining allegiances and traditions, shared histories and political aims, and we shall also explore how they may resist hegemonic renderings. This will lead us to examine the category of 'myth' in the construction of religion, and its relationship with 'history' in particular social and political contexts.

Case study: Ramanand Sagar's *Ramayan*

Figure 4.1 A poster for Sagar's *Ramayan*.

Task

Look carefully at the poster in Figure 4.1 advertising Sagar's *Ramayan*.

- What is your initial reaction? Why do you think this is?
- What claim is being made?
- What further questions would you want to raise to help you understand and assess this claim?

Your initial reactions probably depended on whether or not you were familiar with Bollywood films and their imagery or with the story being portrayed. If not, you will probably have wanted to ask who the characters are, and why one seems to be a monkey in human form and another has ten heads. You may have wondered why this kind of story is claimed to be a universal 'best watch' and have been inclined to think, in a chapter on myth, that 'myth' might imply something that could not be true. The brief synopsis of the story in Box 4.1 should enable you to identify the characters shown. At the end of the chapter you might want to come back to your initial response and see how you would read the poster in the light of the discussion that follows.

These then are the bare bones of the Ram-katha, the story of Rama.

Box 4.1 The Ram-katha

The Ram-katha,[1] the story of Rama,[2] tells of prince Rama, the rightful heir to the throne of Ayodhya, who is deprived of this succession through the machinations of his stepmother Kaikeyi, and banished to the forest along with his devoted wife Sita, and loyal half-brother Lakshmana. During their wanderings in the forest, Sita is abducted by Ravana, the ten-headed demon king of Lanka, who takes her away to his island kingdom. Rama and Lakshmana, with the help of Hanuman the monkey king, defeat Ravana, rescue Sita and return in triumph to Ayodhya. Here Rama assumes his position as king, taking over from another half-brother, Bharata, Kaikeyi's son. He has been waiting nobly to submit to the rightful heir, leaving Rama's sandals on the throne to indicate this. Sita's virtue is compromised by her stay in Lanka, however, and although she has already proved her chastity by undergoing an ordeal by fire (*agni-pariksha*), she is banished to the forest by Rama, where she is eventually swallowed up by the earth, despite Rama's later attempts to reinstate her.

Although it sounds like a classic 'good versus evil' story, and may be told as such, it is not always so straightforward. The story of Rama has existed for centuries in literally thousands of versions. Some reverse the place of the hero, putting Ravana in Rama's place. Some are religious, some political. Some are linked with a particular caste group or region, some sung by women, others performed by men. Some span religious traditions, others have a particular Buddhist, Jain or Hindu orientation. The list is endless (for useful introductions and selections, see Suthren Hirst 1997; Richman 1991a, 2001). For this reason, the south Indian poet and scholar, A.K. Ramanujan (1991: 46), talks of a 'pool of signifiers', a repertoire of characters, plot and relationships that may appear in various forms, yet are recognizable for what they are.

At the same time as having this multiple and dynamic history, the story is also part of the corpus of work known as *itihasa*. This term means 'thus indeed it was', indicating the telling of a tale. It is now often translated as 'history'. Encompassing both these meanings, it is used here to denote the so-called Sanskrit epic tradition, which refers not just to the Ramayana, but also to the Mahabharata, the Great [Tale or War] of Bharat (India), which recounts the conflict between two sets of cousins, the Pandavas, accompanied by Krishna, and their nemesis, the Kauravas. Together these tales in verse represent an enormous body of literature, which has become central to South Asian culture over many centuries. Although the Sanskrit *Ramayana* is attributed to the authorship of Valmiki and the Sanskrit *Mahabharata* to Vyasa, the Religious Studies scholar and Sanskritist, Julius Lipner (1994: 125), comments that 'neither . . . are the work of a single hand. Both . . . took shape by way of numerous interpolations and additions'. This Sanskrit epic tradition has, then, 'taken shape' in South Asia. It is itself a tradition moulded over time by the telling of tales, often in oral form, and through 'numerous interpolations and additions' (p. 125). It also relates to a vast body of other stories, both in Sanskrit and in vernacular languages, told in drama, puppet plays, poetry, hero tales, philosophical explorations and devotional texts, to name but a few genres. These are not simply derivatives of the supposedly 'original' Sanskrit epics, but are related to them, or developed independently of them, in all sorts of complex ways For this reason, to avoid the implication that they are all 'versions' of a single original, in this chapter we will speak most often of different 'tellings', following the example of A.K. Ramanujan (1991).

The *Ramayan* is not the only epic to meet TV fame.[3] The *Mahabharat* was also serialized on Doordarshan in the late 1980s, but only after the serialization of the *Ramayan* had proved, if you will excuse the pun, to be such an epic phenomenon. Shown weekly on Sunday mornings, the *Ramayan* had the largest ever audience figures for a TV programme, drawing viewers across modern religious divides. It has since been watched worldwide in numerous rebroadcasts, video and DVD versions. Many commentators have remarked on the impact that the series had. The scholar Philip Lutgendorf, for example, notes regular media reports of 'the cancellation of Sunday morning cinema shows for lack of audiences, the delaying of weddings and funerals to allow participants to view the series, and the eerily quiet look of many cities and towns during screenings' (Lutgendorf 1995: 224). He also notes various devotional and ritual activities associated with viewings. For example, he cites a newspaper report describing regular activities at a sweetshop in Benaras, where:

> a borrowed television was set up each week on a makeshift altar sanctified with cow dung and Ganges water, worshipped with flowers and incense, and watched by a crowd of several hundred neighbourhood residents, who then shared in the distribution of 125 kilos of sanctified sweets (*prashad*), which had been placed before the screen during the broadcast.
>
> (Lutgendorf 1995: 224)

Such accounts point to this being arguably one of the most powerful tellings of Ram-katha that has ever taken place in South and Southeast Asia and their diasporas. In order to understand this power, we need to explore three ways of contextualizing the series. First, however, we want to comment on the social location of myth more generally.

Myth . . .

In popular usage, the term 'myth' often implies 'untrue'. In European scholars' descriptions of Indian stories it has often had profoundly negative connotations,[4] yet as Ninian Smart pointed out when discussing what he wanted to define as the '*mythic* or *narrative* dimension' of religion: 'The term [myth] may be a bit misleading, for in the modern study of religion there is no implication that a myth is false' (Smart 1998: 15). What then is a myth?

Smart himself talks of myth as 'the story side of religion', of 'vital stories', of 'sacred narrative', and of different types of stories that religious communities may tell. He stresses that a religion's 'seminal stories' (i.e. myths) may or may not be rooted in history, and emphasizes the link between myth and ritual (Smart 1998: 15). Unlike the many writers who have approached the study of myth from psychological, sociological, structuralist and other theoretical perspectives, Smart avoids taking a particular analytical approach; he is more concerned with explaining the significance of myths in shaping religious world views. This is an interesting approach that helps to explain the significance of myths in people's lives, but, at the same time, his world religions framework can confine myths to a specific religion. In such a framework, we might see the Ramayana as part of a corpus of Hindu myths located in a particular range of texts, including the older Vedas and the Puranas (see Box 4.2). The study of Ram stories, however, helps to demonstrate that

Box 4.2 Puranas

The Puranas constitute another massive body of Sanskrit texts that belong, like the Sanskrit epics, to the *smriti* category of texts, according to the brahminical classification that has become widely used (see Chapter 3). Dating them is extremely difficult with much of the material going back earlier than the versions we have now, perhaps to the early centuries CE, and passages appearing in more than one Purana. There are said to be eighteen major and eighteen minor Puranas. They tend to focus on one particular deity as Supreme (whether Vishnu, Shiva or Devi, the Goddess) and reflect the competition between developing devotional traditions. One of the most famous, perhaps consolidated around the ninth century CE, is the *Bhagavata Purana*, which tells the stories of Krishna's birth and childhood and his loving relationships with the *gopi*s, stories reflected in the way the countryside around Mathura is still seen as the place of his continuing play with his devotees (see Chapter 1). For more on the Puranas and their relation to *itihasa*, see Klostermaier (1989: ch. 5).

many stories are common to more than one religious tradition, may have forms that are not themselves apparently 'religious' and may draw on or be merged with much more localized folk tales. We will see some examples of this below. Myths in this sense do not obey the rules of categorization we frequently attempt to impose on them. They weave their way through different localities and linguistic turns as they are told and re-told, acquiring new meanings and drawing imaginatively on other mythic tales as they go.

For this reason, it is difficult to provide a comprehensive survey of South Asian myths, particularly in one chapter of a book such as this.[5] Instead, we will use the Ram stories to demonstrate how myths develop and relate to social life. In terms of defining myth, our preference is for a rather general definition such as Eric Csapo's. Myth, he says, 'might be more usefully defined as a narrative which is considered socially important, and is told in such a way as to allow the entire social collective to share a sense of this importance' (Csapo 2005: 9).

This enables us to look at which group tells a story, how and for what ends, so long as it does not make us forget that, even within communities, and certainly outside particular ones, there will be alternative 'tellings' circulating. This emphasis on communities, their social and political values and the contestation of these values also points us towards Bruce Lincoln's (1999: 147) understanding of myth as 'ideology in narrative form', a means of asserting and challenging particular ways of being. This might lead you to ask: What 'ideology in narrative form' does Sagar's *Ramayan* present? And why might this have proved so popular?

. . . and mythologicals

The poster we have used to introduce our case study refers to the serial as 'mythological'. Although this term has of course a general meaning related to myth, it is also a specific reference to a genre of film in India's enormous film industry known as 'Bollywood'. This is the first context in which we shall consider Sagar's production. Mythologicals are as old as the Bollywood industry itself. In the 1910s the film-maker Dadasaheb Phalke made several films drawing on the epic and puranic story tradition, including a telling of the story of Ram's assault on Lanka called *Lanka Dahan*, made in 1917. The same element of devotional response familiar in the TV *Ramayan* has been noted in audiences attending these early mythologicals (see Lutgendorf 1995: 219).

The mythological genre continued to be reproduced with limited success as the Indian film industry began to grow. One striking example of the genre is the 1975 film *Jai Santoshi Maa*. This film is based on a folk tale (*vrat katha*) related to Santoshi Ma, a goddess who 'seems to have become popular in north India during the 1960s, spreading among lower middle-class women by word of mouth and through an inexpensive "how-to" pamphlet and religious poster of the goddess' (Lutgendorf n.d.). The low-budget film was a surprise box office hit, and as a result the popularity of this goddess increased dramatically, crossing over, as one scholar recently notes, from a localized folk existence to national popularity, almost a new goddess, 'spring(ing) full grown from the head of Bollywood' (Doniger 2009: 677). As another scholar observes, this transition was not so surprising, because of several layers of intertextuality:

> The colours of her clothes and complexion were drawn from a palette standardised by the poster art industry that dominates the iconographic imaginations of most modern-day Hindus. Her characteristic poses showed her standing or sitting on a lotus, as several other goddesses do. And she shared her most prominent implements . . . with the great goddess often named Durga.
>
> (Hawley 1996: 4)

Through a combination of generic and specific references, then, Santoshi Ma settled into a new level of divine popularity, framed by her celluloid narrative.

The reference to the mythological genre in the *Ramayan* poster indicates the conscious debt to the social history that produced Santoshi Ma, and in many ways there is a parallel to be drawn with the dramatic success of the film. The production of the *Ramayan* on television, of course, allowed for a much more detailed exploration of the Ram-katha themes, in successive episodes. The genre of the soap opera is often invoked as an explanation of the gripping popularity of the weekly episodes. There is, however, another vital generic context that helps us to understand the social location of this telling.

Ramlila performances

Ramlila performances became increasingly popular in northern India from the eighteenth century on. These spectacular annual events portray episodes from Tulsidas's sixteenth-century devotional telling of the Ram-katha[6] during the Autumn Nine Nights (Navratri) Festival. They provide another important context for understanding the resonances of Sagar's serial. Culminating on the tenth night, Dassehra, with the slaying of Ravan, a giant papier mâché demon blown up with exploding fireworks, these performances operate simultaneously as entertainment, markers of social status (for the sponsors of the performances) and devotional activity, as the *lila* is seen as making the deities present to the onlookers through the actors.

'Ram-lila' literally means 'the play of Rama'. Borrowing its form from Krishna-lilas, it is 'play' not just in the sense of performance, but also of the freely undertaken 'play of the deity' shown in the human realm on our behalf. The rise of Ramlilas is an indication of the competition that developed in this part of India in the eighteenth and nineteenth centuries, between groups devoted to Ram (especially the powerful Ramanandi order; see also Chapter 11), and those devoted to Krishna, whose play in Mathura we looked at in Chapter 1. Local maharajas would act as patrons of particular Ramlilas, Banaras gaining a reputation for being the most spectacular, so the Ramlilas became embedded in regional issues of prestige and political power (Lutgendorf 1991; Richman 1991a, 2001). All this should alert us to the power of this story, its implication in politics at a number of different levels.

Sagar's many sources

So far we have emphasized the diversity of the Ram-katha, its multiple variations and its significance as a feature of competition and politics related to specific communities. All this may raise the question of how far this is a Hindu story as such. At one level, this might seem a silly or even insulting question, another attempt to insinuate that Hinduism does not even have its own central stories of which this one is key. Yet there is an issue of profound importance here. Just as Jewish, Christian and Muslim traditions tell a story of Abraham/Ibrahim and his two sons, yet in very different ways reflecting their own self-understandings of God and their related religious identities, so too South Asians of different traditions have told the story of Rama for their own reasons. While Jewish, Christian and post-Christian feminists, Church Fathers, medieval scholiasts and others have interpreted Eve and the 'spare rib' or 'side' of Adam variously, so too has the story of Rama enabled different groups to think creatively about their own (theological, social, political) priorities and ends and indeed to construct their own identities on such bases.

Scholars, aware of the great plasticity and openness of myths in general (van Baaren 1984) and the Rama story in particular, have feared that Sagar's version of the Rama story neglected this multiplicity with potentially dangerous consequences (see below and Thapar 1990). Sagar himself has sought to allay this fear, stressing that he consulted and drew from several versions; indeed, this was often emphasized by the narrator in the series (Sagar himself) as a means of emphasizing the theme of the story as a symbol of national integration (Lutgendorf 1995: 222). Although this was treated with scepticism by some critics, and although the powerful influence of his version can indeed not be ignored, we should note that the popularity of the series was very wide. The audience included Sikhs, Jains, Muslims and Hindus across the political spectrum, bound together by the drama of this long-running story. In addition, as we have seen, the TV version simply extends the *lila* tradition, combining it with the 'visual vocabulary' of the mythological, to produce a significant telling, resonating powerfully in the interwoven worlds of politics, business and devotion. This certainly makes it significant, but its resonance with older traditions and contexts mediates its dominance, placing it always within a narrative framework grounded in heterogeneity. And indeed it does seem that multiple tellings do continue to thrive, as we shall see in the next section.

Many Ramayanas: twisting the kaleidoscope on the Rama myth

The term 'many Ramayanas' is taken from the title of a fascinating edited volume by Paula Richman (1991a). It hints at the plethora of tellings of the Ram-katha. Here we give just a few examples.

The first poem?

The great ascetic, Valmiki, wondered: '"Is there a man in the world today who is truly virtuous?"' (1.2). In response, the sage Narada told him the story of Rama (1.7–1.79). Then, wandering in the forest, Valmiki saw a hunter shoot down a male *krauncha* bird just as he was mating, and in his grief he cursed the hunter (2.2–2.14). He proclaimed that the verse he 'produced in this access of *śoka*, grief, shall be called *śloka*, poetry, and nothing else' (2.17). As a result he was commissioned by the god

Brahma to 'tell the world the story of the righteous, virtuous, wise, and steadfast Rāma . . . . No utterance of yours in this poem shall be false. Now compose the holy story of Rāma fashioned into *śloka*s to delight the heart' (2.34–2.35) (from *The Rāmāyaṇa of Vālmīki, Bālakāṇḍa*, in Goldman 1984).

One of the most powerful tellings of the story is Valmiki's Sanskrit *Ramayana*. Told in seven books (*kanda*s), it has long been regarded as the *adikavya*, the first poem, or first work of literature of the Sanskrit tradition. In the extract above, the Sanskrit puns on the terms 'shoka' and 'shloka'. From Valmiki's grief (*shoka*) over the death of the mating *krauncha* bird come the lines of poetry (*shloka*) in which the *Ramayana* attributed to him is told. Scholars discuss the date of this long poem, later regarded along with the *Mahabharata* as one of the two great Sanskrit epics (*itihasa*). Sanskrit scholar, John Brockington, and folklorist, Mary Brockington, present what they see as the original poetic core centring on a martial hero, Rama (dating to perhaps the eighth century BCE) (Brockington and Brockington 2006). On this, they argue, subsequent layers have been built. In these the story has come under the increasing influence of brahmins, who turned it into a story of *dharma* (correct social behaviour), with Rama as its chief exemplar (perhaps by around the second century CE). Finally it became a devotional text as Rama was first identified as an *avatar* (descent) of Vishnu and then as the Supreme Deity in his own right (Brockington 1984; Whaling 1980). Although the last is most clear in later texts, including Tulsi's (see below), Books 1 and 7 of Valmiki, which most scholars agree are later than the rest, already start to shadow this understanding. In one of its most influential forms, then, the story's plasticity and links with different identity constructions – a martial band, an ideal society based on brahmin values, a devotional community remaining under a brahmin wing – is already clear. People tell and retell significant stories, given sanction to do so by the stories themselves.

A Jain manuscript

Although the Valmiki *Ramayana* and many others show clear brahminical influence, the story was also influential in Jain circles from an early date, often cast as an oppositional telling (Thapar 1989). In some Jain tellings, Ravana becomes the ideal Jain ascetic, so that virtues of abstaining from any form of harm, and of truth-telling, become key. Rama may be portrayed as a Jain ascetic in his last life of rebirth, so cannot kill Ravana, a task left to Lakshmana. In the manuscript in Figure 4.2, beautifully digitized on the International Digamber Jain Organization's website, Lakshmana, Rama and Sita are shown approaching four Jain ascetics, with the splendid city of Lanka, over which Ravana rules justly, in the circle behind them. Note the flowers that are blooming in the ascetics' presence.

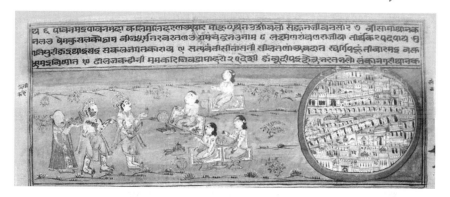

Figure 4.2 A Jain *Ramayana* manuscript. Reproduced courtesy of International Digamber Jain Organization, http://www.idjo.org/Manuscript. asp?id=17&i=2.

A devotional text in wider context

One of the most influential Rama tellings affirms that all the Vedas sing of:

> God who is one, desireless, formless, nameless and unborn, who is Truth, Consciousness and Bliss, who is supreme radiance, all-pervading and with all forms. It is He who has performed many deeds assuming a suitable form. That He has done only for the good of his devotees; for He is supremely gracious and loving to the suppliant. He is excessively fond of His devotees and treats them as his own. (1.12)
>
> The glory of the Name is thus infinitely greater than that of the Absolute (*nirguṇa*). I shall show below how in my judgment the Name is superior even to Śrī Rāma. (1.23)
>
> (Tulsidas, *Rāmcharitmānas*, see Gita Press 1968)

This text was composed by Tulsidas beginning in 15743 in Ayodhya, north India. It has become one of the most influential of all Hindu renderings of the story and has been translated into many north Indian languages; it is also the main basis of the TV serial version. Tulsi's text is often described as written in Hindi (a language that in the late nineteenth century developed a distinctly Hindu association; see Chapter 9). It is, however, more accurate to say that it was composed in Avadhi, a regional form of Hindustani spoken at the time in the eastern Uttar Pradesh area. Tulsi apologizes for his vernacular rendering, commenting that 'the glory of Śrī Rāma is charming indeed, while my speech is rough . . . [but] embroidery of silk looks charming, even on coarse cloth' [1.13 (6)]. The Avadhi context is significant, as it locates the *Ramcharitmanas* ('The Lake of the Doings of Ram') as part of a regional literary culture shared across religious traditions. Avadhi was the language in which the Indian Sufi love poets of the time wrote and the elites communicated; the *Manas*, as it has become known, is located in this rich context. For example, as Thomas de Bruijn (2005) demonstrates, Muhammad Jayasi's 1540 CE Sufi mystical romance, *Padmavat*, uses the story of Rama and Sita as an intertext for its story of devotion between King Ratansen, the Rajput ruler of Chittor, and the beautiful Padmavati. Functioning both as a love story and as a Sufi allegory for the devotee's mystical love of the divine, it also reflects competition between the 'external' Islam of the rulers and the Sufi 'internal' way, as well as the tensions between local kingdoms and the expansionist politics of the Delhi Sultanate (Sreenivasan 2007: 58–9 and see Chapter 1).

Although Tulsi's description of God as nameless, formless and so on chimes with this Sufi context, we can also see how it can easily be read in Advaitin terms (see Chapter 2). Indeed, it draws on the earlier Sanskrit Advaitin *Adhyatma-ramayana* in so doing. Tulsi, of course, thinks that this God takes form as Rama for the sake of his devotees, but also that this formless Reality is transcended by the Name (of Rama), chanted by devotees and mentioned throughout the text. Here he draws on the kind of understandings of 'the Name' found in the north Indian Sant tradition, which also influenced the early Sikh gurus (see Chapters 2, 6 and 9). The Sant tradition was itself probably influenced by Nath Yogi traditions, on which Jayasi drew overtly in telling his *Padmavati* story.[7] This fluidity should not be read incorrectly. The situation was one of competition between religious traditions, but these are not to be straightforwardly identified with the -isms of Hinduism, Islam and Sikhism in World Religions terms. As we shall see in Chapter 6, a model of particular interconnecting and competing teaching and devotional traditions may be a helpful one for understanding religion in South Asia (and indeed beyond).

Women's songs

> All there is for Sita is the lot of a daughter-in-law; a turtledove is standing in her way.
> The life of Rama's Sita was all innocence.
> Sita has left for the forest; wild cows cross her path.
> This harsh lot of a daughter-in-law is all because of that beastly Ravana
> . . .
> To Sita, the harsh lot of a daughter-in-law brought troubles as numerous as the hairs on one's head.
> She sent a share of it to her sisters, country after country.
> To Sita, the harsh lot of a daughter-in-law came a grain at a time.
> She sent a share of it to her relatives, village after village
> To Sita, life in the forest was imposed on her in a thousand ways.
> She handed it out on tamarind leaves to her friends, country after country.
> To Sita, the harsh lot of a daughter-in-law brought troubles as numerous as the hair on one's head.

She sent a share of it to her friends, country after country.

(from Poitevin and Rairkar 1993: 65–7)

In this contemporary song of the millstone, sung by Gujarati and Marathi peasant women as they grind flour, Sita becomes the vehicle for their own expressions of the 'harsh lot of a daughter-in-law', married into a husband's family, distanced from their own (see also Nilsson 2001). Singing together they can express their own hurts, knowing them shared and made safe in this domestic environment. The song demonstrates the way in which Ram-katha is developed to become a part of the everyday struggles of these women. Like other women's tellings, it expresses parts of the story in sometimes stridently resistant terms. One influential telling sees Sita rise up from captivity in Lanka to slay the demon Ravana herself, for she is none other than Devi, the Goddess (Coburn 1995). This telling contrasts quite starkly, as we shall see, with the dominant portrayal of Sita in modern tellings such as the TV *Ramayan*. You might want to compare this approach with that of other groups of women whose appropriation of the story reflects different caste interests (Narayana Rao 1991).

A Muslim interpreter

Justice M.M. Ismail (1921–2005) was the Acting Governor of Tamil Nadu and Chief Justice of the Madras High Court. This eminent Tamil Muslim was also a very influential interpreter of the Ram-katha, and stood in a line of such scholars going back to at least the eighteenth century (Narayanan 2001). He established the Kamban Kazhagan, a Tamil literary festival, named in honour of the possibly twelfth-century poet Kamban, whose *Iramavataram* is one of the most well-known tellings of the Rama story in the Tamil language. In the Rama story, one of the most contentious episodes is the killing of Valin, a monkey king. Rama shoots him from behind a tree, which apparently contravenes the ethics of a warrior code and calls into question Rama's status as an exemplar of correct social behaviour (*dharma*). M.M. Ismail's long book on this subject, comparing Kamban's treatment with Valmiki's, apparently vindicates Rama in Kamban's version, a justification that earned the praise of the Shankaracharya of Kanchi at the time (Narayanan 2001: 278). This is highly significant given that the Shankaracharyas of Kanchi have been involved in the Ayodhya dispute (see Chapter 11), frequently being aligned with the Hindu nationalist position.

Narayanan suggests that one reason why Kamban's telling has been open to Muslim interpretation is that it is seen as a key part of Tamil literary heritage rather than as a religious text, never having achieved liturgical status within the Shrivaishnava Tamil community. Nonetheless, for the Shankaracharya to praise a Muslim scholar who defended the great Hindu hero Rama both challenges the notion that Hindus and Muslims are necessarily divided by such a myth, and alerts us to the way that such agreements or differences are rarely politically or socially neutral. An interesting comparison can be made between Ismail's approach and that of the Tamil campaigner, E.V. Ramasami, who burned copies of the *Ramayana* in August 1956 on the Madras Marina, to protest against what he saw as the northern Hindi-based domination expressed in the story (see Richman 1991b).

The gender twist: Sita, the devoted wife?

> Eternal mythologies like the *Ramayan* are revived and popularised via state controlled media at the mass 'entertainment' level, and the negative values they convey regarding women find more than adequate reflection in textbooks and children's literature at the 'education' level. With Sita as our ideal, can sati [widow burning] be far behind? It is this overarching ideology of male superiority and female dispensability that sanctions sati and leads to its glorification, and accepts the silent violence against women that rages in practically every home across the country.
>
> (Kamla Bhasin and Ritu Menon, *Seminar*, February 1988, quoted in
> Tully 1992: 132)

In his book, *No Full Stops in India*, journalist and commentator Mark Tully quotes these Delhi feminists to show the level of feeling that the TV *Ramayan* generated, but also to reject their powerful claim, pointing out that Sagar does not treat Sita or the females in the series like 'sex objects'. Indeed, Tully compares what he sees as the chaste treatment of them in the TV version with Valmiki's description of the drunken orgy that takes place in Ravana's court between his wives. He also points out that Sagar himself was keen to show that it was Sita's decision to go into exile after the triumphant return to Ayodhya, not simply banishment by Rama. There are then disagreements over the meanings associated with this telling, which are played out by reference to other tellings. Such patterns of debate are as old as the Ram-katha itself. For Bhasin and Menon, it is the 'overarching ideology of male superiority and female dispensability' that is at issue here. This reminds us of Lincoln's definition of myth as 'ideology in narrative form'. The narrative as told in the TV *Ramayan* presents Sita as the *pativrata* supreme. The *pativrata* is 'one devoted to her lord', the attitude that a Hindu woman is widely expected to take to her husband, treating him as her god. When Rama is banished, Sita accompanies him and Lakshmana into the forest. When Ravana kidnaps her, she remains chaste and faithful to Rama. When Rama's side recovers her, she submits to the *agni-pariksha*, the test by fire, to attest her chastity. When Rama banishes her after their return because the people of his realm continue to question her faithfulness, she goes into exile without him and bears his twin sons in the forest.

That figures like Sita have a powerful influence seems indisputable. Hindu girls are still often told, 'Be like Sita', especially as they prepare for marriage, indicating not only that they should submit to their new husband but also to his family, their prospective mother-in-law in particular (Suthren Hirst 1997). This is not then simply a male–female hierarchy, but a more complex one built on patrilineal and patrilocal kinship patterns. It may seem small wonder that, like Eve and Mary, 'the scarlet woman' and 'pure virgin' in Christian tradition (see Warner 1976 and many others), Sita becomes the focus of feminist critiques too. Yet also like Eve and Mary, she has been reclaimed from 'patriarchal' readings, both by close reading of texts such as Valmiki's and Kamban's,[8] and by considering the multifarious tellings that offer widely varying strategies and interpretations.

What these diverse tellings show again is that myth, the 'ideology in narrative form', is contestable, dynamic and inter-textual.[9] It has been argued that the portrayal of Sita as the 'good wife' in a modern context owes not a little to developing late Victorian representations of the woman as 'angel of the home' (Tharu 1989). In arguing that Hinduism itself had ideals recognizable to the colonial power, Hindu reformers could reclaim key stories from critique and shape narratives that both justified and circumscribed women's participation in the nationalist struggle for independence (see further Chapter 10). This leads us to a consideration of politics and myth.

The politics twist: Rama's modern rule?

Long before the TV serial, the Ramayan story was a defining one in South and Southeast Asia. In the modern period it played a significant role in the nationalist struggle for independence from the British. M.K. Gandhi, for example, frequently invoked the idea of *Ram Rajya* (Ram's rule or government)[10] as the ideal form of government, which the freedom movement should strive towards as it fought the colonial rule of the British. In terms of the TV series itself, it is not insignificant that it was screened in the late 1980s. This was a decade in which the assertive, militant Hinduism known as Hindu nationalism was becoming increasingly significant in Indian politics (more on this to come in Chapters 8 and 11). In Chapter 3, we noted the way in which the relatively recent goddess Bharat Mata has increasingly come to be associated with this movement. Ram similarly has come to be associated with Hindu nationalism, although in many ways his association is much more complex, more powerful and more contested, as a result of the embeddedness of the Ram-katha in the multiplicity of South Asian traditions, as examined in this chapter.

Throughout the 1980s, as their political power grew, Hindu nationalist organizations attempted to capture the sacred quality of the land of India through a variety of symbolic ritual acts. In 1983, for example, the Hindu nationalist Vishwa Hindu Parishad (VHP, 'World Hindu Forum') organized a ritual event known as the Ekatmata Yatra. This event co-ordinated pilgrimage-type processions that criss-crossed India, carrying images of the goddess Ganga and also Bharat Mata, and distributing water from the holy Ganga river (Jaffrelot 2004; Lochtefeld 1996: 105–6). It is an example that indicates the trajectory of Hindu nationalist strategy during this period. As the political scientist Christophe Jaffrelot comments, recalling our definition of myth as ideology in narrative form, the 'religious geography of the Indian space was . . . harnessed for the ends of an ideological mobilisation' (Jaffrelot 2004: 212).

Although the strategy met with some success, it was rapidly superseded by Hindu nationalist campaigns developing around the figure of Ram. These have emphasized the relationship between the Ram-katha and the land of India, in terms of both the wanderings of Ram and his companions across the country, and the ubiquitous popularity of the story. Hindu nationalist organizations such as the VHP have projected Ram himself as a symbol of Hindu Indian-ness. 'Through stickers, cut-outs, magazine covers and calendars', the political scientist Manjari Katju (2003: 48) argues, the VHP have 'made a tremendous effort to publicise Rama as a strong warrior, fully armed, standing unmoved and determined before a surging tide, with a stoic expression on his attractive face' (see Figure 4.3).

Figure 4.3 Rama the Hindu nationalist warrior above the imagined Janmabhoomi temple. You can find more about this in Chapter 11. Reproduced courtesy of Christopher Pinney.

Although the TV *Ramayan* was not a project that can be explicitly linked to the organizations of Hindu nationalism, some scholars have noted a cultural association between the serial and the rise of Ram as a kind of national warrior. There are some parallels to be drawn, for example, between this masculine, heroic Ram and the stylized masculinity of Bollywood (Kapur 1993). We have also already noted the nationalist undertones of the series, as each episode opens with an invocation of the Ram-katha as a 'symbol of national unity and integration' (quoted in Katju 2003: 47). Certainly several scholars have noted this association, with the eminent historian Romila Thapar (1990) developing an impassioned argument against what she sees as the homogenization of the Ram-katha tradition, with Sagar's version coming to be seen as 'the national culture of the mainstream' (p. 158), and, further, an 'attempt to redefine Hinduism as an ideology for modernization by the middle class' (p. 159). You can explore these arguments further. You will see, for example, that they are quite different from those made by Philip Lutgendorf, whose work we drew on earlier. It is particularly interesting to view these debates in the light of our definition of myth as 'ideology in narrative form'.

There is much at stake in these debates. In 1992 a Hindu nationalist campaign led to the dramatic destruction of a medieval mosque in the north Indian pilgrimage town of Ayodhya, because it is claimed that it was built on the exact spot on which Ram was born. This act had major ramifications for modern Indian politics, and led to many thousands of deaths. The desire to build a temple at this spot is still very much alive, although the site continues to be the subject of a tense legal and political battle. We will explore Ayodhya in more detail in Chapter 11. Here, it serves to remind us of the sustained power of myth to shape the modern social and political landscape.

The religion twist: Ram-katha, myth and religion

The valorization of Ram in recent history associates the Ramayana with a specific form of religion. We have tried to demonstrate in this chapter that such a view needs to be mediated by a recognition of the continued vitality of many tellings. As we noted in our initial examination, the Ram-katha mythic repertoire defies simplistic classification – a defiance that stretches to its identification as specifically religious. There we saw that even the classic *Ramayana* of Valmiki was not a 'sacred book' in its original form, as historian Romila Thapar demonstrates in her article referred to in the previous section (Thapar 1990: 141; cf. Brockington and Brockington 2006). Rather, it was 'an amalgam emerging out of a number of ballads, folk tales and myths' (Thapar 1990: 145). We need to remind ourselves that, in these early versions, the idea of Ram as a divine figure was not there. Rama was first a human hero, then a personification of the ideal *kshatriya* or warrior (see further Chapter 7A). Only later is Rama seen as divine and identified as an *avatar*, that is, a descent form of the god Vishnu, or even as the Divine Name itself. However, as Lipner (1994: 130) says, 'in a religious sense this is not to the point', as Hindus recognize Rama as an embodiment of the Supreme throughout.

Myths relating to Vishnu's ten (or more) descent forms are well known and multifarious. Our Rama is only one of them. The other forms range from the fish and boar *avatar*s (top left, top right in Figure 4.4) to the human

Figure 4.4 'Vishnu in the Centre of his Ten Avatars'. Jaipur, Rajasthan, Rajput School (eighteenth century). Victoria and Albert Museum, London, UK/The Bridgeman Art Library. SC36441.

forms of Rama-with-the-axe (bottom left, and see Chapter 7B) and Krishna (third down on right) and often include the Buddha (bottom centre) and Kalkin, the avatar on the white horse who is still to come (bottom right) This painting from Jaipur in Rajasthan, entitled 'Vishnu in the Centre of his Ten Avatars', portrays the central figure as playing a flute and with the black colour often associated with Krishna, illustrating the fluidity of concepts of deity we noticed in Chapter 2.

The general thrust of these myths is related to the key concept of *dharma* (see Box 4.3). The relationship between the *avatar*s and *dharma* is explained for us by Krishna.[11] In the *Bhagavad Gita* (which of course is part of the other great South Asian epic, the *Mahabharata*), he tells Arjuna:

> Although I am unborn and have a self that is eternal, although I am lord of beings, by controlling my own material nature I come into being by means of my own incomprehensible power.

Box 4.3 *Dharma*

The Sanskrit term '*dharma*' is almost impossible to translate into English. In the *Gita* passage here, Johnson translates it as 'law' and '*adharma*' as 'lawlessness'. This follows van Buitenen's lead, the latter using it as a 'marker' to indicate '*dharma*' while making it clear that the term itself has a much deeper and broader reach than the English term 'law' (van Buitenen 1973: xli). The fundamental meaning of '*dharma*' is 'order': ritual order, social order, cosmic order, all of which are interrelated. This is what is disrupted at the beginning of the *Gita* and Krishna comes to restore. In the plural, '*dharma*' can also then mean the duties of the different ideal social groups (Chapter 7A) and stages of life (Chapter 5), for it is these duties, properly fulfilled, that uphold this order. These are spelled out in the vast Dharma Shastra literature, which contains many varying views. One of the most famous Dharma Shastra texts is the *Manu Smriti*, probably composed during the first couple of centuries CE around the time that the great epics were being assembled too (Olivelle 2004: 37). It was already influential by the fifth century CE and became more so under the British who understood it to be a Compendium of Hindu Law and used it in making legal decisions. In the twentieth century, untouchables stirred by Ambedkar (Chapter 7B) and anti-brahmin Tamils stirred by Ramasami (see above) advocated burning it since they saw it as a sign of brahmin oppression (Olivelle 2004: 4).

Whenever there is a falling away from the true law and an upsurge of unlawfulness, then, Bharata, I emit myself.

I come into being age after age, to protect the virtuous and to destroy evil-doers, to establish a firm basis for the true law.

(*Bhagavad Gītā* 4: 6–8, see Johnson 1994: 19)

As Krishna says, the supreme lord 'emits himself', that is, descends into the world, whenever there is an 'upsurge of unlawfulness'. In other words, the *avatar*s are believed to operate to restore or preserve order in the world: they are there to affirm *dharma* and act against *adharma* (chaos and disorder – the opposite of *dharma*).

This is an interesting indication of the way in which the epics themselves have become, in one kind of telling, part of an orderly religious cosmology. It is a theme taken up Julius Lipner in his exploration of the epics. He notes the way in which they act as a kind of vehicle for disciplining the many strains of devotionalism (*bhakti*) that were developing from about the first century CE along with the epics themselves (Lipner 1994: 126).[12] Devotional cults that were developing around specific divine figures were seen as threatening to a social environment in which one particular class or *varna* (brahmins) was seen as ritually superior (see Chapter 7A for more on *varna*). This was because *bhakti* often implied that a direct link between the individual and the divine was possible, whoever that individual might be. True devotion can be felt 'by anyone – male or female, high or low, rich or poor, learned or illiterate – without renouncing the world, so that the male Brahmins' claim to privileged access to the divine and to potential liberation through renunciation is subverted', as the anthropologist Chris Fuller (1992: 157) states. Given this and to retain brahmin influence, Lipner (1994: 126) argues that 'the epics have been Brahminised . . . their stories . . . allowed to unfold in a framework of generally Brahminic ideals'. As such, Rama is cast in such tellings as the champion of Vedic *dharma*, upholding the order of things.

This of course takes us right back to the idea of myth as ideology in narrative form. Given that a brahminic view of the ritual superiority of the brahmins is a form of ideology that appears to be naturally conservative, you will be able to understand that it is ripe for subversion by other groups – or, to put it another way, for the propagation of alternative ideologies in other mythic forms. The narrations of E.V. Ramasami's Dravidian Self-Respect Movement linked with the *Ramayana* burning we noted above give a strong example, but there are many others of less aggressive form. The Ram-katha, then, in its flexibility and dialogic dynamism, demonstrates very well how competing ideologies are expressed in myth, and how they continue to be contested by a variety of groups engaged by visions of social reality and issues of political power.

Concluding thoughts: on tellings as twists

In this chapter we have gained some glimpses into just one main mythic tradition of South Asia, that of the Ram-katha. Even from these glimpses it has become clear how a multi-layered approach taking serious account of context is vital to understanding how myths work, not only in South Asia but also beyond. In particular, these glimpses help us to realize the danger of calling the Ramayana a 'Hindu myth', for the 'pool of signifiers' that constitutes the Ram-katha is drawn on in multiple ways across the boundaries of the -isms. In this sense, this chapter forms a core demonstration of our argument throughout this book: for the Ramayana *is* a Hindu text – a devotional one if we look at Tulsi's telling, a mythological devotional if we look at Sagar, a matter of politicized identity if we look at warrior Ram posters and so on. Yet this is only one way of looking. And the twists of the kaleidoscope have shown us tellings that elude categorizations of all sorts, challenging gender norms as well as embedding them, politicizing regional identities as well as transcending them. You will be able to find many more . . .

Questions for further discussion and research

- Going back to the poster, is the picture of the globe just emphasizing the point about record viewing figures? What else could it be signifying in mythical and political terms?
- How would you counter a view like Walker's that dismisses Hindu myth and history as fantastical?
- A stress on the historical birthplace of Ram and other figures from key Hindu stories has developed only in the modern period. Why do you think this might be?
- Discuss why some Hindus find it objectionable when their epics are called 'myth'.
- Love stories form some of the most powerful narratives told in South Asia. In what sense are these myth too? (You might want to compare the *Gita Govinda* on Krishna and Radha, the Sufi *Madhumalati* and the Punjabi folk story of Hir and Ranjha, for example. See Miller 1977; Behl and Weightman 2000; Usborne 1973 for the texts themselves with good introductions).

Further reading

Lutgendorf, P. (1995) 'All in the (Raghu) family: a video epic in cultural context', in L. Babb and S. Wadley (eds) *Media and the Transformation of Religion in South Asia*, New Delhi: Motilal Banarsidass.

> An interesting analysis by a scholar whose 'fil-um' analyses in general are a lively and informative read (Lutgendorf n.d.).

Pandey, G. (1995) 'The appeal of Hindu history', in V. Dalmia and H. von Stietencron (eds) *Representing Hinduism: The Construction of Religious Traditions and National Identity*, New Delhi: Sage (also second edition).

> A useful reflection on the construction of Hindu history from myths such as the Ramayana.

Richman, P. (ed.) (1991) *Many Rāmāyaṇas: The Diversity of a Narrative Tradition in South Asia*, Berkeley: University of California Press.
Richman, P. (ed.) (2001) *Questioning Ramayanas: A South Asian Tradition*, Berkeley: University of California Press.

> Two excellent collections of wide-ranging articles by textual scholars, historians and anthropologists, which demonstrate precisely the point of our chapter.

Sreenivasan, Ramya (2007) *The Many Lives of a Rajput Queen: Heroic Pasts in India c.1500–1900*, Seattle: University of Washington Press.

> An interesting exploration of a different mythic repertoire, which traces this story through Jain, Sufi, Rajput, British and Hindu nationalist tellings and their interrelations.

5   Ritual and worship

A question

The worshipper has bathed. She takes off her shoes and enters. At the shrine, she shows her respect and she, or someone on her behalf, offers water, incense, flowers, fruit, lights, or perhaps a cloth.

- What is she doing?
- And to which religious tradition does she belong?

Whether these questions puzzle you, or the answers seem obvious, you may like to return to them at the end of the chapter, and ask them once again.

Ways of looking at ritual

Ritual and worship lie at the heart of religion, however religion is understood. If belief is prioritized, worship may be seen as an appropriate response. If a focus on practice is preferred, ritual and worship will be key practices to examine, often seen as exemplifying key 'meanings' of a religion or symbol system (Geertz 1993). Alternatively, a stress may be put on their efficacy or power, rejecting the drive to impose cognitive meanings (Asad 1993: 55–79; Dempsey 1999: 174). Finally, in Ninian Smart's (1969) World Religions model, the ritual dimension is one of the six dimensions he initially proposed to characterize a particular '-ism'.

There is a danger, though, in all these approaches if they link particular forms of ritual and worship unproblematically with a single religion (or branch within it). There are, of course, many different forms of Hindu, Muslim, Christian and other worship in and beyond South Asia that are recognized as such by worshippers. We shall see some later. However, in South Asia, as elsewhere, the situation may be much more complex than this suggests. It is not just that particular groups develop and change their modes of worship in different historical and social contexts and in encounter with one another. The models above can, and indeed have to, allow for this. Rather, people from 'different' religions frequently participate in the rituals of others, in ways that have often become fraught with misunderstandings, critique and conflict in modern South Asia. In this chapter, therefore, we carry on with our exploration of the ways in which continually negotiated notions of religion need to be carefully interrogated, this time at points where ritual and worship from different traditions intersect.

To do this, we adopt an ethnographic approach. Our case study is a contemporary *'urs* celebration in Aurangabad, a city refounded in 1681 by the Mughal emperor Aurangzeb as part of mid-seventeenth century Mughal expansion into the Deccan region of south India. *'Urs* rituals surrounding the anniversary of the death of a Muslim saint or *pir* are familiar throughout South Asia. Often they, and the shrines around which they are based, are frequented as much by Hindus and other non-Muslims as by Muslims. They have, though, been criticized by both Muslim and Hindu reformists as respectively non-Muslim and Muslim alike. In particular, they have been portrayed as the popular syncretic practices of those not properly educated in the requirements of proper (elite-directed) religious observance. This has led to their suppression and reformulation in many circumstances, as we shall see below.

Through our case study, however, we shall show that the ritual programme at the Aurangabad *'urs*, like many others, has significant continuities and parallels with 'the Islam of the saints' outside South Asia. This will help to disrupt the notion of a self-sealed ('popular') South Asian culture that has distorted proper Islam. In addition, by examining how worship at such shrines provides one context in which multi-layered South Asian cultural traditions have interacted, we show, first, how veneration of the saints has been an elite, not simply a popular, practice, and, second, how it has been shared by Muslims and non-Muslims alike.

Case study: the *'urs* of Shah Nur (d.1692)

Aurangabad, where Shah Nur's *'urs* takes places annually, has been a major centre of Sufi Islam for well over three centuries. As you read Nile Green's ethnography based on fieldwork undertaken in 1999, it is important to remember that *'urs* means 'marriage' and that the occasion celebrates the re-union of the saint with God at death.

In a vivid account, Green describes the preparations for the festivities as the house of the *pir* and its surroundings are decorated and rich food cooked for the guests, just like in a big South Asian or Persian wedding. During the first days of the *'urs* itself, Sufi musical performances (*mahfil-e-sama'*) attract large crowds each evening as the *qawwal*s, professional praise singers, sing Persian and Urdu songs blending earthly and spiritual love. Later comes the 'wedding' procession: loud drumming announces a young man, representing Shah Nur, riding the white horse at the front. Accompanied by a camel for Muhammad, he leads the car bringing the current custodian of the shrine (the *sajjadah nashin*) and a pot of sandalwood paste, while wildly dancing young men follow on, hoisting one another aloft. As they reach the shrine mid-evening, the saint's wedding night begins. All try to touch the sandalwood pot. Then it is taken into the mausoleum by the custodian and older married males. Outside, the wedding feast is served, vegetarian *biryani* for Hindu guests, mutton *biryani* for Muslims. The music tonight is solemn, males crying and dancing in the heightened spiritual sensibility known as *hal*. Just before dawn, mystical interface between the two worlds, the crowds disperse; the married men offer money, 'wedding gifts' in exchange for the saint's blessing.

Consummating sainthood: the sandalmalī *of Shāh Nūr*

The ritual climax of the *'urs* is the *sandalmalī* or 'sandalwood-rubbing'. It takes place in the saint's mausoleum ritually transformed into his wedding chamber, small, dark and enclosed, scented with incense, softened with silks.

The married men gather closely inside the confined space; the press of bodies is such that it soon becomes extremely hot. No-one can move, the atmosphere compounded by the cries of the *qawwāls* outside the chamber door.

The men crowd around the low railings that surround Shāh Nūr's cenotaph. The grave is covered in bright silks beneath which lies the buried body, a visual metaphor which evokes the double experience that the men are kneeling beside a marriage bed as well as a grave. There is an intense silence within the chamber. After some time the *sajjādah nashīn* reaches for the clay mixing bowl and is passed the ritual ingredients. The rich red sandalwood is supplied by him alone, but every male present may pass a small vial of his own attar to mix into the potion. As the *sajjādah nashīn* sits slowly stirring the bowl, everyone waits in silence. He alone is allowed to place his hands into the mixing bowl. The others must wait.

Now comes the central act of the *'urs*: the uncovering of the cenotaph that literally marks the saint's tomb and symbolically marks both the marriage bed and the bride herself. During every other moment of the year the cenotaph is covered with layer upon layer of silk cloths. The top layers are red, green, occasionally yellow, colours of weddings. As each cloth is slowly removed, the atmosphere in the chamber reaches closer to its climax, for this is the symbolic unveiling of the bride. Yet as the last cloths (*chādar*) are revealed, their sudden white colour – the shroud of death and burial in Islam – reminds the participants that they are partaking in a mortuary ritual too. When every *chādar* has been removed there is a strange and compelling beauty to the brown sandy clay of the naked cenotaph of Shāh Nūr.

Now the earlier tension explodes as the rubbing of the tomb, the *sandalmalī* proper, begins. The tense but constrained scene erupts into one of frenzy, each man trying to rub the red *sandal* paste into the earthen cenotaph. For five brief minutes cries, grunts and gasps fill the sealed chamber. Then, amid the shouts and tears of the participants, the consummation of the wedding is complete. Word is given through the tightly secured doors to the *qawwāl*s outside who immediately strike up song. This reflects the message passed by the groom from the privacy of the bridal chamber that the marriage had been consummated at the premodern wedding. As then, now here, songs and celebrations follow in celebration of love fulfilled. The emotional exhaustion within the chamber passes into relief. The grave cloths are replaced, new ones that devotees have offered placed onto the cenotaph. In the wedding chamber of Shāh Nūr, participants press red *sandal* hand-marks onto the walls. For the rest of the year the marks remind visitors that a wedding has been consummated there.

(Nile Green 2010b)

Explaining terms

pir – Muslim saint or holy man

sajjādah nashīn – hereditary guardian of a shrine, usually a descendant of the *pir*, lit. 'the one seated on the [*pir*'s] prayer carpet'

barakat – blessing/power

Task

- What indications are there that the *'urs* is a Muslim ritual?
- What evidence can you find for the participation of Hindus as well as Muslims?
- What questions would you want to ask to help you understand this celebration in greater depth?

Understanding the *'urs*

It may at first sight appear that the music, drumming, dancing, sandalwood paste and other offerings, along with the worshipful respect that the *pir* himself, and the *sajjadah nashin* as his representative, enjoys, are accretions of Hindu popular practice. They seem far removed from the sober performance of *namaz* or *salat* that characterizes Islamic worship, in the mosque for men or at home for women. For this reason, shrine worship and the '*urs* in particular have been targeted by Islamic reformers as non-Islamic practices. Yet the situation is more complex. We shall demonstrate this by considering two key factors: the links that '*urs* celebrations in South Asia have with the wider Islamic world, and the internal Muslim critique of Sufi practices. Then we shall consider the multi-layered nature of participation in Sufi shrine practices in which Hindus and others frequently join.

The ʿurs, the wider Islamic world and the local community

The key practices and logic of the '*urs* are firmly rooted in Islamic texts and cultural practices outside South Asia, both in the Arabic and particularly the Persian world. The word '*urs* meaning 'marriage' in Arabic, and many of the '*urs* customs – decorating the house, new clothes, the red bridal veil, rose-water perfume, processions, singing and dancing – are highly characteristic of Muslim weddings, especially those celebrated in rich, that is, elite, Persianate contexts. Moreover, the idea of a saint's death as marriage with God, complete union and fulfilment, is already found in classical Islamic sources.

A further layer of Islamic significance is found in the way the processions, singing and dancing echo similar celebrations held in Western Asia to mark the Prophet's birthday, held to fall on the same day as his death. The links between birth, death, marriage and sexuality in wider social and ritual practice and in Sufi poetry thus link South Asian '*urs* celebrations firmly with a wider 'Islam of the saints'.

Sufi musical performances (*mahfil-e-sama*ʿ) also have clear roots outside South Asia. The ritualized audition of music and poetry is aimed at summoning the state of passionate mystical love ('*ishq*), which stands at the core of the Sufi quest. The notion of '*ishq* is also central to Persian love poetry. Such high status poetry strongly influenced sixteenth-century Indian Sufi romances such as Manjhan's *Madhumalati* and Jayasi's *Padmavat* (see Chapter 4), texts that both tell a human romance and portray the worshipper's desire for God. The popular *qawwali*s sung at Shah Nur's '*urs* emerge from this Sufi tradition and complement the more formal praise to Allah, the Prophet Muhammad and the saints.

The '*urs* also builds up local Muslim identity. The route taken by the procession marks out Shah Nur's *vilayat* or sphere of influence. It not only performatively confirms this sphere by visiting places important in his hagiography, but also avoids the routes taken by other '*urs* processions, for example that of Nizam al-Din, showing that the *vilayat* is particular to each saint. The '*urs* thus not only shares in a much wider Islam of the saints but also constitutes a particular Muslim community around the *vilayat* of Shah Nur. This is emphasized by the participation of women and children in the earlier *mahfil*, the young men accompanying the procession, the rose-water contributed by the married men, their participation in smearing the cenotaph and handprinting the wall. As this enables each person variously to share in the *barakat* or power of the saint in union with Allah, we can see this as a fundamental act renewing the participating Muslim community for the coming year. Around them of course is also a much wider crowd that gathers to enjoy the festivities, watch the procession (as one might feel 'part' of a wedding by watching the bride come out of a church), join in the feasting and swell the local economy by buying things at the many stalls set up.

Critiques of Sufi shrine practice

Although critiques of shrine worship were numerous, they were often intra-Muslim, indeed intra-Sufi, rather than targeted against Hindus as such (van der Veer 1992a: 548). The initiator of such critiques in India is held to be the Sufi, Shah Wali-Allah (also written Waliullah) (d.1762), but key critiques of Sufi practice such as those of the Hanbali scholar, Ibn-Taymiyya (1263–1328), are found much earlier. Many of Wali-Allah's views were not very popular in his time. They were, however, picked up by writers such as Rashid Ahmad Gangohi (d.1905) and were carried through into the influential work of Sheikh Ali Thanawi, a Deoband-influenced Sufi, writing in the early twentieth century, as well as in the scathing critiques of Maududi whose writings in this respect have been influential far beyond his native Pakistan (on Deoband, see Chapter 8; on Thanawi and Maududi, Chapter 10).

Wali-Allah was writing during what the historian Rizvi (1980: 111) describes as 'the eighteenth century scramble for political domination' as the Mughal empire collapsed after the death of Aurangzeb in 1707. There was widespread disenchantment with corrupt officials, self-serving *'ulema* (Muslim scholars), cheating *qazi*s (legal experts) and duplicitous 'holy men' (Rizvi 1980: introduction). A key aim of his writing was to propagate a purified form of Islam to halt this decline. To this end he wrote (fruitlessly) to the dissolute Emperor Ahmad Shah (1748–54):

> Strict orders should be issued in all Islamic towns forbidding religious ceremonies publicly practised by infidels (such as *Holī* and ritual bathing in the Ganges). On the tenth of Muharram Shī'īs should not be allowed to go beyond the bounds of moderation and in the bazaars and streets neither should they be rude or repeat stupid things, (that is, recite *tabarra* or condemn the first three successors of Muhammad).
> (*Maktūbāt*, Shāh Walī-Allāh, Rāmpūr Ms, quoted in Rizvi 1980: 294)

Wali-Allah emphasized that true Sufi practice was 'the purification of the heart' (*ihsan*), not simply the relationship between *pir* and disciple, and in this he set a pattern of interpretation influential at the time and subsequently. He argued vehemently against worship at tombs, which he identified with idol worship and hence *shirk*, associating another with God. Like Thanawi and Maududi later, he saw this as one of the many 'sinful innovations' (*bida'*) that had affected Muslim practice. Despite his desire to promote good relations between various Sufi groups (see Box 5.1), he targeted the Chishti shrine of Khwaja Mu'in al Din in Ajmer for specific criticism. A Naqshbandi

Box 5.1 Sufi *silsila*s in South Asia

A *silsila* or lineage is a kind of chain of succession through which a Sufi holy man traces his *barakat* or power back through his own *pir* to the Prophet himself. There have been numerous orders (*tariqa*) with associated lineages active in South Asia. Some of the most influential have been:

- Chishti: founded in Ajmer, Rajasthan, by Khwaja Hasan Mu'inuddin Chishti (d.1236) in continuation of the tradition of the town of Chisht in Afghanistan. The great shrine in Delhi of Shaykh Nizam al-Din Auliya (d.1325) is that of another great Chishti saint. Figure 5.2 is a photo from the shrine of Salim Chishti (d.1572).
- Suhrawardi: originally an urban order with elite connections from around Baghdad, which spread early in its existence to India (thirteenth century CE) and became the other main Indian order of the medieval period.
- Naqshbandi: an order with an emphasis on mental *dhikr* (recitation) and inner concentration, which reached India in the sixteenth century CE from Central Asia; a major influence in the modern period, especially in Pakistan.
- Qadiri: ascribed to 'Abd al-Qadir al-Jilani (d.1166), expanded from the fourteenth century onwards through Arabia to reach Africa, Southeast Asia and India by the late fifteenth century.
- Shattari: founded in India in the fifteenth century, stressed letter mysticism and sometimes incorporated Indian yogic practices. Manjhan, the author of the *Madhumalati* (see Chapter 4), belonged to this order (Behl and Weightman 2000: xix–xxv)

It is not clear to which *silsila* Shah Nur belonged, although now he is regarded as a Qadiri (Green 2006: 9). There has always been a spectrum of Sufis operating outside formal lineages, some of whom known as *qalandar*s purposely defied convention. Others were initiated into more than one *silsila*, sometimes bringing lineages together as a consequence (see Chapter 6, and Trimingham 1971; Rizvi 1978–83; Green 2006).

of a group that did use music, he adopted the older Naqshbandi critique of *sama'* and warned Chishtis against it. In such an atmosphere, in the nineteenth century, although the particular causes are unclear, Shah Nur's shrine declined, but was revived in the early twentieth century as celebrated in Malkapuri's hagiography (see further Green 2006).

Multi-layered participation and barakat

The ethnography above focuses on the 'ordinary' Muslim participants at Shah Nur's *'urs*. However, the Muslim elite were also involved. A senior member of Aurangabad's Muslim elite gave Shah Nur his lodge, now shrine. That shrine has, in both past and present, been variously patronized by the Muslim elite (including the Mughal emperor Aurangzeb) as well as by 'ordinary' Hindus and Hindus holding positions of power (Green 2004a,b 2006). As with many other shrines across South Asia, people come seeking the *barakat* of Shah Nur for a variety of purposes. This blessing or power is (or has been) available to rulers seeking confirmation of their legitimacy; it also cements communities, offers help finding work, cures illnesses and helps women sort issues of marriage and relationships. It operates within a landscape of practitioners recognized to have such powers, who are identified not primarily as Hindu or Muslim (or Sikh, Christian, Jain, etc.), but as those whose own practice or devotion founds the efficacy of the solutions they offer (compare Amma, Chapter 3). It is for such reasons that the anthropologist, Richard Kurin (1983), argues that *barakat* should be made the fundamental category for analysing ritual and devotion at shrines.

Shared shrines are not limited to South Asia. In the Middle East and the Balkans, for example, Christians, Muslims and Jews have sought similar help from those who are believed to have the ear of God (Ayoub 1999; Meri 2002; Bowman 1993). The 'all-embracing' nature of Hinduism and its influence on a pristine Islam cannot therefore be a satisfactory explanation of shared South Asian shrine worship as such. Even a distinction between elite and 'popular' practice falls apart when the specific history of shrines like Shah Nur's is examined. A model of discrete (reformed) world religions does not fit shrine worship well. There are, however, other ways of understanding the multi-layeredness of such worship, which build on the logic of *barakat*.

In Chapters 3 and 6, we see how it can be important to focus on specific devotional traditions to help us understand configurations of religious traditions in South Asia, both modern and earlier. Here, we can see how Shah Nur and his line of *sajjadah nashin*s form the core of such a tradition around which *barakat*, ultimately deriving from Allah, is accessed by devotees, the local Muslim community and others drawn to the shrine. We can develop this further by thinking about Ballard's 'dimensions', particularly here the kismetic. Seeking the *pir*'s *barakat* to help with the intractable troubles of everyday life, people who would adopt quite different life cycle rituals or dharmic identities, and even different qaumic or religio-political identities, and who may be of very different social status, may without contradiction worship side by side at the shrine, recognizing, even if in different ways, the source of its underlying power. Diverse in their social status, practices and desires, they simply recognize that *barakat* is the normal result of a saint's being in touch with the transcendent.

However, it is also important to contextualize this by drawing on Jackie Assayag's (2004) model of participation by dissociation, which we look at in more detail in Chapter 11. This model, which is supported by many other ethnographic studies (such as Searle-Chatterjee 1993; Dempsey 1999; Gottschalk 2000; Tuladhar-Douglas 2005), does not seek to homogenize what is going on at a shrine like Shah Nur's. It accepts that people are conscious of themselves as having different identities (of caste, religious allegiance and so forth), which mediate the shared space of a shrine and, we would argue, its *barakat*. Such a model can accommodate the ruler who comes for political legitimation (whether Aurangzeb, or Indira Gandhi – see Chapter 6), along with the seeker for inner teaching, a regional group re-enacting its identity, folk seeking pragmatic support, a village group that worships at both its own Hindu temple and Shah Nur's urbanizing shrine (Green 2004b). It can also take into account fluctuating patterns of patronage that safeguard, or fail to safeguard, access for different groups (Green 2006). Worship at a shrine is thus clearly seen to be multi-layered, but also susceptible to change. In the following section, we shall not only see some further instances of multi-layered shrine worship, but also examples of how worship defines, links and challenges people's religious identities in different ways.

Kaleidoscopes of devotion

Worship at a Roman Catholic shrine in Bangladesh

The village of Panjora in the archdiocese of Dhaka, Bangladesh, is home to a statue of St Anthony of Padua (Italy), miraculously discovered there. On St Anthony's annual feast day before Lent each year hundreds of thousands of people come to the village (around 50,000 in February 2011). At this and other times:

> devotees of Saint Anthony touch a statue of the saint with their right hand as they ask for special blessings . . . . They also leave money, candles, biscuits, doves, etc, as traditional *manot*, or gifts offered to a saint for granting a favour.
>
> (*Union of Catholic Asian News* 2009)

Santi Rosario writes:

> When I was walking around the outdoor altar with the big statue, put up in preparation for the annual festival of St Anthony [of Padua], I saw a number of high school girls in uniform going over to St Anthony's

big statue, touching his feet and then touching their forehead and chest
[Figure 5.1]. A few also brought some flowers which they touched the
saint's feet with and then took them back. I first assumed they were all
Christian girls. However I found that half of them were Muslims. One
Muslim girl told me her father comes to the festival and that he was a
businessman in the local bazaar. Another Muslim girl said her mother
came and made some *manot* when her younger brother was sick. I spoke
to one of the nuns at the school and she said many Hindu and Muslims
come to make *manots* or to make their offerings of candles, *agarbati*
[incense], milk, money, chicken etc, once their *manot* to St Anthony has
been fulfilled.

(Rozario and Samuel 2010: 361)

The article in the *Union of Catholic Asian News*, quoted above, confirms
that Hindus and Muslims as well as Christians come to make and honour
such *manot*s (vows). Anthropologists Santi Rosario and Geoffrey Samuel
argue that shared practices such as these and their equivalents at shrines such
as the *mazar* of Shah Ali Bagdadi in Dhaka support the 'sustainability' of
everyday social life in Bangladeshi society, and are actually growing with the
pressures of modern life and easier accessibility to linked shrines elsewhere

Figure 5.1 Schoolgirls touch a statue of St Anthony to ask for blessings. Reproduced
courtesy of Santi Rosario.

in South Asia, notwithstanding Islamist purist movements in Bangladesh (Rozario and Samuel 2010: 362; cf. Sébastia 2002, on Velankanni, 'the Lourdes of the East', in Tamil Nadu; Sikand 2002). Rosario and Samuel refer to these shrines as 'heterotopic spaces', which provide an alternative to the rather heavily regulated spaces in which women in particular live the majority of their lives and offer 'some kind of healing or transformative power' (p. 362). In Chapter 6 we look at a further example from Pakistan.

Networks of devotion

> In Fatehpur Sikri, the desert city built by the Mughal emperor Akbar stands the shrine of the great Indian Chisti Sufi saint, Salim Chisti (1478–1572), a descendant of Moinuddin Chisti of Ajmer. Here I, an English Christian, was asked to go by a Hindu Khattri friend of mine, brought up in Uttar Pradesh, India, but at the time living in the UK. Some years before, she had visited the shrine and made a vow (*vrat*) that she would return if she had a healthy child. Her elder daughter was born as a result. Realizing that she was unlikely to be able to return in the near future, she asked me to go in her place, untie a black thread from the lattice [Figure 5.2] and bring it back to her. She would cast it into a river in the UK, as she would have done in the Ganges, had she been in India herself.
>
> (Jacqueline Suthren Hirst)

Vows such as this, as at St Antony's shrine above, play a very important part in women's lives in particular, undertaken as they often are for the stability of the patriline or wider family. It is easy to criticize them as superstitious or simplistically transactional ('Do this for me, and I'll do this for you'),

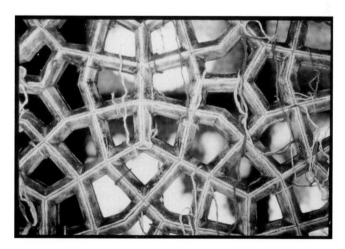

Figure 5.2 Fatehpur Sikri shrine lattice. Reproduced courtesy of Jacqueline Suthren Hirst.

but this misses the deeper understanding of *barakat* or its equivalent, which we discussed above. It also undervalues the gratitude that accompanies the fulfilled *vrat*, the way it contributes to social order and allows heterotopic space from it, and the mechanism of acceptance of misfortune if the fulfilment seems delayed.

A Hindu devotional song

> Om Jai Jagdish Hare/Swami Jai Jagdish Hare
> Bhagat Jano Ke Sankat/Bhagat Jano Ke Sankat/Khshan Mein Dur Kare/
> Om Jai Jagdish Hare . . .

In many modern Hindu temples around the world, from New Delhi, India, through Leicester, UK, to Toledo, Ohio, USA, this song can be heard during the *arati* ceremony (the offering of light), a central part of temple worship or *puja*. It addresses Vishnu as the Lord of the whole world, who takes away the sufferings of his devotees. You can find the words and MP3 download on the web as well as an English version designed to be sung to the same tune (Das n.d.; Bhanot n.d.)

In temples such as these that use a globally recognized style of layout and worship, with shrines to different deities to cater for devotees' preferences, the 'eternal truth of Hinduism' is constructed in marble, mantra and music. The tune to 'Om Jai Jagdish Hare' was made familiar originally through film. The same tune has then been used with other words to different deities in such temples. A similar tune is used in some Swami Narayan temples worldwide with the words, 'Jai Sadguru Swami', addressing Lord Swaminarayan.[1] A form of worship grounded in the specific beliefs and practices of that *sampradaya* becomes linked with the wider globalized Hindu tradition through that tune. It may, however, differ radically from worship conducted according to, say, specific Pancaratra rites in one of the great south Indian temple complexes such as Shrirangam or to a village deity in Nepal or Tamil Nadu, or at a local roadside shrine. Nevertheless, in some cases:

> The village protector worshiped at roadside shrines is now also a multipurpose deity worshiped in the growing chain of non-sectarian, one-stop, full-service temples that increasingly epitomize urban, cosmopolitan Hinduism - like the white marble temple to 'Great Hanuman' (*bare Hanumān*), but incorporating shrines to Shiva, Radha-Krishna, Durga, and Santoshi Ma, that draws thousands of worshipers to the corner of New Delhi's Connaught Place and Baba Kharak Singh Road.
> (Lutgendorf 1994: 244; compare Figures 5.3 and 5.4)

It is important to realize, however, that most Hindu devotional worship is not temple based but offered at the home shrine, whether this is a small corner in the kitchen or a dedicated room in wealthier homes (Figure 5.5).

Figure 5.3 A Hanuman shrine in Uttar Pradesh. Reproduced courtesy of Jacqueline Suthren Hirst.

Figure 5.4 Worshippers in the Hanuman temple, Connaught Place, New Delhi. Reproduced courtesy of Nvvchar.

Figure 5.5 M.H. Gopalakrishnan doing Deeparadhanai (worship with the lamp) at his home shrine in Chennai as part of his Karthikai Pooja, November 2010. Photographer: Vaishnavi Ganesh. Reproduced courtesy of M.H. Gopalakrishnan and Vaishnavi Ganesh.

Usually this is done by the mother or other women on behalf of the family, often very early in the morning as soon as she has bathed. As in a public temple, the deities are treated as honoured guests, offerings of incense, water, food and light purifying both the place where they are and the worshipper herself as well as nourishing the deity. The worshipper in turn receives back the 'leftovers', normally impure (see further Chapter 7A), but for the worshipper pure as even the deity's impurities are pure in relation to her. These are then shared with other family members as *prashad*, signs of the deity's favour and blessing.

At the centre of this and temple worship is the notion of taking *darshan*, literally taking 'sight' of the deity. In *darshan*, the worshipper stands before the deity and both sees and is seen in turn. When a *murti* (image) is installed in a temple, it is at the point when the eyes are 'opened' that a marble or stone sculpture becomes deity manifested in the *murti* itself. There are excellent studies by Diana Eck (1998) and Vasudha Narayanan (1996) to help you explore this further.

A poem of Kabir

Saints, I see the world is mad.
If I tell the truth they rush to beat me,
if I lie they trust me.
I've seen the pious Hindus, rule-followers,
early morning bath-takers –
killing souls, they worship rocks.
I've seen plenty of Muslim teachers, holy men,
reading their holy books
and teaching their pupils techniques.
They know just as much.
And posturing yogis, hypocrites,
hearts crammed with pride,
praying to brass, to stones, reeling
with pride in their pilgrimage,
fixing their caps and their prayer-beads,
painting their brow-marks and arm-marks,
braying their hymns and their couplets,
reeling. They never heard of soul.
The Hindu says Ram is the beloved,
the Turk says Rahim.
Then they kill each other.
No one knows the secret.
They buzz their mantras from house to house,
puffed with pride.
The pupils drown along with their gurus.
In the end they're sorry.
Kabir says, listen saints:
they're all deluded!
Whatever I say, nobody gets it.
It's too simple.

(Kabir, 'Saints', see Hess and Singh 1983: 42–3)

When devotion is offered to deities as above it is often referred to as *saguna bhakti*, devotion to the one who takes characteristics or form. Kabir's poem, by contrast, belongs to the tradition of *nirguna bhakti*, devotion to the one without or beyond form, who is worshipped in the heart. It is scathing of empty ritual. The *Bijak* functions as the sacred scripture of almost all branches of the Kabir Panth, which may have originated in the early seventeenth century, a couple of centuries after Kabir (see Chapter 2) from whom the movement takes its name. Some branches develop Kabir's *nirguna bhakti*; others link it back to Muslim, Sikh or Hindu identities. Many of the most popular songs attributed to him are not found in earlier collections like the *Bijak* (Lorenzen 1996: 205–23), but they do show how similar ideas, carried in devotional singing and films, and often sanitized, continue to be highly influential in contemporary South Asia (Babb and Wadley 1995; Henry 1991; Dwyer 2006: 89–90).

A *Jain form of worship*

The breathtakingly beautiful temple in Rajasthan, northwestern India (Figure 5.6), is a place of pilgrimage for Jains of both main traditions, Shvetambara and Digambara,[2] who practise worship to images of the Jinas. Offerings of milk, water, sandalpaste, flowers, incense, light and sweets may be made by lay people, although brahmin priests also play a ritual role here.

When European observers came upon Jain ritual practice, they found it deeply confusing (Cort 2002: 63–7). Because they regarded the Jain texts that described the often severe ascetic practices of Jain monks and nuns as normative, they looked on Jain lay worship (*bhakti*) as an aberration, especially if its proponents were wealthy. If Jain monks renounce the world

Figure 5.6 Worshippers at Chaumukha Adinath Jain temple, Ranakpur. Reproduced courtesy of Jacqueline Suthren Hirst.

to follow the teaching of the Jinas, who have transcended the world and are neither gods (still part of the world of rebirth) nor God, what are ordinary Jains doing worshipping images of the Jinas as if they are? Why do they have Hindu deities in their temples? Is this just absorption of Hindu customs? Or evidence that Jains are really Hindus? We shall return to these questions below. How might you go about unpacking them at this point, though, given what you have already discovered?

The gender twist: men, ritual and sources of power

The key importance of women in worship has been stressed in numerous contexts, from responsibility for *puja* at the domestic shrine to the performance of particular *vrat*s or *manot*s for the welfare of their husbands and wider family members (e.g. Jacobson and Wadley 1997; McGee 1991; Rosario and Samuel 2010). Women may also function as *pujarini*s (those who conduct the *puja*) at non-brahminical public shrines (Vachani 1990) and play a key role in *bhajan* or *kirtan* groups that meet to sing the praises of a particular deity, or Sikh *shabd*s from the Guru Granth Sahib, for example.

In this section, however, we focus on the construction of masculinity shown in the Shah Nur 'urs and other forms of devotion in modern South Asia. In their study of the massively popular Sabarimala pilgrimage in Kerala, southwest India (about eighty miles from Mattancheri), anthropologists Filippo and Caroline Osella argue that the participants, overwhelmingly male, renew their masculinity as responsible husbands, fathers and family members by becoming temporary renouncers and identifying with both the male deity Ayyappa and their fellow participants during the forty-one days the pilgrimage is meant to take (Osella and Osella 2003; for a clip of the *puja* at the shrine itself, see Sabarimala Sree Dharma Sastha Temple 2010). The Osellas stress that the majority of the participants take the *vrat* (vow) of celibacy required for the pilgrimage in order to achieve very concrete ends such as the well-being of a child, the desire for a son, or business success. Success is granted through the power of the ascetic Ayyappa, whose status as an ascetic able to grant such boons is interdependent on new male devotees making the pilgrimage each year. Although the women perform their own *vrat*s for well-being throughout the year, the Osellas (2003: 739) argue that their role is overshadowed by the men's in this ritual of 'masculine heroism'. This is because the pilgrimage ritual replicates hierarchy both within and beyond itself: new participants submit to the *guruswamy*, the experienced elder who leads a group; all submit to the deity; and women submit to the returned men, whose newly acquired power enables the women's own rituals to have efficacy in their turn.

Using their analysis, which draws critically on the anthropological work of Bloch (1992) and Fuller (1992), we may suggest a further reading of Shah Nur's 'urs. At the crucial parts of the ceremony, the women are not present, their role waiting to be revalidated in the renewal of community that comes through the young men, and specifically through the elders, ready to identify with the death-marriage of the saint in his tomb. However, whereas the pilgrims to Ayyappa temporarily renounce sex, drink and meat eating to participate in their deity's ascetically gained power, the young men in Aurangabad *bring* their virility to the shrine, in turn receiving back through the elders the *barakat* of the saint, whose power comes from his unity with Allah. Their masculinity is renewed through identification with the saint and with the group involved, their sexuality contained by the authority of the elders, to be used in future in marriage and procreation within the reconstituted community itself.

The politics twist: shrines and state power

In Sufi traditions, political and spiritual authority has been held to be separate, the former in the hands of the king or ruler, the latter in the hands of the *pir*s or saints. Nonetheless, the two have often been intertwined, rulers patronizing particular shrines in person and giving land grants, the *pir* of the shrine in turn legitimating the king's rule through his own spiritual authority[3] (Eaton 2000: 252; see further Chapter 6). The *sajjadah nashin*s of the shrines have consequently often been in charge of considerable estates, as well as exercising authority over those gradually brought into their shrine's economic and religious ambit (Eaton 1987). This power base has proved a challenge to those seeking to change patterns of authority in the modern nation-state. Local ties have also affected voting patterns and attitudes to state governments.

Far from being neutral sites, then, shrines with the power they hold have been targets of government reform across the Islamic world, although often for contradictory reasons. In Republican Turkey post 1923, shrines were subject to closure because they were seen as incompatible with the then-government's secularist programme; in Saudi Arabia because contradictory to a Wahhabi form of Islamism that criticizes worship at shrines as *shirk*. In Pakistan, rather than closing shrines, successive governments sought to control them in different ways, as the anthropologist Katherine Ewing has shown. The governments of Ayub Khan (1958–69), Zulfikar Ali Bhutto (1971–7) and General Zia ul-Haq (1977–88) each had their own agendas: Ayub Khan a centralizing modernizing government, Bhutto identification with the 'people's party' and ul-Haq a progressive Islamization. Each, however, used the shrines to lessen the power of the *sajjadah nashin*s, pursue their own agendas and so subtly redefine the purpose of the shrines and what it is to be a true Sufi (Ewing 1983). Their strategies included land reform and continuing legislation regarding the Auqaf Boards set up to govern Muslim endowments; supporting major shrines and linking them and their histories with a national agenda and secular institutions such as hospitals; ensuring participation by politicians in key rituals, such as laying a *chadar* (cloth) during the *'urs*; and stressing the need for the *pir* to be an educated scholar, hence equating the true *pir* with the *'alim* and making Islamic education a goal for the ordinary person.

Ewing argues that respective governments needed to demonstrate that they were more capable of running the shrines than the *sajjadah nashin* to justify their involvement. That this remains a current issue can be seen from reports in *Dawn*, the key Pakistani English-language newspaper, following the suicide bombing at Data Ganj Bakhsh, the major shrine of an eleventh-century Sufi in Lahore, on Thursday 1 July 2010. Rather than the local *sajjadah nashin*, various Islamic organizations are now ready to take on the role of protectors when the government is seen to fail. The Sunni Tehrik mentioned in the following report is a Pakistani political organization founded in 1990, advancing the interests of Barelwi Muslims who have resisted Islamizing rejections of shrine worship while reforming it themselves (Sanyal 2010):

> The Sunni Tehrik organised a protest demonstration outside various mosques after Juma prayers and took out a rally on M.A. Jinnah Road to condemn the shrine bombing. It warned the government that the party would start making its own arrangements for the protection of all religious places and shrines if the departments concerned failed to fulfil their responsibilities in this regard.
>
> (*Dawn* 2010)

Later that week, in an article headlined 'Darbars bombed by Muslims, revered by Hindus', Shafqat Tanvir Mirza contrasted the current Pakistani government's focus on ' "Juma-leaders" and founders of madrissas' and its neglect of the followers and shrines of Sufi poets with the respect accorded to comparable figures and shrines in India, commenting: 'In the country of so-called "kafirs" there is no danger to khankahs, mazars and other holy places' (Mirza 2010). Trying to shame the Pakistani government by comparison with its arch-rivals, India, Mirza and others apply pressure through the mass media in terms of wider regional politics. Political legitimacy and the support of shrines remain clearly interlinked as our case studies in Chapter 11 will also demonstrate.

The religion twist: whose interpretations?

At this point, we return to the common assumption that worship belongs to a single religious tradition or, rather, sub-tradition and that this is what defines it as such. Often, in South Asia, as elsewhere, this is indeed the case, although the way in which worship has come to be defining of that tradition will have been renegotiated in different historical periods and social contexts. A Sunday morning service in the Church of South India in 2010 may look much more like its European Protestant counterparts than like a Roman Catholic Mass celebrated just around the corner, but this may have as much to do with different attitudes to enculturation (e.g. whether shoes are removed, one sits on the floor or chairs, flowers and incense sticks are offered as in *puja*) as with other differences between these two main streams of Christian tradition.

However, as we have seen in this chapter, that is only part of the picture. As well as, or instead of, worship belonging to a specific devotional tradition, many South Asians participate in shared forms of devotion, at shrines, at festival times and in support of vows. They provide crucial forms for sustaining social life. British failure to recognize this in the case of shared Syrian Christian and Nayar festivals in Kerala ripped apart the social fabric there in the nineteenth century as Susan Bayly (1984) documents. The way religion is constructed or imagined affects people's lives in many varied ways. It also affects how they present their worship and devotion, both to themselves and to inquirers.

This is shown very clearly if we look at Jain forms of worship in modern South Asia. To all intents and purposes, these look very similar to forms of Hindu or Buddhist *puja*, to some offerings made at Sufi shrines or in some Indian Christian forms of worship. Yet assuming a similar underlying logic can be deeply problematic.

Evidence for the practice of *bhakti* is already found in very early Jain texts predating the Shvetambara/Digambara split. This should cause us to widen our understanding of how *bhakti* might be understood in different traditions rather than prejudging modern Jain practice (Cort 2002). The anthropologist Lawrence Babb's distinction of three different types of worship practised by the laity of the Kartar Gacch branch of Shvetambara Murti Pujas in Jaipur, Rajasthan, is helpful. *Ashtprakari-puja*, involving eight ritual acts,[4] is performed to images of the Jinas; a similar *puja* with some additions is offered to the Dadagurus, former ascetics now regarded as deities; other forms of *puja* are made to deities shared with or customized from Hindu settings.

The first cannot be transactional as the Jinas are beyond the world of rebirth within which exchanges can take place (although, as in the Ranakpur temple above, the *murti*s are positioned teaching the truth to beings in all four directions of the cosmos, which permits an affective relationship; Johnson 2003). Offerings to them represent the renunciation of the gift and the esteem in which ascetic values are held, both within everyday life and as the means to liberation. The worship is 'reflexive', in that it benefits the one who makes it by enabling the internalization of such values and so binds the laity to the ascetic community. The second continues to value asceticism, in its focus of worship; many of the stories about the Dadagurus emphasize how they converted seekers to a Jain way of life during their previous life as Jain ascetics. The worshipper, acting as one of the Indras or Indranis, gods and goddesses who attended the mother of each Jina as she prepared for the birth of her child, becomes orientated to the renunciation at the heart of Jain tradition. The worship is, however, also 'transactional', as the Dadagurus are able to interact with their worshippers as they are still part of the world of (eventual) rebirth. The worshipper receives boons of various kinds (success in exams, a healthy child, business prowess), which are generated by the Dadagurus' ascetically gained power. The aims and results of such worship are therefore similar to much Sufi and other shrine worship, lending support to theorizing this in terms of *barakat* (power of blessing in its widest sense). The third form, to deities such as the goddess Padmavati, is purely transactional, although even here a 'Jainizing' of the deity as a follower of the Jinas can be found (Babb 1994). Some of Babb's informants criticized deity worship as too 'Hindu' and so to be rejected or at least minimized (pp. 37, 23). Whether this stems from earlier Jain criticisms of brahminical practice or from an absorption of European critiques, it indicates the desire of Babb's informants to present a particular construction of what Jain worship 'should be'. Constructions are important.

So too are underlying forms of logic. After Dadaguru worship, a small proportion of the offerings is taken outside the Jain temple. This *prabhavana* might look like Hindu or Sikh *prashad,* where the food is received back from the deity (or Waheguru) and consumed as the deity's leftovers and blessing. However, the gift is not there to transfer sin or demerit or 'dangerous spiritual materials' from the worshipper to the priest or someone else, as in much Hindu ritual (Raheja 1988), for the Jain aim is not 'transfer' but destruction of *karma* (Flügel 1998). What looks the same or very similar may then be quite differently understood and indeed negotiated in different contexts.

Concluding thoughts and questions for further discussion and research

This returns us to the questions with which this chapter began: the woman making offerings – what is she doing, and to which religious tradition does she belong? As you will now see, there is not a straightforward answer to either of these. The answers will depend on many different factors: where she is, who she is, why she is doing this, whether she accepts dominant ways of explaining her worship or resists the attempts of others to draw boundaries round it in a particular way. This in turn generates a further series of questions, which might provide the basis for your own discussion and research:

- What is happening when a ritual looks the same?
- How important are the meanings people attach to a ritual?
- How might the presentation of those meanings be affected by particular constructions of 'religion'?
- How and why does the study of particular practices push us towards a multi-layered, cross-traditional, carefully contextualized way of understanding them?

Further reading

Eck, Diana (1998) *Darśan: Seeing the Divine Image in India*, 3rd edn, New York: Columbia University Press.
> An anthropologist's perceptive introduction to forms of Hindu worship.

Green, Nile (2006) *Indian Sufism since the Seventeenth Century: Saints, Books and Empires in the Muslim Deccan*, London: Routledge.
> A detailed historical study through which it is possible to trace the evolution of different Sufi shrines in Aurangabad, including Shah Nur's. Read it alongside his 'Oral competition narratives of Muslim and Hindu saints in the Deccan', *Asian Folklore Studies* 63 (2): 221–42 (2004) for further examples of the wide range of worshippers who go to such shrines.

Humphrey, Caroline and James Laidlaw (1994) *The Archetypal Actions of Ritual: a Theory of Ritual, illustrated by the Jain Rite of Worship*, Oxford: Clarendon Press.
> A thought-provoking book by two anthropologists which takes seriously the wide range of Jain views of ritual while trying to develop a broader theory of ritual.

Kurin, Richard (1983) 'The structure of blessedness at a Muslim shrine in Pakistan', *Middle Eastern Studies* 19 (3): 312–25.
> By arguing for the centrality of *barakat* (blessedness) as an analytical concept for understanding shrine participation, this article challenges approaches that classify it as either superstitious or syncretic.

Rosario, Santi and Geoffrey Samuel (2010) 'Gender, religious change and sustainability in Bangladesh', *Women's Studies International Forum* 33 (4): 354–64.
> Examines effects of modernist forms of religion on ritual practice formerly shared by Hindus, Muslims and Christians linked with viability of village life.

6 Teachers and their traditions

In Chapters 2–5 we have focused on four key aspects of 'religion': notions of the divine, sacred texts, myths and devotion. We have seen how each of these becomes shaped and produced in modern South Asian contexts. One of the obvious missing 'elements' from this list is the category of 'founder'. For some religious traditions it is easy (although quite often misleading) to identify an 'original' historical teacher from whose life and/or teachings the rest of the tradition flows: Jesus for Christianity, Gautama Buddha for Buddhism, Mahavira for Jainism, Mohammad for Islam. This then yields a model for a religion of a single, central tradition from which offshoots develop. This is all rather problematic when it comes to 'Hinduism'. Hindu traditions do not have a central tradition or single founder. Some scholars argue that rather than Hinduism, we should speak about Shaivism, Vaishnavism and sometimes also Shaktism as separate, discrete religions, based around the worship of Shiva, Vishnu and the Goddess respectively (see von Stietencron 1995: 51). As the historian Will Sweetman has argued, this approach has many problems. Not least it presupposes a model of religion based on that of Christianity, which requires a religion to have a 'set of revealed scriptures' and assumes that it 'worships the same god as the highest deity' and '*knows its own . . . founders of sects*' (von Stietencron, cited in Sweetman 2003b: 334, our emphasis).

In this chapter, we propose to turn this problem on its head. Our approach will not be to view Hinduism as the exception to a rule of core tradition and single founder, but rather to understand these ideas in multiple terms. As David Miller (1976–7: 527) pointed out, following the great French Sanskritist, Louis Renou: 'The dynamic, sacred centre of Hinduism, is, in fact, the enlightened guru, whose charismatic leadership creates the institution for philosophical, religious, and social change.' This points us towards a 'centre' that is, in a way, decentred, as it refers to the numerous guru–pupil transmission traditions that are so important across South Asia. In fact, we can use this idea to go further. Whereas Miller is referring clearly to what he sees as the 'dynamic, sacred centre of Hinduism', we want to think about this idea in terms of South Asian religious traditions more generally. Because of this, we will speak more frequently of teachers and their traditions, rather than gurus, as 'guru' is a term that tends to be associated with Hindu and

Figure 6.1 SeatGuru Trip Advisor. Copyright: TripAdvisor 2011. Website: http://www.seatguru.com. Reproduced with permission.

Buddhist but not, for example, with Indian Islamic traditions. As in earlier chapters, we want to explore the ways in which religious traditions have frequently crossed such perceived boundaries. The interaction of different teacher–pupil traditions is a significant indicator of this dynamic; indeed, many teacher–pupil traditions function without major reference to such issues, or are more concerned with local contexts. The key question we would like to pose is therefore: How might a model of teacher–pupil traditions disrupt the notion of separate world religions and give us a different way of approaching religious traditions in modern South Asia?

The idea of such transmission traditions has had little place in introductory studies to Indian religions.[1] By contrast, the specific notion of the South Asian teacher as guru has entered into English and other European language usage across a very broad spectrum of contexts. It was used in early Orientalist accounts to epitomize 'eastern spirituality' and freedom from the supposed constraints of Christianity and its dogmas (see Chapter 8). In more recent guises, it has, ironically, come to designate heavyweight business chiefs and their material-economic power,[2] and it has entered into the everyday lexicons of contemporary life as a signifier of professional competence and results-orientated expertise. The first hits in a guru google search, for example, took us to a website designed to get you the best seats on your next flight! (Figure 6.1).

Contemporary gurus, then, reside in some distinctly secular environments, although the term does of course also retain religious connotations. Our aim in this chapter will be to re-situate the guru as teacher in a South Asian context, exploring this relationship and its importance to religious traditions on the basis of both ethnographic and historical evidence. As we shall see, gurus continue to be a vibrant and in many cases increasingly popular element of South Asian religious life. Perhaps because of this, there have in recent years been some interesting and informative studies of modern Guru movements that approach the phenomenon in a number of different ways, some arguing that they form a radical break with earlier guru–pupil formations (Warrier 2003a,b, 2005; McKean 1996; Hallstrom 1999, 2004). In this chapter we will refer to some of this work. Our case study will draw on the work of Lisa Hallstrom, who has studied one particular teacher in depth. This is the Bengali Anandamayi Ma.

Case study: Anandamayi Ma: modern teacher, divine force

We motored to Dehradun on July 12th [1971], reaching the Kishenpur Ashram by midday. My wife and daughter were very near Mother's room. I was allotted a cottage in 'Kalyanvan', the last one in the grounds.

I retired for the night by about 9.30 pm. My bed was near the left hand window of the cottage. Being a good sleeper, I went into deep slumber at once. It must have been around 11.30 or 12 midnight that I became wide awake for some unknown reason. I am absolutely certain that all vestige of sleep had left me. There was a glow outside my window. I sat up and looked out and beheld:

'The entire space, as far as the eye could see was a brilliant blaze of light.'

I recollected the words of the 11th chapter of the Bhagavad Gita, particularly the slokas (verses) 12 and 13 which say:

'If the splendour of a thousand suns were to blaze out at once in the sky, that would be akin to the splendour of that Mighty Being.'

And also sloka 20—

'The space between the heavens and all the quarters are filled by you alone.'

The experience is very clear in my mind but I struggle to find words to convey what I saw. This wondrous sight was Mother – encompassing the boundaries of my vision fully and completely; Mother, magnificent, lustrous and universal; Mother in Her Mahima form but as always seen by us, and most remarkable was the radiance in and around Her hands in which She held Padmanabha Bhagavan.

This experience lasted for about five to six minutes. I was thrilled and so profoundly at peace that I was able later to get the sleep of wonder and joy unalloyed.

(H. H. Marthanda Varma, the Elia Rajah of Travancore, from extracts in *Ananda Varta* magazine n.d.)

Explaining terms

Kalyanvan – 'beautiful forest', the area in which the Dehradun ashram is set; the forest is a standard place of asceticism and renunciation

Mahima form – 'Great' form; Anandamayi as the Great Goddess in her universal form. For a modern depiction of Vishnu in his universal form see Chapter 2

Padmanabha Bhagavan – Lord Vishnu lying on the snake Ananta, with Lord Brahma emerging from the lotus blooming from Vishnu's navel, and holding a *lingam*, the representation of Lord Shiva. The deity of the Rajas of Travancore (compare deity of Rajas of Cochin in Chapter 1)

samadhi – here, deep meditation

Figure 6.2 Shree Shree Ma Anandamayee, sitting in *samadhi*. Reproduced by courtesy of Shree Shree Anandamayee Sangha, Varanasi.

Looking at the photos of Anandamayi Ma alone, it may have surprised you to think that some devotees reject calling her a woman. She clearly is one! At the same time, the Raja's account is revealing in the way that it represents her as Devi, the Great Goddess we encountered in Chapter 2. In this sense she is of course not a woman at all – she has no 'self' and no gender in the normal sense of the word, being universal, the absolute force of the universe. Her relationship to other divine figures is also hinted at by her cradling of Lord Vishnu in her hands. Anandamayi Ma was thus a human yet at the same time a divine figure, in the manner of many such teachers in South Asian traditions. She was born Nirmala Sundari, in the village of Kheora, in largely Muslim rural Bengal, on 30 April 1896. Her parents were Vaishnava brahmins from families claiming Vedic lineage. Both her grandfathers were gurus. At the age of twelve she was married. Hagiographical tales of Anandamayi's life speak

Figure 6.3 Anandamayi Ma, as an older woman, holds the *murti* of Padmanabha. Reproduced courtesy of Shree Shree Anandamayee Sangha, Varanasi.

of the states of ecstasy (*bhava*) she experienced from early childhood. When her devotion intensified from about 1922 on, she was urged to take *diksha* by her husband's (Shakta) family guru. The guru had perceived her as having potential as a disciple, and sought to initiate her as a follower who would subsequently be both a receiver of the guru's teachings and a propagator of his path. However, on 3 August, the full moon day, according to Ma, 'the *yajna* and the *puja* that have to be performed during the initiation were spontaneously carried out by this body' (quoted in Hallstrom 1999: 38). This self-initiation effectively asserted Nirmala's independent assumption of the ascetic life (although compare Box 6.1); henceforth she would be known as Anandamayi Ma.

Five months later, Anandamayi initiated her husband as a disciple; later her parents would be initiated too. In 1924, she and her husband moved with his job to Shahbagh Gardens near Dacca (Dhaka), starting the period of her public recognition. Anandamayi stayed for some days at the over-grown Siddhesvari Kali temple nearby, where her first ashram was later established. The site was a *siddhapith,* a place particularly associated with the power of the Goddess in Shakta traditions, where *yogis* were believed to have achieved realization. 'Realization' is that understanding of 'how things really are', which liberates one from the world of rebirth, although what that constitutes varies widely between traditions.[3] On yogic paths, and ascetic paths more generally, the practitioner is believed to acquire a range of powers enabling him or her to transcend the normal limits of being human. These may range from omniscience to the ability to travel distances instantly, but it is often emphasized that in themselves they are (or should be) of no importance. Devotees' accounts emphasize that Ma herself manifested yogic powers, including the ability to predict and to heal, but rejected using them for worldly ends. She was, however, persuaded to perform *Kali-puja* during this period at the Nine Nights festivals for the Great Goddess, a deity gaining increasing political significance in late colonial Bengal (Kumar 1993; McDermott 2011). Soon such *puja*s were being offered to her as the Divine Mother, after she manifested a 'full *bhava*' or complete appearance as the Goddess, playing and laughing as she did so (for more on 'playing' as possession, see Erndl 2000, 2007).

From 1926 for the rest of her life, Anandamayi Ma travelled throughout India following what is referred to as her *kheyala*, or Divine Will. Her devotees believe this *kheyala* arose from her egoless nature as the Divine and was always exercised for their good, not her need. This included instructing her mother and husband's great niece to take the sacred thread, unprecedented at that point for women. Wherever she travelled, devotees (including foreigners) took *darshan* (see Chapter 5); some were initiated as renouncers. Ashrams were established to give her resting places as she travelled. The Shree Shree Anandamayee Sangha was established as an administrative body in Varanasi in 1950 as the network of ashrams grew, with her blessing but without her involvement. The Sangha continues today, with many projects

Box 6.1 Different stages of life

The ascetic (*samnyasi*, feminine *samnyasini*) is a person who lives a life of austerity or renunciation (*samnyasa*), often but by no means always in pursuit of the quest for release from the world of rebirth. In modern Hinduism this is often portrayed as the fourth of the four stages of life. The four stages are those of:

- student (*brahmacharya*): when the Vedas are to be studied;
- householder (*grihastha*): when a person marries, has children, creates wealth, pursues enjoyment, performs their prescribed duties;
- forest-dweller (*vanaprastha*): the first turn away from society, often presented as retirement;
- renunciation (*samnyasa*): leaving society and one's own name and social identity completely behind in the quest for liberation, a moment marked by the ritual in which the renouncer symbolically performs his own funeral rites (note the way in which Anandamayi refers to herself as 'this body', not as 'I').

These stages, which are part of the brahminical view of *varnash-ramadharma* (the duties of the four ideal social groups and stages of life needed for ritual, social and cosmic order), are found in Dharma texts such as Manu. Just as we shall see in Chapter 7A on *varna* (social group), this scheme effectively tidies up actual social practice, simplifying the relation between householder and ascetic lifestyles and values. Even the Dharma texts vary over whether a person should go through all four stages sequentially or whether this is not required. In Chapter 1 we saw that the historical context in which Mahavira and Gautama Buddha taught over two millennia ago was already one of great variation in ascetic practices and this has been the case in varying ways ever since, including Sufi *qalandar*s and others from across a range of religious traditions (see Chapter 5).

of *seva* (social and welfare services such as schools and hospitals); it also runs a website carrying photos, videos and *Ma-bani*, the words of Anandamayi that devotees regard as authoritative teachings (Shree Shree Anandamayee Sangha 2008). When Ma died in 1982, she had not named a successor. Her devotees experience her as still present, and the swamis refer to themselves as *acharya*s (teachers), subordinate to Ma as *guru* (here signifying divine teacher status).

Locating Ma within teacher traditions

Hallstrom (1999), on whose work this summary is based, emphasizes that the story of Anandamayi Ma's childhood, marriage, *sadhana* (practice) and *bhava* (manifestations) serves to draw the devotee into the Divine Reality she is held to be. The details of Ma's story show how, for devotees, she is embedded in caste, regional, worshipping and renouncer traditions, yet at the same time held to transcend them all. In this way, her story belongs to the genre of hagiography, the stories of 'saints', 'holy men' (or women) and gurus found across every South Asian tradition – Jain, Buddhist, Christian, Sufi and many Hindu varieties (Granoff 1988a,b; Lorenzen 1976, 1987; Ernst 1985; Katz 2000). Typically, these hagiographies convey the multiple, layered significance of the guru, often expressing elements of divinity and humanity at one and the same time.

Anandamayi can also be located in this broader field in terms of what might otherwise be considered a rather inconvenient fact: many of her devotees deny that she is a guru at all. Hallstrom suggests two possible reasons for this. First, that her 'inner circle' of *shishya*s (pupils who have received initiation from her) may wish to keep the nature of this relationship hidden, esoteric knowledge not to be broadcast beyond themselves. If so, this would merely confirm that she is typical of a well-established pattern of teacher–follower relationships in which the teacher is the centre, with an inner circle of initiates who alone receive the highest teaching, surrounded in turn by a greater circle of followers, themselves surrounded by a very large penumbra of people who may have loose connections with the teacher, or centre, or shrine concerned (Miller 1976–7). The Shankaracharyas and Sufi *pir*s we refer to below also exemplify this pattern. Second, Hallstrom suggests that, because Anandamayi actually becomes the devotee's *ishtadevata* (chosen form of God), this supersedes the 'mere' role of guru, understood as a human teacher. Again, this is a well-established pattern. Realized teachers have frequently been held to be manifestations of ultimate reality, however that may be understood. The Buddha and Adi Shankara have certainly been so regarded, but so have myriad teachers whose names are less well known.

In some other ways, however, the case of Anandamayi Ma seems to challenge what might be termed the generic features of teacher traditions in South Asia. One significant issue is the importance of lineage. As we will see in some of our other examples, the teacher is most frequently located as part of a succession of teachers stretching back generations and linking them to critical foundational teachers. This lineage acts as a guarantor of authority, legitimacy and therefore truth, helping to define the identity of the particular tradition as a socio-religious entity. A second, obviously linked, is the importance that is generally placed not just on the teacher but also on the pupil and on the nature of the teacher–pupil relationship. Here the importance and nature of initiation, the types of teaching method used, the pupils' views of themselves in relation to the teacher and the teaching are significant factors in establishing and sustaining the tradition. In relation to both of these points, Anandamayi was rather unconventional. Regarding lineage, we saw in telling her story that Ma was self-initiated, rather than being identified as a successor of a previous teacher. In addition, she named no successor to continue her lineage. In line with this, the current teachers who give initiation distinguish between her as the (continuing) *guru* and themselves merely as *acharya*s passing on her teaching. This subtle difference points up a further difference in the way that many of Ma's followers regard their relationship to the guru: frequently, they see themselves more as *bhakta*s (devotees) than *shishya*s (pupils). That is, they look to her grace as a divine being, rather than seeking to progress spiritually by efforts derived from her teaching (Hallstrom 1999: 160). Ma cannot then be seen simply as a guru from their point of view, or even as an avatar (understood here as only a partial descent of God); she is rather a full manifestation of deity (p. 174). However, that manifestation is veiled in her human body to make it possible for them to interact with her.

Other work demonstrates that there is a tendency amongst modern Hindu gurus to present themselves specifically as what Maya Warrier (2005: 36) has termed 'avatar gurus'. This position is taken up by, for example, Sathya Sai Baba and Mata Amritanandamayi, two gurus based in southern India. The avatar guru makes the self-conscious claim to be a 'descent form' of a divine power (see Chapter 4), appearing on earth in order to perform a particular divine mission.[4] The mission of Amritanandamayi as an *avatar* of the great goddess, for example, is described in her hagiographical biography as 'comforting suffering humanity' (see Warrier 2005: 34). Warrier's view is that this position is critical to reconciling the position of the guru as renouncer with an active engagement in worldly affairs (see further below). Both Sai Baba and Amritanandamayi head vast and sophisticated transnational organizations (unlike Anandamayi Ma, who made no attempt to become involved with the Mission set up by her followers). Although both are removed from the world, their intimate connection with these worldly organizations is legitimate as a means of fulfilling their 'avatar mission'. As *avatar*s, of course, both these gurus also freely receive the deep devotion of their followers, enhanced by *bhava darshan*s (organized visual revelation of the guru in divine mood).[5]

All three are, however, very different from, say, the way current Madhva traditions function, with pupils trained by teachers in the rigorous theological philosophy of this dualist Vedanta tradition going back to the great thirteenth-century Acharya, Madhva. That the correct interpretation matters not only to the pupil seeking liberation but also to the social identity of the tradition is clearly shown on the Dvaita home page (1995–2006), where the claim of ISKCON, the International Society for Krishna Consciousness, to be a Madhva school is rejected point by point (Poornaprajna Vidyapeetha 2006).[6] Clearly these examples indicate that the idea of teacher traditions and teacher–pupil relationships as a means of understanding South Asian religious traditions is one that must remain flexible. The idea of 'teacher traditions' encapsulates a set of related features we can use to understand the dynamics of these movements, but which we must deploy in a nuanced and careful fashion in relation to different situations. The varied examples we will now go on to explore should demonstrate this point.

Exploring diversity in teacher traditions

An ancient Upanishadic story (c.800 BCE)

> A person who lived in the country of the Gandharas was taken, blind-folded and abandoned in a lonely place. Shouting out his predicament, he attracted the attention of someone who took the blindfold off and told him which way to walk back to his home place. Being wise, he followed the instructions and, asking his way from village to village, he arrived back in Gandhara country. 'Just so,' says the text, 'a person here who has a teacher knows.' The delay in being freed from this world only lasts until he is taught by such a person.
>
> (based on *Chāndogya Upaniṣad* 6.14.1–6.14.2, see Roebuck 2003: 179)

This is one of the favourite stories of the eighth-century CE Advaita Vedantin teacher, Shankara, whom we met in Chapter 2. He frequently quotes just a tiny phrase from it, heightening its meaning even further: '*Only* the one with a teacher knows . . .' For him, it is only as the pupil engages with the teacher that liberation from the world of rebirth becomes possible. In the context of this relationship what Shankara calls the 'compassionate Veda' functions: the teacher who knows its correct interpretation, because he himself was trained in the true Advaitin teaching tradition, helps the pupil to realize 'how things really are', namely, that the self within is nothing other than Brahman. The means of knowledge is the Veda (especially the Upanishadic section), which gives methods for stripping away the misconceptions preventing the pupil from understanding this. But like the stranger for the person lost in the forest, the teacher is the key link in 'making the penny drop' (see Suthren Hirst 2005). For Shankara, the Advaitin teacher is human but has overcome misconception. His own pupils praise him highly for the liberating insight he passed on to them. Later hagiographies go much further and portray him as a manifestation of Shiva himself. The modern Shankaracharyas, heads of huge *maths* (ascetic centres) whose lineage documents trace themselves back to Adi Shankara, have become in the late twentieth century self-appointed spokesmen for Hinduism.

The Radhasoami Satsang

> So hard the path of *guru-bhakti* –
> Let the guru make it easy. [Refrain]
> As a man the guru seems to men,
> Yet as a man he's known to someone who knows nothing.
> How can one ever rest? (1)
> The guru sometimes acts just like
> An unaffected child
> And the soul is struck with wonder. (2)
> The *satguru* gives proofs within the body
> And a little faith begins to grow
> But later must be sacrificed.
> Again and again the mind becomes fickle . . . (3)
> The fool doesn't know where his welfare resides
> Or the will of the Lord (5)
> and acts to his own disadvantage.
> Again and again he will hear holy words, and again and again
> will forget them.
> He won't recognize the *satguru*
> Or know his greatness. (6)
> Let that great Lord we know as Dhara Sindhu Pratap
> Watch over us, protect us in all ways
> And give the gift of *bhakti*. (7)
> (Shyam Lal, *Shabdāmrit Dhārā*, see Gold 1987: 45–6)

'Radhasoami' refers to a number of related religious paths established at the beginning of the twentieth century. In his study of the Radhasoamis, Daniel Gold explores current branches of the movement in the context of a much longer tradition, the Sant tradition, which developed in north India during the medieval period (Gold 1987). We have already come across this tradition in Chapter 2, through the poet-saint Kabir (see also Chapter 9). Exploring foci of authority, modes of lineage and historical variations around particular *sant*s and their traditions, Gold gives a clear though complex picture of the many permutations and interpretations of teacher–follower movements in the north Indian milieu from the sixteenth century onwards. He distinguishes between traditions that emphasize disembodied Vedic authority (eternal heritage), iconoclastic *sant* poets like Kabir, and the 'singular personality' of gods like Krishna or gurus more in the 'divine image' we saw above. Gold shows that the phenomenon of teacher–pupil movements has been widespread and prevalent in the past, thus placing the prominence of contemporary Guru movements in historical context.

In the Radhasoami song quoted above, 'Dhara Sindhu Pratap' is the name used for the Supreme Lord. The singer, Babu Shyam Lala, also known as

Guru Data Dayal, was third in the lineage of gurus at the Radhasoami Satsang in Dinod, Haryana (Gold 1987; Babb 1987; see Radha Soami Satsang Beas 2010 for the Beas lineage, which is independent of others). Shyam Lala observed in 1927:

> For success in this matter [spiritual practice] it is essential that [the per-fect] Guru . . . must be given, by the disciple in all his affairs, spiritual or temporal, priority over God, until the disciple himself becomes one with Guru and God.
>
> (cited in Gold 1987: 106)

In this tradition, then, the role of the living guru is distinguished from God (since the devotee cannot grasp his true identity at this stage), and is even considered to be more important than God in terms of a disciple's spiritual progress. Yet when the human teacher is understood, he is none other than God. In the song, Shyam Lala plays on the term *Satguru* ('true teacher', 'teacher who is the Real'). The perfect human teacher is the true teacher because he teaches and indeed embodies the truth of the Lord. Once more this emphasis links the Radhasoami movement to the Sant tradition, and indeed to one particular seam of that tradition, for the term *Satguru* is widely used in Sikh traditions for both the ten Gurus and for God.

Guru Nanak and Bhai Mardana

Guru Nanak (1469–1539) is held by Sikhs to be the first of ten Gurus, each of whom manifested the Guru, that is God, in his life and teachings.[7] In Figure 6.4 he is shown sitting, while his companion, Mardana, plays his stringed instrument, the *rebec*. Mardana was a Muslim of the Mirasi commu-nity, a hereditary caste of minstrels and genealogists who played for various communities across north India (see Chapter 7A). It was not, therefore, unu-sual that a Mirasi would play for someone else. Mardana, however, became attached to the early group around Nanak and would have accompanied them in their *kirtan* (hymn-singing) sessions. Three of Mardana's own songs are in the 'Sikh scriptures', the Guru Granth Sahib,[8] along with those of the first five Gurus, two Sufis, some brahmins, Kabir, Trilochan, Ravidas and others of the Sant tradition. Such apparently cross-community connec-tions seem to defy the logic of religious identification,[9] but by approaching Nanak and his successors through the model of teacher–pupil traditions and bardic groups we can see that the association of Nanak and Mardana has a coherent logic. Nanak is recognized as the teacher, Mardana becomes one of his followers, their particular tradition drawing, like many developing Sant traditions of the period, on the kind of rich repertoire we shall note below.

The importance of the teacher in this tradition is demonstrated in the following passage from the Guru Granth Sahib, in which we can clearly see its interweaving with broader devotional and textual contexts:

Figure 6.4 Bhai Mardana and Guru Nanak, from a Janamsakhi manuscript. Reproduced courtesy of Harjinder Kanwal.

The Guru's word is the sound current of the Naad;[10] the Guru's word is the wisdom of the Vedas; the Guru's word is all-pervading. The Guru is Shiva, the Guru is Vishnu and Brahma; the Guru is Paarvati and Lakhshmi. Even knowing God, I cannot describe him; He cannot be described in words. The Guru has given me this one understanding: there is only the One, the Giver of all souls. May I never forget Him!

[*Sri Guru Granth Sahib*, p. 2, v.5 (page and verse is standard) n.d.]

Gold's analysis of esoteric language in the related north Indian Sant tradition helps us to understand how particular teaching lines emerged from this kind of context. Gold detects four increasingly specific levels of language use that act as clues. At the first, most general level, Hindi *sant* poets shared a general pool of vocabulary and approach with other yogic teachers (including the Nath *yogi*s whose tradition influenced Nanak although he also spoke out against them). Many refer, for example, to the *ida*, *pingala* and *sushumna* channels of energy within the head. At the second level, the *sant*s used particular terms and images that characterized their own approach, for instance the 'whirling cave', to describe aspects of experience that broadly grouped them together as a 'clan', related to but distinct from other yogic groups. At the third, more specific level, *sant*s who shared some kind of spiritual relation in connected lineages used vocabulary to describe the levels of experience of the practitioner in similar if not precisely the same ways – held to derive from a guru's experience or instruction. Finally, at the most specific level, teachers within a particular clearly defined lineage used terms in precise technically defined ways to prescribe a particular path to follow.

Although this part of Gold's work is based specifically on descriptions of esoteric experience, either actual or anticipated, it gives us a useful way of conceptualizing teaching traditions and their interrelations, particularly if linked with his further discussion of *sant*, *panth* and *parampara*. These terms have numerous uses. However, Gold uses them to draw attention to the *sant* as a charismatic individual held to have realized and/or embodied the truth, the *panth* as the group of followers that collects around him, and the *parampara* as the more formally defined line of succession of teachers that concretizes the tradition into a specific lineage. This last may be either through initiation (*nad parampara*, 'sound lineage', that is, through the transmitted mantra) or through biological succession (*bindu parampara*, 'seed lineage', passed down through families). Sometimes the two coincide. You might want to bear these helpful distinctions in mind in reading the rest of this chapter and in your further research.

The Tantric guru

The link between *mantra*, guru and God is found not only in Sikh traditions but also in Hindu and Buddhist Tantric traditions too. The 'Ocean of the Heart' (*Kularnava Tantra*) (c.1000–1400 CE), a compendium drawn on by many different Kaula sects,[11] says:

> Just as words such as 'pot', 'vessel' and 'jar' all mean the same object, so too are god and *mantra* and guru said to be the same object. Just as divinity is, so is the mantra; just as there is mantra, so there is the guru (13.64–65).
>
> (Brooks 2000: 358–9)

Tantric traditions provide an excellent variety of examples to illustrate our emphasis in this chapter on both the importance of the teacher tradition model and the need to keep the model flexible. Incredibly difficult to pin down, and often demonized by European writers, Hindu reformers (including Rammohun) and earlier Indian authors as anti-social or immoral, they have become associated in popular discourse with the five Ms: the acceptance of meat (*mamsa*), fish (*matsya*), wine (*madya*), fermented grain (*mudra*) and sexual intercourse (outside the marital relationship) (*maithuna*), all mentioned in the *Kularnava Tantra* we have just quoted. It is easy to see why these gave opponents a quick target, redolent as the *makara*s are of practices proscribed in many mainstream Indian devotional and ascetic traditions, as well as being offensive to Victorian and early twentieth-century European sensibilities. The *Kularnava Tantra* is already well aware of the transgressive nature of such practices, and makes it very clear that they are only to be practised by 'one who knows the meaning of the Heart treatises directly from the auspicious guru' (5.91, see Brooks 2000: 355). The esoteric side of Tantric traditions, controlled by strict secrecy and initiation by the guru, is crucial. An initiate is to be 'outwardly Vedic, a Śaiva at home, secretly a Śākta [that is, a tāntrika]', or in a Buddhist version of the aphorism: 'externally a Hīnayāna, internally a Māhayāna, secretly a Vajrayāna' (White 2000: 34). What Tantric traditions share is a focus on using desire (*kama*) for both worldly purposes and for liberation (Padoux 1986), the apparent opposite of ascetic paths. Yet both Tantric and ascetic paths are deeply concerned with power and its effects.

David White (2000: 9) proposes that at the centre of Tantric practice lies the *mandala*, the diagram representing the energy of the cosmos, which the practitioner seeks to appropriate through designated ritual means. Not only used for individual ends, such practice has lain at the heart of South and Southeast Asian patterns of kingship. This has been shown very clearly in the case of the Tantric goddess Kubjika, the secret lineage goddess of the royal family of Nepal. She is under the control of her Newar priests along with Newari caste rankings and the political affairs of the Kathmandu Valley itself (White 2000: 33; Dyczkowski 2001). Yet the divine embodiment that the *mandala* represents varies dramatically between traditions; this embodiment could range from a naked female and her sexual or menstrual fluids to a body of sound, a deity, the Tantric guru himself or the empty sky (White 2000: 11; Flood 2005). In these traditions, initiation transfers power from guru to initiate as a kind of 'fluid' matter, the guru's very substance creating the practitioner in turn (as well as very concrete social and political relations), and blurring the difference between 'biological' and 'spiritual' lineage. For a recent example of the way this may be understood in relation to the *Kularnava Tantra*, see the article by a devotee of Satguru Sivaya Subrahmuniyaswami (born Robert Hansen in California), the founder of the worldwide Saiva Siddhanta Church and the magazine *Hinduism Today* (2003).

A Sufi lineage: the Chishtis of Bijapur

From a rather different context, the diagram of the lineages for the Chishti Sufis of Bijapur from the fifteenth to eighteenth centuries (Figure 6.5) shows nicely the way in which 'spiritual' and 'biological' (or familial) succession can both differ and interrelate in Indian (and other) Islamic traditions too. The notion of *isnad* or lineage is extremely important in Muslim contexts and will often be traced back to Muhammad or the family of the Prophet. Like lineages in Indian brahminic and other traditions, the correct (and unbroken) lineage acts as a guarantor of authenticity and truth. It also thereby maintains the authority of the particular line concerned. Sufi

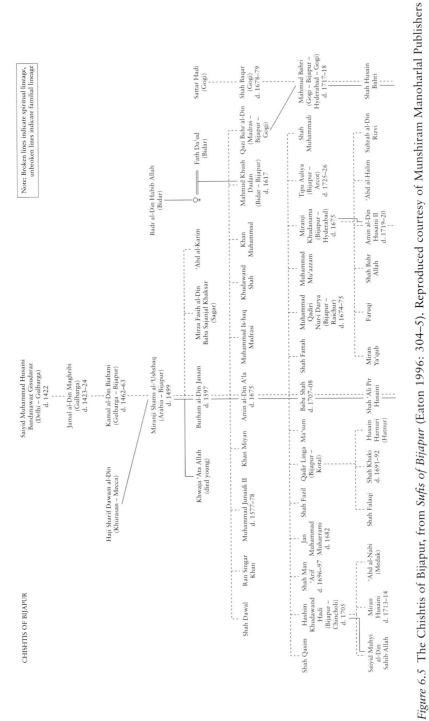

Figure 6.5 The Chishtis of Bijapur, from *Sufis of Bijapur* (Eaton 1996: 304–5). Reproduced courtesy of Munshiram Manoharlal Publishers Pvt. Ltd.

traditions are organized in *silsila*s, transmission lines from *pir* to *murid* (holy man/teacher to disciple). Just as the hagiographies of many Jain, Buddhist and brahminical teachers record their starting out by approaching different teachers initially, so too a particular *pir* may have received teaching in more than one other *silsila* before being initiated into the one he will then head. Some will retain allegiance to more than one, as the identifications on the Aulia Allah (n.d.) website indicate. Identifying the *mazar*s or tombs where *pir*s are venerated across Pakistan, as well as living *pir*s, this site includes Qadria Chishtia, Qadria Qalanderia Noshahia and so on as well as simple Naqshbandi, Chishti and others. (For information on the main Indian Sufi *silsila*s, see Box 5.1 in Chapter 5 and references there.)

Living pirs

One *pir* listed on this site is Hazrat Shah Naqshbandi, or Zindapir, of Ghamkol Sharif in the North-West Frontier Province, Pakistan. As his name suggests, he claimed descent through the Naqshbandiyya order, which traces direct lineage back to Muhammad's companion and the first Caliph, Abu Baqr. 'Zindapir' in Urdu means 'living saint'; Hazrat Shah attained this name, not surprisingly, before his death in 1999. His lodge in Ghamkol Sharif was established in 1951, and it has over the years attained a position as a place of pilgrimage, which has continued after his *wisaal*, that is his 'union with the beloved', or death. Pnina Werbner's ethnographic account of the atmosphere at the lodge during the period that the *pir* was alive is worth quoting at some length:

> People came to see him and bask in his light, and though he kept himself aloof and at some distance from the women supplicants, they were, nevertheless, convinced that he saw into their inner hearts and grasped their suffering. He was said to perform acts of miraculous healing but my own observations were of less dramatic encounters, in which he distributed salt, amulets and prayers, blowing *dam* (a verse from the Koran), advising women to say their prayers, touching a limb with his cane. The intangible moral amity among supplicants was generated by his living presence, and by the ambience of peace it was felt that he cast on the lodge itself, perceived to be a haven of tranquility, *sukun*, a place of healing.
>
> (Werbner 2010: 378)

This atmosphere created by the saint is reminiscent of the power of the presence of other teachers we have looked at, such as Amritanandamayi and Anandamayi (and also Amma; see Chapter 3).

Another example of a living saint in the Naqshbandiyya tradition can be found at Atroshi, about a hundred miles from the Bangladeshi capital Dhaka, in the rural district of Faridpur. The *pir* of Atroshi is Muhammad

Hashmatullah. Although remote, Atroshi is a pilgrimage site that in recent years has attracted hundreds of thousands of devotees. These numbers have meant that the organization of the lodge has become increasingly regimented:

> The *pir* is available to disciples only within a rigid framework of etiquette rules . . . . (He) gives *darshan* (appearance) three times a day, and the disciples who have come to petition him are managed in such a way as to prevent their becoming too burdensome, clinging or obstructive to others waiting behind them. The *darbar* is structured, in effect, as a series of frames around the person of the *pir*, or more exactly, around the experience of seeing and being seen by the *pir*.
>
> (Mills 1998: 38)

In this description of the operation of the Atroshi lodge, I am sure you can see echoes both of forms of worship we have seen operating across the region (Mills even uses the term '*darshan*' to describe the interaction between *pir* and devotee), and of the embodied divine power of the teacher.

The gender twist: making creative spaces

We began this chapter with an example that demonstrated the ability of women to assert their position as teachers in modern South Asian traditions. Anandamayi Ma is by no means exceptional, as there are many other traditions that have been started or revived by women teachers. Mata Amritanandamayi is another good example. In this section, however, we want to focus in on the way in which gender relations, and more particularly the position of women, find an interesting expression on the other side of the teacher–pupil relationship.

Very often, the teacher–pupil model can provide a space for women to assume different roles from those that dominate their everyday lives. Pnina Werbner's exploration of activities at the lodge of the *pir* of Ghamkol Sharif demonstrates this. Werbner explores both the everyday activity of suppliants coming to visit the *pir*, and the annual festival celebrations associated now with the '*urs*, the 'wedding' of the *pir* to his beloved (see Chapter 5). She demonstrates that this context provides 'a creative space for female devotional singing, laughter and enjoyment, as well as for wandering and exploration' (Werbner 2010: 377). Such activities are of course marked by the mingling of different groups of people engaging in interaction focused on the person of the teacher, and the common experience of following his path and expressing devotion through his person. These critical spaces of interaction, she argues, fosters what she calls 'nationwide fraternities and sororities of citizen-devotees, which extend across geographical distances, class and ethnicity' (p. 381). In this sense, then, the spaces opened up by teacher traditions in South Asia produce significant social realities, sometimes in tension with or as an alternative to the realities of everyday life.

Werbner goes further, suggesting that the space of the Sufi lodge and the interactions associated with it can create 'the kind of civic culture that fosters notions of moral obligation, caring and loyalty among stranger-citizens within Pakistan as a nation-state' (p. 381). This of course is a major claim, and her justification for making it is partly based on a recognition that the vibrant *pir*–devotee tradition as it is experienced in Pakistan is a real opportunity for non-elite women in particular to participate in public spaces in empowered ways, that they constitute, as she says, 'an essential part of [the *pir*'s] kingdom and they are accorded respect in their own right as valued members of its far-flung community' (p. 381).

We need to be careful to maintain a sense of perspective in considering such claims in the context of our consideration of teacher traditions in South Asia. Although the lodge at Ghamkol Sharif appears to present opportunities for these alternative roles for some Pakistani women, the saint during his life was very much a patriarchal presence, reflecting the power of the teacher in any model of teacher–pupil relations in which the teacher is regarded not just as a keeper of knowledge but also as a repository of divine power. Just as there are cases in which the model provides such opportunities, there are also cases in which the potential for the male teacher to exploit his position of power is also evident.

It is not just in media coverage of gurus and sex scandals that such concerns come to light. In South Asia, a healthy scepticism of 'false fakirs' is longer than certain colonial roots. Shyam Lala above emphasized the need for a *perfect* guru, that is, one who can be trusted, a theme already employed by Shankara in his criticism of the Buddha as at best untrustworthy, at worst deceptive (*Brahma-sutra-bhashya* 2.2.32, Gambhirananda 1977: 426). Although the grounds for such trust have varied (and are themselves open to abuse), one long-standing one is the observed truth, coherence and efficacy of the guru's teaching. Another is the effectiveness of their power, whether cultivated through ascetic or devotional means. Such power has been exercised in many varying ways in the past, not least by 'warrior *sadhus*' who protected trade routes in the seventeenth and eighteenth centuries, seriously challenging British administrators' views on what it was to be religious (Pinch 2006). Moreover, ascetic and/or devotional power, drawn on by rulers and devotees alike, has at times led and indeed continues to lead to the accumulation of wealth through land grants and donations. This has often seemed paradoxical to European observers. Both male and female gurus in the modern period have had to take account of such puzzlement or condemnation.[12]

The politics twist: spiritual power as political?

As our discussion of gender relations shows, power is not a theme that is restricted to the spiritual capabilities of teachers in the teacher tradition. Although they are frequently presented as beyond the confines of ordinary existence in hagiographical accounts, gurus, *pir*s and other teachers are deeply embedded in webs of social and political relations. The *pir* of Atroshi, for example, was frequently visited by President Ershad of Bangladesh during the 1980s, while Indira Gandhi, who was Prime Minister of India in the 1970s and 1980s, often went to see Anandamayi Ma, her mother's close friend and teacher. In India, the relationships between 'godmen' and figures in the political establishment have been the subject of media attention for many years. An academic study that takes up this theme is a book by Lise McKean (1996), *Divine Enterprise*, which examines relationships between modern gurus and the form of militant political Hinduism known as Hindu nationalism. 'As producers and purveyors of spiritual commodities', she argues, 'gurus assist in propagating Hindu nationalism, an ideology that relies on referents to Hindu India's unparalleled spiritual prowess and moral authority' (McKean 1996: 1). In this approach, then, there is almost a structural link proposed between modern Guru organizations and the development of Hindu nationalism, forged through the opening up of the Indian economy to transnational capitalism in the late twentieth century. The marketing of spirituality is for McKean an integral feature of the rise of a triumphalist and ultimately defensive and exclusivist Hindu common sense, fuelled by the rapid rise of the new middle class.

Although this argument cannot be dismissed, there is evidence to suggest that the projection of a structural link between modern Hindu organizations and Hindu nationalism is over-stressed. For example, Maya Warrier (2005: 126–7) indicates in her study of the Mata Amritanandamayi Mission that this organization encompasses both Hindu nationalist and explicitly anti-Hindu nationalist devotees, even though the main constituency of the Mission is the same middle class at the heart of McKean's claims. It seems that the latter's claims may be to a certain extent accurate, although we should be careful not to over-emphasize the argument. There are other ways in which modern teacher movements operate, and there is also evidence that some are specifically geared towards combating the tendency towards extremism noted by McKean. Karline McLaine's (forthcoming) work on the Shirdi Sai Baba movement in Delhi, for example, points up the way in which some elements in this movement attempt to position the guru's tradition in opposition to contemporary discourses based on antagonism between Hindus and Muslims.

In general, we need to be aware of the different political consequences that can emanate from our initial observation that the world of teacher traditions is intimately bound up with social and political relations. As such, the various teachers are bound to come into contact with political power, to be implicated in the maintenance of established orders or to be associated with challenges to such order. This is not a new phenomenon. It is clearly associated with teacher traditions for as long as these have been recognized as part of the fabric of South Asian society. So, for example, Ibrahim Adil

Shah II, the Muslim Sultan of Bijapur (1580–1627), referred to himself as
Jagat Guru, or World Teacher. He demonstrably showed interest in Hindu
aesthetics and in Sarasvati, the goddess of learning, poetry and music.
Richard Eaton (1996: 104) suggests that he may have wanted to root the
Bijapur court firmly in the local culture, or that he was imitating his Mughal
contemporary, Akbar, in ascribing to himself universal religious as well as
political leadership. Contemporary Qadiri Sufi reformers objected to his
approach, as others reacted to Akbar's eclecticism. But in this context we
can view the claim to guru status and the association with forms of Hindu
learning as appropriate political strategies, drawing on available discourses
of power, which include the realm of the teacher traditions. As the Sultan
demonstrably realized, spiritual power was and still is intimately bound up
with relations of power at other levels.

The religion twist: teacher traditions and the discourse of 'religion'

The ways in which specific modern teacher movements relate to the discourse of religion vary enormously. In Chapter 9 we shall see how the Sikh
Khalsa community marked itself off from other Sikh and Hindu traditions at the end of the nineteenth century, so leading to the formation of
Sikhism as a modern religion. One among many Sikh traditions deriving
from a *sant* background, it has projected itself as normative. By contrast,
Subramuniyaswami's Saiva Siddhanta Church, grounded in a very specific
(though reformulated) Shaiva religious identity, uses this as a platform from
which to speak on 'Hinduism today' (see Kauai's Hindu Monastery 2011).
Other Guru movements that have developed a transnational profile are often
marked, however, by a claim to exceed or bypass religious allegiance. This is
partly because of disaffection with institutionalized religious forms that may
be seen to be the source of conflict or constriction. It is also a way of making
truth claims for one's own religious brand. Gurus such as Amritanandamayi,
Sai Baba and Sivananda all claim to offer a kind of free-floating spirituality that appears to operate in a realm beyond the attachments of specific
religions. Sivananda's 'practical spirituality', for example, 'can be adopted
by Hindus and non-Hindus alike' (McKean 1996: 165). Or as Sathya Sai
Baba says, 'Do not give importance to differences of religion, sect, status, or
color. Have the feeling of one-ness permeate all your acts' (Sai Organization
Sites n.d.: front page). Warrier reports that part of the popularity of Mata
Amritanandamayi amongst middle-class adherents is her lack of concern for
their religious attachments, or even their attachment to other gurus. In some
ways, this emphasis on a kind of non-aligned spirituality works with the
secularization thesis, which perceives traditional religion as less significant
in the modern world.[13] Spirituality provides meaning in the context of this
ostensibly growing secularization. The Divine Life Society, for example,

states that it 'aims to remove the unwarranted distinction between the spiritual and the secular, and endeavors to present an integrated view of life as a whole' (McKean 1996: 183).

In Chapter 8, we will explore the way in which this idea of spirituality is strongly aligned with a discourse of Orientalism that marks India as different, effectively a site ripe for colonial domination because of its perceived inability to negotiate the modern world of material, political and economic progress. We shall also see in that chapter how that same idea of spirituality was transformed into a form of resistance against this domination, although the form of this resistance was ambiguous, marked as it were by the dominant knowledge system. In the identification of modern teacher–pupil traditions as deploying the language of spirituality to escape some of the pitfalls of religious identity, we can see a similar kind of ambiguous or double-edged positioning, partially resistant, partially articulated through dominant structures that tend still to exoticize South Asia and particularly India as a land of spiritual resonance (where Western people have, notoriously, travelled to 'find themselves'[14]). Through this observation, a significant point for our approach to South Asian religious traditions is exemplified. Very often, one can see the presence of, and even the dialogue between, different discourses in the articulation or practice of these traditions. Here we see the idea of religion as both separate and other, alongside and in conversation with teacher–pupil traditions, which have developed without being bound by this discourse of religion over a long period of time. The engagement of a range of different people and different groups exemplifies this latter model. Examinations of contemporary Guru traditions need to take account of these different discursive pressures, this negotiation of positions in relation to different contexts in which such traditions are articulated. Exploring the interplay of these different ways of looking at such traditions is a compelling prospect for further research.

Concluding thoughts

We have seen throughout this chapter how approaching South Asian religious traditions through the model of teacher–pupil traditions can enable the identification of a range of interesting connections and socio-political contexts that help us to understand the continuities and innovations which have shaped such traditions over many centuries. Drawing parallels between Sufi *pirs* and gurus such as Anandamayi Ma is perhaps controversial, as, if we view such traditions through the lens of religion, we can see that they are located in quite different discursive spaces. Using the lens of the teacher traditions model, however, we can see how these exist together in an interrelated space, which has been contested and negotiated by a range of agents over time. The final section in particular demonstrates, however, that it is often important to deploy these different models together when studying teacher–pupil traditions, as they exist in complex social environments that demand careful and considered unpacking.

Questions for further discussion and research

- What are the advantages and disadvantages of grouping together the very different movements mentioned in this chapter as 'teacher traditions'?
- How does Subrahmuniyaswami's definition of 'the true meaning of Vedanta' ('Secrets from the *Kularnava Tantra*', *Hinduism Today* 2003) compare with that of Shankara (Chapter 2 and this chapter) and Rammohun Roy (Chapter 2).
- It appears that there is an obvious contradiction between renunciation and the economic and political power of some ascetic teachers and their organizations. Is there any underlying logic that would make sense of this apparent discrepancy?
- In what senses, if any, do teacher traditions transcend 'religion'?
- Because ascetics have for millennia been supposed to acquire great power through their various practices, they have often been figures of fear. Here are some suggestions for further research:
  - Compare Ravana's ascetic powers in various tellings of the Ram-katha (you could start by looking at Richman 1991a and 2001, both of which have useful index entries on Ravana).
  - Read Jayanta Bhatta's entertaining ninth-century play on the problems of the ruler of Kashmir. He wanted to get rid of some very unsalubrious Shaiva ascetics whose anarchist behaviour was seen as a threat to the society of the day (see Dezső 2005).
  - Study British perplexity at the roving bands of armed ascetics who constituted a worrying source of disorder to the stability of empire (Pinch 2006).

Further reading

Gold, Daniel (1987) *The Lord as Guru: Hindi Sants in North Indian Tradition*, New York: Oxford University Press.
> A historical, literary and ethnographic study of north Indian *sant* traditions in relation to a diverse Indian landscape of yogic, Sufi and other traditions.

McKean, Lise (1996) *Divine Enterprise: Gurus and the Hindu Nationalist Movement*, Chicago: University of Chicago Press.
> A vigorous argument about the Hindu Nationalist connections of many modern Guru movements (see Warrier 2005 for a critique).

Padoux, André (2000) 'The tantric guru', in David Gordon White (ed.) *Tantra in Practice*, Princeton: Princeton University Press.

>   A clear introductory article that contextualizes the Tantric guru in the broader context of Indian teacher traditions with a translation of selected verses from the *Kularnava Tantra* on the guru.

Warrier, Maya (2005) *Hindu Selves in a Modern World: Guru Faith in the Mata Amritanandamayi Mission*, New York: RoutledgeCurzon.

>   A study of a modern devotional Guru movement that cuts across national, cultural and religious boundaries, based on personal interviews and ethnographic research.

Werbner, Pnina and Helene Basu (eds) (1998) *Embodying Charisma: Modernity, Locality and the Performance of Emotion in Sufi Cults*, London: Routledge.

>   An interesting collection of ethnographic essays on Sufi teacher traditions in Bangladesh, India and Pakistan, with an introduction that looks critically at a range of related anthropological theories.

7A Caste: social relations, cultural formations

In Part I, we have looked critically at deity, texts, myth, ritual and worship, and teachers and founders, often considered to be key 'features' of a (world) religion. We have discovered how these categories often group together very diverse phenomena. This prompted us to develop other ways of thinking about religion and religious traditions in South Asia and beyond. In this chapter we look at a topic that at first sight does not appear to fit with this approach: caste. Unlike the other categories, which are held to be common across religious traditions, caste is often seen to be quintessentially Indian, if not the grounding principle of Hinduism (Dumont 1980). In Chapter 7B, which will start Part II of this book, we shall explore how this view of Hinduism as caste-based developed in the modern period, although, as always, with older roots. Here in Chapter 7A,* to conclude Part I, we explore the diversity of social relations and cultural formations that are covered by the umbrella term 'caste'. In doing so, we shall look at both historical and ethnographic approaches and ideological systems. This will help us to contextualize how the umbrella term came to be used, as well as to realize that the diverse phenomena that it covers were and are historically and socially produced, just like other social formations across the world.[1] This will help us to be open to a much more flexible way of understanding such social phenomena, and the many ways in which they are related to the equally complex term, 'religion'.

Case study: the Meos of Mewat

Figure 7A.1 shows a map of an Indian village, drawn in the 1980s. This village, Bisru, in northwestern India, was where the French anthropologist, Raymond Jamous, lived at the time. He was studying the kinship relationships of a particular caste group, the Meos, who integrated him into their own kin networks as the *bhai* (brother) of Abdulaziz, a university-educated Meo, his first contact there. The region in which Bisru is located is called

---

* An explanation of the rationale for calling these two chapters 7A and 7B respectively is provided at the beginning of Chapter 7B.

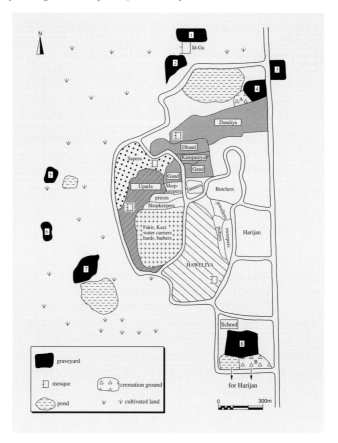

Figure 7A.1 Map of Bisru village (reproduced courtesy of Sophie Archambault de Beaune).

Key: *Bard* (Mirasi): Muslim low-caste singers who retell the past glories of the family they serve at life-cycle events;

Fakir: here, specific caste of Muslim funeral priests (similar to Hindu mahabrahmin funeral priests) – generally, Muslim wandering ascetic;

Harijan: here, 'untouchable' leatherworkers and sweepers;

Id-Ga: the mosque kept for Muslim festivals such as Id/Eid;

Kazi: Saiyads/Sayyids, descendants of the Prophet Muhammad, usually regarded as higher status than Indian-origin Muslims;

Priests: here, (Hindu) Brahmins; *Shopkeepers*: here, Baniyas (see text).

Mewat, 'the land of the Meos'. It forms a triangle between Delhi, Agra and Jaipur. This is said to have been the territory of the Pandavas, the cousins of the great *Mahabharata* epic. An important Meo caste myth, the *Pandun ke kara*, identifies the Pandavas as their own caste ancestors. Like the Pandavas, they see themselves as a warrior and ruling caste, describing themselves by the regional term for ruler, that is, Rajput. Meos are one of the most important groups in the Mewat region and have spread out beyond it in both India and Pakistan. You might wonder why . . .

The map shows that this village, like many in South Asia, is divided into sections. The labels in the different sections are the names of the different castes or segments of castes who live in that part of the village. You might already be looking to see where the Meos live and wonder why you cannot find the label. What you will find are the names of the seven Meo lineages of the village: Haweliya, Dandiya, Dhand, Gand, Kampaniya, Sapera and Uparla. They in fact fall into three groups, centred around three 'lineage houses' in the village where their respective caste-segment *panchayat*s are held. The *panchayat* is the key local group that sorts out disputes, makes decisions about members who go against the caste ritual and social rules, organizes festival processions and so on. Such caste-related *panchayat*s are an essential part of the social fabric of South Asia. Does this then confirm the view that caste is an essential and unchanging aspect of Hinduism?

Task

As you look at the map and key carefully and think about Abdulaziz's name, how many clues can you find that disrupt or at least cause you to question this view? How many different groups can you locate in this village? What other questions would help you understand social groupings and relations in this village and beyond?

Raising questions

Perhaps your first query will have been: If caste is basically a feature of Hinduism, why are there so many mosques in this village, why does Abdulaziz have a Muslim name and why are there Meos in Pakistan? According to Jamous (2003: 17), 'The Meo themselves say that they are at once a caste and a Muslim community.' This clearly suggests that, at least for the Meo, caste and Muslim identity are not felt to be incompatible. We explore this below. Here we note that in this village the Meo are what anthropologists call the 'dominant caste', the most important group in terms of both numbers and status. Locals themselves identify this village as a Meo village, by contrast with other villages in the area where other similar status caste groups, such as (Hindu) Jats or Thakurs, are dominant. The particular dominant caste acts as the *jajman* in the village or area, the patron of the other castes who render service to them. Can you now identify any of these service castes from the map?

Such service may be daily – very low-caste sweepers remove waste from outside Meo and other high-caste houses, for example. Alternatively it may be provided on ritual occasions – travelling Muslim Mirasi lowish caste bards sing the myths of Meo families at birth and marriage; Hindu brahmins from outside Bisru provide 'deeper' genealogies for the Meo, confirming their right to power. Service castes in Bisru, as elsewhere, are divided into clean castes (such as the Mirasi) and unclean castes (including the sweepers); we shall return to the reasons later. See if you can identify other service castes in Bisru, their status and their religious affiliation as you read the rest of this chapter.

Looking back at the map and still querying the caste equals Hindu model, you may also have wondered why one section has funeral priests, apparently high status descendants of Muhammad, water carriers, singing bards and barbers all living together. In this village they are all Muslim (again disrupting the Hindu paradigm) and are also clean service castes in relation to the higher status Meos. Is this then just a Muslim village?

On the other hand, you may have noticed that there are both burial and cremation grounds, the former used by Muslims, the latter generally by Hindus. You may have spotted the brahmin priests and wondered which other groups in the village are Hindu. And whether the Harijans, or untouchables, regard themselves as Hindu, Muslim, or neither. You might also wonder if people who identify with other religious traditions live in this village or the surrounding area and how these different social/caste groups with varying religious affiliations relate to one another locally and in terms of larger regional and global issues. To explore these issues we are first going to look at three different terms that have all fed into the English umbrella term 'caste'. They are not simply interchangeable but are sometimes used as if they are. To show this, we shall interrogate these categories in terms of relations in and around Bisru, centring as they do on the Muslim Meos and their negotiations for stability through the changing politics that have affected local life.

Casta, varna *and* jati

The word 'caste' does not have a simple equivalent in Indian languages. It is an outsider term, a European mode of classification. It comes from the Portuguese word '*casta*', used primarily during the Iberian colonization of South America to hierarchize different 'races' [Europeans, various types of Creole, (local) Indians, Africans and so on]. Early Portuguese travellers in India may have been interested in applying similar notions when they spoke of 'Brahmenes' and others, although whether this was assumed to be a fundamental feature of Indian society by these travellers has been questioned by scholars (see Dirks 2001: 19). However much this was the case, as we move into the British colonial period the idea of caste as a natural hierarchical feature of Indian society – similar to the *casta* taxonomies of colonial South America – became increasingly entrenched. The historian Nicholas Dirks explores the development of what he calls the 'ethnographic state'. Interested in categorizing its subject people for more effective rule, colonial officials used tools such as the census (see also Chapter 9), as well as regional Gazetteer reports and photos (Figure 7A.2) to gain knowledge of caste groupings. Dirks argues that this colonially derived *casta* view of caste as a comprehensive system also became the model for more recent anthropological accounts of caste, driving scholars to look for the fundamental and all-embracing system that distinguished Hinduism as such. The famous French anthropologist, Louis Dumont, provides a key example.

In his classic study, *Homo Hierarchicus*, Dumont (1980) located Brahmins at the top of the hierarchy of castes, by virtue of their superior ritual purity. The lower down the hierarchy, the greater the impurity, untouchables at the bottom being those deemed the most polluting. Dumont stressed that, in traditional Indian societies, even the king's power was secondary to the brahmin's, as it was dependent on the legitimation of the brahmins who

Figure 7A.2 Casta-type photographs under the Raj. These two photographs appear in William Crooke's *The Tribes and Castes of the North-Western Provinces and Oudh*, published in Calcutta, 1896. The one on the left is labeled 'Brahmin Pandit', the one on the right 'Two Chamars' (C.A. Bayly 1990: 293). They are typical of the scientific, taxonomic approach of the 'ethnographic state'. They are also quite strongly reminiscent of eighteenth-century South American '*casta*' paintings, a genre that attempted to record and classify different groups in an elaborate racial hierarchy (see Katzew 2004 for examples). RAI 2722 'Two Chamars'; RAI 2723 'Brahmin Pandit'. Reproduced with permission of the Royal Anthropological Institute.

performed the state rituals necessary to sanctioning the king's position. Similarly, he held that this model worked at more local levels, the brahmins being available as the prime ritual specialists because of their superiority as the purest caste. In Bisru, there are some indicators that might appear to confirm Dumont's view, such as the polluted status of the untouchable castes, but there is an immediate problem with the brahmins who are certainly not the prime ritual specialists for the Meos, even though they recognize the Meos' high status. It would be easy to suggest that this is because the Meos are Muslim, and so 'disrupt' the 'proper' functioning of the caste system. As we shall see below, this approach may be seen to underlie that of both Muslim and Hindu reformers who tried to work on the Meos from the early twentieth century. Below we shall indicate a different approach. Here, however, we note that Dumont's view, although much criticized (see, for example, Dirks 2001: 4–5; Appadurai 1986, 1988; Sharma and Searle-Chatterjee 1994), remains influential, partly because it was also informed by our second key term, *varna*.

'*Varna*' is a Sanskrit term that can mean 'colour'. It is frequently translated as 'caste' but this can be very misleading. In brahminical texts, it refers precisely to the four ideal social groups into which society is to be divided. Its mythological basis is to be found in a hymn from the *Rig Veda*, the 'Purusha Sukta', which tells of the sacrifice of the primal cosmic man (*purusha*). 'His mouth became the Brahmin; his arms were made into the warrior, his thighs the People, and from his feet the servants were born' (*Rig Veda* X.90.12, see Doniger 1981: 31). Like the *casta* view, it too forms a total system, an ideology, not just a social framework, in which the upholding of *varna* is thought to uphold order in the cosmos as a whole. Ritual, social and cosmic order (*dharma*) are guaranteed by people fulfilling the specific duties (*dharma*) of their own *varna*: the brahmins[2] teaching the Veda, the *kshatriya*s protecting and ruling the kingdom, the *vaishya*s producing wealth and the *shudra*s providing service to others. These are spelled out at length in the Dharma Shastra texts such as *Manu* (c. second century CE, Olivelle 2004: 18–25). Later texts such as the *Bhagavad Gita* ground the whole system in the Supreme Lord, Krishna, who says: 'The four-*varna* system was brought forth by Me, in accordance with qualities (*guna*s) and actions' (4.13; on these *varna*-related qualities, see Box 7A.1).[3] Given that this is a Hindu devotional text, and has grown in importance as a defining text of Hinduism since the nineteenth century, it seems reasonable to assume that the 'caste system' is indeed the backbone of Hinduism, and that it is rightly seen as a comprehensive one. In addition, the *varna* system has been used in public rhetoric through the centuries, not least because it represents the interests of those who have promoted it, the brahmins and also, because they have seen it to be in their own interest, Hindu kings. Even Muslim rulers in India have presented themselves as protectors of the four *varna*s and *dharma*, using the ideological language of their subjects to articulate their concern to preserve a correctly functioning social order to the benefit of all (Laine 1999; Chattopadhyay 1998).

Box 7A.1 The three *gunas*

In *Gita* 4.13, Krishna links the *varna*s with actions and 'qualities'. The 'qualities' refer in context to the three *gunas*, the three 'strands' or constituents of mind-matter (*prakriti*). These are:

- *sattva* (purity);
- *rajas* (passion);
- *tamas* (darkness).

These combine together in different proportions, in food, speech, *varna*, rituals, gift-giving and so on, every aspect of material life. Only the self (*atman*) is not affected by them. Brahmins, *kshatriya*s and so on each act according to their own natures and the *gunas* associated with them (18.41). In terms of food, eating pure sattvic food (which has a good flavour, is mild and easy to digest, such as rice) leads to good health, long life and so on (17.8), whereas the passionate rajasic crave pungent and spicy food leading to sickness, and those tamasic by nature eat leftovers and food unfit for ritual offerings (17.9–10). And so on with the whole of material life. In the *Gita*, the wise person understands that the self transcends all this, and dedicates all action to Krishna, the Supreme Self.

Yet three observations of life in India (and elsewhere in South Asia) show the problems of applying *varna* directly to social life. First, although there are only four *varna*s, in actual fact there are thousands of different castes. Bisru itself has at least fourteen labelled on the map, and different regions across the subcontinent have many different local groupings. Second, the *varna* system does not include the so-called untouchable castes, whose members number hundreds of millions and are themselves divided into many hierarchized groups; Chamar leatherworkers now rank above sweepers in Bisru, as we shall see below. Third, currently and historically many groups have simply not been part of the caste system in their local regions at all. The so-called Tribals are a case in point. To cater for these last two vast groups the categories of Scheduled Castes and Tribes were created in Indian law;[4] a different scheme was used in Nepal (see later). Yet the Meos themselves, now a Muslim Rajput high status caste in the Bisru region, were, according to one of their own origin myths, bandits, outside the local social system and preying on it. Although historically it is unclear when they achieved Rajput status, it does seem that Meos in different lineages founded or took over key villages around which locally functioning networks of caste became (re-) organized, notwithstanding the Muslim names and life-cycle rites used by the newcomers who ran the local scene. They were not alone in so doing, either in Rajputana (modern Rajasthan) or elsewhere in the subcontinent. For detailed historical work on how different groups gradually became absorbed into what we might call 'organized caste society' in eighteenth-century south India, see Susan Bayly's (1999) excellent study.

We have then started to see why both '*casta* as system' and '*varna* as ideology' give us problems when we look at 'real life'. Perhaps our third term will help us clarify the umbrella term 'caste' a little more. '*Jati*', literally 'birth' in Sanskrit, also means 'type' or 'specific category'. It has the merit of having modern Indian-language equivalents reflecting long-standing indigenous use: '*zat*' in Punjabi, '*jat*' in Hindi/Urdu, for example. It too is frequently translated as 'caste' and is often associated with anthropological approaches. The social anthropologist, Roger Ballard (1996) and others have argued that, for Punjabis, *zat* has for the most part been the primary form of identity, despite the strong emphasis on identifying groups on the basis of religion during the colonial period. Such a phenomenon of primarily identifying with kinship group is not peculiar to the Punjab and is found in the Bisru region too.

A *jat* or *zat*, then, is a birth or kinship group that links particular families and their descent groups into a larger social whole. The term '*jati*' or 'caste' may, however, be applied at different 'levels' of these kinship groups, which often have very complex internal structures. So again we need to proceed with caution! In this chapter, we retain the Sanskrit form *jati*, which is also used in much anthropological literature, as a construct for 'caste as based on kinship', to remind us that we need to look at particular local terminology and social relations to understand the specifics.

*Jati*s, in the anthropological literature, are characterized as sharing certain features. They are, for example, endogamous, that is, members have a very strong preference for marrying someone from the same *jati*; they are identified as having a traditional or nominal shared occupation, even if particular members are no longer actually engaged in it; and they normally receive cooked food and water only from those who are of higher or similar (ritual) status to themselves. Relative ritual purity relates to body/touch (Sharma 1999: 36). Relatively high ritual purity is associated with vegetarian diet and abstention from alcohol and 'clean' occupations including shopkeeping. Low ritual purity is linked with meat eating and alcohol consumption and 'unclean' occupations, the lowest involving dead animals and human waste.

Let us see how life in Bisru and around relates to such a schema. We will treat marriage last and with it the issue of the different levels at which 'caste as *jati*' can be seen to function. In terms of occupation, then, Bisru (Hindu) jewellers retain their traditional occupation (like, for example, the many jewellers of the Gujarati Soni goldsmith caste who have businesses on the 'Golden Mile' in Leicester, UK); but Bisru Chamars, tanners, have turned their back on dealing with dead animals and tanning them. They have raised their caste status by altering their occupation and becoming vegetarian. Functioning as cobblers, their caste is still Chamar, although they are now able to enter Meo houses, unlike their fellow untouchables, the sweepers.

In terms of food, accepting cooked food and water still marks Bisru social hierarchies. Yet although Bisru brahmins condemn Meos for their recent consumption of buffalo meat and will generally not accept cooked food from them, they continue to respect their high status as the dominant caste and some will take tea with them. Yet this is to risk being labelled 'not a proper brahmin', even by Meos! Bisru Muslim Nais can act as cooks at public ritual occasions for Meos, because in this region they are seen as sharing descent with Meo clans and hence social status. Elsewhere, Nais, who are barbers, and may be Hindu or Muslim, or neither, have very low-caste polluting status, because they deal with human waste products – hair and nails. This reminds us forcibly that we need to look at localized situations to see how such social relations work. It warns us not to read what is indeed an important local preoccupation, purity, as the only criterion affecting status, nor to read caste relations in terms of a single overarching Hindu system.

Let us now turn to marriage and the different levels of 'caste as *jati*'. We focus first on the Meos. The Meos form a caste at the broadest anthropological level (they are endogamous), and in self-identification as Meos. Within that, they have a complex system of twelve clans or *pal*s (some of which have links with specific territorial units) and fifty-two *got*s (agnatic kin units, that is, those who share common male descent groups). The territory-linked *pal*s are further divided up into sub-clans or *thamba*, linked with a village purportedly founded by the *thamba*'s common ancestor. The term *thamba* also designates that founding village and its surrounding villages as a political area, within which may live Meos from other descent groups as well as other caste groups, as Bisru shows. Meo marry *outside* their *got* or clan and *outside* their village. They marry *within* the Meo 'caste'.[5] By contrast, the term 'Baniya' (a general term for merchants and shopkeepers, including those who live in Bisru) covers an even broader 'caste' group, not strictly a *jati* in the anthropological sense. For although Baniyas in this area intermarry, they do not form intermarrying groups with, say, Baniyas in Gujarat, a state to the west. Within a particular *jati*, sections may break away and marry only within their own particular section, effectively splitting the endogamous unit in two or more. Pocock (1972) demonstrates this for Patidars in Gujarat. This was linked with other strategies to improve the status of the section that broke away.

This returns us to the question of the interrelations between *casta*, *varna*, *jati* and other aspects of social groupings that contribute to the notion of 'caste'. The *varna* ideal is used as a kind of measure against which particular *jati*s can negotiate their relative status compared with other local groups. We have already seen the Chamars' change of diet and lifestyle. The Meos' own location of themselves as Rajputs with ancestry going back to the Mahabharata Pandava heroes shows a similar strategy, aligning themselves with the *kshatriyas* of the past as many other Rajput and other groups have done. Working in the other direction, 'brahmin' as *varna* rarely unites brahmins of different brahmin castes who are not endogamous and have very marked differences in status. Some of these are linked with occupation, the so-called *mahabrahmin* funeral priests being an extreme example through their association with dead bodies. Those who act as *purohits*, or priests, are also generally thought to have lower status than those who do not, an important point as brahmins are often perceived primarily as 'the priestly caste'.

Finally, it might be thought that these finer points of caste would break down in urban situations, where people's intimate backgrounds in terms of region, village and local caste status are less easily open to constant scrutiny. Yet the evidence is to the contrary for many reasons. These include the fact that links between kinship groups and hence between people in different locations remain important, especially in terms of support, whether financial from city back to village, living accommodation and introductions for kin moving to a larger conglomeration, visits back home on ritual occasions or when the dream of employment elsewhere terminates in a slum. In addition, marriage within one's caste remains an important choice for many, not least because, for example, a caste negotiating higher status provides economic and emotional security of many kinds (Gooptu 2001).

So where does this exploration leave us? We have shown the complexity of the phenomenon often simply referred to as caste. We have seen that it has operated in terms of administrative systems and the demands of those seeking political power, in terms of ideologies and the desires of those wishing to shape society in particular ways, and in localized situations where groups have moved in and out of social relations with one another in terms marked by factors including, but not limited to, ritual and economic power. We have also started to challenge the idea that caste is only 'properly' a Hindu phenomenon. The following examples illustrate how caste cuts across religion in South Asia and has also been challenged by pre-modern Hindu voices.

Twisting the kaleidoscope on caste

The rejection of jati? *A poem from the twelfth century*

> God, O God, mark my prayer:
> I shall call all devotees of Śiva equal,
> from the Brāhmaṇa at one end
> to the lowest-born man at the other end;
> I shall call all unbelievers equal,
> from the Brāhmaṇa at one end
> to the untouchable at the other end;
> this is what my heart believes!
> In saying this – should I have any doubt,

be it so small as a sesamum bud,
O *Lord of the Meeting Rivers*,
chop off my nose so that the teeth stick out!

                       (Basava, 'God, O God', see Schouten 1991: 26)

This poem is by the twelfth-century Shaiva poet, Basava. According to the fifteenth-century poem-biography of his life, he became the trusted minister of King Bijjala in Kalyana (modern Karnataka, south India), a person of political power. Probably born a brahmin, he rejected his background to worship Lord Shiva, the *Lord of the Meeting Rivers*, in whose name he signs his poems. We saw in Chapter 3 how Basava's followers, male and female, wore a small stone lingam around their necks, this community of '*jangamas*' known for its egalitarian attitude to caste, class and gender, at least within its own ranks (Ramanujan 1973: 62–3). Yet Basava's poems also show that low and indeed high brahmin caste was for him part of society. Only Shiva's touch reversed this within the community, not necessarily outside it. It appears though that Brahmins and tanners, washermen and women, did all belong. However, by the fifteenth century the Virashaivas, or Lingayatas, although really consisting of a medley of castes, started to function as a caste group, striving for caste status, rejecting lower caste Lingayat groups. Nonetheless, at the end of the nineteenth century, Lingayatas became heavily involved in educational projects, not least to challenge brahmin monopoly in British government service, while their women do have higher ritual status, education and fewer purity restrictions than in other communities (Mullatti 1989).

A Christian fishing caste

In the village of Kodimunai in southern Kerala (Figures 7A.3 and 7A.4), the majority of the people belong to the Mukkuvar fishing caste. Latin Catholics probably converted in the sixteenth century by Portuguese Jesuits, the Mukkuvar intermarry with Tamil Mukkuvars, and function like any other caste group in that respect. They have a matrilineal system, which means that the husband comes to live with the wife's family, at least for the first few years of marriage. High-caste Hindu Nayar groups in Kerala are also matrilineal. The Mukkuvar are an untouchable group, however.[6] The women tend to sort and sell the fish that the men catch and are vital to the local and caste economy (Figure 7A.5).

Another systematization: a nineteenth-century Law Code

From 1854 to 1963 the categories in the 1854 Muluki Ain (see Box 7A.2) were used in both civil and criminal law in the Kingdom of Nepal and affected people's personal and political rights. The most powerful and highest ranked category (cord-wearers), for example, were subject to lighter

Figure 7A.3 The church at Kodimunai. Reproduced courtesy of the photographer, Loyola Ignatius.

Figure 7A.4 Kattumarram used for fishing. Reproduced courtesy of the photographer, Loyola Ignatius.

penalties for the same crime than other groups. In 1963 this Code was repealed. The revised Muluki Ain rejected the category of untouchability and recognized all Nepalis as citizens with equal rights under the law.[7] It thus changed the principle of a Nepali having 'ascribed status' in terms of birth and legal category to one of having 'achieved status' via education and 'national integration' (Guneratne 2002: 78). Nonetheless, caste continues to be important in negotiating relations with the state, as we shall see below.

If you look at Box 7A.2 carefully, you will see how a single set of categories,

Figure 7A.5 Fisherwomen on beach, Marina, Chennai. Reproduced courtesy of Jacqueline Suthren Hirst.

specific to Nepal, and politically constructed (see below), incorporates aspects of what we might identify as *casta*, *jati* and *varna*. It also brings groups such as 'tribals' or 'Europeans' within the same system. Its *casta*

Box 7A.2 The five hierarchically-ranked categories of the Muluki Ain, the Legal Code of 1854, Nepal (Gunaratne 2003: 98)

Cord-wearing (twice-born)
 Brahmins, Thakuri, Chetri, comparable Newar groups
Non-Enslaveable Alcohol Drinkers
 'tribal' groups, e.g. Magar, Gurung, Rai, Limbu, from which army largely drawn
Enslaveable Alcohol Drinkers
 'tribal' groups, e.g. Tharu, Tamang, Bhote (of Tibetan origin)
Impure Touchables
 Newar service castes; includes Muslims and Europeans

....

Untouchables
 including blacksmiths, tanners, musicians, Newar sweepers

aspect is shown in the very way a total hierarchized system was imposed on Nepali society (through its locally devised principles of high and low status with alcohol drinkers in between). *Varna* is explicitly recognized in the top category: the 'cord-wearing' groups are the top three *varna*s entitled to wear the sacred thread of the twice-born. Different endogamous service *jatis* are incorporated into the lowest two categories. Perhaps most importantly we can see how this clear legal framework sought to impose uniformity on people whose actual forms of social grouping were fluid and varied enormously. It can therefore make us alert to other processes of totalizing and negotiation that have happened at local, regional, state and national levels for centuries in South Asia as elsewhere.

The gender twist: caste, religion and women as gateways

Broader issues of gender, religion and kinship are also entangled with those of 'caste'. Here are three brief Meo examples.

As in many other castes, Meo women act as a kind of gateway protecting the honour of the patriline into which they marry. A key ritual in which they maintain its continuity is *kuan puja*, worship at the well, performed at life-cycle rituals such as birth, circumcision and marriage (Jamous 2003: 29). The worship is given to the Bheru, the god found in stone form beside the well; both well and Bheru are linked with the woman's marital lineage. The well-being of the patriline is the worship's clear focus.

By contrast with their ritual importance, Meo women found themselves expendable to larger political, caste and religious ends during the early twentieth century and partition. From the 1920s, Meos were proselytized by the Tablighi Jama'at, an Islamic movement growing out of the Deoband school (see Chapter 8). The Meos' minimal Islamic practices – some mosque attendance, circumcision, burial and the use of Muslim names – were deemed insufficient. Men and women alike were urged to adopt 'proper' Islamic norms. Women in particular were urged to give up Hindu practices such as *kuan puja* and singing songs.

Targetted by the Arya Samaj and Sanatan Dharma movements in response, many Meo women were subjected to enforced *shuddhi*, the Arya Samaj's purification ritual designed to reincorporate men and women into the Hindu fold (see also Chapter 7B on this ritual). In the abduction of women, which was a widespread phenomenon of partition (as in conflicts across the globe), Meo women were taken into Jat and Gujjar families following *shuddhi*, often in fear of their lives. Meo men were evicted to Pakistan (where they were not welcome either), their extensive lands the target of their caste competitors. As one participant told the anthropologist Shail Mayaram (1997: 191): 'This was a time of communal frenzy and passion when people forgot humanism (*insaniyat*). We took away women. That was the system. Women do not have any religion (*dharam*).'

Nonetheless, when Jamous did his research in the 1980s, Meo women were still 'resisting regimes':[8] performing *kuan puja* and singing songs including a satire blaming the Jama'at for all their household and village troubles; and cooking water buffalo despite brahmin rebuffs.

The politics twist: caste status and the state

There are all sorts of ways in which politics and caste are intertwined, not least the many ways in which political impulsions mould and shape what is seen as 'caste' and how it functions in different social and historical contexts. In her discussion of the Meos up to partition, Mayaram (1997) shows very clearly the political influence on caste formations of the Princely States of Alwar and Bharatpur, in whose territories many Meos lived.

Here, we focus on a different example of the interrelation of politics and caste. The Muluki Ain (Chief Law), as we saw above, was brought into force in Nepal in 1854. Jang Bahadur Rana, the Prime Minister, aimed to create a legal system integrating the smaller independent kingdoms forcibly brought under the kingdom of Gorkha in the late eighteenth century. He also wanted to mark the emerging nation of Nepal off from India under the British. In formulating the Code, he drew on aspects of British law as well as Newar (Buddhist) and other local customs (Guneratne 2003). If we look at its ranking, it is apparently based on the purity of the different groups' presumed lifestyle. Alcohol drinkers (*matwari*) were incorporated between high-caste Hindus and untouchables. Yet the two categories of *matwari* clearly show the interest of the state: a higher ranking was given to those useful in military terms to its preservation. They were also those the British identified as 'martial races' (including the Gorkhas). The lower, including the Tharus, marginal forest-dwellers, were seen as insignificant to the state. The *Oudh Gazeteer* said Rana Tharus 'will on no account take service as soldiers', being 'a cowardly race' (Government of Oudh 1877: 208–9, cited in Guneratne 1998: 755). The state could also change a person's (caste) categorization. A brahmin who infringed the law could be made to drink alcohol or eat pork, forcing him into the 'Non-Enslaveable Alcohol Drinkers' category. His children would then be classified as such. Because a person's personal and public rights were linked to his *jat* as defined in the Code, this identity became key to participation in the state and to negotiations to improve *jat* status. Thus, political processes homogenized a series of differently conceived identities into a set of categories that shaped political and personal identities in turn. In the twentieth century also, culturally widespread endogamous Tharu *jat*s came to conceive of themselves as a single *jat*, as a result of the changing economic and political policies of the Nepali state (Guneratne 1998).

The religion twist: alternatives to 'proper' religion

The map of Bisru shows several mosques, each of which tends to function as a neighbourhood and therefore caste-related mosque, much as many Hindu temples do. You probably identified the village as Muslim originally, but may now be a little more puzzled about the Meos' religious identity. As we saw above, the Meos have been targeted by both Hindu and Muslim reforming groups, resulting in their political marginalization around partition, although with subsequent revival as the dominant caste in some Mewati villages since. We have seen how their practices span ones very similar to Hindu practices and others that are clearly Muslim. Mayaram (n.d.) therefore asks the question: In what ways is it possible to be simultaneously Hindu *and* Muslim in South Asia? (or Hindu and Christian, Muslim and Sikh). She draws not only from her work on the Meos of India and Pakistan, 'today one of the largest Muslim communities of the sub-continent' (p. 4), but also on the Merat, a complexly differentiated group. Together, Rawat, Chita and Merat *jati*s make up the Merat *jati* at the wider level. Each separate *jati* also has Hindu, Muslim and Christian sections. They intermarry within their *jati* and share a cosmology incorporating gods, goddesses, *pirs* and ancestors. Both Hindu Rawats and Muslim Merats have been criticized for not manifesting 'proper' religious identity. Yet Mayaram argues that such 'liminal' groups should be more properly seen as having identities relating to at least one religious tradition. She acknowledges that they have to withstand huge pressures by those who want to 'singularize, reform and domesticate' them, because they are seen as contestatory and 'dangerous from the perspective of state and religious authority' (p. 8). Yet she finds in their creative theologies and very existence a source of alternative ways of living together. In this, the Meo and Merat pose a strong question to a normative, over-arching model of World Religions, which in Part I of this book we have been seeking to contextualize.

Concluding thoughts: diversity, religion and religious traditions

In Chapter 1, we asked you to bear with our definitions of 'religion' and 'religious traditions', to enter the worlds of our approach as you would if you were watching a play. We hope that you have not sat through Act I as a mere spectator, but have been drawn into it, through the lives and practices of those we have glimpsed, people affected by the ways others represent them, people negotiating and affecting the ways they are represented, agents shaped by their particular contexts, as we all are, yet shaping them in turn. We hope that you have glimpsed just a little of the enormous diversity of South Asian religious traditions, 'the panoply of ideas, practices and objects that today are commonly recognized as belonging to a religion', as we said in Chapter 1. Finally, we hope that you will now see why it is so important to look at these ideas, practices and objects in different networks of contexts and through different twists of the kaleidoscope. The World Religions model is an important one. We have seen how some features of it emerge in South Asia in the modern period in relation to ideas of divinity, sacred texts, myth and so on. In Part II we will see how particular views of Hinduism, Buddhism, Indian Islam and Sikhism come to be formed. However, much of the 'available data' we have looked at in Part I do not easily fit with such a model. That is why we have looked for alternative ways of 'cutting across' the data, to recall Will Sweetman's (2003a: 50) phrase. Our final discussion point for Part I invites you to think back over the material you have encountered so far to consider some of those alternatives.

Discussion point to end Part I

> In this context [the Meos' attitude to 'the act of faith'], Islam is merely one dimension of local social and religious life.
>
> (Jamous 2003: 31)

From the point of view of a World Religions model, Jamous' statement about the Meos and Islam might seem highly problematic. In this chapter, however, we have seen various perspectives from which we could understand it. Thinking back over the whole of Part I now, what alternative models for looking at the intersections between different aspects of religion and social life have you come across? How, if at all, might they provide a helpful corrective to the World Religions model? What can a stress on diversity and the need to understand specific contexts bring to our understanding of religion in modern South Asia? You may want to bear these questions in mind as you turn to Part II. We shall return to them in Chapter 12.

Further reading

Dirks, N. (2001) *Castes of Mind: Colonialism and the Making of Modern India*, Princeton: Princeton University Press.
  A challenging text that presents a view of caste as a colonial construct.

Mayaram, Shail (1997) *Resisting Regimes: Myth, Memory and the Shaping of a Muslim Identity*, Delhi, Oxford University Press.
  A careful historical study of the Meos through changing modern periods examining the political, religious and other influences in relation to which they have resisted others' regimes.

Ram, Kalpana (1991) *Mukkuvar Women: Gender, Hegemony and Capitalist Transformation in a South Indian Fishing Village*, London: Zed Books.
  A nuanced ethnographic study helping to deconstruct essentialisms of caste, religion and gender.

Sharma, U. (1999) *Caste*, Buckingham: Open University Press.
  A useful, nuanced introductory text rooted in anthropological method.

Thapar, Romila (2002) *Early India: From the Origins to AD 1300*, Berkeley: University of California Press.

   The comprehensively revised work of a major Indian historian, dealing with issues of caste throughout and particularly in Chapter 2.

Part II

Shaping modern religious traditions

7B The confluence of caste and religion

To present a chapter in two sections, A and B, and put each in a different part of a book, I and II, is a rather unconventional thing to do. We have chosen to take this approach partly to emphasize continuities between Parts I and II of this book. Having a split chapter in this way seemed to us to suggest a kind of overlap, which is appropriate to our desire to see the two parts as complementary and integrated. At the same time, we wanted to signal a key shift in the book's focus at this point. We have done this by taking the same general theme (caste) and approaching it according to two different foci. It is central to our argument that any of our themes can be approached in multiple ways. Chapters 7A and 7B demonstrate one important way of doing this.

So, what is the shift in approach or focus that we are making? Our movement is away from exploring the variety and social embeddedness of South Asian religious traditions, which has frequently led us to recognize patterns of practice and ideas that seem to defy our normative understanding of how religious traditions should operate. It is towards mapping the ways in which these kinds of practices and ideas have been organized, or aligned, in relation to just such normative understandings, through a range of specific historical processes. You will find that we are still very strongly wedded to the idea that, to understand South Asian religious traditions, you must get a sense of the contexts within which they are enacted. But if our emphasis in Part I was on diversity as context, our emphasis in this part is on these historical processes as context. We want to develop themes that explain how contemporary South Asian religious traditions have come to be seen as they are seen. Of course, it is impossible to do this comprehensively in one volume (let alone half a volume!), so our focus will again be on specific issues, particular themes we see as significant to developing such an understanding. At the heart of this has to be the issue of religion itself. So much of what we saw in Part I appeared to subvert the idea of religions as clearly identifiable systems. 'Religion' is nevertheless a critical concept in modern South Asia – it provides a very significant lens though which many people understand and interpret South Asian societies, politics and so on. How have the multiple traditions of South Asia encountered the category of 'religion'?

What synergies and tensions have developed through this encounter? In Part II of the book we explore these general questions.

To begin this change of focus, we return to the issue of caste, the theme of Chapter 7A. Here, however, we want to explore the ways in which caste has contributed in particular to the construction of particular religious identities in the modern period. Most significant here is the religion called Hinduism. Caste in the modern world is undoubtedly perceived most immediately as a phenomenon associated with Hinduism as a religion.[1] But this statement is one we need to treat with caution. First, we have of course seen in Chapter 7A that caste practices sometimes seem to cut radically across the boundaries of what we would normally consider to be discrete religious traditions. Second, we shall see in Chapter 7B that modern perceptions of caste have also had a major impact on the way that other, 'non-Hindu' religious traditions are conceptualized. Third, we should note the ambiguity that informs the relationship between Hinduism and caste. Some Hindus, Hindu organizations and representative groups are keen to downplay the importance of caste, saying that this institution is not a part of genuine Hinduism.[2] Others claim that caste has degenerated from a former 'pure' *varna* form, and that the future of caste is to work towards a reinstatement of that pure ordering of society.[3] Still others see caste as a form of political consciousness to be deployed against (and sometimes, paradoxically, in coalition with) the domination of other caste groups. Such consciousness has become a major feature of modern Indian politics, with some political parties developing clear caste identities, and winning elections on the basis of especially low-caste assertion.[4] This variety of evidence suggests a social phenomenon that by no means has a settled, uncontroversial existence in modern environments. Despite the idea of caste being a fixed, immoveable feature of an individual's identity, the evidence rather suggests that its significance and meaning shifts from situation to situation. This should be a familiar idea to you from Chapter 7A. Our key aim in Chapter 7B will be to explore the ways that this shifting significance and meaning has related to and influenced the development of particular religious identities, especially that of Hinduism. We will see that low-caste identity has been particularly significant here.

Case study: Jotirao Phule on the origins of caste

Our case study is a piece of writing produced in the late nineteenth century by a social activist from western India (present-day Maharashtra) called Jotirao Phule. This particular piece of writing, produced in 1885, refers to an issue that frequently preoccupies students studying the idea of caste: Where does it come from? How has it developed? This is an issue that we have already commented on in Chapter 7A; we look at it here as an example of how caste has been self-consciously debated by Hindus and others in the modern period. You might also note that issues examined in earlier chapters

are also apparent here: issues such as the Aryan 'invasion' and the culture of the Aryans, discussed in the introduction and in Chapter 3, and the importance of myths, explored in Chapter 4.

Gulamgiri *(1885)*

> The extreme fertility of the soil of India, its rich productions, the proverbial wealth of the people, and the other innumerable gifts which this favourable land enjoys, and which have more recently tempted the cupidity of the Western nations, attracted the Aryans . . . . The original inhabitants with whom these earth-born gods, the Brahmans, fought, were not inappropriately termed Rakshasas, that is the protectors of the land. The incredible and foolish legends regarding their form and shape are no doubt mere chimeras, the fact being that these people were of superior stature and hardy make . . . . The cruelties which the European settlers practised on the American Indians on their first settlement in the new world had certainly their parallel in India in the advent of the Aryans and their subjugation of the aborigines . . . . This, in short, is the history of Brahman domination in India. They originally settled on the banks of the Ganges whence they spread gradually over the whole of India. In order, however, to keep a better hold on the people they devised that weird system of mythology, the ordination of caste, and the code of crude and inhuman laws to which we can find no parallel among the other nations.
>
> (Quoted in Omvedt 1995: 17–18)

Explaining terms

Rakshasa – normally translated as 'demon', and frequently portrayed fighting the gods in puranic literature

---

Task

Discuss or make some notes on the view of caste presented by Phule here. What is his view of the origin of caste? What strategies does he use to develop his argument? How might this approach resonate with people in nineteenth-century India? What questions would you like to ask about Phule himself to help broaden your understanding?

It may be clear to you that Phule is engaged here in an exercise that might be described as 'debunking established myths' through the provision of 'rational', or historical, explanations. He refers to the 'incredible and foolish legends' that depict the original inhabitants of India as demons (he interprets '*rakshasa*' as developing from the Sanskrit term '*raksh*', to protect), and compares the coming of the Aryans to the decimation of indigenous American cultures by Europeans in the fifteenth and sixteenth centuries and beyond. You might also note that the narrative he is presenting is all about domination, and the subjection of the 'original inhabitants' of India to a 'code of crude and inhuman laws', otherwise known as caste. The overall impression is of the construction of a system of oppression by an invading force, designed to keep the indigenous inhabitants in a state of what, in other contexts, he described straightforwardly as slavery. In this narrative, the brahmins – the archetypal high castes – are the descendants of those invaders; the low castes in particular are the descendants of the indigenous inhabitants.

Reading this short extract may raise questions for you about Phule's own social location, his caste status and how and why he developed this strong public voice about caste in the nineteenth century. More generally, we might pose questions about how this vision of the origins of the caste system relates to other versions, and how myths support or challenge the system. Phule certainly alludes to the way in which myths relate to caste. Having noted that Phule was from Maharashtra, and on the basis of material in Chapter 7A that emphasized the localized understanding of caste, we might also reflect on how far his views were rooted in the Maharashtrian experience, and the extent to which his critique had an impact in this region and beyond. From the latter point, we might ask how far his views were singular, or whether they reflected a more general questioning of established ideas about caste in this period. First, however, we will see how our understanding of Phule himself helps us to contextualize the evidence from *Gulamgiri*.

Social activism in the colonial arena

As we saw in Chapter 7A, caste operates on the ground as a connected web of social groups that are often related, at least nominally, to occupational tasks. Jotirao Phule (1826–90) was a Mali – this is a gardening caste, which in many areas (including Maharashtra) was seen as a relatively low caste. Growing up in the city of Poona, Jotirao was educated in the 1840s at a Christian Missionary school. Very soon after he left school himself, he went on to open several schools, first for girls, and then for low castes and untouchables. These activities brought him very much into the public sphere in Poona, particularly as there was a degree of opposition to the education of these social groups. Phule became engaged in a variety of social activist movements, and in 1873 he established the Satyashodak Samaj – the

'Truth-seeking Society' – as a focus for his activities. The Samaj was a classic organization in the colonial milieu, reflecting the formation of similar social activist organizations such as the Prarthana Samaj in western India (see Jones 1989: 137–44). These organizations were distinctly modern: they had membership lists and subscriptions, officers and regulations, and one of their key activities was to present petitions to the local colonial administration in relation to their concerns. The only difference was that, whereas the Prarthana Samaj, for example, was exclusively high caste in its membership, the Satyashodak Samaj had a membership that was mixed in terms of caste, with both low castes and radical high-caste members. Because of this modern form, the Satyashodak Samaj provided Phule with a platform on which to develop and present his views in a way that had resonance in the context of colonial public space. His views were, in this sense, 'heard' both by agents of the state, and, more importantly for us, by a public that was primarily made up of the literate middle classes, those who had established themselves socially and economically through the expansion of colonial influence.

Phule's critique of Indian society, developed and reiterated in a series of publications, was fairly straightforward. He opposed social inequality and the domination of high-caste groups. He was concerned in particular with the way in which brahmins and other high castes controlled knowledge in society, and saw the education of disempowered groups as a key means of breaking this monopoly. Significantly, Phule understood caste inequality as rooted strongly in what he perceived as the religion of Hinduism, and saw this as a key barrier to both social and political progress in India. The latter half of the nineteenth century was a time of developing activism, both political and social, amongst mostly high-caste elites, and Phule was aware of the claims that such organizations were making to represent Indians (or 'Hindus') more generally. His response was clear, bold and challenging: 'if our learned Aryans really want to build unity amongst all the people, and improve the country, then they will have to get rid of this vile religion of winners and losers' (as quoted in O'Hanlon 1985: 267). This 'vile religion of winners and losers', as he called it, was inextricably linked to what he perceived as the source of Hinduism in Vedic culture. The extract with which we began demonstrates this point, as it makes reference to the Orientalist account of Vedic culture deriving from an 'Aryan invasion' from the north. The difference here, however, was that whereas the Aryan invasion was generally perceived in Orientalist accounts as the harbinger of the 'Golden Age' of Vedic civilization in India – the 'true', unsullied Hinduism of ancient times – Phule interpreted this set of events as the end of ideal society in India, the disruption of indigenous culture and the beginning of caste oppression.

This simple strategy of inversion was one that Phule deployed time and again in his analysis not just of history, but also of myth. An example of this is provided by a long poem called 'Priestcraft Exposed', published by Phule in 1869. Here is an extract:

Lawless men leagued together
They made Brahma their chief
They plundered and caused chaos
Beating the people and bringing them to their knees
Degrading them into slaves
See, these are the Shudras
The rest left over, a tiny number
Rose up and challenged Parashuram
They took care to remain united
Of their countrymen, their beloved brothers
Many were slain
The Shudras no longer cared for unity
The maha-ari attacked Parashuram
Many women became widows
Parashuram routed the maha-ari
In constant fighting he broke their spirit
He did not spare pregnant women
He killed the newborn children
The great enemies of the twice-born
Came to the end of their strength
Thrust down and defeated
Those that were left were punished severely
Abused as Mangs and maha-aris, great enemies
See, these are the Kshatriyas of the olden days

(Quoted in O'Hanlon 1985: 142–3)

Explaining terms

Brahma – a significant deity (see Chapter 2); Phule innovates here by including Brahma as a leader of the Aryans

Maha-ari – 'the great enemy' in Marathi; Phule deduces this as the meaning
of Mahar, the name of one of the principal untouchable castes of Maharashtra

Mang – another untouchable caste of the region

Parashuram – 'Rama with an axe', one of the descent forms (avatars) of
Vishnu

In the same manner as the opening extract from *Gulamgiri*, this extract
tells a story of indigenous inhabitants being oppressed by an invading force.
In the second half of the nineteenth century, when elements of the middle
classes of different regions of British India were beginning to develop a
strong critique of British rule, this was a story with a certain piquancy. But of

course the invading force Phule was referring to was not the British; rather it was the Aryans, who as we have noted were believed to have invaded India from the north. In this extract in particular, Phule weaves well-known mythic narratives into this story. He refers to Parashurama, 'Rama with an axe', who is an *avatara*, or descent form, of Vishnu. We saw in Chapter 4 how *avatara* myths, although many and varied, are generally related to the idea of the restoration of *dharma*. *Dharma*, of course, is a multi-layered concept, which encompasses what in Chapter 7A we understood as *varna-dharma* – in its loosest sense, the order of different castes in relation to one another. In order to live a dharmic life, one is required to fulfil duties associated with one's caste status, and *dharma* is threatened when castes do not act in accordance with their duties. The restoration of order explored through the avatar myths is frequently related to this form of *dharma*. Parashurama, for example, who features in the extract above, was the sixth *avatara*. He is particularly associated in a number of narratives with the suppression of *kshatriya* rulers who had apparently exceeded their *dharma*, restoring the supremacy of brahmins in the process. Phule's inversion strategy represents Parashurama as a brutal suppressor who enforced his rule by degrading *kshatriyas*, forcing them into servitude as a means of preserving brahmin domination.

An interesting feature of this inverted story is its particular resonance in western India. Myths associated with Parashurama are strongly associated with the Konkan coast, which stretches between the present-day states of Maharashtra and Karnataka, and with the restoration of a Brahmin-dominated order in the face of the adharmic actions of a particular set of rulers, the Haihaya-Kshatriyas. In the extract from Phule's poem, *kshatriyas* are brutally suppressed, leading to the creation of both *shudras* and the Mahars and Mangs, two of the principal untouchable castes of this region. Phule's narrative, then, is regionally specific, looking to provide a common *kshatriya* past for low castes and untouchables. Interestingly, the history of Maharashtra in the nineteenth century demonstrates that there was a great deal of debate over the status of a group of castes covered by what Rosalind O'Hanlon (1985: 15–49) describes as the 'Mahratta-*kunbi* caste complex' during this period. Claims to *kshatriya* status amongst elements of this low-caste cluster were contested by dominant brahmin castes. Phule's poem builds on this debate, whilst at the same time drawing on the genealogical traditions through which specific *jatis* build their caste identities by linking them with broader mythic narratives. Phule's inversion of the Parashurama narrative appeared to present an alternative mythology for low castes in Maharashtra. His innovation was to make this mythology inclusive of a range of caste groups, including the untouchable Mahars and Mangs, in order to support a broad anti-brahmin front. He was able to do this, of course, because of the power of print. Whereas traditionally such caste narratives would be carried primarily in oral form, told and retold in specific localities to support the local status of particular caste groups (as we saw with the Meos in Chapter

7A), Phule's poems and prose accounts were published and distributed more widely, projecting broader identities and critiquing the notion of brahmin oppression in a more global sense.

Low-caste politics

We will explore the impact of 'print culture' in more depth in Chapter 10. Here, the example of Phule's quite forceful critiques and mythic inversions in print is useful for demonstrating how, during the period of the late nineteenth century, we see the emergence of a kind of corporate low-caste consciousness, defined to a greater or lesser extent against a projected corporate high-caste oppression. From this period onwards, low-caste identity began to develop into a major feature of Indian politics. A succession of low-caste leaders entered the political sphere of colonial India. They argued that institutions like the Indian National Congress – which was established in 1885 and developed into the main nationalist organization – simply could not represent the oppressed because they were dominated by high castes.

The most famous of these was undoubtedly Dr B. R. Ambedkar (1891–1956), another leader from western India, who had a profound impact on national politics in the lead up to and aftermath of Independence in 1947. Ambedkar was an untouchable from the Mahar caste, who nevertheless worked his way through college and then on to education at Columbia University, United States, and the London School of Economics, before qualifying as a barrister. Ambedkar was a fierce critic of caste privilege, and he drew heavily on republican ideals and notions of equality framed by his knowledge of global history in order to inform this critique. In terms of religion, he linked caste oppression directly to Hinduism, describing the latter at one stage as a 'veritable chamber of horrors' ('What Gandhi and Congress have done to the Untouchables', see Hay 1988: 331). He also performed dramatic symbolic acts, such as the public burning of the *Manu Smriti*, the Dharma Shastra text that was perceived by many educated lower castes as the textual source for many oppressive caste regulations (e.g. *Manu Smriti* 8: 270–2, see Olivelle 2004: 182). This kind of performative act drew much from the strategies employed by his contemporary and at times rival M.K. Gandhi.

Ambedkar's political success and wide popularity is indicated by the existence of statues like the one in Figure 7B.1, which inhabit squares, roundabouts and educational institutions across India. He has inspired a great number of low-caste people to become involved in politics, and today in India there are some very prominent political parties who claim his inspiration. One of the most important of these is the Bahujan Samaj Party, or Majority People's Party, which is particularly prominent in the populous north Indian state of Uttar Pradesh, and which defines itself as a party of 'Social Transformation and Economic Emancipation'. A brief review of the party's website (http://

Figure 7B.1 A statue of B.R. Ambedkar at a road junction in Pune. Reproduced courtesy of James Madaio.

bspindia.org/) will demonstrate to you the sustained power of Ambedkar's
name, image and ideas in contemporary politics.

One further factor, however, is particularly interesting to us here:
Ambedkar's dramatic decision, first signalled in the 1930s, to convert from
Hinduism to Buddhism. This eventually occurred in 1956, at a very public
ceremony in Nagpur in central India, accompanied by nearly a million of
his followers who were also, like him, untouchable Mahars (Omvedt 1995:
51). In fact, Buddhism, although a tradition strongly associated with India
because of the significance of the life of Gautama Siddhartha, is a compara-
tively minor religion in terms of actual practice in contemporary India. By
far the majority of Buddhists today are those who followed Ambedkar into
conversion during or after 1956, most of them being Mahar untouchables.
The act of conversion is marked by twenty-two vows, which Ambedkar and
his followers took during the ceremony in 1956. Below we have reproduced
a selection of these vows:

1. I shall have no faith in Brahma, Vishnu and Maheshwara nor shall
   I worship them.
2. I shall have no faith in Rama and Krishna who are believed to be
   incarnation of God nor shall I worship them.

3. I shall have no faith in Gauri, Ganapati and other gods and goddesses of Hindus nor shall I worship them.
4. I do not believe in the incarnation of God.
5. I do not and shall not believe that Lord Buddha was the incarnation of Vishnu. I believe this to be sheer madness and false propaganda.
6. I shall not perform Shraddha nor shall I give pind-dan.
7. I shall not act in a manner violating the principles and teachings of the Buddha.
8. I shall not allow any ceremonies to be performed by Brahmins.
9. I shall believe in the equality of man.
10. I shall endeavor to establish equality.
. . .
19. I renounce Hinduism, which is harmful for humanity and impedes the advancement and development of humanity because it is based on inequality, and adopt Buddhism as my religion.

(Jai Bhim Network n.d.)

We have, of course, purposefully selected these vows from the full list of twenty-two, and I am sure you will have noticed the prominent insistence on a separation from facets of Hindu tradition. Vow five, for example, explicitly denies that Buddha is an *avatara*, a descent form of Vishnu, which most Vaishnava Hindus claim to be the case. You will see also in vow six the rejection of key rituals (both *shraddha* and *pind-dan* refer to rituals associated with death). Also prominent, in vows nine and ten, is a focus on universal equality. What has become known as Mahar or Ambedkarite Buddhism is largely defined by its rejection of what are perceived as the inequalities of Hinduism, and an affirmation of equality which draws on the republican ideals that Ambedkar held dear. It is, then, a religion that developed both out of perceived inequalities and on the basis of developing ideas about the rights of man. These two issues formed the basis of emerging low-caste consciousness in nineteenth- and twentieth-century India.

The religion twist: caste and the fashioning of modern Hinduism

The case of Ambedkarite Buddhism is a particularly stark example of the way in which perceptions of caste, and relations between castes, have had a deep impact on the development of modern religious identities in South Asia. In some ways contemporary Islam and especially Christianity have also been influenced by a similar kind of social critique. We saw in Chapter 2 how Dalit theology, for example, has helped to shape the profile of contemporary Indian Christianity. This theology is rooted in the experience of suffering amongst the lowest castes, many of whom converted to Christianity explicitly as part of an attempt to escape discrimination and social stigma. As we saw in Chapter 7A, however, the shift across religious boundaries does not necessarily mean an 'escape' from such stigma. Caste identities and relations clearly work across these boundaries. Indeed, one might argue that the emphasis of movements such as Ambedkarite Buddhism and Dalit theology is all about emphasizing rather than escaping from specific caste identities.

The underlying reason why there was, in a sense, no escape from caste identity by taking such a course should again be clear from Chapter 7A. Caste, as it is conceptualized in the dynamic between *varna*, *jati* and *casta*, is intimately bound up with everyday social and political relations, which simply cannot be constrained by the concept of religion. At the same time, we cannot avoid the modern positioning of caste as an institution particularly linked with Hinduism. We have seen that social activists such as Phule and Ambedkar related caste discrimination to what the former called the 'vile religion of winners and losers'. Partly, these views responded to the Orientalist identification of caste as fundamentally related to Hinduism, projecting these two as 'twin' features of Indian society (Inden 1986: 402). In addition, they were part of a debate that had emerged over the course of the nineteenth century amongst middle-class Indians (also influenced by Orientalist thinking) about how to conceptualize Hinduism as a modern religion. We saw some elements of this debate in the work of Rammohun Roy in the 1820s. As the century progressed, a succession of mostly high-caste, middle-class elites contributed, developing a range of ideas about the parameters of the Hindu religion.

The issue of caste, and the position of low castes, was a central feature of these debates. A good example is provided by the activities of the Arya Samaj. In Chapter 3 we discussed the approach to the Vedas developed by the founder of the Arya Samaj, Dayananda Saraswati. As part of his advocacy for Vedic culture, Dayananda was extremely critical of contemporary caste practices, especially what he saw as the venal practices of contemporary brahmins (Jones 1976: 40). Rather than using this, like Phule, as a base from which to condemn Hinduism outright, however, Dayananda argued for what he perceived as the restoration of Vedic *varna*s, which he claimed had been a system based on individual merit, rather than birth.[5] This approach was one of the reasons for the popularity of the Arya Samaj in Punjab, where many middle ranking castes (rather than brahmins) had taken advantage of colonial education opportunities and formed the rump of the burgeoning middle class. The Samaj's meritocratic approach to religious authority was naturally attractive to this socially mobile elite.

As the Samaj developed towards the end of the nineteenth century, some of the more radical elements within its Punjabi branches attempted to take the vision of meritocratic *varna* to its logical conclusion by 'reclaiming' low castes, effecting a change of status through a mixture of education and ritual purification (*shuddhi*). This move was opposed resolutely by many caste Hindus. In particular, a self-styled 'orthodox' opposition to the Samaj, known as the Sanatana Dharma movement, was vocal and sometimes physical in its attempts to prevent such processes of reclamation (Zavos 1999: 69–70).

In the elaboration of these positions, we can see the playing out of a kind of reforming versus orthodox model of debate, focused around the issue of low-caste groups. How far could such groups be considered a part of Hinduism? If they were a part of Hinduism, how could their lowly position be justified? These questions were persistently significant in press and pamphlet debates between representatives of self-styled reforming and orthodox organizations, reinforcing the link between the status of low castes and general concerns about the form of Hinduism in the modern world. Phule's rasping critique, resonant in the same kind of public spaces, provided significant momentum to this trend.

In the early twentieth century, the work of Dr Ambedkar and others ensured that these issues remained prominent features of political debates about the nature of both the Hindu and the Indian community. Leaders such as M.K. Gandhi were deeply engaged by the problem of untouchability. Indeed, Gandhi regarded the abolition of untouchability as a prerequisite to true liberation. At the same time, his approach was quite different from that of Ambedkar, In particular, whereas Ambedkar saw caste oppression as inexorably linked to the form of Hinduism (hence his conversion), Gandhi was convinced that it could be eradicated, and that Hinduism as a religion would be enhanced as a result.[6] Many other Hindu activists have sought similar ways to ameliorate the position of low castes, and the difference between these and the more assertive, militant approach taken by some low-caste groups themselves continues to demonstrate a faultline that runs through modern conceptions of Hinduism.

Conclusion

> Untouchability still exists and bids fair to last as long as Hinduism will last.

This quotation, attributed to Dr Ambedkar, is featured on the website of an organization based in the United States called the Dalit Freedom Network (Dalit Freedom Network n.d.). The term '*dalit*' is one that we came across in Chapter 2. It means 'oppressed' or 'broken' in Marathi, and was, according to some authors, first used to refer to low castes by Jotirao Phule (Mendelsohn and Vicziany 1998: 4). In more recent years it has been used as a self-signifier by untouchable groups and individuals, generally indicating the adoption of an assertive politics of social justice, inspired by the work of Ambedkar. As the quotation demonstrates, Dalit consciousness continues to be defined against the idea of Hinduism.

In the nineteenth century and after, this positioning contributed pointedly to debates in print and other public fora about Hindu practices and ideas. In this sense, caste and in particular the activism of Phule, Ambedkar and others became a critical feature of the dynamics that have shaped modern Hinduism.

Questions for further discussion and research

- Is it correct to say that Jotirao Phule was a Hindu?
- How does the approach to caste in this chapter differ from that in Chapter 7A?
- Compare the politics of Phule and Ambedkar and account for any differences.
- Discuss the significance of Ambedkar's conversion to Buddhism in 1956.

Further reading

Ciotti, M (2010) *Retro-Modern India. Forging the Low-Caste Self*, London: Routledge.

> Anthropological account focused on contemporary low-caste consciousness in Uttar Pradesh.

O'Hanlon, R. (1985) *Caste, Conflict and Ideology: Mahatma Jotirao Phule and Low-caste Protest in Nineteenth Century Western India*, Cambridge: Cambridge University Press.

> The most comprehensive account of Phule's life and work, including many excerpts from his writings.

Omvedt, G. (1995), *Dalit Visions*, Delhi: Orient Longman.

> A short account of the emergence of low-caste politics in the modern period, with an interesting introduction on the relationship between low-caste identity and Hinduism, and chapters on both Phule and Ambedkar.

Zavos, J. (2000) *Emergence of Hindu Nationalism in India*, New Delhi: Oxford University Press.

> Chapters 2 and 3 explore the development of debates about Hinduism in the late nineteenth century, including sections on the Arya Samaj and Sanatana Dharma Sabha.

Zelliot, E. (1996) *From Untouchable to Dalit: Essays on the Ambedkar Movement*, New Delhi: Manohar.

> Authoritative source on Dalit movements. Includes an essay comparing Ambedkar with Gandhi.

8   Encounters with the West

In the course of this book, we have quite frequently noted the impact of colonialism on the development of modern religious traditions in South Asia. In addition to our discussion of the concept of 'religion' in the introduction, Chapters 2 and 3 in particular have demonstrated this impact. They showed how colonialism encouraged the articulation of Hinduism as a supremely rational monotheism, and the assertion that the Vedas may be seen as the 'true scripture' of that religion. These chapters were, however, primarily designed to explore different aspects of social and religious life in South Asia, rather than being specifically directed at assessing the way in which the colonial encounter produced change. In Chapter 7B, we altered this focus and explored how colonial conditions created the space for the representation of low castes as an identifiable group, defined by their position in the so-called 'caste system', now identified increasingly as a defining feature of Hinduism. In this chapter, we address the issue of colonial encounter even more directly, looking at interactions with Europe (especially Britain) and America during the nineteenth century, first in relation to the emergence of different modern representations of Islam and 'the (Indian) Muslim community', and then more broadly.

But first a couple of caveats. By focusing on the nineteenth century, we are not supporting a view that it is only at this juncture and because of colonialism that Hinduism or forms of Islam that radically break from the past are created. In the first part of this book, we have constantly given examples from the *longue durée* to indicate not just the rich diversity of religious expression and behaviour in South Asia but also how the roots of modern forms go back much further than British India. However, this is not to deny that certain colonial forms become intertwined with modern presentations of religion, whether these are projected as modern, or as 'traditional', and this is what we investigate in this chapter.

Second, in the chapter title, we have used the vague term 'the West', even though we have some misgivings about it (which we will explore when we review the work of Edward Said later). Our main justification for using the term is that, if you look at evidence from the nineteenth century and beyond, many people did and still do use it as a means of capturing their sense of a perceived flow of ideas, practices, people or just general 'forces' from Europe and America into South Asia (as to other parts of the world). We will be qualifying the term as we go along, but there is a sense in which this generalized idea of 'the West' itself captures some of the concerns of people reflecting on traditions and changes in South Asia, as we shall see. We have also used the term 'encounter' in our title, because of our concern that the flow of ideas, practices, people or indeed 'forces' referred to above has never been only in one direction, even during those periods of the greatest imbalance of power between South Asia and aspects of 'the West'. We hope, then, to demonstrate not how South Asian religious traditions have been changed by the force of 'Western power', or the impact of 'Western ideas', but rather how they have been influenced by the complex cultural interactions that both informed and developed out of the colonial experience.

You may reflect that there are quite a lot of disclaimers already in this chapter. Is there any need to be this cautious? Our answer to this is yes. There is every need for caution, because of the power imbalances mentioned above. In recent years postcolonial theory has uncovered the deep-seated operation of power in the way that colonial societies have been thought about, or represented. In fact, the sociologist and cultural critic Stuart Hall has identified what he calls a 'system of representation', which he refers to as 'the discourse of the West and the Rest'. 'By this strategy', he says:

> the Rest becomes defined as everything that the West is not – its mirror image. It is represented as absolutely, essentially, different, other: the Other. This Other is then itself split into two 'camps': friendly–hostile, Arawak–Carib, innocent–depraved, noble–ignoble.
>
> (Hall 1992: 308)

Watch out for legacies of such dichotomization in South Asian contexts in the rest of this chapter.

Case study: Sayyid Ahmad Khan and Islamic learning in the colonial milieu

Our initial case study in this chapter acquaints us with the work of a distinguished Muslim figure of the nineteenth century, Sayyid Ahmad Khan (1817–1898) (Figure 8.1).[1]

Sayyid Ahmad was an elite Muslim: a member of the so-called *ashraf* class that saw itself as descending from the Persian aristocracy associated with the Mughal empire.[2] In fact, Sayyid Ahmad's family was directly associated with the Mughal rulers, as his grandfather had served in the Mughal administration of Emperor Akbar Shah II. From the early 1830s Sayyid Ahmad was employed by the East India Company in the judicial branch, rising to become a member of the Imperial Legislative Council towards the end of his life. Sayyid Ahmad's public profile rose after the rebellion of 1857, also known as the Indian Mutiny. Not only had he been an active supporter of

Figure 8.1 A photo of Sir Syed Ahmad Khan Bahadur. Reproduced courtesy of Afzal Usmani.

the British during the rebellion (therefore endearing himself to the colonial administration), he also became increasingly active in its aftermath as a self-styled spokesperson for Indian Muslims. In particular, Sayyid Ahmad was concerned that Muslims should not be disadvantaged in relation to the colonial state, because of their perceived association with the previous dominant power on the subcontinent. One answer to this concern was to promote the idea of Islamic learning in a colonial milieu. This excerpt from a letter to an associate demonstrates his approach.

Extract from a letter to Mawlawi Tasadduq

I have been accused by people, who do not understand, of being disloyal to the culture of Islam, even to Islam itself. There are men who say that I have become a Christian. All this I have drawn upon myself because I advocate the introduction of a new system of education which will not neglect the Islamic basis of our culture, nor, for that matter, the teaching of Islamic theology, but which will surely take account of the changed conditions in this land. Today there are no Muslim rulers to patronize those who are well versed in the old Arabic and Persian learning. The new rulers insist upon a knowledge of their language for all advancement in their services and in some of the independent professions like practising law as well. If the Muslims do not take to the system of education introduced by the British, they will not only remain a backward community but will sink lower and lower until there will be no hope of recovery left to them.

. . . It is not only because the British are today our rulers, and we have to recognize this fact if we are to survive, that I am advocating the adoption of their system of education, but also because Europe has made such remarkable progress in science that it would be suicidal not to make an effort to acquire it. Already the leeway between our knowledge and that of Europe is too great. If we go on with our present obstinacy in neglecting it, we shall be left far behind. How can we remain true Muslims or serve Islam, if we sink into ignorance? The knowledge of yesterday is often the ignorance of tomorrow, because knowledge and ignorance are, in this context, comparative terms. The truth of Islam will shine the more brightly if its followers are well-educated, familiar with the highest knowledge in the world; it will come under an eclipse if its followers are ignorant and backward.

The Muslims have nothing to fear from the adoption of the new education if they simultaneously hold steadfast to their faith, because Islam is not irrational superstition; it is a rational religion which can march hand in hand with the growth of human knowledge.

(Sayyid Ahmad Khan, Letter to Mawlawi Tasadduq,
see Hay 1988: 188–90)

Task

What connections do you see between this approach to religion and colonial control and that of Rammohun Roy, explored in Chapter 2?

It is clear from this excerpt that Sayyid Ahmad faces criticism for his approach to education, and perhaps for his approach to Europe more generally. Some people have accused him of turning away from the 'culture of Islam', or even of becoming a Christian. The reason for this is that he is advocating an opening up to European knowledge, rather than a reliance on Arabic and Persian learning, although he was well schooled in the latter. His reasoning is twofold: first, Muslims in India will not be able to progress within the parameters of colonial society – key avenues of employment, in particular, will be denied to them; second, if Muslims want to remain true to their religion, they should embrace new forms of learning – education is paramount, because Islam is 'a rational religion'; it does not rely on superstition or blind faith.

A great deal of this reasoning is reminiscent of Rammohun Roy's approach to colonial rule; he was also keen to embrace new forms of learning, and received criticism from more conservative elements within society. He also claimed that rationality was a key facet of his religion, and that as such it was particularly suited to the encounter with Western learning. He similarly invoked the idea of, in his case, 'the Hindus' as a recognizable group in Indian society, and much of his writing was concerned with the development of this group and its approach to religion.

It is no coincidence that both Rammohun and Sayyid Ahmad Khan were part of an elite class who had the opportunity to gain access not only to new forms of learning, but also to new forms of employment opened up by the development of the colonial milieu. Together, they represent a particular elite response to colonial control that places emphasis on a willingness to acknowledge the value of Western knowledge, whilst not conceding the comparative value of indigenous knowledge. This approach provides legitimation for engagement with colonial authority in the name of one or another community identified as indigenous. In Sayyid Ahmad Khan's case, of course, this community was 'the Indian Muslim community', or *qaum* (we shall see below how this idea, like that of 'Hindooism', was itself contested). In particular, he aimed to provide modern leadership to the *qaum* through his strategy of engagement. He did this primarily through the founding of an Islamic centre of learning, the Muhammadan Anglo-Oriental College of Aligarh, later the famous Aligarh Muslim University, first established in 1875. As historian Kenneth Jones (1989) notes, the college aimed to provide 'elements of English education in an Islamic context' (p. 67), in order to fashion 'educated, honest, public-spirited leaders able to work with the English government, and to protect the Muslim community. In time this elite would lift the Muslims into a cooperative dominance, ruling India in partnership with the British' (p. 68).

A key point about this project was that it sought to fashion a modern lay leadership for Indian Muslims (Ahmad 1967: 37). This in itself was a rather new kind of idea: a sign of the times that seemed to identify the Muslims of British India as a discrete community in and of themselves, at least nominally linking together the vast numbers of diverse people across the subcontinent who in one way or another identified themselves as Muslim. In reality the constituency of the college was limited to 'the north Indian Muslims literate in Urdu who formed the reservoir of Muslim intelligentsia and government servants' (Lelyveld 1978: 123). This was the group that Sayyid Ahmad perceived as natural leaders who could then speak 'in the name of all the Muslims of India' (p. 123), on the basis of what the historian Barbara Metcalf terms 'the Aligarh thesis': 'that the Muslims of British India had been rulers; had now declined in comparison to non-Muslim Indians; but could, through English education and Islam, once again be great' (Metcalf 2002: 327). The idea of a lay leadership to this putative Muslim community also implicitly encroached on existing authority within these diverse Islamic communities; as such, it was largely opposed by the *'ulema*, the Muslim clerics who constituted that traditional Islamic authority.

To understand the social and political location of Sayyid Ahmad's educational project in a bit more depth, we need to look further at the way educational systems in South Asia had changed in the first half of the nineteenth century. Under the Mughal empire and successor states, families of scholars, whether Muslim *'ulema*, Sufis or brahmins, were patronized to teach their particular specialisms on an individual or small group basis, either in their own accommodation, in *madrasa*s or *gurukul*s, or as home tutors for elite families. Specialist artisans inducted the next generation into needed skills, mothers nurtured young children, cultivated courtesans shared in musical and literary education, trading routes opened up long distance travel for people to seek teachers elsewhere.

In this great plurality were two key features: personal or family inclination, and informality – not that strict codes of behaviour were not inculcated, but there was no 'organized sector' of education as such. Sayyid Ahmad Khan was himself taught by his mother, Azizunnissa Begam (a woman in *purdah*, see Chapter 10), who spoke and read Urdu and Persian, and had studied the Qur'an. She and her husband held interesting, reformist positions that undoubtedly had an impact on their son: they followed a Sufi Naqshbandi Mujaddidi reformer, Shah Ghulam Ali, who was opposed to practices such as making offerings at the tombs of *pir*s (Minault 1998: 16). They were also influenced by the significant eighteenth-century reformer Shah Wali Ullah (see Chapter 5). Sayyid Ahmad went on to study with influential *'ulema* families in Delhi, Kandhla and Chiryakot (Lelyveld 1982: 88), was educated in both an Islamic curriculum and Persian literature, became familiar with British educational methods through his juridical work for the East India Company and later admired the 'Oxbridge' model. He then applied a critical, enquiring approach acquired through this eclectic education to the four sources of Islamic knowledge (Qur'an, Hadith, reasoning through analogy, and consensus). In particular, he emphasized the possibility of *ijtihad*, or independent reasoning. *Ijtihad* refers to individual reasoning based on a rational approach to the four sources of Islamic knowledge.[3] It was, importantly, through an emphasis on this reasoning as 'the inalienable right of every individual Muslim' (Ahmad 1967: 54) that Sayyid Ahmad saw the possibility of rapprochement with Western forms of knowledge, and so it was partly to this that many of the *'ulema* of the time objected (Jalal 2000: 68).

The thrust of British education policy in India was towards the development of a formal, institutionalized system, perceived as a necessary basis for 'progress' and 'civilization'; this formed quite a contrast to the diverse, inclination-led, informal spectrum of possibilities referred to above. From the Madrasah 'Aliyah (Calcutta Madrasa), set up in 1780 by the East India Company to train *qazi*s for local courts, through missionary schools, Macaulay's notorious Minute of 2 February 1835 decreeing the use of English (rather than 'native' or classical Oriental languages) for instruction in government educational institutions, and on to the work of individual European reformers later in the century, colleges and schools were set up variously to produce suitably trained officials and administrators, to convert people to Christianity, to extend the reach of the colonial authorities, to foster citizenship and to promote and control bourgeois interests, in parallel with developments in education in Britain. The principles and techniques of these institutions, a 'crucial weapon of rule', were then adopted and adapted by those educated in them (still a small elite) in order to establish their own institutions (Kumar 2000: 20; see also Lelyveld 1978: 113–18). These covered a wide range, from traditionalist establishments such as one we will look at in the next section, to reformist ones such as the Aligarh college. They all sought in various ways to negotiate curricula deemed suitable for both current progress and faithfulness to their own (often re-presented) traditions of learning (and belief), and to participate through these new organizations in projecting particular, often religious, identities in a newly forming public space (see Chapter 10).

In such a context, Sayyid Ahmad Khan's was one particular way in which the encounter with Western knowledge was translated into an approach to religion and community in South Asia. In one sense, this was by no means a radical move; Sayyid Ahmad was indeed anything but a radical in his approach. In his own eyes, the historian Ayesha Jalal comments, he acted only to 'shepherd a straying flock of co-religionists into greener pastures within the colonial system', in the process producing 'a conception of Muslimness consistent with the colonial state's epistemology of communitarianism' (Jalal 2000: 61). At the same time his approach did represent a kind of Islamic modernism (Ahmad 1967), placing a particularly strong emphasis on individual Qur'anic interpretation and promoting the need for a modern, rationalist intelligentsia capable of leading an identifiable Muslim community, distinct in its projected political and social aspirations from the perceived Hindu majority. As the historian Aziz Ahmad (1967: 38) says, Sayyid Ahmad's work consequently had significant effects on the conceptualization of Islam and Muslims in the region.

Other Islamic encounters

Parallel developments during this period demonstrate the diversity of ways of negotiating this encounter with the West. One of the most interesting alternative developments in the field of Islamic education was the Dar ul-Ulam of Deoband, which was established in 1867 (Metcalf 2002, 2004). Unlike Sayyid Ahmad's institution, destined to become the Aligarh Muslim University, the Dar ul-Ulam was a *madrasa* – that is, a school specifically designed to deliver theological education and Islamic law. In this sense the Deoband school, as it became known, was more closely related to the traditional concerns of the *'ulema*.

At the same time, there were some crucial differences in the approach of the Deoband school that we need to take into account. In the first instance, the *madrasa* was established independent of any particular mosque or locally prominent family, as was the norm in northern India at that time (and indeed

more widely than this). As an independent institution, the *madrasa* acquired
its own buildings that housed classrooms and a library, and it employed its
own staff to deliver classes and administer the organization. The students
were admitted to a fixed course of study over a fixed period of time, and
their period of study was assessed by regular examinations. If this is beginning to sound rather familiar, there is no coincidence in that. The Deoband
madrasa was really distinctive in the way in which it emulated the structure
of British educational institutions, even whilst its curriculum remained resolutely Islamic.

Another key difference was that the *madrasa* was funded not through a
system of patronage, but through the very modern principle of public sub-
scription. The historian Barbara Metcalf (2004: 33) explains:

> The Deobandis solicited annual pledges from their supporters, a method
> learned from missionary associations. The system was complex, requir-
> ing careful records and dependent on the new facilities of postal service,
> money orders, and even the printing press. Thanks to the last, the
> annual proceedings were able to publish widely the list of donors who
> thus received recognition for their generosity. The donors were listed in
> the order of the size of their gift, but even the humblest contributor was
> included.

You will note the reference to the missionary model here. The Deoband
school drew a kind of structural lesson from Christian missionaries, emu-
lating the way in which they located themselves in social space. This also
extended to the idea of the school itself as a mission, in the sense that the staff
who worked there were encouraged to see their work as a kind of religious
service, the public who contributed were encouraged to see their contributions as *zakat* (i.e. the Islamic requirement to give charitably), the school's
relatively impecunious state was positively encouraged,[4] and the graduates
of the school (as modern *'ulema*) were encouraged to take the message of
Deobandi Islam to different localities, perhaps setting up approved branches
of the *madrasa*, structured on the same basis as the Deoband institution. In
this way, the distinctive approach of the Deoband school spread exponen-
tially, and today it is a major force not just in South Asia, but also in countries
such as Britain and the United States where many South Asians have settled.

In contrast to the Aligarh movement's accommodationist stance, the
Deoband school did not embrace Western knowledge in the same way, nor
did it attempt to engage the state through the possibility of acquiring grants-
in-aid to support the institution. Rather, it placed emphasis on the careful
exploration of Islamic law and theology, with particular emphasis on the
hadith as a source of knowledge and guidance. The programme of study
at the *madrasa* was a full six years long. Graduates were religious specialists who could mediate Islamic knowledge and provide judgments (*fatwa*)
for less well-educated Muslims. Although religious experience was valued,

this experience needed to be supported by learning. The implication here is that the unmediated experience of the devotees of Sufi *pir*s, as explored in Chapter 5, is not recognized as appropriate religious practice. Sufism, the mystical path that is so strongly rooted in the Islamic traditions of South Asia, was therefore recognized as legitimate by the Deobandi school only inasmuch as Sufi saints were recognized as learned individuals. The reverence and devotion directed towards these individuals was shunned. This carefully articulated attitude towards Sufism reveals that even the Deobandis' conscious rejection of the paths of Western knowledge was in some ways nevertheless a product of the colonial encounter. Sufi devotionalism was partly rejected because it was perceived as superstition, an accretion that did not represent the 'true' form of Islam, as articulated in the Qur'an, and elaborated through the words of the prophet in the Hadith. This approach is very reminiscent of those noted in Chapters 2 and 3 as associated with Rammohun Roy and Dayananda Saraswati. The very different approaches to religion developed in these three instances share a common structure based on the recognition of 'authentic' religion in 'pure', textualized forms. As we have seen, this common structure was a key component of the developing, modern notion of 'religion' as an objectified category of human experience. Indeed, the very structuring of 'real' Hinduism and Islam along these lines was a critical factor in the development of the category. In this way, we can view Deoband's self-conscious, studied traditionalism as distinctively modern.

We want to look briefly at one further interesting Islamic movement that emerged in a similar time and space as Deoband: that which has become known as 'Barelwi'. The Barelwi tradition coalesced around the scholarly figure of Ahmad Riza Khan (1856–1921) of Bareilly (hence the name, Barelvi), a town that, like Deoband, is in the northern Indian state of Uttar Pradesh. Ahmad Riza Khan was a *shaykh* of the Qadiri Order of Sufis. Like Deoband, the Barelvi movement was identifiable institutionally through a *madrasa* (and subsequent 'branch' *madrasa*s), although the initial impulse to develop the movement was much more clearly focused on the figure of Ahmad Riza Khan and his forthright refutation of the approach of movements like the Deobandis (Sanyal 2010: 231–67), whom he described as 'followers of Satan the rebel' (p. 236).

In contrast to Deoband, the Barelvi movement is strongly associated with the defence of what we might perceive as traditional devotional practices. These include the celebration of *'urs* and other ritual practices associated with the tombs of recognized Sufi saints, and a general respect for established customs and localized practices. In this sense Barelvi Islam seems rather unfocused, and you might reasonably ask why one would see this position as a 'movement'. Like Deoband, however, Barelvi has become a very widely recognized movement in South Asian Islam, and it has a particularly strong presence amongst British Muslims. Its life as a 'movement' is really predicated on its context, emerging in the north Indian milieu in which a range of more recognizable movements such as Deoband and Aligarh developed. One might even say that this context invoked the idea of Barelwi as a movement: in order to be meaningful in the colonial milieu, Barelvi was fashioned as a 'movement' against what were perceived as innovatory practices. In this sense, just like Deoband and Aligarh, Barelwi was distinctive because it was clearly focused on the idea of Islam *as a religion*. As Metcalf states, this approach meant that Barelvis were 'not . . . representing a continuity with the past but rather, in their very self-consciousness, representing a departure from it' (Metcalf 2002: 296).

The World's Parliament of Religions

This 'self-consciousness' about religion is reflected far more widely during this period than just amongst the Muslim intellectuals of northern India. It is, we would say, again evidence of that emerging modern notion of 'religion', an objectified category, populated by a series of roughly comparable sub-sets (the 'World Religions'), which many commentators have located as developing gradually out of the encounters between 'the West' and other parts of the world, a pervasive feature of global geo-politics from the seventeenth century onwards (see Chapter 1 on this issue). Another example of the developing global impact of this process is provided by the famous 'World's Parliament of Religions', held in Chicago in 1893. The objective of this event, as described by its Chair, the Reverend John Henry Barrows, was to 'bring together in conference, for the first time in history, the leading representatives of the great Historic Religions of the world' (Barrows 1893, quoted in Zavos 2008: 51). The august gathering opened with the tolling of the great Columbian Liberty Bell ten times, one for each of the 'Ten Great Religions' of humanity (Ketalaar 1993: 269). The opening ceremony then proceeded with representatives of different religious traditions on the main platform, 'a bewildering kaleidoscope of tints, punctuated and emphasized by the still black and white of the American and European' (*Chicago Times*, 12 September 1893, quoted in Ketelaar 1993: 275).

South Asia was of course represented at the Parliament by a range of individuals.[5] Amongst them was Swami Vivekananda, a Bengali devotee of the mid-nineteenth-century mystic Shri Ramakrishna. Vivekananda's appearance at the Parliament provides us with an interesting further example of the 'encounter with the West'. This example is rather different, in that the encounter occurs not in India, the site of colonial domination, but in America, a land with an identity that was both part of 'the West', and predicated on release from colonial domination by Europe. This rather uneasy double image was reflected in the character of the Parliament, which was both dominated by white Christians and yet keen to embrace what Barrows saw as the 'fact, which is indisputable, that there are on this planet a number of religions, among which Christianity numerically counts one' (Barrows 1893, quoted in Zavos 2008: 50). In addition, Vivekananda's appearance at the Parliament demonstrated a very independent agency: he arrived at the Parliament uninvited, having travelled from India with the financial assistance of Indian patrons, and proceeded to represent Hinduism in a very public and forthright manner.

Vivekananda's approach to Hinduism was heavily based on the philosophy of Advaita Vedanta (see Chapter 2), and to this extent we can link his approach to others we might recognize as being developed through the encounter with the West, in particular the rational monotheism of Rammohun Roy. At the same time, the presentation of these ideas in Chicago was pitched at quite a different level. Vivekananda presented Advaita Vedanta as the universal religion, encompassing all others. He presented it not as an arcane set of practices and ideas from a distant and subjugated land, relevant in Chicago only as a matter of curiosity, but as a vital and enduring force that could reinvigorate the hollow spiritual existence of the industrial, alienated West. This was a combative, assertive approach, in which India was projected as a critical resource for global development. As Vivekananda is reported to have commented in the wake of the Parliament, 'The Parliament of Religions, as it seems to me, was intended as a heathen show before the world; but it turned out that the heathens had the upper hand' (see Vedanta Center of Atlanta n.d.).

By the end of the nineteenth century, there is plenty of evidence to demonstrate this self-confident, resistant approach to the encounter with the West in the development of South Asian religious identities. As we will see in Chapter 10, the development of the ideology of Indian nationalism was strongly bound up with the identification of religion not only as a realm beyond the reach of the colonial state, but also as a key site for the development of an independent national culture. As Vivekananda exemplified in America, many middle-class Indians were developing a self-image of superior spirituality, as an antidote to what appeared to be an evident Western superiority in material realms. This apparent dualization points us towards a critical area for understanding what we have called the encounter with the West: that is, the idea of Orientalism and the development of what has become known as 'postcolonial theory'.

Encountering Orientalism and postcolonialism

In exploring the key themes of this chapter (and indeed more broadly), it is important to take this influential body of theory into account. 'Orientalism', of course, is a term we have come across before. It was used in Chapter 3 to refer to the range of European intellectuals who engaged in study about India in the late eighteenth and nineteenth centuries. People like William Jones have become known as Orientalists because they developed European knowledge about 'the Orient'. Often these men were highly sympathetic towards India and other regions of the East, and critical of the development of European cultures. Nevertheless, the idea of Orientalism has developed a negative, almost pejorative inflection. This is largely the result of the influential work of Edward Said, a Palestinian academic who published a book called *Orientalism* in 1978 that explored the phenomenon of colonialism and the complex modes of power associated with it.

In the first chapter of his book, Said lays out three meanings of the term 'Orientalism' (pp. 2–3). The first relates quite clearly to Orientalist intellectuals like Jones; it denotes an 'academic field' developed, as we have noted, in the late eighteenth and nineteenth centuries, but with an enduring influence in academic and research circles since this time. Indeed, we might reasonably make a connection between this field and some of the 'area studies' fields that are now quite common in universities, such as, of course, the field of South Asian Studies.

The second meaning highlights the idea of an Orient/Occident dualism as a means of categorizing the world. This idea, of course, is important in this chapter, as it invokes the notion of 'the West' as a homogeneous phenomenon, just as much as it invokes 'the Orient' or 'the East' in a similar way. There are many ways in which this meaning has cropped up in the examples we have been looking at; perhaps most straightforwardly we can see it operating in the approach of Vivekananda to Indian 'spirituality', in contradistinction to the materialism of the West, and we will explore this idea in more depth below. It is also apparent in Sayyid Ahmad Khan's desire to emphasize Islam as a rational religion, as opposed to 'irrational superstition'. This is also a highly resilient dualism, very much in evidence in the contemporary world, where it frequently operates in a wryly resistant fashion, echoing to some extent the attitude of Vivekananda. An example is provided by the 2002 film *The Guru*. One aspect of this film is its portrayal of the feckless fallibility of rich New Yorkers when they are confronted by the mystical spiritualism of India – as represented by the resourceful migrant, Ramu, whose 'spiritualism' is lifted surreptitiously from a fellow performer in the pornographic film industry. Another example is that of the Guru played by Sanjeev Bhaskar in the British Asian television show, *Goodness Gracious Me*. Bhaskar's Guru is regularly presented as teaching a group of, as he calls them, 'spiritually flatulent westerners' about the wonders of Hinduism, which he describes in one sketch as a 'fascinating network of philosophies, legends . . . and nice tunes' (Bhaskar 2007).

The third meaning of Said's Orientalism is as a body of knowledge by which, he says, the Orient was managed (Said 1978: 3). This refers to what is otherwise known as discursive power, the power to structure the way in which ideas, objects and practices are known and understood. This discursive power, Said argues, acts as the ideal companion to the economic and military power of colonial control. Through it, a regime of truth is established that privileges certain ways of seeing the world over others. Perhaps Said's most radical idea was that this discursive power operated not just to manage and control colonial possessions, but also to *produce* the reality of colonial, or more broadly, 'Oriental' society. 'The Orient', he argued, 'was

Orientalized not only because it was discovered to be "Oriental" in all those ways considered commonplace by an average nineteenth century European, but also because it *could be* – that is, submitted to being – *made* Oriental' (Said 1978: 5–6).

The responses to the West we have examined in this chapter may all be seen as in some sense developing from the 'production' of the Orient posited here by Said. The Aligarh movement was predicated on the idea that Islamic knowledge was 'old' or traditional (the Oriental 'other' of modern, Western knowledge); the approach of both Deobandis and Barelvis responded to the identification of devotional Sufism as a distinctive feature of South Asian Islam (was this, or was this not, 'real' religion?); and as we have seen, Vivekananda presented Hinduism at the Parliament and more broadly as fundamentally different from Western ways of knowing. In addition, we may go on to say that, inasmuch as all these examples had a self-conscious understanding of diverse traditions as 'religion' at their heart, they were symptomatic of a new form of reality in which the idea of religion itself was perceived as a central feature of South Asian society, a key idiom for the structuring of social relations.

It is this third meaning of Orientalism that is most closely associated with the burgeoning body of work known as 'postcolonial theory', which has developed not just in the study of literature (Said's initial data source), but also across the arts and social sciences. Postcolonial theory has some similarities to that other major force in recent intellectual history, postmodernism – primarily because both of these approaches are premised on the social construction of knowledge, and so on the power of discourse to discipline the subject. Postcolonial theory begins with a recognition that the discursive power outlined here was not relinquished at the point of Independence. The aftermath of colonialism is rather marked by what the author Leela Gandhi (1998: 15) describes as the continued domination of 'minds, selves, cultures', and some 'enduring hierarchies of subjects and knowledges' (G. Prakash, cited in Gandhi 1998: 15). Postcolonial theory has developed as a kind of critical resistance to the continuation of these relations of power. It aims, on the one hand, to recognize, explore and analyse the structures of knowledge associated with the colonial project, and, on the other hand, to retrieve and exemplify what Leela Gandhi calls 'disqualified or subjugated knowledges' (p. 53) – those ways of thinking that have been suppressed through the domination of colonial knowledge systems. In this sense postcolonialism, as it has become known, is an avowedly political project, as well as an academic one. It has as its objective a transformation of the relations of power that currently dominate global geo-politics, relations which, it is argued, are based on the history of colonialism and the Orientalist structures of knowledge that supported it.

There have, of course, been some very trenchant critiques of postcolonialism (for a summary, see Gandhi 1998: 54–8). Postcolonialists are often accused of producing a caricature of 'Western power', based on the very same (East/West) dichotomy that they seek to critique. In addition, rather like postmodernism, postcolonialism is often presented in language that is difficult to penetrate. Although this in itself may be seen as a form of resistance to the dominant structuring of knowledge, it is used by critics as evidence to argue that postcolonialism has been developed by intellectuals mostly based in Western universities (a key source of the production of colonial knowledge that postcolonialists seek to critique), and that it has little impact on the real structures of power under which people work, suffer, starve in the postcolonial world.

There is plenty to be said for this criticism, but at the same time we can see the development of forms of knowledge in resistance to colonialism that have had a direct impact on people's lives. The emergence of Deoband might be viewed in this manner, as might Vivekananda's presentation of Indian spirituality. But as these examples suggest, the workings of this resistance are not straightforward. They are frequently bound into webs of colonial discourse, and their effects in terms of 'hierarchies of subjects and knowledges' are difficult to predict. In the final section we will explore this point in more depth by looking more closely at that idea of Indian spirituality that Vivekananda so vigorously propagated.

The religion twist: spirituality and rationalism

> 'Wherever virtue subsides and vice prevails, I come down to help mankind,' declares Krishna, in the *Bhagavad Gita*. Whenever this world of ours, on account of growth, on account of added circumstances, requires a new adjustment, a wave of power comes; and as a man is acting on two planes, the spiritual and the material, waves of adjustment come on both planes. On the one side, of the adjustment on the material plane, Europe has mainly been the basis during modern times; and of the adjustment on the other, the spiritual plane, Asia has been the basis throughout the history of the world. Today, man requires one more adjustment on the spiritual plane; today when material ideas are at the height of their glory and power, today when man is likely to forget his divine nature, to be reduced to a mere money-making machine, an adjustment is necessary . . . and again the place from which this power will start will be Asia.
>
> (Swami Vivekananda 1896a, 'My Master', in *Complete Works* 1962: 154)

In this declaration, given in 1896 during his first European tour and after the World's Parliament of Religions, Vivekananda states clearly his view of the dichotomy between the material West (Europe, America) and the spiritual East (Asia), and the associated claim of Eastern superiority and leadership of the globe in spiritual matters. By grounding his view that the needed spiritual revival will come from Asia in *Gita* 4.6 (a passage we have come across before; see Chapter 4), he asserts its cosmic, ancient and universal authority. Yet as we have seen, his is, to some extent, a 'Western message from the East'

(Killingley 1998). In this section we will explore the way in which this idea that 'Eastern' religion was especially spiritual was constructed and developed as a facet of the religion discourse. As we shall see, the classic Occident/ Orient dichotomy apparent in this characterization has some complex and entangled roots.

One root was in the work of the German Romantic writers. In particular, the philosopher Arthur Schopenhauer (1788–1860) was deeply attracted to the classical Upanishads and their message of 'pristine spirituality'. Yet Schopenhauer's Upanishadic source was a Latin translation, the *Oupnek'hat*, published by the French Orientalist, Anquetil du Perron (1731–1805) in 1801–2. This was itself a translation from the Persian rendering of the Upanishads commissioned by the Mughal emperor Akbar (see Halbfass 1988: 35). The claimed 'spirituality' of the Sanskrit Upanishads had therefore already been mediated through several languages and cultural contexts. But it became a powerful trope.

The Theosophy movement, established in New York in 1875, was one of several to take up and develop this trope of Indian spirituality. In the cosmopolitan environment of the late nineteenth century, their activities and writings had more direct links with India than those apparent in Schopenhauer's work. Their leaders included the American colonel Henry Olcott, the colourful Russian Madame Blavatsky, and Annie Besant, an English woman who was to become first woman President of the Indian National Congress in 1917. The Theosophists gave Vivekananda significant direct support, even though he tried to distance himself from them in later years (Baumfield 1991: 42–60). It seems more than likely that they formed one significant influence causing him to adopt the vocabulary of India's 'spirituality'. Another may have been the work of his Bengali contemporary, Keshab Chandra Sen, also working in a cosmopolitan environment. Keshab was a significant leader of the Brahmo Samaj, the organization established by Rammohun Roy earlier in the century. His 1883 'Asia's Message to Europe' pointed out that 'cultured souls in the East treat spiritual realities as things that can be seen and felt' (cited in Killingley 1998: 142). Vivekananda may also have been influenced by Schopenhauer's disciple, the major Orientalist scholar, Paul Deussen (1845–1919), who promoted Advaita Vedanta in the late nineteenth century. They certainly met and spoke together in 1896 (Killingley 1998: 146). Yet as the historian Tapan Raychaudhuri (1998: 16) points out, Vivekananda's ideas also grew out of his own experience as a pupil of the Bengali mystic Ramakrishna Paramahamsa, whom he saw as the realization of Advaitin truth, and he frequently drew on Indian texts to develop these ideas, as the initial quotation in this section demonstrates. So the influences are complex.

Through such interactions, the idea of religion as an assertive spirituality with a strong ethical component, an emphasis on tolerance, and an engagement with social and political realities became increasingly influential not just in Vivekananda's thinking, but more broadly as well. It became, for example, a creative force for nationalism (see Chapter 10). It is also clearly evident in the philosophy of the important twentieth-century academic and statesman, Sarvepalli Radhakrishnan (1888–1975). It is also apparent in the philosophies of numerous modern Gurus (see Chapter 6). A further legacy is identifiable in the idea of the 'mystic East', central to the 1960s American counter-culture, when hippies travelled to India in search of a spirituality they found lacking in their own society, and in the UK the Beatles and others became attracted to Maharishi Yogi (on this trend, see Mehta 1990). During this period also, Swami Prabhupada brought the Hare Krishna movement, the International Society for Krishna Consciousness (ISKCON), to the West, initially to New York in 1966. ISKCON is now a major Hindu presence in the UK, the US and other parts of the world.

Such trends seem far removed from what has been mooted as another key development through the encounter with the West, namely the stress on the rationality of religion. This seems much more congruent with Sayyid Ahmad Khan's response and, as we noted earlier, echoes Rammohun's concern to demonstrate the true rationality of Hinduism by contrast with the spurious rationality of the Three in One dying God of Christians and their intolerance of the views of others. Does, then, the work of Vivekananda and Sayyid Ahmad represent two divergent responses to the encounter with the West, the one spiritual, the other rational? Although this may seem persuasive, the picture is again more complex. The Theosophists, cited above as an influence on Vivekananda, provide a good example. They rejected institutionalized Christianity and engaged in séances, where people tried to contact spirits of the dead, seeking in India a form of spirituality compatible with these interests. The anthropologist and historian, Peter van der Veer (2001), however, reminds us that, at the time, séances were regarded as a form of empirical experimentation, a rational scientific method. In contrast to what we might call this spirit of scientific enquiry, the Theosophists rejected mainstream Christianity precisely because it was legitimated by appeal to revelation (with this rationalist approach, perhaps echoing the critique of Rammohun Roy). The Theosophist view was that rationality, spiritualism, spirituality and political action complemented rather than contradicted one another. Their objection was to what they saw in Europe and America as the mystification of oppression, apparent in centuries of institutionalized Christianity.

The Religious Studies scholar Richard King has commented in relation to the idea of the 'mystic East' associated with India that 'colonial stereotypes . . . became transformed and used in the fight against colonialism.' 'Despite this', he continues, 'stereotypes they remain' (King 1999b: 93). The evidence we have presented here suggests that the image of dichotomization between spirituality and rationality in the presentation of modern religion in South Asia is just such a stereotype. There is no doubt that it has been an influential and significant image, which has had its impact not just in the fight against colonialism, but in a range of different environments both in South Asia and more widely. Nevertheless, a stereotype it remains, masking a far more nuanced and entangled set of historical processes. Consider the following quotation from Vivekananda, again asserting the role that India can play in global development: 'The salvation of Europe depends on a rationalistic religion, and Advaita – non-duality, the Oneness, the idea of the Impersonal God – is the only religion that can have any hold on any intellectual people' (Vivekananda 1896b, 'The Absolute and Manifestation', in *Complete Works* 1963: 139). It is only by recognizing those nuanced and entangled historical processes that such a statement can be reconciled with the Swami's equally forthright assertions about the spiritual superiority of India. For Vivekananda, Advaita Vedanta is both spiritual and rational, and it is on this basis that it is suited to the demands of the modern world. Sayyid Ahmad Khan may have said something similar, in fact, about Islam. As in Chapter 2, where our evidence led us to question the apparent binary opposition between monotheism and polytheism, we must here be similarly cautious with ideas of spirituality and rationality. Discourses of domination and resistance may present these as binary opposites, but as students of religion we need both to explore the operation of such discourses, and to look beyond appearances to the complex processes that have produced them.

Conclusion

In this chapter, then, we have explored the various ways in which the 'encounter with the West' has occurred in relation to both the representation and the development of South Asian religious traditions. It is clear from the evidence that there is again a great deal of diversity apparent in this scenario. Our examples of Islamic movements from the late nineteenth century have demonstrated this diversity. Although we may detect both 'modernist' and 'traditional' responses to the fact of colonial domination, we need to be aware that both these responses demonstrate interaction, and, through this interaction, various forms of innovation and adjustment; this is a point we may place within the wider framework of the dynamism of 'tradition' and 'modernity' as categories more generally, which we commented on in our first chapter. One common development apparent in these examples has been evidence of a consideration or consciousness of Islam as a religion, comparable to other religions, and of the idea of Muslims as a community, comparable to other religious communities in British India. As we shall see in the next chapter, this was a persuasive and significant idea, in relation not just to Islam and Muslims, but to religious communities more generally. Indeed, in this chapter, we saw how such self-conscious approaches to religion played out in the dramatic environment of the World's Parliament of Religions, and how they have contributed to the articulation of multilayered forms of resistance to colonial domination. Even whilst acknowledging this role, however, we should remain sensitive to the complexities through which such ideas about religion have been produced, and the unpredictable consequences that develop as they are deployed in diverse modern contexts.

Questions for further discussion and research

- How would you define 'the West' and 'the East'?
- Comparing Aligarh Muslim University and the Dar ul-Ulam at Deoband, do you see one as modernist and the other as traditional?
- What is postcolonial theory? Does it help or hinder us in trying to understand the examples of 'encounter' explored in this chapter?
- Is South Asia a uniquely spiritual place?

Further reading

Chowdhury-Sengupta, I. (1998) 'Reconstructing Hinduism on a world platform: the World's first Parliament of Religions, Chicago 1893', in W. Radice (ed.) *Swami Vivekananda and the Modernisation of Hinduism*, New Delhi: Oxford University Press.

> An informative article exploring the role that Vivekananda played at the Parliament in Chicago in 1893.

Gandhi, L. (1998) *Postcolonial Theory: A Critical Introduction*, Edinburgh: University of Edinburgh Press.

> Introducing the main features of postcolonial theory, although no particular emphasis on religion (see King for this).

Jalal, A. (2000) *Self and Sovereignty: Individual and Community in South Asian Islam since 1850*, London: Routledge.

> Chapter 2 provides a broad perspective on the development of notions of Muslim community in the late nineteenth century, placing the work of Sayyid Ahmad Khan in perspective.

King, R. (1999b) *Orientalism and Religion: Postcolonial Theory, India and the 'Mystic East'*, London: Routledge.

> Some challenging and forthright arguments about the development of South Asian religions (primarily Hinduism and Buddhism) on the basis of postcolonial theory.

Metcalf, B. (2002) *Islamic Revival in British India: Deoband 1860–1900*, New Delhi: Oxford University Press.

> A comprehensive account of the early development of the Deoband movement.

9 The construction of religious boundaries

This chapter is in many ways a continuation of the themes of Chapter 8, in that it explores further ways in which the encounter with 'the West' impacted on South Asian religious traditions. Here, however, we are focused on one particular area that is of critical importance to the way in which these traditions are practised and represented in the modern and contemporary era: the ways in which definite boundaries have been constructed or developed between these traditions. This process has been critical to contemporary understandings of South Asian religions. The 'construction of religious boundaries' is actually a term deployed by the Punjabi academic Harjot Oberoi (1994) in his study of the development of Sikh traditions in the Punjab over the period from the sixteenth century up to the present. Oberoi's thesis is a rather startling one at first sight, and has led to him being aggressively targeted by some Sikhs as an apostate (as he is himself a Sikh). It is, briefly, that the religion of Sikhism was not established by Guru Nanak in the sixteenth century and subsequently developed through the work of the nine Gurus who succeeded him. Rather, the notion of Sikhism *as a religion* was really established at the end of the nineteenth, beginning of the twentieth century, through a number of socio-economic and cultural changes associated with colonialism. In this sense, he presents it as part of a broader process of religious boundary construction, in which different traditions coalesced through similar processes in order to form the different religions that we now understand as 'the religions of South Asia'. In short, the Oberoi thesis suggests that this period saw the creation of religions in South Asia.

The thesis is problematic for a range of reasons. Perhaps most significantly, it seems to deny the antiquity of South Asian religious traditions, and prioritize (yet again) the agency of Western traditions, their ability to provide a kind of model or blueprint for the cultures of South Asia and other parts of the postcolonial world. This is a critique that we will examine in this chapter; but we should also look at the kind of evidence that Oberoi produces, and other evidence which may provide us with a perspective on this interesting and indeed critical area. In line with the pattern of the book so far, however, we should begin with an example, from which to work outwards to explore the various dimensions of the issue at hand. Here, we follow Oberoi (1990: 153) by focusing on an event he describes as a 'watershed in the history of modern Sikhism'.

Case study: the Anand Marriage Act, 1909

In 1909 the Imperial Legislative Council in Calcutta passed what was known as the Anand Marriage Act. A part of the Act is reproduced here:

THE ANAND MARRIAGE ACT, 1909
An Act to remove doubts as to the validity of the marriage ceremony common among the Sikhs called Anand.
Whereas it is expedient to remove any doubts as to the validity of the marriage ceremony common among the Sikhs called Anand;
It is hereby enacted as follows:
1. Short title and extent. –
(1) This Act may be called The Anand Marriage Act, 1909; and
(2) It extends to the whole of India
2. Validity of Anand Marriage. – All marriages, which may be or may have been duly solemnised according to the Sikh Marriage ceremony called Anand shall be and shall be deemed to have been with effect from the date of the solemnisation of each respectively, good and valid in law.
3. Exemption of certain marriages from Act. – Nothing in this Act shall apply to –
(a) Any marriage between persons not professing the Sikh religion, or
(b) Any marriage, which has been judicially declared to be null and void.
(Government of India 1909)

Task

What questions might reading this text generate? Discuss with a peer or jot down what the text does or does not tell you about Sikhism and marriage practices associated with this religion in the early twentieth century.

A reasonable question to ask in exploring this text is what it really can tell us about religion. What importance do legal texts, or, to be more precise, Legislative Acts, have for those of us who are interested in religious traditions? You might also have asked why this particular Act was passed at this point; why was it perceived to be necessary? The preamble to the Act speaks of 'doubts' that need to be removed in relation to this Sikh ceremony. What kind of doubts existed about this practice, and why was a law needed to dispel them? What exactly was the 'Sikh marriage ceremony called Anand',

and how did it relate to other forms of ceremony? Was it the only ceremony associated with Sikh marriage, or were there others? The reference to 'professing the Sikh religion' may also have invoked you to ask what it meant to 'profess' the Sikh religion at this time – or, perhaps more pertinently in the context of this book, was there anything different about 'professing the Sikh religion' during this time, or was it much the same as doing so at any other point in history?

Obviously, given what we have already said about Oberoi's thesis, there is a suggestion that 'being Sikh' was perhaps conceptualized differently at this time. To understand how this might be the case, we need to get a broader sense of the idea of 'being Sikh', and the evidence associated with the historical development of this idea. This, then, is one form of contextual data that will help us to understand the Anand Marriage Act. But to understand the precise timing of the Act, at the beginning of the twentieth century, we also need to explore a variety of contexts from this period. These include dynamics associated with Sikh identity, and also associated with religious identity more broadly during the period. The objective, then, is to provide several twists of the kaleidoscope in order to examine the Anand Marriage Act in different ways, and hence help us to answer some of the questions generated by reading this short historical text.

Sikh organizations in the late nineteenth century

As noted above, Oberoi cites the 1909 Act as 'a watershed in the history of modern Sikhism'. The passing of the Act in 1909 in fact was the result of a quite concerted political campaign, the success of which owed a great deal to the emergence and development of a series of Sikh organizations, known as Singh Sabhas. These organizations had spread across Punjab from the early 1870s, first being established in the major urban centres of Amritsar and Lahore. By the turn of the century there were more than 100 Sabhas across the northwest, and, although there was a great deal of differentiation and competition between these organizations, it was this basic network of organized Sikh identity that was to inform the campaign in support of the Anand Marriage Bill. Between October 1908 and September 1909, more than 300 meetings were held in support of the Bill, and some 700,000 Sikhs petitioned the colonial administration in order to persuade them to pass the Bill into law (Oberoi 1990: 153). These demonstrations of concerted action were supported by vigorous print campaigns in newspapers and journals associated with the Singh Sabha movement. In short, the Anand Marriage Bill agitation was a very modern form of protest and mobilization, in which recognizable civil society techniques were deployed to achieve a specific political objective. As this implies, the organizations behind the agitation were equally modern in their form, and well suited to this kind of deployment.

Oberoi argues that the emergence and growing public profile of these organizations was indicative of fundamental changes in the structure of Punjabi society in the second half of the nineteenth century. In particular, he points to the emergence of a new social elite during this period – 'a restless new elite who cut across kin ties, neighbourhood networks and even caste affiliations', ushered in by a combination of colonial patronage and what Oberoi (1990: 149) calls 'the lethal armies of advancing capitalism'. The processes that were intensified by these 'lethal armies' were similar to those in other areas of the empire: the commercialization of agriculture, increasing urbanization, the development of rapid communications technologies were all factors that had a profound impact on colonial societies. In Punjab the impact of these factors was intense. Agricultural land was particularly productive here, and became more so as a result of a network of irrigation canals built by the British.[1] The market in agricultural land became increasingly competitive in the late nineteenth century, with urban commercial classes profiting as small-scale farmers relinquished their holdings (Barrier 1966).

Allied with these processes were some very particular colonial patterns of social development, instigated by a developing British approach to Sikhs as a group. From early on in the colonial period in Punjab, Sikhs were identified as especially suitable recruits for the British Indian army. There were practical and historical reasons for this. The fact was that Punjab was close to a region of India where the British most anticipated deploying the army, that is, the North-West Frontier, where in the late nineteenth century there were real concerns about an invasion from Russia. As such, recruiting in Punjab was pragmatic and cheaper, as troops from this region would be paid at a local service rate if deployed in the northwest. Punjab had also largely remained loyal during the rebellion of 1857, when large parts of northern India had been engulfed by a violent uprising against British rule. This loyalty was valued greatly by army commanders. In addition to these reasons, however, it was generally recognized during the second half of the nineteenth century that Sikhs were a 'martial race'. Based on the burgeoning race science of the time, the British understood Sikhs, amongst others, to have a particular propensity for military valour and fighting skill.[2] As a result, Sikh communities were fostered through administrative policies such as the granting of valuable land in canal colonies (Ali 1994: 8–9). Interestingly, the army also engaged in the explicit promotion of what was perceived as normative Sikh identity. For example, Tony Ballantyne refers to the 1896 *Handbook on Sikhs for Regimental Officers*, written by recruiting officer R.W. Falcon (published in Allahabad). In the handbook Falcon identifies 'true Sikh tribes', noting of 'Singhs, the members of the Khalsa': 'These are the only Sikhs who are reckoned as true Sikhs . . . the best practical test of a true Sikh is to ascertain whether in calling himself a Sikh he wears uncut hair and abstains from smoking tobacco.' Falcon goes on to warn officers away from recruiting Sikhs whose identity was 'very diluted by Hinduism'

(Ballantyne 2006: 65). These clear ideas about what constituted proper Sikhism were reinforced by the insistence that Sikh recruits maintained their external symbols of Sikhism (the so-called five Ks) and accepted the authority of the army-appointed *granthi*s, or ritual readers and interpreters of the Sikh text. In this way, then, the difference of Sikhs was reinforced by social and economic practices associated with colonial rule. The social mobility and competition that these processes instigated informed the formation of groups such as the Singh Sabhas.

The approach of Falcon and the implication of a different form of Sikhism projected by the Singh Sabhas begs the question of what exactly changed in terms of Sikh practice and identity during this period. Falcon's reference to the 'true Sikhism' of the Khalsa suggests that there was a range of other approaches to the idea of Sikh-ness, a point that also reminds us of the 'doubts' about Sikh ritual referred to in the Anand Marriage Act. The Khalsa is a particular Sikh tradition, established by the tenth in the succession of Sikh Gurus, Guru Gobind Singh, at the turn of the eighteenth century. Gobind initiated the formation of this semi-military 'brotherhood' at a time of political instability in Punjab, marking membership through an initiatory 'baptism' ceremony and a commitment to maintain the five Ks. The most noticeable of these 'Ks' is of course *kesh*, the commitment to leave the hair uncut, a tradition that has led to the wearing of the turban and beard, perhaps the most visible sign of modern Sikhism. What is frequently overlooked, however, is that this tradition is one amongst many, most of which are not bound by these specific ritual elements. Thus there are Sikhs of, for example, the Udasi, Nirmala, Suthreshahi, Jitmali and Sahajdhari traditions. All these have, in one way or another, claimed to follow the teachings of the succession of Gurus that began with Guru Nanak in the sixteenth century. Most, however, have not necessarily been constrained by this allegiance, taking part in a constellation of ritual and devotional activities extant in the region. This entangled history leads Oberoi to claim that:

> the territories in which Sikhs lived, the languages they spoke, the agrarian festivals in which they participated, the ritual personnel they patronised and the symbolic universe of their rites of passage – all these were shared by numerous other communities in Punjab.
>
> (Oberoi 1994: 48)

This environment is what Oberoi (1994: 141), drawing on Max Weber, refers to in his book as the 'enchanted universe' of Punjabi popular religion. This 'universe' provides the context, for example, for Sikhs to be 'deeply involved in the worship of miracle saints' (p. 147), for the worship of Devi as 'an integral part of Sikh sacred practices' (p. 162) and for engagement with 'a wide variety of sacred resources and the intermediaries who managed them' (p. 201).

The activities of the Singh Sabhas were primarily geared towards marking out a particular notion of Sikhism in the context of this diversity. In particular, Khalsa Sikhism was increasingly identified as normative, as it represented a distinctive sense of religious identity in a manner that was, as we have seen, recognized and valued in the context of colonialism, and suitably reflected the aspirations of the emerging new elite. In particular, the emerging ethos of what was to become known as 'Tat' (true) Khalsa seemed to reflect the desire to fashion a religious identity that spoke of authenticity, universality and an unmediated relationship with God, free from the apparently obscurantist machinations of brahmin priests. This was to be an identity appropriate to the self-image of an elite that was educated, independent, urban and empowered by the new technologies of the colonial milieu (most immediately, of course, the printing press). In this sense, the ethos of Tat Khalsa was fashioned quite self-consciously against Hinduism, represented as the epitome of that obscurantist traditionalism.

It is no surprise that one of the most striking early articulations of Tat Khalsa thinking was a tract by the author and publicist, Bhai Khan Singh Nabha, called *Ham Hindu Nahin*, or 'We are not Hindus'.[3] In this text, Singh asserted the distinctiveness of Sikhism, its rootedness in the Guru Granth Sahib, the importance of the distinctive signs of Sikhism and the separation of Sikhism from Hindu forms of image worship. He also emphasized independence by asserting that Sikhs should not rely on brahmins and other traditional castes when undertaking life-cycle rituals, but should look instead to deploy distinctive Sikh rituals. This argument was supported by the steady production by a range of Tat Khalsa intellectuals of a series of *rahit nama*s, or codes of conduct related to ritual practices. Oberoi examines these in some depth, exploring the changes they invoked to specific lifecycle rituals. For example, death rituals were to be focused on the recitation of the Adi Granth and the maintenance of the five Ks, and ashes were not to be scattered on the holy river Ganga. The naming of a newborn child was to occur through consultation of a Granthi rather than a brahmin. Marriage rituals were also to be transformed. Traditionally in Punjab, the precise details of marriage ceremonies would be configured by caste and locality, but they would almost certainly include a consultation with a brahmin to determine an auspicious date, and on the day the recitation of Sanskrit mantras by a brahmin, and the circumambulation of a sacred fire. The ceremony advocated by the Tat Khalsa stipulated no astrological consultation, a simple recitation of verses from the Adi Granth during the ceremony and a circumambulation of a copy of the Granth rather than the fire. This ceremony was known as the Anand marriage ceremony, making reference to the Anand Sahib verses of the Granth, associated with the third Sikh Guru, Amar Das. This revised ceremony is of course the ceremony referred to in the Anand Marriage Act. Its acceptance by the imperial legislature was in effect a legitimation of the Tat Khalsa campaign to fashion a new form of normative Sikhism, a distinctive religious code emerging from the multiple traditions of nineteenth-century Punjab.

Constructing boundaries, counting communities, claiming rights

These radical developments in the perception of Sikhism during the late nineteenth and early twentieth centuries did not, of course, occur in a vacuum. They were part of a general trend towards what we are, with Oberoi, calling the construction of religious boundaries in late nineteenth-/early twentieth-century India. We have already touched on some of these changes. Chapters 7 and 8 have alluded to them in relation to Hinduism and Islam. In addition, Chapter 3 touched on the emergence of the Arya Samaj. This was a dynamic, activist movement amongst Hindus of a particular class, which seemed to echo the form of the Singh Sabhas in many ways, and was initially most successful in that very region where the Singh Sabhas flourished: Punjab. It is clear from the evidence presented above that the emergence of such movements was strongly related to broader social and economic processes affecting the Punjab region (and, we might add, much more widely across British India). Processes of change related to the emergence of new class identities, changes in agricultural production, and urbanization have been emphasized. In addition to these, the colonial encounter provides the context for some more specific changes related to government policy that have been identified by a range of scholars (for example, Dirks 2001; Cohn 1987; Zavos 2000) as important forces in the construction of religious boundaries. In this section we want to explore some of these changes.

A particularly dramatic innovation in this period was the decennial census. The colonial state experimented with taking censuses in different regions of its Indian territories during and before the 1860s, amalgamating these to produce the first complete census of colonial India in 1872. The decennial series based on a single enumeration exercise across the whole territory of British India was then established from 1881. The first census of British India collected only eight pieces of information (age, name, caste, religion, kind of dwelling, race or nationality, literacy and infirmities). Although it was to get more elaborate in later years, the key elements for our purposes were already in place: religion and caste. These categories of information may seem straightforward enough (although you may disagree if you have read the introduction, or Chapter 7A!), but it is notable that nothing like them was apparent in the census in Britain during this period (and indeed right up until 2001, when a voluntary question regarding religion was introduced[4]).

This difference is indicative of what some scholars have detected as a broader intent in the colonial census exercise. As we noted in Chapter 7A, the colonial state developed an ethnographic impulse (Dirks 2001), driven by a desire to construct a kind of scientific picture of cultural, social and economic relations in its territories. Part of this exercise was the production of the *Imperial Gazeteer* and the voluminous provincial *Gazeteer* series that detailed the topography and daily patterns of social life in districts across British India. Part of it also was the identification of certain groups (such as the Sikhs, as we have noted) as possessing particular characteristics. And part of it was the decennial census, which, amongst other things, sought to uncover the extent of and relationships between castes and religious communities. In the age of scientific advance and industrial technology, such information would, it was assumed, enable effective rule, and mediate the uncertainties of 'native society'. As Dirks says:

> numbers were elegant, discrete, comparable, meaningful within and across categories and units. . . . In India, numbers could be readily compared and analysed to suggest reasons for political unrest or disaffection, to demonstrate the 'moral and material progress' of India under political rule, to control crime and disorder by numerical demonstration.
>
> (Dirks 2001: 199)

Several authors have demonstrated the difficulties that arose in translating this desired enumeration of society into a representative reality. In particular, the difficulty of identifying and classifying religious and caste affiliations and relations has been documented. Complaints about the difficulty of identifying Hinduism in particular, and the puzzling answers of some who were assumed to be Hindu, are a regular feature of census reports well into the twentieth century. The comment of the Berar Census Superintendant in 1881, E.J. Kitts, is prescient:

> When the hill people were pressed for a reply as to what their religion was, sometimes after much parleying, they said either they were Hindoos, or that they knew nothing about religion; that they were *arani log*, ignorant people. All they knew was, they were Korkus by caste . . . . Nowhere, as far as I can discover, did a single individual assert that there was such a distinct and separate thing as a Korku religion; he merely answered to the effect 'I am a Korku, but I do not know what my religion is called. I worship Mahadeo, Hunuman, Byram-Bai, Chand, Suraj and the Bhagwant, who is the author of my religion, call it what you please'.
>
> (Report on the Census of India 1881, volume 1, quoted in Zavos 2000: 74)

Of course, not all interlocutors were as perplexing to the census superintendents as these hill tribes of central India. But the response is nevertheless revealing, as it indicates an epistemological gap between the expectations of the British and some of those they ruled when it came to the idea of religion.

What significance can we attribute to this gap in the context of the construction of religious boundaries? As the scholar Michael Hann comments (2005: 16) about the actual experience of the census for most Indians: 'after a 10 minute interlude, all would go back to their daily affairs, marking the onset of a ten year intermission.' 'Indeed,' he continues, 'compared with the big events of Indian colonial history, . . . the census ranks low in any list of confrontational colonial occurrences.' There are two particular ways, however, that the census can be said to have had an impact in a manner that is important to us. The first is objectification, as discussed by the anthropologist Bernard Cohn (1987: 224–54). Cohn is precisely interested in that ten-minute interchange, as it invokes reflection for those involved on 'who they were and what their social and cultural systems were' (p. 248). Asking the question 'What is your Religion?', for example, invokes a reflection upon the category as it is presented to you, and how you relate to it. The idea of 'Religion' in such an exchange is rendered as an object apart from the self. In a sense this is just the process indicated by the hill tribes of Berar above, even if they ultimately appear to be uninterested in the category. Cohn argues that the effect of objectification is cumulative and part of a broader set of situations in which social and cultural practices had to be explained (p. 230). Although his argument is more focused on caste than religion, these categories are of course related, and the same process of examination and questioning is apparent, as our example indicates.[5] In a sense, then, the census represents an important conduit through which that self-conscous notion of religion, noted as associated with different Muslim and Hindu movements in Chapter 8, becomes a feature of Indian social life.

The second point we should draw from the census is not so much to do with the actual act of census-taking; it is more to do with the census as a cultural product. The census as we know it exists as a set of statistics accompanied by commentaries on these statistics. The quotation above is taken from one of these commentaries, the Report on the Census of India 1881, volume 1. This information, statistics and narrative were of course published, and so became a feature of the colonial public sphere. Unsurprisingly, the census was published in English, so its accessibility was limited, but it was certainly open to those emerging professional classes active in establishing the Singh Sabhas. They were largely English educated, and so had access, not so much to the census reports themselves, but to comment and commentary inspired by interactions with these reports. Newspapers and tracts were to become key arenas for debates over the information and interpretations contained in the census. These debates were frequently inspired by the problems of categorization discussed in census reports, and in particular the issue of whether low castes and tribals should be classed as belonging to one or another religion (usually, of course, Hinduism; but discussion of the relationship between Sikhism and caste was also evident in census reports). These discussions invoked debate about just where the limits, or boundaries, lay between different religions.

In addition the census reports placed an obvious emphasis on comparative numbers. Objectified religions were measurable through the census in relation to one another. As the decennial series grew, this placed emphasis, for example, on the success of Christian missionary campaigns in particular regions, and on the comparative birth rates of different religious communities. A pamphlet produced by a prominent and radical Arya Samaji, Swami Shraddhananda, in 1926 demonstrates the point. Shraddhananda's pamphlet was entitled *Hindu Sangathan*: *Saviour of the Dying Race*, and in the preface he recounts an episode that inspired him to write on this subject:

> It was in February 1912, while standing in the spacious hall of the Arya Samaj in Calcutta, that a Bengali gentleman . . . Colonel U. Mukerji . . . was introduced to me. . . . Colonel Mukerji read out to me the following extract from 'Census of India report' for 1911, vol 1, page 122: 'In the whole population of India the proportion of Hindus to the total population has fallen in 30 years from 74 to 69 percent . . .'. Thus did Colonel Mukerji work out the problem: taking 5 per cent to be the actual proportion of the decline of Hindus within thirty years, their present number of 69 per cent will be swallowed up within $14 \times 30 = 420$ years, if no efforts were made to put a stop to the present decline.
>
> (Shraddhananda 1926: 14–15)

Here, then, we can see the impact of the census in certain public spheres of colonial India. Shradhananda's concern is for the very existence of 'the Hindus', and this concern was very much framed by the comparative development of other religious communities, increasingly seen as competitors in an emerging game of numbers and power.

Debates over numbers in the census, then, provide one very pertinent means of articulating what was becoming, during this period, an increasingly intense focus on the relationship between religions and the boundaries between them, a focus that we have seen emerging in the distinctive assertions of difference represented by the growth of Singh Sabhas. Another way in which these concerns articulated themselves was through what we might call the language of religious rights. In the wake of the rebellion of 1857, the Queen Empress Victoria had issued a Proclamation in which she famously pledged, amongst other things, a form of religious freedom. 'None', she pronounced, '[shall] be in any wise favoured, none molested and disquieted, by reason of their religious faith or observances, but . . . all shall enjoy the equal and impartial protection of the law' (Philips 1962: 11). This statement appears to have been designed primarily to defuse a perceived 'native volatility' around the issue of religion, which was understood to be the main reason for the 1857 rebellion.[6] However, in the late nineteenth century, it came to be used increasingly by middle-class Indians as what one Hindu organization in 1894 called a 'Charter of Religious Liberty',[7] a reference point for the assertion of community rights in the public spaces of colonial India. Nowhere was this more evident than in the rumbling agitations around cow protection.

Cow protection and religious boundaries

The cow is of course considered a sacred animal by many Hindus. This sacredness is multi-faceted, but key elements include the perception of cow products (especially milk) as pure, and therefore appropriate for use in a range of brahminical rituals, and the association in mythical stories with Krishna, the divine cowherd. It is clear from historical evidence that, despite these associations, cows have not always been considered sacred in ways that they are today (Jha 2002). Although there is plenty of evidence to demonstrate that some rulers in precolonial Indian states banned the slaughter of cows for a range of reasons (van der Veer 1994: 90–1), cow protection and inter-community tensions around them really emerge as a major feature of Indian society in the colonial period. In particular, the late nineteenth century sees the emergence of cow protection societies, or Gaurakshini Sabhas. As with other organizations emerging during this period (such as the Singh Sabhas), these were modern organizations run by mostly professional, middle-class individuals. Gaurakshini Sabhas were concerned partly to promote good husbandry techniques amongst the rural population, because, as one English language paper put it in 1889, 'our animals, as they appear, are wretched looking skeletons fit for shooting'.[8] At the same time, these organizations were committed to the protection of cows from slaughter, in particular by Muslim butchers, and especially ritual slaughter in relation to Muslim festivals such as *Bakr Id*.

The language of cow protection disputes that subsequently emerged during this time was the language of rights and religious liberty. On the one hand, the religious liberty of Hindu cow protection societies would be infringed by cow slaughter. On the other, the religious liberty of Muslims would be infringed by the prevention of such slaughter. Although such disagreements were most often expressed through petitions to local authorities to adjudicate on the issue of 'rights', the tensions that developed around these disputes did sometimes spill over into violence. These scenarios were, then, powerful arenas for the construction of religious boundaries, and for the iteration of community identities in relation to those boundaries, and it is no surprise that the technologies of the colonial public space were deployed to support these ideas. The printing press was of course key here.

Christopher Pinney (2004) has explored the role played by chromolithographic images in the development of colonial politics. The image shown in Figure 9.1 was produced in 1912 by the Ravi Varma Press, but it is similar to those produced in the 1890s, which are described by Pinney through primary sources from the period. Many of these images, he says, 'share the common feature of the presence of 84 gods within the body of the cow and a group of figures kneeling beneath the udders. One sees in these images the literal inscription of the sacred onto the body of the disputed sign' (Pinney 2004: 107–8). Going on to comment specifically on the Ravi Varma image, he explains that:

Figure 9.1 The Cow with 84 Deities. Ravi Varma Press 1912. Reproduced courtesy
of Christopher Pinney.

the figure with the drawn sword is clearly labelled . . . as a representative
of the *kaliyug*, presumably the demon *kali*. The caption above his head
reads *he manusyaho! Kaliyugi mansahari jivom ko dekho* ('mankind,
look at the meat eating souls of the *kaliyug*'), and the figure in yellow
(labelled as *dharmaraj*) beseeches him with the words *mat maro gay sarv
ka jivan hai* ('don't kill the cow, everyone is dependent on it').

(Pinney 2004: 107–8)[9]

Here then, we can see the way in which Hindu imagery is brought together
powerfully in the chromolithographic image of the cow to represent simultaneously the idea of Hinduism and the universal morality of cow protection.
These powerful images achieved greater impact because of other technologies present during this period. For example, the Viceroy in the early 1890s,
the Marquess of Lansdowne, commented in 1893 that increased tension over
cow protection was caused partly by 'the greater frequency of communication and the interchange of news by post and telegraph between different
parts of the country' (see Pinney 2004: 106). In this way, the community of
Hindus was imagined in ways that have a real collective resonance, reiterat-
ing the idea that religious boundaries between Hindus, Muslims, Sikhs were
social realities which bound communities together across the vast, multi-
dimensional social geographies of India.

Hindi, Urdu and religious boundaries

Cow protection was one of several ways in which such ideas of community were projected. A further example, briefly explored here, is provided by the so-called Hindi–Urdu controversy. This emerged particularly in United Provinces, what is today Uttar Pradesh and Bihar, during the second half of the nineteenth century, and became more broadly apparent in the twentieth century. The controversy focused on the relative status of Hindi and Urdu as languages.

Linguistically speaking, Hindi and Urdu are very closely related, part of a group of dialects and language registers spoken across northern India with a complex history. Part of this history involves the integration of Persian and Arabic elements, roughly consonant with the political history of the Delhi Sultanate and Mughal rule (i.e. from the thirteenth century onwards). By the nineteenth century English was also an influence on this language group. This entangled history has been characterized by the linguist and historian Christopher King as a spectrum:

> at one end of this spectrum comes English and at the other, local dialects. In between we have, first, the classical languages Sanskrit, Arabic and Persian; then, Urdu followed by Hindi; next, Hindustani (in the sense of a language style less Persianized than Urdu, and less Sanskritized than Hindi); and finally, the regional dialects such as Bhojpuri and Awadhi.
>
> (King 1989: 186)

Hindi and Urdu are largely distinguished by the use of a different script (Devanagari and Perso-Arabic respectively) and vocabularies that are influenced, at least in more literary forms, by Sanskrit and Persian/Arabic respectively.

In the late nineteenth century these differences were teased out in order to assert the two registers as entirely separate languages. In a move that will now be familiar to the reader of this chapter, this development was accompanied (if not produced) by the emergence of modern organizations designed to 'protect' the language, and accompanying petitions to authorities to ensure official recognition. In effect, these languages came to be seen as symbolic of Hindu and Muslim communities, in a similar manner to that noted around the use and protection of cows.

Religious boundaries and communalized religions

South Asia is a region of the world that has been marked by some fierce incidences of violence related to religious identities. Independence and partition in 1947 was, of course, a tragedy as much as a cause for celebration. As Sugata Bose and Ayesha Jalal (2004: 164) have very poignantly noted, 'the dawn of independence came littered with the severed limbs and blood-drenched bodies of innocent men, women and children.' Since this time, the subcontinent has periodically been the site of violent clashes between religious groups, and indeed the wars that have been fought between India and Pakistan have been suffused with religious ideologies intertwined with the political and economic forces underpinning their conduct.

Very often, these violent encounters are presented as a result of irrevocable differences between these religious groups, honed and reproduced over centuries. Behind such claims of sustained antipathy lies the phenomenon that has become known as 'communalism', a term which in the Indian context roughly refers to hostility between identified social groups (especially, but not exclusively, religious groups) on the basis that their interests and/or characteristics are antagonistic. There has been a good deal of debate about when and how communalism emerged in India, but Gyanendra Pandey's work has been useful in identifying what he calls the journey through which the term 'communal' became 'an adjective derived not from "community" but from "tension between the [religious] communities"' (Pandey 1990: 9). He locates this journey very much in the modern period (with the key transitions occurring in the 1920s), when Hindu–Muslim riots became an increasingly regular feature of Indian political life. Pandey notes that for many nationalist activists this trend was symptomatic of the residual power of reactionary forces in Indian society: 'feudal elements' collaborating with a colonial state bent on propagating a policy of divide and rule. As Jawaharlal Nehru, who was later to become the first prime minister of India, stated, 'Communal leaders represent a small upper class reactionary group . . . these people exploit and take advantage of the religious passions of the masses for their own ends' (cited in Pandey 1990: 241).

This kind of approach seems to deny agency to all but the smallest 'reactionary elements' within society, whilst the large majority of people are projected as simply acting on the basis of primordial religious passions. Looking at the evidence does not support this view. Work by historians such as Nandini Gooptu (2001) and William Gould (2004), for example, shows the vigorous action of manual workers in *bazaars*, artisans and transport and construction workers, as well as agents of the Congress itself, in the production of communal politics. These scenarios are frequently driven by local contexts in which the language of communalism becomes a useful tool to propagate particular positions of power. This is reminiscent of our analysis of cow protection in the 1890s; indeed, cow protection did emerge as a major element of communal antagonisms as they developed in the twentieth century. The language of religious identity and religious boundaries was a significant element of the cow protection debates. More generally it should be noted that the idea of communal conflict as a conflict between essentialized group identities is largely dependent on the existence of such categories. In this sense, the construction of religious boundaries we have examined through the Anand Marriage Act and other markers is an important prerequisite for the development of religiously based communalism as a feature of modern politics in India.

In fact, the example of Sikh identity with which we began is apposite, as, although it is communal conflict between Hindus and Muslims that has dominated understandings of this concept in modern South Asia, one of the most notorious instances of this phenomenon involved the Sikhs. This was the sequence of events set in train by the Indian Army's Operation Bluestar in 1984 (Figure 9.2 references these events).[10] During the course of this operation, the Golden Temple in Amritsar was desecrated, and many innocent Sikh pilgrims were killed, caught in the crossfire between the Army and the armed followers of Jarnail Singh Bhindranwale, who had taken refuge in the temple precinct. This event had a deep impact on Sikhs around the world, and some months later the Prime Minister Indira Gandhi was assassinated by her Sikh bodyguards. In the days after the assassination, the capital of India, New Delhi, was the site of a terrible slaughter of Sikhs. For four days in early November Sikhs were targeted, some say systematically and with the collaboration of state institutions, by armed groups who burned their houses and businesses and killed what official estimates put at nearly 3,000 people. During these days, the idea of a distinctive community of Sikhs, argued for so strongly by the Singh Sabhas of the late nineteenth century, and by Khan Singh Nabha in his pamphlet *Ham Hindu Nahin*, became an explosive idea.

Of course, these horrific scenes are not the only ways in which distinctive religious identities have manifested themselves in modern South Asia. The phenomenon of communalism, however, does demonstrate that social processes associated with the construction of religious boundaries can have the most deadly effects, and that alternative histories which put these processes in context may be useful correctives in understanding the continued development of religious traditions in South Asia.

The religion twist: Sikhism/Nanak Panth

One way of approaching this challenge of producing 'alternative histories' is to consider the idea of Sikhism as a religion. Of course, in one sense this question seems rather absurd. Sikhs across the world have a strong consciousness of religious faith, and to question the status of this consciousness as 'religious' may just appear to be an extension of that persecution which was revealed so brutally in 1984. Applying a critical approach to the idea of religion, however, may help us to unpack this as a valuable area of reflection. We began this chapter with an examination of the Anand Marriage Act, which prompted us to ask questions about what it meant to 'profess the Sikh religion'. An examination of vigorous organizational dynamics in the late nineteenth century enabled us to see that there were indeed some quite dramatic changes to 'professing the Sikh religion' advocated by some socially powerful Sikhs during this period. The success of these Sikhs led, in fact, to the Anand Marriage Act and the consequent legal recognition of

Figure 9.2 Nineteen Eighty Four, a painting by London-born artists, The Singh Twins. Reproduced with permission of The Singh Twins (http://www.singhtwins. co.uk).

Sikh identity as distinctly religious. This distinctive identity, which equates a particular reading of Khalsa practice with Sikhism, appeared to marginalize a whole range of associated traditions that Oberoi (1994: 92) brings under the umbrella term 'Sanatan Sikh'. Interestingly, Ballantyne (2006: 66) notes that, despite what he calls 'the productivity of Singh Sabha pens and presses and the devoted efforts of the reformers to regularize religious practice in the villages of Punjab', nevertheless 'long-established cultural patterns were not immediately displaced nor were heterodox identities entirely erased.' This revealed itself in marriage ceremonies, for example, where 'Brahman(s) continued to officiate' long after the passing of the Anand Marriage Act (Ballantyne 2006: 66). As much as we have argued that it acted as a force in the construction of religious identities, the census also reveals that diverse identities continued to thrive, with Ballantyne (2006: 67) noting that the 1901 census included more than 130 different designations that it categorized as 'Sikh'.

The diversity that such evidence uncovers demands attention from the scholar of religion. In particular, a twist of our kaleidoscope may enable us to see the relationship between Sikh traditions and religion differently. One twist in Chapter 6 has already encouraged us to view the Sikh lineage in the context of teacher–pupil traditions. Here, we want to deploy one of Roger Ballard's alternative methods for understanding Punjabi religion (see introduction), *panth*. *Panth* is most easily translated as 'path', and in the Punjabi context it is particularly interesting because of what is known as the 'Sant' or Saint tradition. This tradition was mentioned in Chapter 2 and again in Chapter 6 as referring to groups of devotional poet philosophers operating across the Hindi-speaking areas of north India,[11] roughly between the fifteenth and the eighteenth centuries. Drawing on a range of *bhakti* devotional and Nath yogi traditions, these inspirational figures are distinctive for their devotion to a single God who was conceived without attributes. This approach is known as *nirguna bhakti*, contrasted to devotional traditions that are focused on a specific divine figure such as Krishna or Shiva, known as *saguna bhakti*. The tensions implicit in the idea of devotion to an attributeless God, which were pointed up in Chapter 2, are an indication of the inward-looking, contemplative trajectory of this tradition. It is also distinctive because of the strong representation of low-caste and untouchable figures who were to become leaders of the tradition. Guru Ravidas, for example, was a Chamar, a leatherworker perceived as untouchable; Kabir, as indicated in Chapter 2, was a weaver, another low-caste occupation, and he may well have been a Muslim. The lack of regard for the trappings of caste identity was consonant with the inward focus of the tradition, the search for god in the inner self.

Although he was not of a low caste, Guru Nanak (1469–1539) is very much a part of this tradition. He famously eschewed caste and spoke of equality before God. His approach to the divine was *nirguna*, as he criticized the idea of image worship, and advocated meditation on the name of god. He preached through poetry/songs that his followers sang together (*kirtan*). W.H. McLeod (1987: 230) describes the path taken by Nanak:

> following some years of itinerant preaching, (Nanak) eventually settled in Kartarpur . . . . This village evidently became the focus of attention

and devotion, earned by the appeal of his teachings and by the sanctity of his own life-style. The master thus attracted disciples. Nanak became Baba Nanak and those who were thus attracted to him became his disciples or *sikhs*. The Nanak Panth was born.

Over time, this *panth* was increasingly institutionalized. A succession of gurus provided guidance to the followers of the *panth*, and various specific acts associated with these gurus may be identified as contributing to the particular processes of institutionalization associated with the Nanak Panth. The third guru Amar Das was significant in that he provided some systematic structure to the Panth through the appointment of territorial deputies or *masand*s. The fifth guru Arjan Dev is credited with compiling the Adi Granth. As we have seen in Chapter 3, this was to become the key text of the Panth, and the acknowledged guru after the demise of the tenth and last living guru, Gobind Singh. The Adi Granth is interesting for the range of verses it contains. Nanak is of course the chief contributor, but, as well as the verses of the succeeding gurus, the Adi Granth contains the verses of other *sant*s such as Kabir and Ravidas, as well as Muslims such as Mardana (see Chapter 6). Gobind Singh, as we have seen, was a distinctive contributor to the institutionalization of the Panth through the creation of the Khalsa.

Such aspects as these, then, have certainly led to the emergence of the tradition as strong and distinctive, but the diversity of contributors to the Adi Granth serves also to reiterate that the Panth is embedded in the broader traditions of the region. Emphasizing its identity as the Nanak Panth, rather than Sikh-ism, the religion, provides an opportunity to recognize this important embedded quality, enabling us to understand the entangled history of this tradition, and its multiple relationships with other ideas and practices developed in the region. This example may help us to see that, rather than distinct religious systems, this idea of a kind of interconnected web of traditions may sometimes provide a useful alternative metaphor for the social realities of Indian life.

Conclusion

In this chapter, then, we have seen how the social dynamics of the late nineteenth-/early twentieth-century period have contributed to the distinctive emergence of religious identities in modern South Asia. It is useful to trace the activities of specific organizations and the movements associated with them in order to see how such identity notions were explicitly articulated, and how significant it was to fashion this articulation through difference. Religion develops as a modern concept defined through difference. A lot of the activities of the organizations we have examined here were strongly focused on elaborating boundary markers that emphasized this sense of difference. Cows, languages, marriage rites. All these were vital 'lines in the sand' that dramatically exemplified the difference between one group and another. Communalism emerged in the twentieth century as a kind of hyper-extension of such exemplifications, variously producing, amplifying and providing a language for speaking about the dynamics of power between different groups within society. Our examination of the Nanak Panth demonstrates how different perspectives (and different languages) can help to put these historical processes in context.

Questions for further discussion and research

- To what extent was the Anand Marriage Act 'a watershed in the history of modern Sikhism'?
- Is it correct to attribute the 'construction of religious boundaries' to the 'encounter with the West'?
- Discuss the impact of the 'construction of religious boundaries' on South Asian religious traditions. What limitations do you see in this impact?
- 'Nanak Panth'/'Sikhism'. Which term do you see as more appropriate for describing the traditions associated with Guru Nanak and the lineage of Gurus that followed him?

Further reading

Hann, M. (2005) 'Numbers in nirvana: how the 1872–1921 Indian censuses helped operationalize "Hinduism"', *Religion* 35 (1): 13–30.
> A focused discussion of the impact of the census on understandings of Hinduism.

McLeod, W.H. (1987) 'The development of the Sikh panth', in K. Schomer and W.H. McLeod (eds) *The Sants: Studies in a Devotional Tradition of India*, Delhi: Motilal Banasidass.
> Exploration of the idea of the Sikh *panth* by an authoritative scholar.

Oberoi, Harjot (1990) 'From ritual to counter ritual: rethinking the Hindu–Sikh question, 1884–1915', in J. O'Connell, W. Oxtoby and M. Israel (eds) *Sikh History and Religion in the Twentieth Century*, Toronto: University of Toronto Press.
> A succinct explanation of Oberoi's core arguments.

Oberoi, Harjot (1994) *Construction of Religious Boundaries*, New Delhi: Oxford University Press.
> In-depth exploration of changes in Sikh traditions before and during what the author identifies as the critical period of development, the late nineteenth century.

Pandey, G. (1992) *Construction of Communalism in Colonial North India*, New Delhi: Oxford University Press.

>   Discussion of the development of communal consciousness. Chapters 1 and 7 discuss the term and its establishment as a feature of political discourse. Chapter 5 discusses cow protection.

10 Public and private space

When we think about 'religion', the ideas of public and private space may not spring immediately to mind. The notion of space seems rather, well, empty. When you compare it with some of the key concepts we looked at in Part I of this book, such as deity, text and myth, it does not seem to carry a specifically religious value. If you have got this far, you will have realized that our intention in this book is to challenge some of the accepted ways of thinking about religion and how religious traditions operate in the context of South Asia; this chapter is no different. Our initial contention is that thinking about public and private space is a useful way of approaching religion – precisely because these are not explicitly 'religious' concepts! As with teacher–pupil traditions examined in Chapter 6, public and private space can help us to see beyond the dominating constraints of the World Religions model, which influences so many analytical concepts deployed when thinking about religious traditions. In this chapter, then, we will be exploring a number of different examples of how public and private space is conceptualized as religious, and drawing comparisons in ways that challenge the association of particular ways of thinking about such space with discrete religious traditions.

As this chapter sits in Part II of the book, it is also very much about historical processes and the development of modern ways of thinking about South Asian religious traditions. We will demonstrate that changing notions of public and private space have been deeply influential in these processes. If in the last chapter we looked at the ways in which boundaries were constructed between different religious traditions, in this chapter we want to demonstrate how negotiations of public/private space have exemplified and reinforced these boundaries in ways that have been fundamental to our comprehension of South Asian religious traditions. In Chapter 11, we will be looking at these issues in a contemporary context; in this chapter, however, we want to start off by remaining in that critical late nineteenth-/early twentieth-century period, when South Asian societies were experiencing rapid and dramatic change. As we shall see, social change was often reflected in the ways that public and private space was imagined. We use this word 'imagined' advisedly, as public and private space is not concrete and immutable, but fluid and negotiated; it is imagined *as* public or private in accordance with a range of social and political pressures. It also happens to be a useful word at this particular point, as our initial case study is formulated very much in the world of the imagination.

Case study: Sultana's dream

One evening I was lounging in an easy chair in my bedroom and thinking lazily of the condition of Indian womanhood. I am not sure whether I dozed off or not . . .

All of a sudden a lady stood before me . . . I took her for my friend, Sister Sara . . .

I used to have my walks with Sister Sara, when we were at Darjeeling. Many a time did we walk hand in hand and talk lightheartedly in the botanical gardens there. I fancied Sister Sara had probably come to take me to some such garden, and I readily accepted her offer and went out with her.

When walking I found to my surprise that it was a fine morning. The town was fully awake and the streets alive with bustling crowds. I was feeling shy, thinking I was walking in the street in broad daylight, but there was not a single man visible . . .

[Sister Sara] felt my fingers tremble . . . as we were walking hand in hand.

'What is the matter, dear?' she said affectionately.

'I feel somewhat awkward,' I said, in a rather apologising tone, 'as being a purdahnashin woman I am not accustomed to walking about unveiled.'

'You need not be afraid of coming across a man here. This is Ladyland, free from sin and harm. Virtue herself reigns here.' . . .

I became very curious to know where the men were. I met more than a hundred women while walking there, but not a single man.

'Where are the men?' I asked her.

'In their proper places, where they ought to be.'

'Pray let me know what you mean by "their proper places."'

'Oh, I see my mistake, you cannot know our customs, as you were never here before. We shut our men indoors.'

'Just as we are kept in the zenana?'

'Exactly so.'

'How funny.' I burst into a laugh. Sister Sara laughed too.

'But, dear Sultana, how unfair it is to shut in the harmless women and let loose the men [. . .] You do not think it wise to keep sane people inside an asylum and let loose the insane?'

'Of course not!' said I, laughing lightly.

'As a matter of fact, in your country this very thing is done! Men, who do or at least are capable of doing no end of mischief, are let loose and the innocent women shut up in the zenana! How can you trust those untrained men out of doors?'

'We have no hand or voice in the management of our social affairs. In India man is lord and master. He has taken to himself all powers and privileges and shut up the women in the zenana.'

'Why do you allow yourselves to be shut up?'

'Because it cannot be helped as they are stronger than women.'

'A lion is stronger than a man, but it does not enable him to dominate the human race. You have neglected the duty you owe to yourselves, and you have lost your natural rights by shutting your eyes to your own interests.'

'But my dear Sister Sara, if we do everything by ourselves, what will the men do?'

'They should not do anything, excuse me; they are fit for nothing. Only catch them and put them into the zenana.'

'But would it be very easy to catch and put them inside the four walls?' said I. 'And even if this were done, would all their business – political and commercial – also go with them into the zenana?'

Sister Sara made no reply. Perhaps she thought it was useless to argue with one who was no better than a frog in a well . . .

(Rokeya Sakhawat Hossain 1905, *Sultana's Dream*, see Jahan 1988: 7–10)

Explaining terms

purdahnashin – one who observes *purdah*. There were many different degrees of strictness. In Bengal, where this piece was written, women who were kept in strict seclusion, rarely leaving the house, were known as *abarodhbasini*

zenana – the women's quarters, into which the men of the house were generally not allowed to enter

Task

Before you continue reading, jot down all the contrasts you can find in this piece between public and private space in (1) the world the storyteller normally inhabits and (2) the world of her dream walk with Sister Sara. What questions would you ask to help you understand this piece more?

The author of this piece is a woman called Rokeya Sakhawat Hossain. You will probably have realized that she writes tongue in cheek and with rather scathing irony. The men in her depiction are portrayed with exactly the same characteristics and weaknesses as women were thought to have in her experience. They are in *purdah* (see Box 10.1), to be confined to the private space of the *mardana*, men's quarters, to keep them out of harm's way, and are to be deprived of their power in public spaces – whether this be in the physical space of the town and its business, the space of exercising physical strength and therefore authority over women, or the space of political and commercial activity. By contrast, as the *Dream* goes on to show, in Ladyland women run the country peacefully and efficiently, properly educated under the auspices of the Queen and turning scientific inventions to both domestic and public benefit.

By now, you will be familiar with raising questions such as: Who was the author and what was the context of this piece? Who was she writing for and in what language? You might also want to ask: How was her own life affected by *purdah*, and prevailing attitudes to public and private space? Was there any difference between this fantasy and other things she wrote? Were understandings of the public and private changing in her period in South Asia? And if so, what factors affected these changes? Were they economic? Political? To do with religious identity? To do with social status?

To help us answer these questions, and then to broaden the discussion to the ways in which religion is related to public and private spaces in other South Asian contexts, we turn first to our author's context.

Rokeya Sakhawat Hossain – challenging the bounds of seclusion

Rokeya Sakhawat Hossain is pictured in Figure 10.1 in the dress of a woman maintaining modesty in the public sphere. However, when a journal editor

---

Box 10.1 What is *purdah*?

The term comes from a Persian word, '*parda*', meaning 'curtain'. It initially referred to the hanging separating the women's quarters in a house from men's. Its meaning now covers a whole range of different ways of separating off female from male space, of ensuring that women do not come into contact with inappropriate men. These ways may be spatial, physical, behavioural and/or attitudinal: withdrawing into the women's quarters, veiling, keeping eyes downcast, behaving in a modest way and so on (Khan 1999). *Purdah* practices thus include, but are not restricted to, forms of dress.

asked to print such a photo of her, Rokeya refused. The author of the feisty *Sultana's Dream* was afraid that publication of such a photo in the public domain would damage the cause of women's education. Her experience of *purdah* may give you a clue as to why.

When Rokeya wrote of *purdah*, she wrote from personal experience and a particular social context. She was born in 1880 in Pairaband, a small village in district Rangpur (now in northern Bangladesh). Her father was the *zamindar*, the local landholder. Rokeya thus grew up in a very well-off Bengali-speaking *ashraf* family that observed strict seclusion for its women. Girls in families like hers were confined to the *zenana*, the women's quarters, from an early age. Although the family encouraged education, including sending at least one of her brothers to England, for the girls this was limited to learning the Qur'an in Arabic by rote. So Rokeya gained her own education through a younger brother who was tutored at home, learning to read Bengali and some English secretly with him. At the

Figure 10.1 Rokeya Sakhawat Hossain (1880–1932). Reproduced from Jahan (1988) with permission of the Feminist Press at CUNY.

time of the publication of *Sultana's Dream* (1905), she was living with her Urdu-speaking husband in Bhagalpur, modern Bihar, which like Calcutta and Rangpur was then part of the Bengal Presidency under British imperial rule. Her husband strongly supported her desire for education and it was with his encouragement that she wrote *Sultana's Dream*, first in English, later translating it into Bengali. That she chose to write in English probably indicates that her first audience was intended to be the British and Western-educated elites, including those Muslim reformers who advocated a 'modern' education for men but were often keen to limit the curriculum for girls. We will return to this below.

In 1909, after her husband's death, Rokeya set up a girls' school in memory of him, near where they lived in Bhagalpur. However, she faced great local opposition and so moved the Sakhawat Memorial Girls' School to Calcutta in 1911. Although she faced great tensions there as well, the school flourished, is still in existence and was key in the training not only of future Muslim women teachers but also of some of the most influential women in public life in Bengal, including the writer and feminist activist Shamsunnahar Mahmud and the Urdu novelist Mohammadi Begum. She was thus a woman who moved out of the private space of strict seclusion into the public realm, not only in founding the school but also in setting up the first Bengal branch of the Anjuman-i-Khawatim Islam (All-India Muslim Ladies' Conference) in 1916. Through this she worked with Muslim women from less prestigious backgrounds than her own to raise their aspirations for education and by providing 'uplift' for the poor (Hossain 1992: 9, 18). She was not, however, a lone figure in all this. Sultan Jahan Begum, the third generation of female rulers of the Princely State of Bhopal, spoke to convince Indian Muslims of the need for girls' education, helped establish elite schools for girls in Bhopal and also patronized educational institutions for girl children of the poor (Lambert-Hurley 2007: 74).

Another piece Rokeya wrote shows clearly the tightrope she and others had to walk when they campaigned for women's education and involvement in the public sphere. It comes from a series of accounts she kept of the worst excesses of *purdah* she came across. The accounts were serialized in the Bengali monthly, *Mohammadi*, in 1929 and later published as the first book in Bengali by a Bengali Muslim woman in 1931, entitled *Abarodhbasini* (*The Secluded Ones*). Incidents include doctors required to make diagnoses of female patients from behind a blanket without touching them, a women killed by a train because she refused a helping male hand, and Account 47 about the *purdah* bus for Rokeya's own school:

> Only three years ago, we had our school bus. The day before the bus came, one of our teachers, an English woman, had gone to the auto depot to inspect the bus. Her comment was, 'This bus is horribly dark inside. Oh, no! I'll never ride that bus!' When the bus arrived, it was found that there was a narrow lattice on top of the back door and the

front door. Excepting these two pieces of latticework, three inches wide and eighteen inches long, the bus could be called completely 'airtight'!

(Jahan 1988: 34)

Various adaptations were made to improve its comfort but still ensure that the girl students who were conveyed in this vehicle to Rokeya's school were kept in proper *purdah*, invisible to men in the street, private despite their excursion into public space. But while the (mainly Muslim) parents complained about the intolerable conditions this caused for the girls, other (male) 'well-wishers' wrote to Rokeya, one in English, others in Urdu, the languages of the upcoming Muslim male elites in Bengal, who tended to scorn the Bengali language as common and fit only for women:

> For the continuing welfare of my school they were informing me that the two curtains hanging by the side of the bus moved in the breeze and made the bus purdahless. If something better was not arranged by tomorrow, they would be compelled, for the benefit of the school, to write in the various Urdu newspapers about this purdahlessness and would stop the girls from riding in such a purdahless bus.
>
> (Jahan 1988: 35)

The English letter was signed 'Brother-in-Islam'. Although Rokeya herself in *Sultana's Dream* speaks of the condition of 'Indian womanhood', not Muslim women in particular, the letter writer makes keeping *purdah* a matter of religion, with a barely veiled threat that the school will suffer if Rokeya does not comply with the strict interpretation of Qur'anic injunctions that he and his fellows think necessary. These male Muslim writers act as guardians of public space and religious virtue in the name of their community. The boundaries of the public and the private are clearly drawn. At the same time, however, they are being contested. Rokeya cautiously negotiates the operation of her school on the one hand, and subversively challenges the constraints of *purdah* in the realm of the imagination.

But is this contestation an 'internal' debate about the status of women 'within' Islam? Let us consider some evidence from a slightly earlier period that challenges this perception:

> And you, what lords you are, naturally so bold, courageous, strong, learned . . . . But just because you happen to be strong, does that make it right? You label women with all sorts of insulting names, calling them utterly feeble, stupid, bold, thoughtless . . . You shut them up endlessly in the prison of the home, while you go about building up your own importance, becoming Mr, Sir and so on . . . . Starting from your childhood you collect all rights in your own hands and womankind you just push in a dark corner far from the real world, shut up in purdah, frightened, sat on, dominated as if she was a female slave . . . . Learning

isn't for women, nor can they come and go as they please. Even if a woman is allowed to go outside, the women she meets are ignorant like her, they're all just the same. So how's she ever going to get any greater understanding or intelligence?

(Tarabai Shinde, see O'Hanlon 1994: 87–8)

This is an extract from Tarabai Shinde's *Stree-purusha-tulana* ('On a Comparison between Women and Men'), published in 1882. Her accusations are very similar to Rokeya's, but the author was not a Muslim. Tarabai came from a well-off Maratha (agriculturalist) family in western India. She referred to herself as having been 'kept locked up and confined in the proper old Maratha manner' (Tarabai Shinde, Introduction, in O'Hanlon 1994: 77). She addressed men with sarcasm every bit as bitter as Rokeya's.

As you can see, both women link the practices of seclusion with exclusion from proper education.[1] Both attribute this to men's attempts to keep powers and privileges in their own hands. Both clearly link the practice of seclusion to notions of status and social respectability in their aspiring communities. It is therefore a matter, in their eyes, of gender, community status and social class rather than religion as such. Neither foregrounds religion, although both recognize religious texts are used as sources of authority that men will draw on to justify their own advantages. Tarabai, for example, makes derisive references to the way in which Krishna, *Ramayana* and *Mahabharata* stories, and the gods themselves, enforce the role of *pativrata* (devoted wife, see Chapter 4) to just do whatever a husband tells her to. 'O congratulations, all you gods! And three cheers for pativrata!' she writes (Tarabai Shinde, in O'Hanlon 1994: 79f, 84 and throughout).[2] We will return to this area of texts as justification for *purdah* later in this chapter. Here, however, it is worth noting one critical point about these debates about the relationship between women and their access to public space. They are all occurring very much in a particular, and particularly new, *kind* of public space; that is, they are all in one way or another in print. The development of print culture and the proliferation of journals from the second half of the nineteenth century was a vital way of empowering women, enabling them to gain access to debates in the public sphere. At the same time, the public discussion of these issues in a sense brings the figure of the secluded woman, the epitome, as it were, of the private, into the public space as well! Not so much the actual women, of course (for those like Rokeya were to some extent no longer secluded), but the *purdahnashin* as a kind of sign. This is particularly so for the kind of men referred to by Rokeya and Tarabai, for whom the ideal of the secluded woman becomes a crucial symbol of different types of (publically significant) identity. In a curious kind of way, then, the private becomes a feature of the public, as new forms of public space are opened up in the context of colonial control.

This complex idea needs a little more explanation. In the following section, we will explore the contexts within which the tensions apparent between the positions of Rokeya, Tarabai and their opponents played out, and how they relate to critical social and political developments during this period.

The home and the world

The title of this section is drawn from a famous novel by the Bengali litterateur and Nobel Laureate Rabindranath Tagore (1861–1941). Written in 1916, the novel weaves a complex story of love and politics, nationalism and religion in early twentieth-century Bengal (Tagore 2005[3]), the very time and place in which Rokeya Hossain was also writing. As the title suggests, these themes are viewed through an exploration of the divisions between private and public space. This is by no means a clear division; much of the complexity of the plot revolves around the ever-shifting nature of these divides, as they are interpreted at different levels: the private space of the home and the public space of the world outside, of course, but also the family and others, the rural homestead and the cosmopolitan city, the familiarity of local traditions and the attractions of westernized modernity, the nation and the colonizer – but also, conversely, the 'home' of deeply held religious beliefs and the dangerous world of political activism. There is also the division between women and men, as the plot revolves around the home of the Hindu heroine, Bimila, and the world of her husband, Nikhil, and his friend and radical nationalist, Sandip. This radical worldliness inspires transgression, as Sandip enters into the private world of Bimila, drawing her out into the public world of nationalism. The novel is a fascinating exploration of politics and social transformation in this exciting period of Indian history. It is also an engaging text for understanding the nuances involved in the operation of Orientalism as a facet of colonial power (see Chapter 8). At this juncture, it is primarily interesting because of these interwoven and sometimes contradictory dynamics of homeliness and worldliness, private and public. Tagore unveils, so to speak, the ways in which rapid social and economic changes were manifesting themselves as new uncertainties in the boundaries between private and public.

This is a process that had been developing over many decades during the nineteenth century, attributable to a range of factors, many of which we have commented on in Chapters 7–9. The development of codified law practices; the emergence of new social classes defined by professional or bureaucratic engagement and new forms of education; increased mobility of people (both geographical and social); economic integration both within India and more broadly across the empire (a form of 'globalization'); infrastructural developments such as the railways and telegraph; and, as we have already suggested in this chapter, the development of print culture – these were all influential factors in the opening up of new public spaces during this period. Many of these spaces were heavily constrained by limitations of class, as well as the vigorous surveillance practices of the colonial state. At the same time, they provided the space for a range of unpredictable developments in social life.

As an example of how this relates to religion specifically, let us consider briefly an example from an earlier period: the newspaper *Samachar Chandrika*, first published in 1820s Bengal. Editorials, articles and correspondence in the paper have been analysed by the historian Brian Pennington (2005). He emphasizes that the *Chandrika* presented itself as traditionalist, set up to protect religious ideas and practices from 'the corrosive effects of a pervasive reformism – both western and indigenous' (p. 140). Don't forget that this was the age of Rammohun Roy (see Chapter 2), when many new ideas about how to conceptualize Hinduism as a religion were being discussed, and comparisons were being made between what were perceived as the characteristic aspects of different religions in public fora such as the press. Significantly, Pennington demonstrates how the *Chandrika's* traditionalism translated not as straightforward conservative resistance or rejection of colonial modernity. On the contrary, the *Chandrika* was driven by 'an urgency to shape a modern, popular Hinduism through emergent discourses promoting a centralization of authority and a common, socially cohesive Hindu identity' (Pennington 2005: 149). This cohesive identity was achieved by remaining strategically 'silent on issues of doctrine and deity', whilst focusing on 'patterning a general structure for Hindu action, social and ritual' (p. 140). Already in the 1820s, then, we can see ways in which notions of corporate 'Hindu action' were being discussed and debated in the new public arena of the press, not just by modernists such as Rammohun, but by self-proclaimed traditionalists who seemed, paradoxically, to be equally concerned about the 'modern'. Just as we noticed the emergence of the private in the public above, we can see here the emergence of the traditional within the modern.

This is a point that is developed by the historian Partha Chatterjee (1993), who has written extensively on the emerging resistance to colonial rule in India, expressed of course in terms of nationalism. The figure of Sandip in *The Home and the World* exemplifies the idea of a modern, radical nationalist, committed to active political mobilization and violent resistance against the colonial oppressor. At the same time, however, his approach relies on a fiery religious rhetoric, and he is drawn increasingly to the figure of Bimila through an entangled combination of sexual and political desire, the latter based on her identification as a personification of the land, the object of nationalist aspiration. Tagore's characterization exemplifies Chatterjee's argument that the growth of nationalist consciousness in colonized India is complex, shot through with contradictory patterns in terms of the relationship between the public and the private. Although he does not explicitly use Tagore's terms, Chatterjee develops a similarly critical distinction in emerging nineteenth-century nationalist consciousness between the home and the world, the inside and the outside. He argues that the home was equated with the spiritual, the world with the material. The material world of scientific and economic development was the realm of the British colonial power, where mastery had to be conceded. By contrast, the home was the place where the spiritual superiority of India could be preserved and nourished.

The material world was the one in which men functioned in competition for employment and financial success, while the 'spiritual world' of the home was the domestic sphere over which women had the primary influence. The former involved compromise with the colonial powers; the latter, it was contended, should not. In developing nationalist positions in the realm of contested public political discourse, the home, and women within it, therefore became crucial. They came to represent various ideals of Indianness, and, increasingly, the identity of particular religious groups and the ability of their members to function as proper citizens within the public sphere.

This developing pattern of consciousness meant that colonial interventions in the 'spiritual' or 'inner' world were fiercely debated. Interventions occurred most frequently through legislation. Throughout the nineteenth century, the British had passed laws affecting women and the family: the Abolition of Sati in Bengal Act (1829), the Hindu Widow Remarriage Act (1858) and the Age of Consent Act (1891) are examples. It is easy to read this simply as 'white men saving brown women from brown men', as Gayatri Spivak (1988: 296) acidly puts it – that is, a justification for the civilizing hand of the colonial power – but there are many complexities, trivialities[4] and counter-productive effects deriving from such legislation, which have been explored in a number of historical accounts (see, for example, Kumar 1993; Nair 1996; Mani 1998. For a clear summary, see Forbes 1996: ch. 1).

The rhetoric over the need to improve the treatment of women ensured that 'the Women's Question' became central to the way in which different groups and individuals defined, differentiated and aligned themselves politically in relation to the colonial power. Crudely, the British identified the problems as follows: for Muslims, the institution of *purdah*, for Hindus, *sati*, child marriage and the prevention of widow remarriage.[5] The evidence presented in this chapter demonstrates that it was not so straightforward. Tarabai Shinde, for example, may have disagreed with the identification of *purdah* as a Muslim problem. Nevertheless legislation, as we saw in Chapter 9, was an influential force. The Acts above relate directly to the specifically Hindu side of the stereotype,[6] and key Hindu higher class (usually male) actors supported, pressed for and criticized this legislation amongst much else. They of course made their various cases in the growing public realm and in relation to idealized constructions of the family. To do this, they used the burgeoning print culture of the press, pamphlets, homiletics and moral handbooks, as well as face-to-face public debates. The private space and affairs of the family, it seems, had become a very public matter.

Correct moral conduct in the 'public–private' sphere

As well as the pressure of legislation, other factors were influential in this process of bringing the private, and women as a sign of the private, into public environments. The historian Faisal Devji (1994) has carefully traced the historical development of the idea of *adab*, or correct moral conduct, in relation to *ashrafi* Muslim identity. Under the pre-British Mughal states, he argues, this was the responsibility of elite men operating in public spaces such as the marketplace and the court, in the courtly language of Persian. Women were largely onlookers, from the less constrained and more vernacular space of the household. Devji argues that, with the onset of British rule, the public realm functioning in the elite language of Persian was no longer the preserve of male Muslim leaders (until the 1830s, the key administrative language of British rule was still Persian), so a radical shift in the location of authority and *adab* had to take place. Increasingly, the home came to be seen as the place where *adab* was still under the control of Muslims themselves. It became incumbent upon women, as bearers and first teachers of children, to be those who embodied and transmitted correct moral conduct, for the well-being not only of the family but also of an imagined Muslim community, an idea that, as we have seen, began to emerge in the second half of the nineteenth century (Chapters 8 and 9). Because of this critical link to the idea of the Muslim community, those who now represented *adab* in the private space of the home had to be projected as such in the changing and growing public realm. So their demeanour and behaviour there had to be policed, as Rokeya and her contemporaries found. Public respectability linked with religious identity (especially for women) became an increasingly political issue.

A contemporary of Rokeya's, the Deobandi writer Maulana Ashraf 'Ali Thanawi (1864–1943), tried to shape the behaviour of (male and female) Muslims in both private and public through his famous and still influential handbook, the *Bihishti Zewar* ('The Heavenly Ornaments') (see Metcalf 1990). This book appears to portray a very restrictive life for (upper-class) Muslim women. To stem 'the ruination of the religion of the women of Hindustan' (Thanawi, First Book I, see Metcalf 1990: 47) and to stop it from passing on to their children and husbands, Thanawi regarded it as vital that relatively privileged and respectable believing women be literate in sufficient Qur'anic Arabic, and Urdu. This would enable them to pass on an educated way of life to their families, yet within what Thanawi saw as the proper bounds of *shariah*-based seclusion. His handbook was extremely influential at the time, as the spread of public print culture made cheap versions easily available to women and men within the domestic sphere.

If we move further on into the twentieth century, we can see how the matter of *purdah* became increasingly a matter of public control in new political contexts. The writings of Syed Abul Al'a Maududi (1903–79) were particularly influential. Maududi was the founder and first president of the Jamaat-i-Islami, an influential religio-political organization, even today, in India and Pakistan and further afield amongst Muslims. Maududi's (1987) *Purdah and the Status of Women in Islam* was originally published in 1939. Quoting *Qur'an* 24:27, Maududi stressed the prohibition on a male entering a house without alerting the female members, after the latter had attained the age of puberty and active sexual feelings. Although he emphasized that 'the object is to differentiate the house from the outside world, so that men and women may live in peace inside their own homes and protected from the gaze of other people' (he quotes a *hadith* included by both Muslim and Al-Bukhari on Muhammad's response when people tried to peep), the control of sexuality is clearly his first concern (Maududi 1987: ch. 12, p.8). In particular, he wanted to place the sexual modesty required in Islam in stark contrast to the permissive sexuality of the West, comparable to that in pre-Islamic Arabia in his view. Speaking to a wider audience than Thanawi, he acknowledged that there might be reasons why women need to move outside the home – for example in order to go to work for those who cannot afford otherwise – yet he clearly favoured their remaining in a separate sphere where possible. Here, then, the emulation of the values of the well off resurface in a different way as the lines between public and private became redrawn yet again. The idea of *purdah* as *adab,* which had become a critical form of moral conduct for all Muslim women, was increasingly institutionalized. This meant that the critiques of commentators such as Tarabai and Rokeya, of *purdah* as a practice related to the economic and social power of men (of whatever religion), were increasingly marginalized, despite the possibilities provided by the radical opening up of public space from the late nineteenth century onwards. The ramifications of processes such as these for religious identities are apparent across the globe today.

The religion twist: purdah, Islam and the public sphere

Take a moment to analyse the cartoon we have reproduced in Figure 10.2. How might the preceding examination of public and private space help you understand the meanings of this cartoon?

It is a commonplace in the Western media, particularly prevalent since 9/11: the conflicted image of the veiled Muslim woman, oppressed yet threatening. You might have reflected that what seems at first glance to be a matter of domestic arrangement, private choice and religious identity has become an intensely public issue. The woman in the cartoon has become iconic in multi-layered and contested ways: a faceless person who is a threat to society; a person under suspicion in an Islamophobic age; a person of faith identifying herself as such; a woman conforming to dress standards expected of a proper Muslim; a woman oppressed, unable to wear what she likes; a person arousing antipathy in a society in which her 'community' is not the norm. The list is endless. She is not a private individual. She is a figure who bears the meanings of others in the public domain.

In the preceding sections, we have seen in the context of South Asia (*purdah*, of course, is not just a South Asian practice) how these meanings have developed through complex histories. *Purdah* has come to be seen there as a key feature of Muslim religiosity. And yet we have seen from the evidence of Tarabai Shinde that such a straightforward correlation is problematic. *Purdah* seems to have been, in the not too distant past at least,

Figure 10.2 Cartoon by Peter Brookes (from *The Times*, 17 October 2006). Reproduced with permission of NI Syndication Ltd.

a practice also associated with certain Hindu social groups. The evidence of Rokeya Hossain and Ashraf Ali Thanawi also indicates that such practices even amongst Muslims were confined to particular social groups. Such evidence gives rise to the question: How far is this practice of seclusion a religious practice?

One way of answering this is to explore religious texts to see how far such practices are sanctioned. We have already noted how Maududi made reference to the Qur'an in his work. There are several relevant passages:

Qur'an 7:26
'O children of Adam, We have provided you with clothing and finery *to cover your private parts*. But the attire of piety is the best.' Such are Allah's signs, that they may take heed.
Qur'an 24:30–1
Tell the believers to cast down their eyes and guard their private parts. That is purer for them. Allah is conversant with what they do.

And tell the believing women *to cast down their eyes and guard their private parts* and not show their finery, except the outward part of it. And let them drape their bosoms with their veils and not show their finery except to their husbands, their brothers, the sons of their brothers, the sons of their sisters, their women, their maid-servants, the men-followers who have no sexual desire, or infants who have no knowledge of women's sexual parts yet.

Qur'an 33:53
If you ask them [the wives of the Prophet] for an object, ask them *from behind a curtain*. That is purer for your hearts and theirs.
(All quotations from *The Qur'an: A Modern English Version*, translated by Majid Fakhry, 1997, emphases added)

These verses, interpreted in the light of further traditions from the *ahadith*, have been widely taken to enjoin both full covering of women, and women's separation from men. Others, however, point out that these verses do not advocate the kind of covering that a full *burqah* with *nikab* provides, allowing only the woman's eyes to be visible in public. Nor do they have to be read as supporting rigid seclusion of a particular kind. We shall return to this below. What does seem to be clear from *Qur'an* 24:30–1 is that these verses do advocate (sexual) modesty, for both men and women; they do specify in whose presence a woman does not need to cover herself (however understood) or keep eye contact from; and importantly, they do link this kind of modest behaviour with 'believing', the appropriate behaviour of a Muslim, a person who submits to God. It would then seem reasonable to read *purdah* as a matter of religion. In interpreting these verses, the issues have been held to turn on what constitutes male and female 'private parts', and what it means that men should approach women 'from behind a curtain'. In addition, the issue of who has the authority to interpret such verses and the principles on which valid interpretations should be based cannot be ignored. Taking verses in isolation is highly problematic from many points of view, while the right of the individual, untrained in the mass of Islamic jurisprudence, to interpret the Qur'an directly has been regarded as deeply suspect. We have already seen such issues arising with Sayyid Ahmad Khan's stress on *ijtihad* (Chapter 8).

In her book, *The Veil and the Male Elite*, the Moroccan Muslim feminist, Fatima Mernissi (1991), seeks to address this critically from a Muslim perspective. She has studied much of the voluminous Hadith literature, taking into account its own discussions of what constitutes a legitimate *isnad*, or chain of transmission. She points out that to take a Qur'anic verse in isolation disregards the context of its revelation (and the passage in which it appears) and so abrogates a fundamental principle of Islamic interpretation. *Qur'an* 33:53 should then, she argues, be understood as a prescription for the rather specific circumstance of Muhammad having withdrawn from a long evening's entertainment at his wedding to Zaynab, when the last straggling guests refused to take the hint and go home. Finally, the last three went. Then the Prophet let fall the curtain mentioned between himself and his Companion, Anas, so at last he could be with his bride in privacy (Mernissi 1991: 84–7). Far, then, from prescribing universal seclusion of women from men, the passage, she argues, is recommending sensitivity and decorous behaviour in regard to others' needs. In a similar vein, 7:26, from the Qur'anic version of the Garden of Eden story, is not so much about dress code, as about the recommendation of 'piety' or 'right behaviour', although what this constitutes, particularly in terms of the public and private, is of course itself not straightforward. As we saw above, the idea of right conduct (*adab*) in South Asia was transformed quite radically over the course of the nineteenth century. Understanding this transformation is dependent on historical context: the shifts in relations of power in colonial India, and the development of new types of public space. In a sense, this point is a reiteration of a key point we have made throughout this book: the meaning of a text (or event, or idea) is constructed in dialogue with context. Mernissi might agree that, without context, it is difficult to gain perspective on the resonance of particular textual passages.

However, even if the interpretation of these Qur'anic verses is contested, the link with Islam appears clear. Indeed, many Hindus, particularly those who sympathize with a Hindu nationalist understanding of Indianness (see Chapter 11), hold the view that veiling and seclusion practices were the result of the Islamic conquest of India[7] and are an Islamic accretion that should be rejected. On such a reading, Tarabai as a Marathi *brahmin* woman, confined to the private space of the home, was simply suffering from the legacy of this, and her reference to 'age-old' customs might be seen as supporting this view. Against such a reading, it has been argued that in the *Arthashastra*, a brahminical text of possibly the fourth century BCE, and no later than 150CE (well before the arrival of Islam in India), the seclusion of high-class women is already mentioned (Basham 1985: 179).[8] The relevant passages in the *Arthashastra* appear to give instructions for the construction and running of the royal harem. The context is of protecting the king from intrigues that may occur in this private space of women, a space which therefore has the potential to damage security in the public realm. So the public/private issue is certainly there, but it does not seem to be a matter of religious identity as such, but of correct practice in a particular situation. This, then, appears to be similar to Mernissi's argument about the context of relevant passages in the Qur'an. In any case, we saw that Tarabai, who makes no anti-Muslim point, appears to find plenty of other support from Hindu epic and other texts for the construction of the *pativrata*, the devoted wife who accepts the private boundaries placed upon her. Her polemic is directed towards men in her own community who deploy such texts in order to keep women secluded and marginalized.

On this evidence, then, our conclusion would be that *purdah* is not a practice one can associate with one particular religion unilaterally. This is not to deny that *purdah has become* intimately related to Islam in the modern era, as indicated in the cartoon at the beginning of this section. But this is a process of history, in which notions of private and public space – and the role of women in marking these – are deeply implicated. The cartoon just as surely demonstrates that the correlation between *purdah* and Islam is understood very differently by different groups of people (the woman in *purdah* acts as a sign, layered with meanings related to the idea of Islam in the modern world). In such circumstances, one might be forgiven for wondering what the woman herself might be thinking about all this. In this context it is worth noting that many women decide themselves to take the veil in one way or another. This decision is often taken with a full understanding of the symbolic nature of this act, the way it is read differently by different groups of people. Consider, for example, this British woman of South Asian heritage talking about her decision to take the veil as she left home to attend a UK university:

> wearing the veil makes me feel special, it's a kind of badge of identity and a sign that my religion is important to me. Some of my friends . . . had the impression that my father or family had a kind of rule that forced girls to dress like this at a certain age. But it was my decision and my choice.
>
> (cited in Watson 1994: 148; see also Tarlo 2007, 2010)

The veil, then, can be an important marker of religious identity, and this marker is intimately bound up with notions of public and private space. We hope to have shown in this chapter that understanding shifts in the division between public and private can help us to think carefully and analytically about the dynamics of religious identity in their complex social contexts.

We want to introduce one last piece of evidence before leaving this topic. Consider the image in Figure 10.3. This image shows construction workers on the site of the Commonwealth Games 2010, which was taking place in Delhi, India, as we wrote. You will note, of course, that both men and women are present in this public space. Men and women work alongside one another, the women out of *purdah*, men working and walking by as a matter of course. We do not, of course, know the religious identity of these women (and men), but we may nevertheless be certain that these are working-class and poor women, paid very little and living in difficult conditions (Jha 2010). For these women, the key issue in the public space is likely to be earning the money that will keep them and their families alive. In this sense we may again make the point that *purdah*, very frequently, is a class-bound activity. It is worth emphasizing that Tarabai and Rokeya came from and addressed well-off brahmin and Sayyid families respectively. Rokeya, despite all her other awareness, and her later work with the Anjuman-i-Khawatim Islam to help poorer women, seems blind in her accounts of *purdah* to the many low-class servant women who crossed *purdah* boundaries all the time, invisible in her analysis of 'women'.[9] We can go further, in fact, and say that public spaces themselves are also (and not just) class bound. The public and the private are concepts that are experienced differently by different groups of people. In this sense you may reflect on public and private space as multiple, a complex web of related, overlapping and dynamic spaces through which

Figure 10.3 Stadium construction. Credit: Daniel Berehulak/Getty Images.

Conclusion

In this chapter, we started with an apparently simple differentiation between public and private space. As we have progressed, however, we have argued three things from the example of *purdah*, which initially seemed only to do with domestic, individual and private choices. First, that there were massive shifts in definitions of 'private' space in the nineteenth century, as the (initially high status) home became associated with the site of religion in complex ways. Because of these, the home and *purdah* were made to bear public significance in terms of developing community identities. There was a shift in who were perceived to be the upholders of public morals. Second, the whole emergence of a public political sphere was linked to a burgeoning print culture and the development of particular religious and educational institutions, ensuring a penetration of the private realm with issues hotly contested in terms of public debate and legislation, and an ability from that private realm to express views in the public domain. Third, these processes were and are inflected by factors of social class, contested interpretations of authoritative texts, sect, region and so forth, indicating that the boundaries between public and private, as between religions, are not fixed but are continually being renegotiated, as is the authority to carry out such negotiations.

Questions for further discussion and research

- What is *purdah* and how does it relate to South Asian societies?
- Why and how does thinking about private and public space help us to understand the development of South Asian religious traditions?
- Was Rokeya Hossain/Tarabai Shinde a feminist?
- To what extent is *purdah* a religious practice (both in South Asia and more generally)?

Further reading

Chatterjee, P (1993) *The Nation and Its Fragments: Colonial and Postcolonial Histories*, Princeton: Princeton University Press.
> Chapters 1–3 explore the development of public space in the late nineteenth-/early twentieth-century period.

Freitag, S. (2005) 'Contesting in public: colonial legacies and contemporary communalism', in D. Ludden (ed.) *Making India Hindu: Religion, Community and the Politics of Democracy in India*, 2nd edn, New Delhi: Oxford University Press.
> The first part of this article discusses the dynamics of public and private space in the colonial era. It then goes on to discuss cow protection and Ayodhya, providing links to Chapters 9 and 11.

O'Hanlon, R. (tr. and intro.) (1994) *A Comparison between Women and Men: Tarabai Shinde and the Critique of Gender Relations in Colonial India*, Delhi: Oxford University Press.
> A lively translation of this sharp-tongued piece with an excellent historical introduction.

Sarkar, M. (2008) *Visible Histories, Disappearing Women: Producing Muslim Womanhood in Late Colonial Bengal*, Durham, NC: Duke University Press.
> An important argument about the way Muslims of similar social status were excluded from the Hindu Bengali *bhadralok* with the implications that this had for women. Challenges the view that Muslim women were 'behind' Hindus because they were more oppressed or backward.

Tagore, R. (2005) *The Home and the World*, London: Penguin.
> A stimulating novel that explores the complex development of private and public space in colonial society.

11 Conflicting paradigms

In this chapter, we continue to contemplate the importance of space in the construction of modern South Asian religion. Our focus shifts, however, from the turn of the century period to consider how religious space 'becomes public' in contemporary contexts. In making this shift in time, we need to develop a point made right at the end of the previous chapter: that notions of the public have developed rapidly over this period. The channels through which debates over religious space – and images and sounds associated with such space – are communicated have expanded and otherwise developed immeasurably since the days of Rokeya Hossain and Taribai Shinde, even if we have presented the work of these two as entering into very modern public spaces themselves. The case study of the TV *Ramayan* in Chapter 4 also gives us some idea of the impact of new forms of media on the representation of religious traditions. We might even say that these forms of media construct new public spaces. This is an idea that has been taken up by the influential social theorist Arjun Appadurai (1996), who uses the concept 'mediascape' to speak about the influence of forms of media on globalized imaginings of the contemporary world, particularly in relation to connections across diaspora communities. The potential implications here for the imagining of religious space are dramatic, and indeed some authors have worked with Appadurai's 'scape' notion to produce the idea of 'religioscapes' (McAlister 2005) as religious maps formulated subjectively in global terms, through different contexts of media and mediation. The TV *Ramayan* is a good example of this, as it demonstrates the power of such new public spaces to shape broad perceptions of mythic texts (like the Ramayana) into representations 'of religion', in this case 'of Hinduism'. As we move through this chapter we will deploy this idea of a religioscape as we look at how particular religious spaces have been imagined in global terms.

Our analytical focus also shifts in this chapter, returning to our overall theme of how to conceptualize religious traditions in modern South Asia. We want to work outwards from the case study to consider what we will term 'conflicting paradigms'; that is, different and competing models for understanding religion, in the context of specific religious spaces. In the first part of this book we have seen how South Asian religious traditions consistently challenge established ways of thinking about religion – issues such as ritual, myth and even notions of the divine do not seem to conform to a clear, orderly pattern configured by discrete systems of belief and practice. In the second part of the book, we have examined ways in which ideas about such discrete systems have begun to provide a template (or paradigm), a way of organizing religious traditions in South Asia that has become increasingly influential. This of course is the dominant mode of understanding religion in the modern world, but it is one that much of our evidence suggests has only partial relevance to understandings of South Asian religious traditions. In this chapter we are going to consider different ways of looking at contemporary religious phenomena, and ask directly if one or another is more valid. That this is a significant exercise in terms of contemporary politics and social relations in the region is amply demonstrated by our case study.

Case study: Ayodhya, a north Indian pilgrimage town

Ayodhya is a town in Uttar Pradesh (UP), very close to the city of Faizabad. It is well known as a pilgrimage town, as it has a plethora of Hindu temples as well as other religious sites. You might also know the name from the Ram-katha, as Ram's kingdom in that story is known by that name. Ayodhya is the realm from which Ram is banished, and to which he returns in triumph, after the defeat of Lord Ravana and the rescuing of Sita. It is important to recognize, of course, that there is what might be termed a generic difference between Ram's Ayodhya and the town of Ayodhya in UP. Ram's kingdom exists in the multi-layered, mythic world of the Ram-katha. The Ayodhya in UP is a town that has developed over several centuries; it was previously known as Saketa, before assuming the name Ayodhya by the seventh century CE. It has significance as a site of Buddhist and Jain pilgrimage, as well as being marked as an important Hindu pilgrimage town from the eighteenth century (van der Veer 1989: 37). Ayodhya is recognized as a *tirtha*; that is, a place that acts as a contact or crossing (literally, a ford) between the divine and the human worlds, often associated with a sacred river (in this case, the Sarayu).

Because of its link with Ram's kingdom, there are several sites in the town that are associated with the epic tale. In particular, various sites have claimed the status of the place of Ram's birth, including one on which a mosque has existed since the sixteenth century. During the late nineteenth- and twentieth-century period, and especially since the 1980s, this site has become a flashpoint for communal tension between Hindus and Muslims. In 1992 the mosque, known as the Babri Masjid, was destroyed by a large group of Hindus, allegedly with the assistance or tacit agreement of certain state forces. This was a major event in modern Indian politics. In the wake of the destruction of the mosque, many thousands of people were killed in riots that took place in towns and cities across north and western India. The stated objective of those who destroyed the mosque was to build a temple to

Lord Ram on this site. As we write in 2010 this has still not been achieved, and the matter is still the subject of legal dispute.[1]

This rather long introduction provides some background to our case study material, which consists of two short vignettes set in Ayodhya, the north Indian pilgrimage town.

A: A report by the BBC journalist Mark Tully

On 6 December 1992, I was standing on the roof of a building with a clear view of the Babri Masjid in Ayodhya. A vast crowd, perhaps 150,000 strong, had gathered and was listening to speeches given by BJP and right-wing Vishwa Hindu Parishad (VHP) leaders. Trouble first broke out in the space below us when young men wearing bright yellow headbands managed to break through the barriers.

The police stood by and watched, while some men wearing saffron headbands and appointed by the organizers to control the crowd did try to stop them. They soon gave up, however, and joined the intruders in beating up television journalists, smashing their cameras and trampling on their tape recorders. Encouraged by this, thousands charged towards the outer cordon of police protecting the mosque. Very quickly, this cordon collapsed and I saw young men clambering along the branches

Figure 11.1 Ayodhya, 6 December 1992: *kar sevak*s on top of the Babri Masjid. Credit: Douglas E. Curran/AFP/Getty Images.

of trees, dropping over the final barricade, and rushing towards the mosque.

The last police retreated from the mosque, their riot shields lifted to avoid being hit by stones the crowd was throwing at them, and two young men scrambled on top of the mosque's central dome and started hacking away at the mortar.

(Tully 1992)

B: *A report by Indian journalist T.K. Rajalakshmi on Sufi shrines in Ayodhya, which appeared in the Indian news magazine* Frontline *in 2003*

The Dargah of Sayyed Mohammad Ibrahim, named after a seventeenth century figure, was fiercely protected by the local people, including several Hindus, when its dome was attacked in December 1992. Sayyed Mohammad Ibrahim is believed to have been born during the reign of the Mughal emperor Shah Jehan and ruled a small principality. Influenced by Sufi teachings, he renounced his worldly pursuits. According to

Figure 11.2 The Dargah of Sayyed Mohammed Ibrahim Shah. Reproduced courtesy of Vidya Bhushan Rawat.

local legend, he arrived in a boat, pictures of which are depicted on his shrine. A large number of Hindu *halwai*s, or confectioners, from the Hanumangarhi area visit the shrine every Tuesday and make offerings and distribute *prasad*.

(Rajalakshmi 2003)

Task

Examine the two vignettes and jot down or discuss what questions they pose to us about religion in Ayodhya.

These two scenarios obviously depict very different views of religious life in Ayodhya. You may have been prompted to ask which is more representative. Does vignette A represent an approach to religion that has been influenced much more by outside pressures, whereas B reflects a longer, internal tradition of religiosity? You may also have asked whether scenario A reflects Hinduism, and B Islam. Considering this issue, you may have noted that scenario B includes reference to Hindu involvement with the shrine, even if it is nominally Islamic as the shrine of a Sufi saint. This includes protecting the shrine during the dark days of 1992 when the Babri Masjid was being destroyed. Such evidence points us away from the stark and simplistic qualitative division implied by a Hindu/Muslim dichotomy between these vignettes.

One question you might have raised is what scenario A has to do with religion at all. Many commentators have indicated that the dispute over the Babri Masjid is really the work of politicians, and its objectives more to do with enabling certain political forces to gain power than with religious conviction. Certainly this is a view that is expressed by some local people as recorded in Rajalakshmi's article. It is also a common view of communal conflict in general: that it is largely caused by power-hungry elites who are able to manipulate the emotions of the general public as and when they need to (see also Chapter 9 on this). In order to test such statements, we really need to understand the context within which the specific actions described in vignette A came about. We will do this below. As with the idea that one reflects Hinduism and the other Islam, we need to be careful here of the conceptual binary that lies behind this marking out of religion and politics as two separate spheres. As we have seen in Chapter 10, the way in which religion enters the public sphere is frequently contested, subject to the play of a range of discourses. The idea that shrine worship is a kind of 'traditional', or quietist, activity, as implied by this binary, is also something that has been challenged in Chapter 6. We will see a reiteration of this idea in some of the instances we look at in this chapter. At the same time, we need to ask whether these two scenarios do indeed represent two different paradigms of modern South Asian religion: the one configured by practices based on relationships between gurus and their followers, and on spiritual pathways associated with divine forces; the other configured by religious systems marked out as discrete and even conflicting in terms of belief and practice. As we explore Ayodhya and other sites in more depth, we will see how far such paradigms can help or hinder our understanding of the realities of South Asian religious traditions.

Babri Masjid/Ram Janmabhoomi

As indicated above, several sites in the town of Ayodhya have claimed to be the birthplace (*janmabhoomi*) of Lord Ram, the hero of the Ram-katha. The site we are concerned with, of course, is distinctive, in that it had been occupied by a mosque since 1528. This mosque was established by Mir Baqi, a general of the Mughal emperor Babar, in the wake of the pacification of the region, then known as Awadh. It is alleged by Ram Janmabhoomi supporters that Mir Baqi destroyed a temple in order to build the mosque, and one dimension of the dispute has subsequently been detailed argumentation over archaeology, as the veracity of this claim has been explored and tested (Mandal 1993; ASI 2003).

For many, the destruction of a temple and building of a mosque is perceived as symbolic of a wider idea: that the period of Mughal rule was accompanied by the mass destruction of Hindu temples as a means of oppressing and exerting power over the 'indigenous' population. This view is indicative of a particular paradigm of religiosity at work: one that perceives Hinduism and Islam as two different religious systems, associated with separate communities who act in relation to one another on the basis of that difference (for examples from press reports that place this confrontation in a broader, global perspective, see Ludden 2005: 2–4). As we noted above, this kind of essential binary is suspect when exploring the messy pathways of human history and social relations. Certainly, the idea that the Mughal dynasty was responsible for this kind of systematic action is highly debatable. Richard Eaton (2000, 2004), the distinguished historian of the medieval period in northern India, has demonstrated that temple destruction, where it did occur, was most often the result of particular political circumstances associated with conquest and patterns of patronage. For the most part, he says, 'temples lying within Indo-Muslim sovereign domains . . . were left unmolested' (Eaton 2000: 127). The historian Peter van der Veer concurs, noting that 'there seems to be nothing definite to say about the attitude of Muslim rulers and officials in the Mughal period towards Hindu institutions' (1987: 287). In addition, the representation of medieval Hindus as 'indigenous' and Muslims as 'outsiders' is also highly dubious, as by far the largest number of Muslims across India were people who converted to Islam or otherwise assumed a Muslim identity over time (on conversion, see also Eaton 2000); only a very small minority of the ruling Mughal elite could trace their ancestry to the Persian origins of this dynasty. On the projection of Indian Muslims as outsiders, Eaton refers to a much earlier eminent historian, Mohammad Habib, who comments rather wryly and with some feeling:

> the peaceful Indian Mussalman, descended beyond doubt from Hindu ancestors, was dressed up in the garb of a foreign barbarian, as a breaker of temples, and an eater of beef, and declared to be a military colonist in the land where he had lived for about thirty or forty centuries.
>
> (Eaton 2000: 95)

Important though it is, however, in one sense this historical work is beside the point, as the Babri Masjid has, in a manner similar to that noted about the veil in Chapter 10, assumed larger, symbolic meanings in different public contexts. A key force in the development of this process has been the so-called Sangh Parivar, or 'family of organizations'. This network, led by the Rashtriya Swayamsevak Sangh (RSS), or National Volunteer Force, is the principal exponent of Hindu nationalism, the form of militant Hindu identity we have referred to at various points in this book. For the Hindu nationalists of the Sangh Parivar, the existence of the Babri Masjid was symbolic of the dishonouring of the Hindu nation. As the female Hindu nationalist politician Sadhvi Rithambara noted in a speech in 1991, 'the Ram temple is our honour. It is our self-esteem. It is the image of Hindu unity' (quoted in Kakar 1996: 221).

The *kar sevak*s (volunteer activists) mentioned by Tully as the protagonists in the destruction of the mosque in 1992 were mostly members or supporters of this network. The two organizations mentioned, the Bharatiya Janata Party (BJP) and the Vishwa Hindu Parishad (VHP), are key institutions in the network. In the decade prior to the mosque's destruction, these organizations were highly instrumental in bringing the issue to a national stage, particularly through a series of processions that sought to locate the Ram Janmabhoomi site at the heart of a sacred Hindu geography (Jaffrelot 2004: 212). Other campaigns looked to mobilize Hindus worldwide, through, for example, the provision of blessed bricks to be used in the building of a magnificent new temple (Davis 2005) (Figure 11.3).

As we noted in Chapter 4, it has also been argued by some commentators that Ramanand Sagar's screening of the Ramayan on national television during the late 1980s was influential in popularizing the Sangh's campaign. Overall, this panoply of strategies has been flagged by the Religious Studies scholar John Stratton Hawley (2006: 259) as signifying the development of 'a sleek new Hinduism that could circumvent, cut through, repackage and obscure the old', in which the figure of Ram is situated at the heart of a glorified, assertive Hindu identity.

Figure 11.3 Bricks imprinted with the name of Ram, to be used in the building of the temple. Credit: DIPTENDU DUTTA/AFP/Getty Images.

Constructing history

Although Hawley has marked this out as something new, we should remember that the dispute at the Babri Masjid does have a history. During the nineteenth and twentieth centuries the site became a focus for tensions in the locality, which sometimes developed into full-blown dispute. A key moment occurred in 1855. Ayodhya was at this time under the control of the Nawabs of Awadh, a succession of rulers who had replaced the Mughals as the dominant regime of the region in the eighteenth century. Peter van der Veer (1987: 288) argues that it is during the period of Nawabi rule that Ayodhya flourished as a pilgrimage town. By 1855, however, real power lay with the dominant force in the subcontinent, the British, and Awadh was to be annexed in 1856 to become part of the British empire. In these last, unstable days of Nawabi rule, a dispute developed at another major religious site in Ayodhya, the Hanumangarhi temple complex. Some familiar themes emerged. A group of Sunni Muslims under the leadership of one Ghulam Hussain claimed that a mosque had earlier been present at this site, and that it should now be re-established. This dispute spilled over to include the Babri Masjid site, where violence between followers of Hussain and Ramanandi *naga* ascetics resulted in the death of about seventy Muslims. Subsequent unrest threatened to develop across Awadh, but a potential retaliatory assault under the leadership of Maulvi Amir-ud-din was quelled by British troops. Soon afterwards, Awadh was annexed by the British, with the events in Ayodhya seeming to indicate the Nawab's loss of control of the region.

Some writers have suggested that the focus on the Babri Masjid site in this early dispute is misplaced – it was a dispute about Hanumangarhi, with the role played by the Babri site being inconsequential, only to become more central in subsequent years as an act of retaliation (Panikkar 1990). Whatever was the case, by 1859 the colonial authorities had constructed a railing at the Babri Masjid site, with the perceived objective of bringing some order by dividing Hindu from Muslim worship. This strategy provided a kind of spatial re-ordering of religious practice at a site where, as the then-commissioner P. Carnegie observed, 'up to that time the Hindus and Mahomedans alike used to worship in the mosque-temple' (quoted in van der Veer 1992b: 98). Note here that Carnegie refers to the site as a 'mosque-temple', evoking a sense of cross-tradition worship that is reminiscent of the Dargah of Sayyed Mohammad Ibrahim. Of course, the key point of installing the railing was to attempt to prevent further disorder in the wake of 1855, but behind this motivation we may detect a deeper assumption: that the idea of a 'mosque-temple' is itself threatening, as it cuts through an understanding of Hindu and Muslim practice as discrete and separate. In this sense, we might see the installation of the railing as an attempt also to install a different paradigm of religiosity in Ayodhya, one that fitted more clearly with established British understandings of what religions are. You may see this as a little fanciful (after all, it was only a railing!), but a key theme of Part II of this book has been to consider how the 'encounter with the West' in the modern era (from the nineteenth century onwards) has instigated some quite radical changes to the ways in which religions are perceived and organized. If, then, in Chapter 9 we focused on the construction of religious boundaries, the railing in Ayodhya is a kind of physical manifestation of this process.

One of the arguments we put forward in Chapter 9 was that these boundary-constructing processes were related to the development of antagonism and the notion of communalism in South Asia. Notwithstanding the apparent motivation behind the installation of the railing to diffuse tension at the Babri Masjid site, we can see that here also the 'construction of religious boundaries' appears to have encouraged some measure of antagonism and separation. Even though Ayodhya was by no means a communal hotspot in the late nineteenth and early twentieth centuries, it did suffer major riots related to cow slaughter/protection in 1912 and 1934. In both these instances, the Babri Masjid was attacked. In the immediate post-Independence period, the situation came to a head with the placing of an image of Ram within the mosque itself. In the wake of this act, the site was locked and public worship disallowed, apart from Hindu worship once a year. This situation remained unchanged until the mid-1980s, when the cause of Ram Janmabhoomi was taken up so vociferously by the Sangh Parivar.

The site, then, has a history that includes both dispute and cross-community co-operation, interwoven with and responding to the history of other sites in the locality, which also include incidents of dispute and co-operation. The actions in the 1980s and early 1990s of the Sangh Parivar, and in response the hastily formed Babri Masjid Action Committee, are part of this history. In the contemporary era, however, the implications of these dynamics are projected onto a radically broadened stage, as the media techniques of the Sangh and the interest of global news agencies engender the dispute over the Babri Masjid/Ram Janmabhoomi site as symbolic of larger truths, involving much larger imagined communities. As the historian K.N. Panikkar (1990: 33) remarks, 'a local tradition . . . is now sought to be made into a matter of national faith.'

During this same period, the Dargah of Sayyed Mohammad Ibrahim continued to function, providing a focus (one of many in the town) for the devotional activities of both Hindus and Muslims in Ayodhya. There are two differences between these sites that we can point out at this point. First, of course, the Dargah has not been 'made into a matter of national faith' – that is, it does not exist in the same kind of religioscape as the Babri Masjid/Ram Janmabhoomi, and so perhaps does not carry the same kind of symbolic value. Second, the Dargah continues undemonstratively as a shared space, whereas the Masjid/Janmabhoomi dispute is increasingly articulated in terms of monopoly – the site is claimed exclusively by two apparently mutually exclusive communities. We will return to the idea of the religioscape in the final section of this chapter. First, we should focus in on that idea of the organization and ownership of space.

Space and power in South Asian religious traditions

The dichotomy between a shared and a monopolized perception of religious space seems to be at the heart of the conflicting paradigms we have proposed in this chapter. Moreover, the history of the Babri Masjid/Ram Janmabhoomi site seems to suggest that shared space is giving way to monopolized space as religious traditions in modern South Asia develop. Is this the dynamic through which we should understand contemporary, postcolonial traditions? To address this question, we explore two further examples of shared space in a contemporary context. Examining trends in these spaces will give us some indications of how we might understand the significance of our conflicting paradigms.

Madhu

The first example provides us with another context of conflict, although this conflict has developed rather differently from that at Ayodhya. The shrine at Madhu in northwestern Sri Lanka has in recent years been caught up in the civil war that has raged on the island since the early 1980s. The shrine is constituted through the presence of 'Our Lady of Madhu', a statue of the

Virgin Mary that is said to have been present at the site since the seventeenth century, even though the church on the site dates back only to the 1870s. The shrine and the community around it is said to have suffered persecution in the mid-seventeenth century, from a combination of Dutch colonists and the local ruler of Jaffna. In the context of this persecution, the statue was removed and concealed, only then to be miraculously rediscovered in the trunk of a tree on the site of the current church compound. The spot where the tree is said to have stood is now one of the focal points of the shrine, as the earth is recognized as carrying healing power.[2]

The recent conflict provides the context for a kind of echo of this sacred history. In 2008 the compound came under fire from government troops as Tamil Tiger forces stationed themselves within the compound itself. At this point the statue was removed again, sharing, as the Sri Lankan journalist Amantha Perera (2009) states, 'the fate of many Sri Lankans, becoming a refugee as it was carried from church to church'. The statue was restored to the Madhu shrine in November 2008, and in July and August 2009 it was the site of major celebrations, attracting an estimated 500,000 pilgrims (Perera 2009) who travelled to the site in the wake of the war. Although the statue itself was unharmed, other parts of the Madhu shrine were damaged by shelling during the war, including the side church of the Sacred Heart of Jesus, where the image of Jesus and the structure of the church have both suffered severe damage – in this state, this area has now become a key focal point of the shrine, with pilgrims tying coins to and taking blessing from the broken statue.

Sri Lankan Catholics are drawn from both the Sinhala and the Tamil communities, and both attend the shrine. More than this, however, the shrine is very much a cross-tradition space, with Buddhists, Hindus and Muslims also attending the festival. At the 2009 festival, the symbolism of this cross-tradition experience was very much apparent, in terms of both comment in the press and reflection amongst pilgrims at the site. Here, then, the shrine's power is presented as a kind of pathway to reconciliation, as the country reflects on the terrible consequences of the civil war.

At the same time, there are some signs of contestation over this space. Part of its power emerges from its recognition as sacred to the Buddhist goddess Pattini Amma, a fertility goddess associated with smallpox and protection against other dangers.[3] For many, this multiple perspective is of course simply a reaffirmation of the sacred power of the site itself, a space of spiritual power. There is, however, some indication of dispute at Madhu, associated with the Catholic Church's initiative in the early twenty-first century to have the site recognized both nationally and internationally as a Catholic institution of special significance. At this point, some Sinhala commentators objected to the idea that the site should be 'claimed' by one religion in this way, with one contributor to a Sri Lankan social networking site commenting that Madhu is 'equally sacred to Buddhists, Hindus, Mohammedans and non-Catholic Christians'. The Catholic church, the article continues, should 'tender an apology for misappropriating a place sacred to other religions and return the site to its original incumbents, the Sinhala Buddhists and move their Church somewhere else' (Gamage n.d.).

Here, then, we can see different tendencies at the Madhu shrine. On the one hand, its modern trajectory is as a shared space, symbolizing reconciliation in the wake of the war. On the other hand, there are signs of contestation, which are articulated in terms of both resisting and claiming monopolization over this space.

Saundatti

Our next example is drawn from the work of the anthropologist Jackie Assayag (2004) on shrine worship in the state of Karnataka, south India. Assayag describes the myriad interactions in a sacred space near Saundatti, where the shrine of the Sufi saint, Bar Shah, exists side by side with a variety of Hindu sanctuaries, dominated by the temple to the goddess Yellamma. The shared nature of this space is demonstrated at a range of different levels – physical, yes, but also architectural, mythical and in forms of worship. Importantly, however, the nature of this sharing is mediated by specific identifications amongst devotees.

For example, Assayag (2004: 200) recounts two local myths about the establishment of the site as sacred. One of these tells of how the goddess, afflicted with leprosy by her vengeful husband, the ascetic Jamadagni, came upon Bar Shah, who took pity on her and cured her leprosy (Yellamma is a goddess much associated with leprosy and other diseases of the skin). In gratitude Yellamma served Bar Shah faithfully for twelve years, after which time the saint granted her space to settle freely at Saundatti, where she had remained ever since. However, when Assayag recounted this story to some local devotees of Yellamma, belonging to the low Banajiga caste, they denied any knowledge of it, and instead recounted a story whereby Bar Shah antagonized Yellamma through his constant cursing of her. In response the goddess blinded the saint, who thereafter realized his mistake and began to worship the goddess faithfully. Through this constant devotion Bar Shah was able to regain his sight, and remained indebted and devoted to the goddess from then on. Here, then, we can see the entanglement of mythic tales at Saundatti, whilst they remain quite separate in some ways for different groups. Even in the localized environment of Saundatti, as you can see, this group of Banajiga devotees appears not to have heard the alternative myth of the establishment of the sacred space, nor of course would they countenance its authenticity.

This kind of 'discrete entanglement' is also evident in forms of worship. Observing Hindu practice at Sufi shrines such as that of Bar Shah, Assayag (2004: 197) comments that they:

readily visit Muslim shrines, where they break coconuts, burn incense, offer flowers and clothes and give money. For example, the saris given by these devotees are used to cover the poles of the *panjahs* when they are taken out in procession during *Muharram*. Just as the Muslims 'describe a circle' (*hajj*) around the *dargah*, Hindus too make a *pradakshina* of the shrine. While the former go right inside the *dargah* to touch the saint's tomb, the latter only go there to have a *darshana* at the figure they treat as a god. But whether it is just by looking or by direct touch, the result is the same. They both absorb a part of the extraordinary charisma.

Assayag comments that this is an important form of cultural adjustment. It does not work by some form of syncretism, but precisely by a differentiation that works by dissociation: particular groups retain (or reshape) their underlying values and practices to preserve their distinctness while participating along-side one another at the same shrine, in a manner reminiscent of the reports of 'Buddhist' and 'Hindu' involvement at the Madhu shrine in Sri Lanka.

Rather than essentializing the underlying identities at Saundatti as Hindu and Muslim, we need to see them as locally inflected. This is not to deny that the person who also participates in *namaz* at a particular mosque does not recognize him- or herself as differentiated from the person who performs *puja* in a particular temple, but that the grounds for differentiation may themselves be multiple – based on caste, area inhabited and so on – as also may be the ways of thinking about the self. This multiplicity enables groups and individuals engaged by these sacred spaces to develop a common, related yet also separated tradition. As Assayag (2004: 206) says, they do this by 'devising stories to suit their interests, adjusting behaviour and adapting opinions and practices according to varying needs and circumstances'. What this demonstrates, he continues, is that 'neither religious symbols nor social behaviour remain static as systems inherited from the past and followed mechanically', but rather that 'ideological and pragmatic patterns are being periodically renegotiated by the protagonists' (p. 206).

This then is a nuanced view of the dynamics of religious identification and practice; these are frequently in a process of 'renegotiation', in dialogue with the various contexts that inform and embrace them, including of course the contextualization provided by other protagonists sharing the space. Our examples have demonstrated that these dialogues include disputation and claims to monopolization in the act of sharing, as well as (at Madhu) projections of shared space that are informed by the discrete ideas of reli-gious identity we have earlier identified as paradigmatic of a possible trend towards monopolization. The paradigms with which we began this chapter, it seems, move in mysterious and unpredictable ways. Although we began by presenting them as a binary, two opposed models for South Asian religious traditions, it seems that as we look at actual practice, this dichotomization is not clear. Ideas of shared and monopolized space seem to overlap each other and lead to different trajectories of development in different contexts. This evidence, then, suggests that the answer to our question about whether shared space is giving way to monopolized space is a cautious 'no', simply because the patterns of practice and associated pronouncements do not preclude the presence of one or another understanding of religious space: they seem to exist and operate together.

The religion twist: looking across religioscapes

From the point of view of the student of South Asian religious traditions, then, you may be quite justified in asking where this leaves us. In Part II of this book, we have seen how notions of specific, discrete religions have gained influence in South Asia in the modern period. In Part I, we explored the evidence of equally modern religious practice and ideas, some of which emphasized the relative *lack* of significance of these discrete religions. Monopoly and sharing. What the evidence in this chapter shows is that these are not so much two ways of being; more that they are two (or more) ways of seeing. In exploring the reality of South Asian religious traditions, there are times when approaches based on recognizing and working to explore layers of connection and diversity will bear rich fruit. There are other times when recognizing the operation of distinct and discrete religious systems is the only way to understand the logics behind particular ideas and practices. These models (paradigms) act as heuristic devices. The point is to remember that they are devices, that they constitute ways of seeing, rather than mistaking them for reality itself. In the examples provided in this chapter, we can see that both have a value, both can be deployed in a way that develops understanding, but neither is sufficient. Even when considering the dispute over the Babri Masjid, which seems to epitomize the paradigm of discrete religions, understanding the value of shared space is important, as it enables us to see the dynamics of Carnegie's 'mosque-temple' in a broader context, part of a much wider and deeply rooted tradition. A critical approach to the issue of the dispute in Ayodhya needs to acknowledge multiple contexts, rather than allowing any particular one to constitute an absolute reality.

This point brings us back to an issue with which we began this chapter: the spaces we have been studying are constituted differently 'in reality', because they are contextualized in different religioscapes. To recap, the idea of the religioscape develops from the theoretical work of Arjun Appadurai (1996), who has recognized the influence of different forms of media on the ways in which people understand or construct social life. Some scholars have articulated this idea in terms of religion, to represent the notion of layers of meaning for different forms of religiosity, formulated in the context of different media spaces. Earlier in this chapter, we noted that the Babri Masjid seems to carry a very different symbolic meaning from the Dargah of Sayyed Mohammad Ibrahim, because they are projected in different religioscapes.

Task

A useful and very quick task that might illustrate this idea is to google three of the terms used quite frequently in this chapter: 'Babri Masjid', 'Madhu shrine' and 'Yellamma'.

In carrying out this task, the first thing you will notice is the dramatic contrast in the number of hits between the first, which figured for us at nearly 8 million, and the last two, which numbered in the tens of thousands. Beyond this, you might have noted the range of issues to do with law, politics, communalism, Islam and Hinduism that are immediately apparent in the Babri Masjid hits. This contrasts with the narrower results that come up for both Yellamma and Madhu. The Babri Masjid, it seems, exists in an entirely different set of spaces. It has a range of meanings that resonate much more broadly than those associated with the Madhu shrine or the Yellamma temple in Saundatti. This is ironic in one way, as it is the only one of these three buildings that does not have a physical existence. Its meanings are nevertheless resonant in forms of politics and social relations that are perceived as significant to people not just in India, but across the region and indeed the globe. It has been put in this position, of course, because of the influence of a range of powerful groups who view it as a building with a wide significance, much beyond its (erstwhile) physical dimensions.

Understanding religion in South Asia means taking account of these differences, acknowledging the power of such projections. In particular, we should acknowledge that the global religioscape in which the Babri Masjid exists is one that is deeply influenced by the dominant discourse of 'religion'. In 1855, the difference expressed in the vicinity of the Babri Masjid may be understood in terms of the varying practices and counter-claims of local Ramanandi *naga*s and Sunni Muslim groups. In the context of a global contemporary religioscape, the dominant lens through which these differences have been articulated is this discourse of religion. The totalizing tendencies of this discourse, the vast resources of the groups involved and their ability to deploy a range of media techniques mean that the manifestations of difference at this site have had a very wide and at times deadly significance. The power of these factors also means that the identification of this dispute as indicative of an inexorable difference between Hindus and Muslims is quickly constituted as reality. It is important, however, to maintain the capacity to see these events in a different way, as part of a broader history of contestation and negotiation in South Asian religious traditions. In this context, we hope that you will see the value of our conflicting paradigms as heuristic devices that can be deployed effectively to maintain critical distance and provide a range of perspectives on this most contentious of examples of modern South Asian religious traditions.

Concluding thoughts

About ten kilometres from Ayodhya lies the small village of Shahnawan, with about 2,500 Muslim and 1,000 Hindu inhabitants. Amongst other small shrines, you will find here the *mazar* (tomb) of Mir Baqi, the general of the Mughal emperor Babar who constructed the Babri Masjid. It so happens that the army general was also a Sufi practitioner, and his burial place has since become a shrine, attracting devotees amongst the villagers and further beyond from a range of different communities. Interestingly, in recent years the villagers of Shahnawan have been approached by the Vishwa Hindu Parishad, who have offered to rebuild the Babri Masjid at the site of Mir Baqi's *mazar*, as long as all Muslim claims to the site of the Babri Masjid/ Ram Janmabhoomi are dropped. These offers have been resisted, with one Muslim villager commenting, 'We already have two mosques and three mazars. We don't need any more. Besides, these people cannot be trusted. Our village will become a hub of VHP activities if we agree to their offer' (Srivastava 2010). Another villager, Shamsher Singh (a Hindu), is recorded as commenting:

> We have a strong oral history. Muslims of this village used to maintain not only the Babri Masjid but also the temples, including Hanuman Garhi in Ayodhya. . . . My father Kanhaiya Baksh Singh was village chief for 45 years because Muslims voted for him. He would clean the mazars every day. We clean it even today whenever we get time. Our sons and daughters offer prayer there.
>
> (Srivastava 2010)

How do different ways of looking, the application of different paradigms and an awareness of the idea of different religioscapes help to analyse and understand the predicament of Shahnawan, and the comments of these villagers? We will close this chapter in, as it were, an open fashion, by leaving this as a discussion point, bearing in mind our discussions of the contested perceptions and multiple meanings of religious space explored in this chapter.

Questions for further discussion and research

- What reasons do you see as underlying the dispute at the Babri Masjid/ Ram Janmabhoomi site?
- What is Hindu nationalism and what impact has it had on religious identities in South Asia?
- Are shrines in South Asia paradigms of religious harmony?
- Assess the role of diverse 'religioscapes' in the development of religious identities and practices in South Asia.

Further reading

Assayag, Jackie (2004) *At the Confluence of Two Rivers: Muslims and Hindus in South India*, New Delhi: Manohar.
>A wide-ranging anthropological analysis of shrine worship and other contemporary religious practices in Karnataka.

Eaton, R. (2000) *Essays on Islam and Indian History*, New Delhi: Oxford University Press.
>A range of essays based on careful historical work that explore the relationship between different social groups in medieval South Asia.

Hawley, J.S. (2006) 'Militant Hinduism: Ayodhya and the momentum of Hindu nationalism', in J.S. Hawley and V. Narayanan (eds) *The Life of Hinduism*, Berkeley: University of California Press.
>A short but very thought-provoking account exploring different approaches to Ayodhya.

Ludden, D. (ed.) (2005) *Making India Hindu: Religion, Community and the Politics of Democracy in India*, 2nd edn, New Delhi: Oxford University Press.
>Some interesting and challenging essays on the development of militant Hindu nationalism.

Van der Veer, P. (1987) '"God must be liberated!" A Hindu liberation movement in Ayodhya', *Modern Asian Studies* 21 (2): 283–301.
>An early but stimulating essay on the Ayodhya dispute, based on ethnographic work in Ayodhya.

12 Twisting the kaleidoscope
Reflections in conclusion

In this book, we have explored a range of issues that are central to an understanding of South Asian religious traditions in the modern era. In Part I, we
chose to focus first on what have often been considered essential features
of 'a religion' or indeed of 'religion' as a generic category: notions of deity,
sacred texts, myth, ritual and founders or teachers. You will find such head-
ings in many books discussing specific religions or analysing religion as a
whole. They appear to generate a fairly clear-cut and generally accepted view
of what 'religion' is like. In response, our book has tackled these themes,[1]
but perhaps not always in the expected manner. This is because, as we have
argued throughout, our approach has been marked by an attempt to disrupt
a *single* notion of religion and to show that there have been in the past, and
can be in the present, multiple ways of looking at religious traditions in
South Asia. This led us in Part I to trace these themes across the landscapes of
South Asian diversity in a range of contexts both past and present, so that we
could examine both continuities and ruptures without privileging particular
ways of seeing. Our stress here has been on multiplicity and diversity, on
getting you to question how to make sense of what you are looking at in the
light shed by many different contexts and perspectives.

Chapter 7A showed this nicely. Here we turned to what has been seen
as a key feature of the social structures associated with religious ideas and
practice in South Asia and in Hinduism in particular, namely caste. As well as
demonstrating that modern ideas about caste are partly a conflation of three
rather different ideologies – caste-as-*casta*, -*varna* and -*jati* – and challenging
a simple 'religions' model, our case study of the Meos enabled us to disag-
gregate notions of deity, sacred texts, myth, ritual and founding teachers as
features of 'a religion' that Meos practise. As we did not present the material
explicitly in this way in the chapter, you might like to reflect on it further
before comparing your views with those suggested in Box 12.1.

It could, of course, be suggested that this example is an easy one to pick
as the Meos have a 'liminal' identity anyway. You might want to test our
approach out further by taking an example from one of the other chapters,
researching it in more detail and then trying to see what happens if you use
different ways of looking (see our summary below). Do not forget that, just

Box 12.1 Different ways of looking at the Meos of Bisru

Notions of the divine

Facts: Male Meos in Bisru sometimes attend mosques and the Idgah for Eid ul-Fitr where they will worship Allah saying the Kalima: 'There is no God but Allah . . .'. Women periodically worship the deity Bheru in stone form at the caste well.

If we read these facts at face value in the light of a 'religion and its features' model, what might we conclude:

- Men and women Meos have different ideas of God (Muslim and Hindu respectively)?
- Meos have syncretic ideas about God (mixing Hinduism and Islam)?
- Worshipping Bheru is *shirk* and should be rejected (as Islamic reformers to the village have taught)?
- Men's spasmodic attendance at mosque shows their belief in Allah is just a veneer (over perhaps a Hindu grounding)?

If we look at them from other perspectives, what might we suggest?

- Meos, like many other people, are not that consistent in thinking out a theology?
- Meos take a pragmatic view of deity and worship what works?
- Meo understandings of the divine have developed in a context in which Sufi, Nath and *nirguna bhakti* traditions intermixed, and so allow for an understanding of a single divine that may manifest in different ways for specific purposes?
- Meos have a creative theology in which their understandings of the divine are not static but are reshaped in different historical, economic and political contexts?
- or . . . ?

Sacred texts/myth

Fact: A key Meo oral text is an origin myth that links Meos with the Pandavas from the *Mahabharata*.

On a 'religion and its features' model, might we conclude:

- Meos are Hindus who use the *Mahabharata* as a sacred text?
- Meos seem to be Muslims so the Qur'an ought to be their sacred text?
- Meos do not have proper sacred texts, only myths?

Alternatively:

- Telling this story is more about legitimating claims to a particular homeland than about religious allegiance?
- The travelling Mirasis who tell this story have helped to create religious formations that make sense across their area where a particular group will have its own narrative patterns?
- Meos' stories have been variously told in different contexts, like many others we have come across in Part I?
- or . . . ?

Rituals

Facts: *Kuan puja* is an important form of Meo worship as it takes place at key life-cycle rituals. Meo boys are circumcized. Meo bury their dead.

On a 'religion and its features' model, might we conclude:

- Meos are inconsistent, mixing Hindu and Muslim practices?

Alternatively:

- The correct specialist functions are observed to ensure the well-being of the patriline and the identity of the wider group rather than as features of 'a religion'?
- Meo sources acknowledge that key practices that are negotiable have changed over time but have in the past century prioritized Meo identity when the views of Muslim or Hindu others have variously contradicted their understandings of how being Meo goes with being Muslim?
- or . . . ?

as in this book we have taken a particular approach, so other sources will also have their own 'filters' on the way they present their data. We hope that Part I has both made you aware of ours and enabled you to become aware of your own, and that these together will help you in your critical reading of other sources that deal with the religions of South Asia.

The challenge of modernity

When we examine religion in modern settings, however, we need not just be aware of the great diversity of contexts in which religious traditions are played out. An additional challenge is provided by the need to explore specifically the impact of aspects of modernity on traditions that have endured and developed over many centuries. Part of the challenge here is to resist the temptation to perceive modernity as all-encompassing. We need to acknowledge the emergence of new systems of knowledge, new methods of communication, new forms of social mobility, without seeing these as producing an entirely new world order. Rather, the challenge is to identify the complex interactions that fashion development in multiple and sometimes contradictory ways. In Part II, our book has been focused on capturing these complex interactions, exploring the varied ways in which our landscapes of diversity have engaged with and developed through them. This included in the last chapter a consideration of whether these landscapes may be being eroded by the power of a particular, dominant, modern way of seeing, through which religions are marked off sharply as separate, often competing 'systems', defined strongly against each other in terms of values, history, cultural norms. That is why in Chapters 7–9 we looked at aspects of the ways in which (actually quite radically varying notions of) Hinduism and Buddhism, Islam and Sikhism have emerged in South Asia in the modern period, before looking at two spatial ways in which religions have been marked off from one another through the concepts of public and private space, and space at shrines, in Chapters 10 and 11 respectively.

We concluded Chapter 11 by noting the unpredictable ways in which even this paradigm of competing 'systems' operates on the ground, and the resilience and plasticity of the landscapes of diversity. We must, however, at the same time acknowledge the relationship between this 'systems' paradigm and the powerful discourses that have structured our understanding of what religion 'is'. More broadly, as we argued in the very first chapter, religion has been fashioned in the context of modernity as the flipside of the secular. The religion/secular dichotomy has been influential in representing the social worlds in which we live through a projection whereby all societies are conceived as more or less religious, and less or more secular, in a directly inverse relationship. The implication here is that religion (and, as it happens, secularism) operates as a single, global category, albeit experienced differently by different people around that globe. This difference is config-ured largely by the operation of sub-categories, a variety of 'systems' that constitute comparable examples of the general category, religion. What we have come to know as the World Religions model has been a critical force in the construction of knowledge and understanding about religion.

In writing this book we have tried to maintain an awareness of this process of construction, and its effects both on the way that religious tra-ditions have played out in modern South Asia, and on the perception of these traditions in the context of the study of religion. One of the most valuable things about researching South Asian religious traditions is that they provide us with an excellent opportunity for this critical reflexive turn. The encounter of established but dynamic traditions with the power-ful discourses and material incursions of European nations in and around the period of colonialism enables us to explore the categories, terms and concepts that we use to think more broadly about the idea of religion. So as we indicated in Chapter 8, studying modern South Asian religious traditions can be a critically important postcolonial project. Not only can it involve the recovery and resituating of marginalized ways of being and doing 'religion' in South Asia; it also helps us to uncover and perhaps even critique the architecture of knowledge systems through which the modern world has been constructed. This is, of course, a rather grand claim! What we hope is that Part II of the book has provided opportunities to reflect on such issues, from the particular perspective of South Asia.

Kaleidoscopic ways of looking

Framed by these broad issues, our strategic intention has been to provide, in the course of this book, the means for a nuanced examination of the realities of South Asian religious traditions. This strategic intention is important, because we could not have, and have not, attempted to provide a comprehensive survey or review of the landscapes of diversity. Doing justice to this range would be a lifetime's work, and even then we are unsure if it would be possible, because of the multiplicity of experience, the nuances of practice that are apparent across this vast and heavily populated region of the world. Our objective has rather been to provide you with the means to develop a confident approach to this multiplicity. In pursuit of this, we have referred to a variety of ways of looking, models and perspectives that can be applied to this task. Our key analogy has been the kaleidoscope: look at the scintilla and you will notice a certain pattern; twist the wrist, and you will see a rearrangement, a different way of looking at the materials you have in front of you; twist it again and yet another pattern appears. Such an image is, we think, crucial to maintaining a nuanced, critical and multiple approach to our field. We invite you to apply it with us now as we look at the kaleidoscope twists once more.

The World Religions model

The first model to consider is of course the World Religions model. We hope to have made clear that, although we are critical of the impact of this model on the perception of South Asian religious traditions, at the same time its influence cannot be ignored. The domination of this model over the past century or so has certainly marginalized certain practices and ways of thinking in the region, and some authors also argue that it has been a destructive force, contributing greatly to the emergence of so-called communalism, that antagonistic essentialism which has so often contributed to ethnic violence in recent years. Under such circumstances, this line of reasoning continues, we should argue against using it and its derivatives in the context of South Asia. As Robert Frykenberg (1989: 29) comments about the idea of Hinduism in particular, 'a continued and blind acceptance of this concept . . . is not only erroneous but, I would argue, . . . dangerous'.

The danger alluded to by Frykenberg, of course, is in perpetuating or contributing to forms of violence related to religious identity. There is a certain political significance to this line of reasoning, then, by which you may be persuaded. There are, however, other approaches to be considered. Most importantly for us, it is important to take account of these concepts as a way of understanding the dynamics of social reality in contemporary South Asia. The World Religions model may be a construct; it may also, in the first instance at least, be an imported, outsider model applied with a certain conceptual violence to the traditions of the region. But it has become a key element of contemporary social reality. Not to use it would, we argue, be in itself a kind of violence towards the way in which people live their lives in the region. No religious or cultural tradition is (or indeed has been) sealed against interaction with others; in fact, the very idea seems to suggest the existence of such traditions as discrete objects, an assumption that takes us back to the problems we have noted throughout with the idea of objectified 'religion'. Traditions, rather, develop: they become distinctive, endure and decline only through interaction, and through processes of recognition or categorization *as traditions* that take place in a range of contexts. The incursion of the World Religions model into South Asia forms a part of these interactions, and provides a critical contextual environment for understanding the idea of traditions in this context. We cannot escape it. We need to understand the processes by which it has become a part of the landscapes of diversity. Our approach in this book has been to move towards this understanding by providing other models that help us to place these processes in context. The World Religions model is certainly there, operating in our field. We need to do that field justice by thinking carefully and critically about how it operates, but also how other discourses and ways of looking contribute to the dynamics of religious practice and the development of ideas in that context.

Panth, kismet, dharm te qaum

In Chapter 1 we introduced Ballard's model of four 'dimensions' of Punjabi religion: *panth*, *kismet*, *dharm* and *qaum*. This approach seeks to operate as an alternative to the World Religions model, providing different lenses for understanding religious dynamics in Punjab. In the course of the book, we have referred to elements of this model as appropriate for developing our understanding. For example, in Chapter 5 we found Ballard's perspective illuminating in providing an approach to worship at shrines that does not see it as aberrant or syncretic: people whose backgrounds cause them to celebrate life cycle rituals in very different (dharmic) ways visit the same shrines as one another to help them cope with the (kismetic) difficulties life throws up. In Chapter 9, we considered how a panthic view of Sikh traditions might alter our understanding. We might also think about our case study in this chapter, the Anand Marriage Act, in terms of how a politicized Sikh (qaumic) identity was helped to develop around the re-fashioning of (dharmic) marriage rituals. At the same time, our approach to this model has been cautious, as we see certain problems with its full deployment. In particular, it might appear that the model operates by breaking down what is perceived as Punjabi religion into four or more dimensions.[2] This approach is very useful in terms of making sense of practices that cut across the notional boundaries between religions (Sikhism, Hinduism, Islam). However, it could implicitly reinforce the idea of religion as a separate category of social existence to be analysed in and of itself (*panth*, *kismet*, *dharm* and *qaum* being all dimensions, or aspects, of Punjabi religion or religion itself more widely). There is also a danger that these dimensions can blind us to historical specificities if we forget that their schema is *heuristic*, that is, designed to give us a way of understanding diverse material, and imagine it is *descriptive*, that is, of the material itself.

Much of our argument has been geared towards moving beyond such constraints, exploring the dynamics through which religious traditions are negotiated in multiple economic, social, political and cultural contexts. We recognize that this is challenging, because of the way in which it radically broadens the scope of enquiries associated with the study of religion, but at the same time we hope that we have been able to provide some ways into this broader field of enquiry.

Models for the arrangement of social space

One very influential model for analysing the colonial impact has been that which looks at social space and differentiates it into the public and the private (Chatterjee 1993). A way, then, into a broader field of enquiry, which does not start with religion, is to look at the arrangement of social space, and the ways in which ideas associated with religious traditions (including ideas configured by 'religion', the World Religions model) have been organized in relation to it. As we saw in Chapter 10, there is no single or established way in which the boundaries of public and private are marked, nor by which religious traditions are positioned in relation to these arenas. Rather, boundaries are variously drawn through processes of negotiation, the assertion of and resistance against particular modes of power. Interestingly from our point of view, the idea of 'religious tradition' in the sense of age-old or even eternal practices that need to be preserved is deeply bound up with such processes, so analysing the movement of these boundaries can be a useful means of recognizing the ways in which particular traditions are actually identified, formulated and maintained by different social groups.

A different model that also looks at the dynamics of how social space is arranged is found in Jackie Assayag's analysis of processes of dissociation as explored in Chapter 11. Different social groups engaged in worship practices in the shared space at Saundatti are perceived to dissociate themselves from other groups. This process can occur on the basis of a range of different markers, such as caste, geographical grouping and, yes, religious identity. As with the boundary between public and private, this process of differentiation is, as Assayag (2004: 206) says, 'periodically renegotiated by the protagonists'. Explorations of the ways in which such renegotiations occur enable interesting and revealing analysis of the location of religious traditions in a broader network of social and political relations, in any given time or space. Such explorations demand a different way of looking, a sensitivity to the dynamics of group interaction in a locality that may or may not involve the invocation of (World) religious identities. The important thing is to see the way that this discourse interacts with others to formulate particular social positions.

Teacher tradition models

Another twist of the kaleidoscope produces a different way of looking at our materials. Throughout the book we have seen ways in which a teacher–pupil model provides a useful alternative means of looking at structured interaction and worship traditions across South Asia (see especially Chapters 3, 5, 6, 8 and 9). Although often different in their particularity, there is, we have argued, a continuity provided through this model that links, for example, Sufi and guru lineages, in terms of the ways in which they operate in broader social and political contexts. In particular, a model of teacher–pupil traditions enables us to gain a nuanced understanding of many of the ways in which power is legitimated, diffused and contested in South Asia through such social formations. These range from the ruler or contemporary political leader who seeks legitimation of their political power through the sanction of particular lineage heads, alive or dead, to the words of past teachers, which become the authoritative texts of the movement; from the not inconsiderable economic power wielded by lineages in charge of large teacher–pupil-based organizations, to the contestation of succession claims in the court and public press. They include ways of creating the space for women to challenge the norms of social life, at least temporarily, and different ways of conceiving how national identity may be fostered, as well as providing the path to liberation from rebirth or intimacy with Allah for those initiated therein.

Teacher–pupil traditions are often referred to as sects. Although this may be for a variety of reasons, one key point is to suggest that as such they are branches of a 'religion'; thus, Hinduism is the religion under whose auspices all Hindu sects may be grouped, for example. In our view though, the model enables us to start from the other end and to take seriously particular teacher–pupil formations, seeing how they participate in shared worlds of discourse, yet differentiate themselves from one another in various ways (Chapter 6). We can then see how particular lineages or teacher traditions choose to align themselves with a particular religion, or indeed to resist identification (Radhasoami traditions give us interesting examples of both)

This then links with a third use of the model, for it also provides us with some interesting insights into the ways in which modern Guru traditions sometimes seek to 'exceed' religion, by claiming that they are open to those of any religious affiliation, or of none. This fascinatingly is a strategy that develops partly from the competition between religions emerging as systems in the nineteenth century and trying in the process to demonstrate their superior rationality and tolerance over others (Chapter 2 and 8), partly from the distaste of Europeans such as the Theosophists for forms of organized religion (Chapter 8), and partly from earlier roots in which a claim to truth or being the true tradition was a way of subordinating other religious traditions to one's own (Suthren Hirst 2008). These traditions thus draw on the logics of teacher–pupil relations as they have developed over many centuries in South Asia, even if their approach in the contemporary context is framed by a kind of conscious rejection of religious affiliation as significant. Again we can see here the way in which different discourses operate through interaction, providing interesting and sometimes unpredictable twists to the ways in which such traditions are articulated.

The gender twist

If above we have recapitulated a variety of models suggested in this book as different ways of looking at the material, we turn now to the twists that we have applied at the end of each chapter in Part I (and in terms of the religion twist, also in Part II). It is important to see these not as a sort of add-on, but as twists that need to be applied to the material through and through. First we go back to gender. You might expect the gender twist to enable us to see ways in which dominant forms of understanding religious traditions are frequently bound up with forms of patriarchal power. The most obvious example we give of this would be the understanding of the *pativrata*, or devoted wife, which we looked at in Chapter 4 through Sita, a key character in the Ram-katha. It would also be possible to read the Meo women's *kuan puja* to the Bherus as a way of embedding patriarchal values through the focus on the well-being of the patriline (Chapter 7A). Or to see the abuse wielded by certain male gurus as confirming patriarchal oppression (Chapter 6). But we urge caution in seeing the gender twist only in these terms, not least because, although oppression should indeed be identified and challenged (see Chapter 10), there is a danger if we write the agenda for this in Western feminist terms and ignore, say, the positive advantages to women of rituals that strengthen the patriline (Bennett 1983; Balzani 2004). Using a twist on masculinity (Chapter 5), we were able to see both how practices renewing masculinity by chastity might re-entrench male authority over women (as in the reading of the Sabarimala pilgrimage in Osella and Osella 2003) and how masculine vitality brought to the shrine of Shah Nur (see Green's reading of the *'urs*, Chapter 5) might revitalize a local Muslim community for the year and enable us to understand how such an identity intersected with or sat alongside multiple others being played out in the same context.

The gender twist also, however, gave us a window on the way in which notions of religion (whether governed by or attempting to resist the World Religions model) may themselves unwittingly entrench patriarchal ideas. When, for example, Hinduism is presented in terms of the 'composite halves' of Shaivism and Vaishnavism, that is, Shiva-worshipping and Vishnu-worshipping traditions (von Stietencron 1989; see also Chapter 2), this implies that each focuses on the Supreme imagined as male. Yet in most of these traditions the male Supreme has a female counterpart who is almost always mentioned first. For example, in the Shrivaishnava tradition (Chapter 3), Shri (Lakshmi) is worshipped alongside her husband Vishnu. Such male-centric approaches also blind us to seeing the many different ways in which the divine is worshipped in female forms across different religious traditions, including those Shakta traditions where the Devi encompasses all male forms (Chapter 2). This is not to imply that powerful female conceptions of the divine necessarily have particular (liberative or other) implications for women themselves. This would again be to import Western agendas (Sunder Rajan 2000). But nor is it to deny that they might have such potential (Kishwar 1997, 1998). It merely highlights how easy it is for a model developed in a cultural context in which God is almost always referred to as He[3] to impose its assumptions on the way other religious traditions are labelled. Moreover, as the goddess is frequently seen as one and many in the same instant (Devi on the one hand, and Lakshmi, Kali, Durga, Saraswati, Yellamma and many others on the other), she provides us with a powerful model for disrupt-ing the opposition of monotheism and polytheism in South Asian religious traditions. As we saw in Chapter 2, the idea of these as opposites is itself a construction associated with the 'coming of religion', and in particular the critique of observed practices by Christian missionaries.

The politics twist

Like gender, the politics twist is not an optional add-on. Using politics as a key twist has enabled us to root our investigations consistently in the context of relations of power. Of course, this aspect has appeared in any case as we have contextualized our case studies, and it would have been quite impossible to keep it out of the discussions in Part II. However, we hope that our systematic return to this theme in Part I has provided an example of another, significant way of looking at the fabric of South Asian religious traditions, one that, in its interest in power, often intersects with issues of gender too. In Chapter 5, for example, we saw the role that successive governments have played in supporting or suppressing certain shrines in Pakistan. In Chapter 4, we saw the implication of myth in the political project of specific groups within Indian society, and the development of a sometimes oppressive approach to religious identity. A similar example is explored in Chapter 3, where we saw this idea developing from an excerpt from a nineteenth-century text (Bankimchandra Chatterjee's 'Bande Mataram'), through the discourse of anti-colonial nationalism and on to become, in the contemporary period, symbolic of a particular, exclusivist form of nationalist politics. By contrast, in Chapters 2 and 7B we explored religious identity deployed as liberation in the specific context of an emerging consciousness of caste oppression.

These examples demonstrate a point that is in many ways unremarkable: that religious traditions are deeply bound up with issues of political power, to the extent that it is often not fruitful to identify them as separate spheres of social activity. Indeed, we might ascribe the idea of these as separate spheres as an effect of the emergence of modern religion, as indicated above. Certainly, the work of Richard Eaton on the medieval period in South Asia, which we have referred to at various points in this book, demonstrates that the division is not really valuable in analysing pre-modern history, tending rather to obscure the dynamics through which, for example, particular caste groups adopted practices associated with Sufi shrines, as with Jats and the shrine of Baba Farid at Pakpattan in Punjab (Eaton 2000: 203–48). In exploring the modern period, we need to acknowledge these patterns as significant, even as we also acknowledge the power of a dominant discourse that explicitly marks out religious identity as a discrete site of politics, articulated by many commentators as irrevocably opposed to and somehow qualitatively different from the site of secular politics. These discourses, we argue, operate together, contributing to the complex realities of both modern South Asian politics, and modern South Asian religious traditions.

The religion twist

It should by now be more than apparent that the religion twist does indeed run through the whole book, and our acknowledgement of the significance of the World Religions model as a way of looking has already indicated that we see this as a key factor in understanding contemporary South Asian societies. Why then devote a separate section to this in each chapter? We have used this device to explore how the diversity demonstrated in our examples has been integrated into a religions model in various ways. In Part II, of course, this was the overt emphasis of our chapters. We nevertheless retained a separate section focused on the religion twist here, as a means of drawing out specific points related to the impact of looking 'through religion' in the modern period. In Chapter 7B, for example, we pointed up the role played by low-caste mobilization in enabling the representation of Hinduism as a religion with reforming and orthodox tendencies. In Chapter 10 a similar kind of relationship was examined, between Islam and the veil, asking whether and why this symbol has been so strongly associated with Islam, and how the public–private model that forms the focus of this chapter enables a different perspective. In Chapter 8 we explored the idea of South Asian religions as distinctively 'spiritual', contrasted through Orientalism with the 'pragmatic West'. Again, our examination of the mechanics of the encounter with the West in this chapter provided the basis for a consideration of how and why this specific configuration has become established. In Chapter 9 the focus was on different ways of looking at Sikh traditions, asking questions about how the notion of the *panth* could unsettle established ideas of Sikh-ism. Similarly, in Chapter 11 the religion twist enabled a methodological consideration of the potential of the religioscape as a different way of understanding the significance of space marked out as religious, and the disputes that may occur between communities using such space, or claiming it as their own.

In Part I of the book, the religion twist enabled us to examine how Rammohun re-read the Advaitin Vedantin interpretation of the Upanishads as a means of presenting 'Hindooism' as a religion that demonstrated the Christian requirements of rationality and tolerance better than Christianity itself (Chapter 2). In Chapter 3, we traced the roots of a modern 'textualizing' of religion through the work of Dayanand Sarasvati (noting, however, that the Vedic texts he prioritized were different from those chosen by Rammohun). It might be objected that this prioritization of texts was largely a preoccupation of a small male educated elite, and it should have been the intention of this book to decentre such an account. In the multiple other examples we give, we do indeed try to do this. But the focus of the religion twist has been on how this way of looking has influenced and become part of multiple traditions. In this case, the twist precisely emphasizes how such elite, texualist concerns have come to have a profound influence on ordinary people's lives, not least in the development of legal systems, including Hindu and Muslim personal law, which continue to shape legal and political contexts in South Asia today. A similar point was made in Chapter 4, where we saw how the vibrant Ram-katha stories have been disciplined, fashioned as 'one of the two Hindu epics'. Although this is not just a modern phenomenon (brahminization of the epics being seen from before the turn of the Common Era), contemporary technologies radically change the reach of such dominant narratives. Yet, as we saw, multiplicity still burgeons. In Chapters 5, 6 and 7A, we have used the religion twist to demonstrate how such multiplicity continues to challenge assumptions often made on the basis of a view of religions as discrete text-based systems: Jains as contradictory in pursuing image worship (Chapter 5), Gurus looking self-consciously to transcend the perceived limitations of religion (Chapter 6), and Meos as mixed up all the way through their rituals and myths (Chapter 7A).

Multiplicity and contextualization

Different models, different means. The kaleidoscope shifts and the scintilla gleam, changing our view, catching our breath, causing us to question. Crucially, our understanding of the value of these different ways of looking is that they provide us with multiple perspectives on – in effect, multiple analytical ways of approaching – our field of study. This multiplicity is key, as it enables a more careful and critically edged understanding of South Asian religious traditions. To return to a statement highlighted in the introduction from the work of Peter Gottschalk (2000: 4), 'If we find that only one map is enough . . . we should suspect ourselves of oversimplification.'

This is why we have approached each of our chapter themes through grounded case studies. These enable us to invoke multiple maps, multiple ways of looking. The vital first step in each chapter has been to locate our case studies initially within layered networks of contexts. For these show us precisely the need for developing different perspectives on the case study that can be sensitive to diversity, resist a single 'packaging' and yet help us understand the case study's particular resonance with the respective chapter theme.

Setting multiplicity and contextualization at the centre of our approach does not, however, imply comprehensive coverage, as we argued in the introduction. We are well aware of the limits of our coverage both geographically and in terms of religious traditions, and want you to be clear about them as well. We have not attempted to cover the development of all contemporary South Asian religions, partly because of considerations of space, but also because we want, even in the exploration of these developments, to resist the dominant paradigm of World Religions. It is this paradigm that provokes the desire to provide a 'total' account, covering not just the three major religions of Hinduism, Islam and Sikhism, but Buddhism, Zoroastrianism, Christianity, Jainism and possibly even Bahai as well.[4] Everything in this book is about resituating this totalizing discourse (as one of many), because we see the idea of this totality as a fantasy. As we have shown, the actuality of South Asian religious traditions cannot be encompassed by such a discourse, because this 'single map' provides only one route through the many landscapes of diversity.

That is why once again, and in concluding, we invoke the idea of the kaleidoscope – our objective has been to encourage the twisting of the wrist, to provide a range of ways of looking, enabling the development of critical and nuanced approaches to these multiple landscapes of diversity. The kaleidoscope is in your hands.

Modern South Asia: a timeline

1707 Death of Mughal emperor Aurangzeb – post 1707 gradual weakening of Mughal empire, replaced by proliferation of regional polities such as those of the Marathas and Sikhs in western and northern India respectively.

1724 Asif Jah becomes first Nizam of Hyderabad, establishing state independent of Mughal control.

1757 Battle of Plassey; direct British control established across much of Bengal through the administration of Robert Clive, previously a captain in the army of the East India Company. East India Company had been trading in India since its establishment by royal charter in 1601 (Elizabeth I).

1757–63 Third Carnatic War intensifies conflict between Britain, France and their respective allies in southern India and Bengal. French influence in South Asia greatly reduced.

Late 18th century East India Company gradually extends its influence through a network of alliances and service provision (e.g. mercenary troops, commercial and financial services).

1773 Warren Hastings appointed as first governor general of India; seeks to establish control on basis of indigenous ('Hindu and Muslim') legal systems.

1793 'Permanent Settlement' of land in Bengal by Cornwallis administration.

1796 East India Company takes control of Dutch territories in Ceylon (Sri Lanka).

1802 Ceylon territories declared a Crown colony, no longer under control of East India Company.

1813 Renewal of East India Company Charter by British Parliament leads to abolition of monopoly over trade, and missionaries permitted into East India Company territories (previously banned).

1820s Rammohun Roy active in Calcutta – translating Upanishads into Bengali, opposing Christian missionary critics of Hinduism, campaigning for outlawing of *suttee*.

1828 Roy establishes first Brahmo Samaj (then called Brahmo Sabha) in Calcutta.

1829 Suttee outlawed.

1833 East India Company ceases to trade.

1835 'Macaulay's Minute' on Education; after much debate, English instituted as language of education and administration across British India (previously primarily Persian).

1849 Treaty of Lahore; Punjab becomes part of British empire.

1857–9 Major rebellion against British control across north India (sometimes called the Indian Mutiny).

1858 East India Company dissolved; Parliament takes control of British India; last Mughal emperor deposed; Queen's Proclamation guaranteeing religious freedom in India.

1861 Indian Councils Act leads to limited franchise for some measure of local government.

1867 Dar ul-Ulam of Deoband established.

1873 Satyashodak Samaj established in Poona by Jotirao Phule – promoting low-caste consciousness: Amritsar Singh Sabha established.

1875 Aligarh Muslim University established (Sayyid Ahmad Khan); first Arya Samaj established by Dayananda Saraswati in Bombay; Theosophical Society established in New York by Madame Blavatsky and Colonel Olcott.

1877 Queen Victoria proclaimed Empress of India; Dayananda in Punjab; Lahore Arya Samaj established.

1879 Lahore Singh Sabha established.

1885 First meeting of Indian National Congress.

1891 Age of Consent Bill.

1892 Indian Councils Act extends participation in local government.

1893 Widespread cow protection agitation; World's Parliament of Religions in Chicago, attended by Vivekananda.

1897 Vivekananda establishes Ramakrishna Mission in Calcutta.

1905 Partition of Bengal; boycott and *swadeshi* movement leads to extension of nationalism; Rokeya Sakhawat Hossain publishes *Sultana's Dream*.

1906 Muslim League founded.

1909 Morley-Minto Reforms (Indian Councils Act) extend representation in government and institute the principle of communal representation. First Hindu Conference held in Lahore, organized by Hindu Sabha; Anand Marriage Act passed.

1916 Tagore's *Home and the World* published. Lucknow Pact between Congress and Muslim League = Congress acceptance of principle of communal representation.

1919 Rowlatt *satyagraha*; Montagu-Chelmsford Reforms; Amritsar massacre.

1920–2 Non-co-operation/Khilafat movement.

Early 1920s Emergence of Hindu nationalist Hindu Mahasabha; increasing communal violence; Meos become the target of both Hindu and Muslim reforming groups, seeking to 'normalize' their practices.

1922 Nirmala Sundari 'self-initiates' to become a *samnyasini*, henceforward known as Anandamayi Ma.

1925   Hindu Nationalist organisation the Rashtriya Swayamsevak Sangh (RSS) established in Nagpur.

1926   Ambedkar leads Mahad *satyagraha*, publicly burns *Manu Smriti*.

1930–5   Civil disobedience campaign against British rule.

1932   Gandhi and Ambedkar public disagreement over separate political representation of 'depressed classes' (lower castes/untouchables).

1935   Government of India Act cedes some provincial power to indigenous administrations; recognition of Scheduled Castes; Act becomes basis of later Indian Constitution.

1940   Muslim League Lahore Resolution calls for independent state of Pakistan.

1946   Calcutta communal riots; Constituent Assembly elections lead to Jawaharlal Nehru becoming Indian Prime Minister-in-waiting.

1947   Independence and partition of India and Pakistan; mass migrations and major violence ensues; beginnings of first Indo-Pak war over Kashmir.

1948   Gandhi assassinated by an ex-RSS member; death of President M.A. Jinnah of Pakistan; ceasefire in Kashmir ('line of control' established); independence in Ceylon (Sri Lanka).

1949   Image of Ram appears in Babri Masjid in Ayodhya.

1950   Indian Constitution passed.

1951   Bharatiya Jana Sangh – a Hindu nationalist political party – established at instigation of RSS.

1956   Ambedkar converts to Buddhism; first Pakistani constitution passed.

1958   Military coup in Pakistan; constitution suspended; Ayub Khan takes power.

1962   Indo-Chinese war.

1964   Nehru dies. Vishwa Hindu Parishad (VHP) established at instigation of RSS.

1965   Second Indo-Pak war over Kashmir.

1967   Indira Gandhi becomes Indian Prime Minister for first time.

1971   Third Indo-Pak war, developing out of separatist movement in East Pakistan, which becomes independent state of Bangladesh as a result.

1971–7   Zulfikar Ali Bhutto Prime Minister in Pakistan; launches idea of 'Islamic socialism'.

1975–7   Indira Gandhi suspends Indian Constitution during 'Emergency'.

1977   Zia-ul-Haq takes power in military coup in Pakistan.

1979   Zia institutes Islamization programme in Pakistan.

1980   Bharatiya Janata Party (BJP) established in India as new Hindu nationalist party, heir to Bharatiya Jana Sangh.

1982   General H.M. Ershad comes to power in Bangladesh through military coup.

1983   Civil war in Sri Lanka commences between government and separatist Tamil Tigers.

1984   Operation Bluestar sees Indian army storming Golden Temple in Amritsar to root out armed followers of Jarnail Singh Bhindranwale;

assassination of Indira Gandhi by Sikh bodyguards, followed by anti-Sikh pogrom in Delhi. Hindu nationalists re-launch the Ayodhya issue through a resolution at the first Dharma Sansad, a VHP-sponsored 'religious parliament'; Ayodhya issue gains prominence steadily through thte 1980s.

1985   Rajiv Gandhi becomes Indian Prime Minister with huge majority in wake of mother's death.

1987   Doordarshan, the Indian state television company, begins broadcasting Ramanand Sagar's *Ramayana* series.

1988   President Zia of Pakistan dies in plane crash; Benazir, daughter of Zulfikar Bhutto, becomes Pakistani Prime Minister after elections.

1989   Popular uprising against Indian rule in Kashmir begins.

1990   L.K. Advani of the BJP launches 'Rath Yatra', a 10,000 mile pilgrimage in a vehicle designed to represent Ram's chariot, in order to publicize Ayodhya campaign; Ershad resigns in Bangladesh, return to democratic rule.

1991   First steps in liberalization of Indian economy begins period of rapid economic growth.

1992   Destruction of the Babri Masjid in Ayodhya; communal riots.

1998   BJP comes to power in India at the head of a coalition of regional forces, the National Democratic Alliance (NDA).

1999   General Parveez Musharaf's military coup ends period of democracy in Pakistan.

2002   Major communal violence in western Indian state of Gujarat.

2004   BJP-led NDA coalition in India is ousted by a Congress-led coalition, the United Progressive Alliance (UPA).

2008   General Musharaf resigns, democratic government returns to Pakistan; Nepali monarchy is abolished, Nepal declared a republic.

2009   Sri Lankan government declares end of civil war, defeat of Tamil Tigers. Congress-led UPA coalition returned to power in Indian general election for second term.

Glossary

abarodhbasini   Bengali term referring to strict *purdah*, in which the woman will barely leave the house.

adab   Moral conduct.

adharma   The opposite of *dharma*; social chaos, or behaviour that leads to it.

advaita   'Non-dual'.

Advaita Vedanta   Form of Vedanta identified with Shankara and others that holds *brahman* to be the sole reality; Shankara understands the conventional world to be a 'superimposition' on *brahman* caused by our ignorance and misconception; form of Vedanta and of Indian philosophy generally prioritized by nineteenth-century European scholars.

Ain-i-Akbari   Of Abul Fazl written in Persian; commissioned by the Mughal emperor Akbar; a sixteenth-century extensive report on multiple aspects of Indian customs and laws, from weights and measures to philosophical schools, compiled as an aid to good governance.

'alim **(singular)**   Muslim scholar. See also *'ulama* (plural).

Allah   God (Arabic); used in many north Indian traditions as a name for deity.

arati/arti/aarti   Offering of light in worship; also called *diparadhana*/Deeparadhanai, especially in south India.

Ardhanarishvari   'half-woman, half-male Lord'; a form of Shiva and Parvati conjoined.

Arya   'Noble one'; term used in Vedic texts by Vedic transmitters to refer to themselves by contrast with those they called *dasyu*, enemy of the gods, or '*dasa*', barbarian, 'other'.

Ashraf   High class; an Indian Muslim of foreign descent (singular: *sharif*).

atman   Self, conscious principle.

Avadhi   Important north Indian dialect.

avatar/avatara   Hindi and English/Sanskrit forms; 'crossing over' or descent; a form of the deity intervening in the affairs of the cosmos usually to re-establish the correct way of acting, or make deity graciously available. Usually of the ten (or more) *avatar*s of Vishnu, although it is also used in other devotional traditions who see Shiva or Krishna, for example, as Supreme.

Bakr Id Also known as Eid/Id ul-Adha; major Islamic festival commemorating Ibrahim's willingness to sacrifice his son Isma'il.

bandhu Connection/correspondence between microcosm and macrocosm; basis of Vedic meditations, Tantric practices, etc.

Baniya General term for merchant and shopkeeping castes.

barakat/barkat Blessing/power (from Arabic).

bhadralok 'Gentle folk'; the growing (largely Hindu) middle class in Bengal in the late nineteenth century.

bhajan Devotional song.

bhakta Devotee, worshipper.

bhakti Devotion.

Bharat Mata 'Mother India', goddess who has gained in significance over the past century.

bhava Lit. 'Being'; state of being; state of ecstasy.

bhava darshan Viewing of the deity/teacher in divine mood/ecstasy.

bida' Sinful innovation (against practice of *shari'a*) Different Muslim schools/groups vary in what they regard as *bida'*.

biryani A rice-based dish.

Brahma Creator god.

Brahman/*brahman* Ultimate reality.

Brāhmaṇa/**Brahmana** One of the four 'layers' of Vedic texts.

brāhmaṇa/*brahmana* An explanation of a *mantra* in the Vedic texts, hence, *Brāhmaṇa* as above; the specialists who pass down the Vedic texts.

brahmin Anglicization of *brāhmaṇa* (also spelled Brahman by some authors quoted in this book), that is, the first of four Vedic *varna*s, those with responsibility for teaching the Vedic texts; umbrella term for the many different brahmin *jati*s found in South Asia today; sometimes equated with priests, but most brahmins are not priests.

brahminical Relating to brahmin; used to refer to schools of thought and traditions rooted in the Veda and in brahmin hands (as they alone had the right to teach the Veda).

casta Portuguese term referring to hierarchized system of races; root of English term 'caste'.

chadar Cloth, veil.

Chamar Leatherworker; a major untouchable caste in central and northern South Asia.

Cord-wearers Highest ranked category of the 1854 Nepali legal code, the Muluki Ain.

Dadaguru Ascetic now regarded as a deity in some Jain traditions.

Dalit 'Oppressed'; term preferred by many who others refer to as untouchable, or even Harijan.

darbar Court (as of an emperor); a formal public session at which a *pir* or other may be seen/consulted.

dargah 'Threshold'; shrine of a Sufi *pir*.

darshan 'Seeing' ; seeing and being seen by the deity (or guru) in worship.

dasi   Female servant or slave.

Deeparadhanai   Offering of light (Tamil).

Devi   Goddess.

dharma   √*dhṛ*, to make firm; order – ritual, cosmic, social; duties, correct social behaviour.

dharm   In modern Indian languages, '(a) religion'; one of Ballard's four dimensions (divine norms for society to which all should conform).

Dharma texts   Term used to indicate the enormous body of texts on *dharma*, the social duties and responsibilities of the four ideal social groups (*varna*) and stages of life (*ashrama*), that is, *varnashramadharma*. Earliest Dharma Sutra texts are probably to be dated from the beginning of the third to the middle of the second century BCE, with elaborating *shastra*s (treatises), such as Manu, from the first or second centuries CE on.

Dharma Shastra   Treatises relating to *dharma*; major body of Dharma texts (see above).

diksha   Initiation (by a teacher).

Eidgah/Idgah   Mosque or ground reserved for communal prayers on the Eid festivals.

Eid ul-Adha (Id al-Adha)   See Bakr Id above.

Eid ul-Fitr (Id al-Fitr)   Festival that falls on the day after the Islamic fasting month of Ramadan ends.

fakir   A term used for any ascetic or wandering holy man.

fatwa   Legal ruling/judgment.

Gayatri Mantra   Mantra from the *Rig Veda* repeated three times daily by brahmins.

gopi   In Krishna myths, the *gopi*s are the girls who looked after the cows, and were attracted to play with Krishna when they heard the sound of his flute..

got   Sub-*jati* kin unit; generally exogamous.

guna   'Quality' or 'strands' of mind-matter that constitute material life; there are three *guna*s, *sattva* (purity), *rajas* (passion) and *tamas* (darkness).

gurbani   The authoritative words of the Guru/God; in Sikh traditions the words of the Guru Granth Sahib; compare Ma-bani.

gurdwara   Lit. 'door of the Guru'; Sikh place of worship (replaced earlier assembly places).

guru/guru   Lit. 'heavy'; teacher. We have not usually italicized this as it has become adopted into English usage.

Guru   Capital used especially of the Sikh Gurus, or as a title; also a title for God.

guru bhakti   Devotion to the teacher (who may be God).

Hadith (*ahadith* – Arabic plural)   Narratives about the life of Muhammad; significant texts for interpreting the Qur'an.

hajj   'Describe a circle'; as also in Hajj, pilgrimage to Makka (Mecca) involving circumambulating the Kaaba.

Harijan Children of God; Gandhi's name to replace 'untouchable', rejected by Dalit followers of Ambedkar.

hal State of heightened spiritual sensibility.

Holi Spring festival celebrated by throwing coloured powder at those normally considered one's superiors; frowned on by Wali-Allah and other Muslim reformers.

ijtihad Individual reasoning, whose relation to the four sources of Islamic legal knowledge has been much debated .

ishtadevata Chosen deity/form of God, in Hindu devotional traditions; this is usually a matter of personal (rather than family or group) choice and may be because of some particular blessing experienced at the hand of that deity.

itihasa 'Thus it was'; Epic (especially Mahabharata, also Ramayana); in modern Indian languages, history.

'ishq Love; especially of the passionate mystical love that is the goal of the Sufi quest; also used of romantic love in Persian and other north Indian poetry.

Jagat Guru World Teacher; a title ascribed to important teachers such as Shankara in the hagiographies of his life; a title taken for himself by a Muslim Sultan of Bijapur.

Jagatmoyi Comprising the (whole) world; a name for Kali.

jajman Patron caste, to whom other castes in a particular area render service.

Janamsakhi Birth stories, or hagiographies, of Guru Nanak.

jangama In Lingayat/Virashaiva usage, a human assistant on path of faith, sometimes referred to as a priest.

Janmabhoomi Place of birth (as in Ram Janmabhoomi, the alleged place of birth of the god Ram).

jat Hindi term for *jati*; birth or kinship group that links particular families and their descent groups into a larger social whole.

jati 'Birth' or 'type' in Sanskrit; endogamous social groups; often translated as 'caste'.

Jinn Invisible beings created by Allah with particular powers; may use these powers malevolently.

Kaaba Black stone and mosque built around it in Mecca (Makka); gives the direction for Islamic prayer (*salat* is performed facing towards it); holiest place in Islam (compared by Kabir with Kailash as holiest place in Hindu practice of his day and region).

Kabir Panth The collection of those who follow the teachings of Kabir.

kabirpanthi One who belongs to the Kabir Panth.

kafir Unfaithful one; infidel.

Kailash Shiva's divine abode in the Himalayas.

Kalima The word of God, the basis of Shahada, the declaration of faith that constitutes one of the five pillars of Islam.

kaliyug The fourth of the great world eras in each world cycle; the current world cycle; a time of *adharma* although it has the advantage that a mere calling on the name of God may be sufficient for liberation.

kar sevak 'Volunteer activist', normally associated with the Hindu nationalist movement, the Sangh Parivar.

khankah/khanaqah Type of building around which Sufi networks were organized; Sufi place of hospitality.

kirtan Praise song; hymn singing.

kismet/qismat Fate; one of Ballard's four dimensions (ideas and practices for dealing with adversity).

kshatriya Warrior class, one of the four *varnas*.

kuan puja A Meo life-cycle ritual performed by women.

kufr Infidelity.

kuldevi Lineage goddess.

kulin Of a lineage.

kulin brahmins A particularly high status brahmin caste.

langar Shared meal of food blessed through its association with worship or service; usually linked with Sufi shrines across South Asia and also a Sikh practice but common across the Punjab, for example.

lingam Lit. 'sign'; aniconic form in which Shiva is worshipped, in the form of a phallus united with a womb (*yoni*) – the male and female powers of the universe united; some Puranic myths explain its form in terms of a fiery pillar in which Shiva manifested showing his infinite supremacy over Brahma and Vishnu.

lila 'Play'; the play of the gods, e.g. Krishna's play with the *gopis*, implying free action unconstrained by the results of past actions; a person possessed by a goddess (or god) may also 'play', hair flailing. See also Ramlila.

Lingayat Caste group based in the Indian state of Karnataka, developed out of particular Shaivite religious tradition (see Virashaiva).

Ma/Mata 'Mother'; an honorific often attached to the name of a goddess or of a female guru, even, or especially, when they are celibate. They are Mother to the whole cosmos or to their devotees.

Ma-bani The words of Mother; the authoritative teachings of Anandamayi Ma. See also *gurbani*.

Madrasa A traditional Muslim school, specializing in a range of Islamic subjects, from grammar to philosophy and Qur'anic studies.

Mahabharata Great epic of India; story of war between two sets of cousins, the Pandavas and the Kauravas.

mahajanapada Kingdom during the Vedic period.

Mahar An untouchable caste prevalent in western India; B.R. Ambedkar was a Mahar.

mahfil-e-sama' Sufi musical performance.

Mali A lower (Shudra) caste; Jotirao Phule was a Mali..

mandala Diagram of the cosmos used in worship or meditation, especially but not exclusively in Tantric traditions.

mandir   Shrine or temple.

Mang   An untouchable caste prevalent in western India.

manot   Vow (Bengali term).

mantra   Formula for chanting; Power is believed to reside in the sound; may be a single syllable, a short phrase or a deity's name.

Manu   Title given to a key Dharma text attributed to Manu; originally titled *Manava Dharma Shastra*, now more often known as *Manu Smriti*.

math/a   Hindi/Sanskrit; an ascetic centre, place of learning surrounding a renouncer teacher.

maulvi   Arabic: 'my master'; Islamic legal scholar and authority figure.

mazar   Tomb of a Sufi *pir*.

Meo   Important *jati* grouping originally located in northern area of Mewat, just south and west of Delhi.

Mirasi   Low-caste itinerant bards in northwestern India responsible for singing genealogies and creating links across the region; Nanak's minstrel was a Mirasi; Meo genealogies are sung by Mirasi (see Chapters 6 and 7A).

mudra   Hand positions taken in meditation or in representations of deity, each of which has a particular meaning, e.g. blessing.

Mukkuvar   Keralan untouchable fishing caste (note that they seem to ignore rather than want to change this ascribed status).

mulfuzat   Collections of saints' teachings especially in Chishti Sufi traditions.

Muluki Ain   Legal code established in Nepal in 1854, categorizing people into five groups – see Chapter 7A.

munshi   Personal clerk.

murid   Disciple, especially of a *pir*.

murti   'Form'; sculpted image of a deity, especially as the place where deity is/manifests once the image has been ritually installed and eyes 'opened'; image of a Buddha or Jain Tirthankara.

namaz   Persian, Urdu; formal Islamic prayer, synonym for *salat* (Arabic).

nirguna   Without qualities; for Shankara's Advaita Vedanta, *brahman* is without any qualities at all, for these would constitute a limit, a form of duality; for Ramanuja's Vedanta, *brahman* is without any inauspicious or bad qualities; for *nirguna bhakti* traditions, the Lord is worshipped without an image, for example in the transcendent Name.

nirguna bhakti   Devotion to a Lord without qualities.

oleograph   A picture produced in oils by a technique similar to lithograph printing; especially as used in the brightly coloured devotional posters or 'photos' of the gods made popular in the twentieth century.

pal   Clan system linked with territory.

palkhi   Palanquin; covered rest for Guru Granth Sahib.

Pandun ke kara   Meo caste myth, linking the group to the Pandava clan of the Mahabharata.

panja   'Hand', relic or emblem of Muslim saints.

panth   Group around a teacher, such as Kabir Panth, Nanak Panth; one of Ballard's four dimensions (commitment to a spiritual teacher).

parampara   Teacher–pupil succession; sometimes used in modern Indian languages for 'a religion'.

Parashuram   'Rama with an axe', one of the descent forms (*avatar*s) of Vishnu.

parda   Lit. 'curtain' (Persian).

pativrata   'Vowed to lord'; of a woman devoted to her husband, who is to be treated as god.

patriline   Ancestral line traced through male line, i.e. father, grandfather, great-grandfather, etc..

pind-dan   Ritual performed by many Hindus on behalf of those who have died.

panchayat   'Assembly of five'; a village-level group, traditionally of elders, designed to adjudicate in local disputes and make local decisions.

pir   Saint or holy man, often a Sufi.

pirani   Holy woman.

pradakshina   Circumambulation of a shrine (clockwise for most deities; anti-clockwise usually for Shiva).

prashad/prasad   Lit. 'favour', food or other offerings made to a deity and then received back as blessed.

puja, pooja   Worship, either at home or in a temple; often includes *arati*.

puja pandal   Pavilion set up for worship, especially at Durga Puja.

Purana   Lit. 'ancient'; ancient story; name given to many texts that contain myths of key Hindu deities, chronologies and so forth; traditionally eighteen major and eighteen minor Puranas.

purdah   A range of ways of separating male from female space, including wearing the veil.

purdahnashin   One who observes *purdah*; there are many different degrees of strictness.

purohit   (Hindu) temple priest or family priest.

qalandar   Sufi ascetic, generally independent of any particular *silsila*.

qaum/qawm   Community; one of Ballard's four dimensions (community identity, especially that of a politicized religion).

qawwal   Professional praise singer.

qazi   Islamic legal expert.

Qur'an (also Koran)   Islamic scripture, believed to have been revealed by Allah through the angel Jibra'il (Gabriel) to the Prophet Muhammad.

Raja/Rajah   Ruler (especially Hindu rulers of what became Princely States under colonial rule).

rajas   Passion, one of the three *guna*s.

rakshasa   Normally translated as 'demon', and frequently portrayed fighting the gods in puranic literature.

Ram/Rama   Hindi/Sanskrit forms of the names of the Ram-katha's key character.

Ramayan/a Hindi/Sanskrit forms of titles of particular texts of Ram/a story.

Ram-katha 'The story of Ram/a', used to designate the entire repertoire or pool of Rama stories.

Ramlila 'Play of Ram'; refers to north Indian performances of Tulsidas's telling of the Rama story, which developed their own form corresponding with Krishna-lila, Krishna's play with the *gopi*s.

rishi Sage.

sadhu Good person; saint; may be used of ascetics; Kabir addressed many of his poems, O Sadhu, to the listener as the true saint who understands the message of the Sant tradition; a kind of signature to many of his poems.

saguna bhakti Devotion to a Lord with attributes; associated with image worship (*murti puja*).

sajjadah nashin Custodian of a Sufi shrine.

salat Formal Islamic prayer to be said five times a day in specified prayer periods; one of the five pillars of Islam; often called *namaz* in South Asia.

samadhi Profound state of meditation; the realized/liberated state of a great teacher; the shrine marking the place of that realization.

sampradaya Lit. something that is handed down; the teaching of a particular tradition; the teaching tradition itself.

samnyasa Renunciation; the fourth Hindu stage of life; or may be interpreted as renunciation of the rewards of actions at any point in a person's life.

samnyasi Male renouncer or ascetic; in the fourth Hindu stage of life.

samnyasini Female renouncer.

sandalmali 'Sandalwood-rubbing', a ritual carried out at the '*urs* festival at Muslim shrines throughout South Asia, including Shah Nur's shrine.

Sanhita-Mantra Dayanand's definition of the true Veda; the hymn collections (*samhita*) only, excluding the explanations or *brahmana*s.

sant/Sant 'Saint'; especially of those in various north Indian traditions that emphasized *nirgun-bhakti*; grouped together as 'the Sant tradition'.

satguru True teacher.

Satguru Title for God especially in Sant and Sikh traditions.

sati, see also *suttee* Lit. 'a good woman'; one who follows *pativrata*.

sattva 'Purity', one of the three *guna*s.

shabd Verse especially from the Guru Granth Sahib (Punjabi form of Sanskrit *shabda*, meaning 'sound', especially powerful chanted sound).

shakti/Shakti Power; female power within universe and within human beings; especially the power of the Goddess; alternative name for the Goddess.

Shakta Worshipper of Shakti; a tradition that views Shakti/the Devi/the Goddess as the Supreme.

shaykh/sheikh/shaikh Sufi master.

shastra Treatise; authoritative teaching.

Shia/Shiʻi   Branch of Islam that traces itself through Ali, Muhammad's son-in-law, who is regarded as the first Imam; they reject the first three Caliphs, *khalifah*, recognized in Sunni Islam (Ali is the fourth Caliph for Sunnis).

shirk   (The sin of) associating another with Allah.

shishya   Pupil.

shraddha   Ritual performed by many Hindus in honour of ancestors, especially dead parents.

shruti   Lit. 'hearing'; the most authoritative brahminical texts, 'heard' or 'seen' by the Vedic *rishi*s; the Veda (all four layers).

shuddhi   'Purification', a ritual process associated in the late nineteenth/early twentieth century with Hindu organizations' attempts to 're-convert' Christians and Muslims, and/or 'reclaim' untouchables as Hindus.

shudra   Servant class, one of the four *varna*s.

silsila   Sufi teaching tradition or lineage.

Sikh   Lit. pupil (Punjabi form of *shishya*); person who follows a Sikh tradition.

smriti   'Remembering'; second brahminical category for ordering Sanskrit texts – texts that are authored by human or divine beings and whose authority is generally held to be dependent on that of *shruti* texts or to represent remembered *shruti* traditions. Includes Epics (including *Bhagavad Gita*), Dharma texts, Puranas, Tantras.

Sunna/Sunnah   The words and actions of Muhammad and his Companions, which form the exemplar for Muslims to follow.

Sunni   'One who follows the sunna'; most numerous and widespread branch of Islam (see Shia above).

suttee, **see also** *sati*   Anglicization of *sati*, used to refer to the practice of a woman burning herself on her husband's funeral pyre (a practice that is permitted in limited circumstances by some Dharma texts and condemned by others, called, for example, *sahamarana* – going to death with); widow burning.

tabarra   Statement dissociating oneself from 'enemies of Allah'.

tamas   Darkness, one of the three *guna*s.

Tantra (1)   Texts belonging to particular devotional traditions, which along with the Puranas were rejected as degenerative by many nineteenth-century Hindu reformers..

Tantra (2)   The name given to an enormous range of Buddhist and Hindu traditions using the power of *mantra, mandala, mudra*.

thamba   Village-level clan grouping, generally exogamous.

tirtha   Crossing point between the human and divine worlds, often marked by a sacred river.

twice-born   Refers to members of the first three *varna*s who are permitted to study the Veda; the ceremony that begins Vedic study, the *upanayana*, is the student's 'second birth', after which he is entitled to wear the sacred thread.

'ulema/'ulama (singular: *'alim*)   Muslim scholars learned in *shari'a/shariah* and sometimes in wider philosophical traditions; used to designate the aggregate of religious leaders.

Upanishad   Fourth layer of Vedic texts, developing from meditations on the Vedic ritual to a search for the reality that underlies the cosmos as a whole; Rammohun's preferred texts.

'urs   Lit. 'marriage'; the union of a Sufi saint with Allah at the saint's death, his marriage to Allah; the annual ritual commemorating that day.

vachana   Particular form of metrical verse preferred in Lingayat tradition.

'Vande Mataram' ('Bande Mataram' in Bengali)   'Praise to the Mother'; Bankim Chandra Chatterjee's poem to Bengal as Mother, later applied to India.

vaishya   Wealth-producing classes, one of the four *varna*s.

varna   Ideal social class: brahmin, *kshatriya*, *vaishya*, *shudra*, described in Vedic and Dharma texts; sometimes features as a standard for ranking *jati*s; important in modern reformers' discourse on the caste system.

varnashramadharma   Duties of one's social class and stage of life (from Dharma texts; important as a framework in modern Hinduism).

Veda   Texts of the Vedic corpus, the first layer of which, the Samhitas ('collections' of hymns), were Dayanand's preferred texts; in brahminical usage includes the four layers of Samhitas, Brahmanas, Aranyakas and Upanishads.

'Veda'   Term used by Lipner to distinguish texts called Veda by their followers from the Vedic corpus proper, hence Tamil Veda and so on.

*Vedanta Sutra*s   Aphoristic verses that provide the foundation for the Vedanta school.

vilayat   Sphere of influence, especially of a Sufi *pir*.

Virashaiva   Shaivite religious tradition originating in Karnataka and associated with the teaching of Basava.

Vishvarupa   Universal form, especially of Vishnu's universal form manifested to Arjuna in *Bhagavad Gita* (ch. 11).

vrat/a/–   Vow (Hindi/Sanskrit term).

yajna   Sacrificial ritual (Vedic); ritual often based around a fire.

yaksha/yakki   Semi-divine beings associated with the earth and trees.

yoga   Lit. 'joining'; physical and mental discipline; forms of meditation.

yogi   A person who practises *yoga*.

zakat   Alms giving, one of the five pillars of Islam.

zat   Punjabi term for *jat*, birth or kinship group that links particular families and their descent groups into a larger social whole.

zenana   The women's quarters, into which the men of the house were generally not allowed to enter.

Notes

Preface

1 Fitzgerald (2000) has pointed out the numerous different ways in which even scholars use the term 'religion'. In Chapter 1 we shall clarify the sense in which we will use the term, and others like it, in this book.

1 Introducing South Asia, re-introducing 'religion'

1 For more information see Hewitt (1997: 5–7).
2 As you read further in this introduction, you will discover that we intend to use the phrase 'religious traditions' in a rather specific sense, making a distinction between it and the perhaps more conventional term 'religion'. A full explanation of this differentiation can be found on pp. 20–1.
3 Because the Muslim calendar is a lunar one, the dates of Ramadan and Eid ul-Fitr move 'backward' through the Julian (international) solar year, and so Eid and Durga Puja may sometimes fall many months apart. Most Hindu calendars are also lunar, but they are 'solar adjusted' so that the lunar festivals only move within a month or so in relation to the Julian calendar (like Christian dates for Easter).
4 Muslims, that is, from this particular locality of Punjab. Overall, India remains the third largest Muslim country in the world.
5 Sites have recently been excavated down to Gujarat (modern India), and traces of the civilization found from Baluchistan (Pakistan) in the west, to past Delhi (India) 1,000 miles to the east, from the Himalayas in the north to Mumbai (Bombay, India) in the south (see the website Harappa 1995–2010), testimony to trading interactions with food foragers, pastoralists, agriculturalists and craft producers within this area (Shaffer and Lichtenstein 2005: 84).
6 One theory is that ecological change led to the Ghaggar-Hakra waters being 'captured' by adjoining river systems, leaving the main centres arid, but there is no consensus yet on this.
7 We use the term to indicate the way of life of those who passed on the Vedic texts, but warn that this in itself was much more varied than the picture we receive from these texts, and that, over the centuries, these people operated within complex milieux of different social groups (Olivelle 1995).
8 Although both historical – and roughly contemporary – figures, the evidence for dating them and so this period is not straightforward. As Sheldon Pollock (1996: 201) points out, many of our historical data for South Asia are problematic. Buddhist texts themselves were interested in dating issues, but the chronicles vary in the length of time they think occurred between the death of Siddhartha Gautama and the reign of Ashoka. See Ruegg (1999) for a summary suggesting a dating of the fourth century BCE; Shrimali, however, returns to the date of 484 BCE for Gautama's death (Jaiswal 2007).

9 Or, by contrast, to present Jainism and Buddhism simply as offshoots of Hinduism.

10 See also Chapters 3 and 4. It is important to note that, regardless of brahminization, these devotional cults were neither straightforwardly 'egalitarian', nor 'anti-northern', as some modern European scholarship and Tamil assertion movements have claimed (see Jaiswal 2000).

11 Romila Thapar's (2004) study of accounts concerning Somnath demonstrates this particularly clearly.

12 The Congress Party evolved out of the Indian National Congress movement, the main organization involved in the fight for freedom from British rule. Between Independence and the end of the twentieth century, the Congress was undoubtedly the dominant force in Indian national politics. In the immediate post-Independence period, the Congress pursued a kind of non-aligned socialism, also known as 'Nehruvian Socialism', after the freedom fighter and first prime minister of India, Jawaharlal Nehru.

13 Estimating the actual numbers is rather difficult, as the category 'the middle class' has been defined in many different ways. A rough estimate would put the figure somewhere between 200 and 300 million. For a discussion of this point, see Brosius (2010: 1–16).

14 As we shall see, neither is really comparable in classical Sanskrit usages: *dharma*, a term of great significance, fundamentally concerns 'cosmic order' or 'duty', whereas *parampara* denotes a teacher–pupil 'succession'.

15 The lack of a word does not in itself imply the lack of a concept straightforwardly ('economics' being a good example).

16 On interesting ramifications of such objectification, see Cohn (1987) and Hefner (1998).

17 For analysis, see Masuzawa (2005).

18 For a fifth dimension, see Ballard (2011). Although the formations he looks at are clearly indigenous, and the terms drawn from Punjabi, Ballard uses them in his own analytical sense, building on the work of Mark Juergensmeyer (1982). For further discussion, see Suthren Hirst and Zavos (2005).

19 For a critique of this idea and its application in a South Asian context, see Stewart (2001) and Stewart and Ernst (2003).

20 We would like to thank our colleague, Alan Williams, for stimulating us to make this clarification.

21 A good place to start would be Mittal and Thursby (2006) or Kitagawa (2002).

2 Deity

1 On caste, see Chapters 7A and 7B.

2 See, for example, H.D. Sharma (2002).

3 It is important to note that this practice has always been limited both to certain regions (including parts of Bengal, close to Calcutta) and to certain caste groups (especially relatively high-caste groups). Despite this, it was read as a characteristic feature of Hindu tradition during the colonial period, and this interpretation has been very influential in modern understandings of *suttee/sati*. *Sati* in Sanskrit simply means 'good woman/wife'. Its colonial anglicized form, *suttee*, identified it simply with this particular limited practice. For some further interesting reading, see Mani (1998).

4 We have to remember when judging such critiques that writers home often portrayed Hinduism in the light that they thought would generate the most funds to support their mission. Individuals also changed their views. Also, Protestant writers had for some centuries used critiques of 'paganopapism' to castigate Roman Catholics. As with Rammohun's Chinese converts piece, their obvious target was not necessarily the actual one.

5 In the early nineteenth century, 'Hindoo' and also 'Hindooism' were common spellings used by missionaries and others, including Rammohun, indicating that at this time the notion of Hinduism was still in a process of crystallization; see Chapter 1, p. 19.

6 A Puranic trio of deities gives another way of stressing the unity of the divine manifested in different forms, a way that is often presented as normative in modern accounts of Hinduism. The Trimurti (three-formed, sometimes very misleadingly translated as 'Trinity') comprises Brahma (the creator deity), Vishnu (the preserver deity) and Shiva (the destroyer deity). Each plays his part at a different stage in successive world cycles (on which see Lipner 1994: 252–4). Brahma, however, rarely has temples dedicated to him (the city of Pushkara in Rajasthan is the one key exception) and many of the Puranic texts are preoccupied with showing that the others are *really* only forms of Vishnu, or of Shiva (depending on the Purana's leaning). In many devotional traditions, the other deities may be almost insignificant demi-gods or ministers of the Supreme (understood as, say, Krishna, or a form of Shiva), or ignored almost entirely.

7 This is a reference to a useful source on modern imagery in South Asia: Pinney (2004). See also the illustrations in Chapter 3.

8 For an introduction to the many schools, see King (1999a).

3 Texts and their authority

1 Although for variations on what is included, see below.

2 'Sacred text' is a term that is frequently used in the study of religions as an alternative to 'scripture'. This is to try to avoid the particular theological overtones of 'scripture' as revealed or of divine origin and to focus on the status that the text has for the communities that use it instead. It has the merit of being able to include oral and visual texts as well as written ones ('scripture' coming from the Latin '*scribere*', to write). However, it is itself weighted with the implicit contrast of 'sacred' and 'secular', which may itself distort the way using communities view the world (see Chapter 8 on the development of the 'religion'/'secular' divide). It can also force texts into categories that do not fit them well. For this reason, we prefer to speak of 'authoritative texts' and look at the nature of their authority for particular groups.

3 For more on birth groups, see Chapter 7A.

4 The *Aitareya Upaniṣad* is a good example. Its Chapters 1–3 are found 'inside' the *Aitareya Āraṇyaka* as *Aitareya Āraṇyaka* 2.4–6 (see Keith 1909: 39).

5 See the glossary for the connections between brahmin, Brāhmaṇa, brahman and Brahmā.

6 The term 'Veda' means 'what is known'. Although the notion that these texts were the foundation of all knowledge is ancient, the view that this means comprehensive and specific knowledge of every kind is a quasi-scientific modern one.

7 Different traditions of Christian have recognized slightly different contents to the Bible, Roman Catholics adding the Apocrypha to the Old and New Testament, which Protestant Christians recognize, for example. Nonetheless, both groups hold to the fixed collection of their own tradition. The text of the Qur'an was carefully fixed in the years after the revelations to Muhammad were written down. The Guru Granth Sahib of Sikhs is not only a fixed text, but is also always written or printed with exactly the same number of pages.

8 *Kesh* (uncut hair), *Kangha* (comb to keep hair in place), *Kirpan* (mini-dagger), *Kacch* (loose undershorts) and *Kara* (steel circle worn around the wrist), given by Gobind Singh as a sign of belonging to the Khalsa.

9 Often spelled Nizamuddin Aulia.

10 'Bande Mataram' is the Bengali spelling/pronunciation; 'Vande Mataram' is the Hindi.

11 After the 1998 General Election in India returned no majority party, the Hindu nationalist Bharatiya Janata Party (BJP) was able to form a government at the head of a centre-right coalition known as the National Democratic Alliance (NDA). Although this government collapsed in 1999, the NDA was returned at the subsequent election and remained in power for one full term. In the 2004 election the NDA was defeated, and a new coalition came to power, the left-leaning United Progressive Alliance (UPA), led by the Congress Party. The UPA held power in the following election in 2009, and remains in power as we write in 2011.

12 Persian for 'Lord', that is, Allah.

4 Myth

1 'Ram-katha' means 'story of Rama'. We follow Richman (1991a) in using this term to denote the entire corpus of Ram stories. It is not the title of a single text, so we do not italicize it. We use Ramayana and Mahabharata (no italics) to indicate the various epics that go under such names. We use *Ramayana* and *Mahabharata* (italics) to indicate the titles of the specific texts attributed to Valmiki and Vyasa.

2 Rama, Lakshmana, Bharata, Ravana and so on are the Sanskrit forms of these names. Ram, Lakshman, Bharat, Ravan are the Hindi forms. We try to be consistent with the particular context to which we are referring.

3 *Ramayana* and *Mahabharata* are the Sanskrit spellings, *Ramayan* and *Mahabharat* the Hindi ones.

4 See, for example, Walker's (1968: 455) dismissal of brahminical court chronicles as the 'fanciful outpourings' of mythology, cited in Suthren Hirst (1998: 105).

5 For a treasure chest of synopses and further reading, see Mills, Claus and Diamond (2003).

6 On Tulsi's telling, see further below.

7 The north Indian Nath tradition traced itself back to Lord Shiva (Adinath) and historically to Gorakhnath. A Tantric tradition influenced by Buddhist Tantra, this Shaiva tradition was influential in medieval western Maharashtra amongst lower castes in particular (Vaudeville 1987: 217) and was in competition with Jains for patronage (Dundas 2000: 235). Nathyogis were often regarded as rather anti-social by their competitors. The classic treatment of them remains Briggs (1938).

8 For example, Valmiki's Sita goes *against* Kaikeyi, her step-mother-in-law, who wishes her to remain in the palace, urging her need to accompany her husband wherever he goes. This is an interesting point not just in terms of the narrative ideology of *pativrata*, but also in terms of a woman's access to public space, an issue explored in depth in Chapter 10.

9 In her excellent study comparing Radha, Krishna's consort, with Sita, Heidi Pauwels (2008) argues that there has been an increasing 'Sita-ization' of Radha in twentieth-century portrayals of her.

10 Established once Ram returned in victory from Lanka to assume the throne relinquished by his half-brother Bharata.

11 The term '*avatara*' is not actually used in the *Gita* itself, but this verse is widely held to be the origin of the *avatara* doctrine. In fact, in the *Gita*, Krishna is understood as the Supreme Lord himself, not just as a descent of Vishnu.

12 For more on *bhakti*, see Chapter 5.

5 Ritual and worship

1 We are grateful to Professor Raymond B. Williams and Sadhu Paramtattva Swami for clarification on this point. On Swaminarayan as 'the human face of God', see Williams (1996: 145).

2 Literally 'white-clad' and 'sky-clad', the names of these two main traditions (which split in the early centuries CE; Cort 2002: 72) refer to the white clothing of the Svetambara and the nakedness of the Digambara ascetics. Each has different divisions, some of which accept the worship of *murti*s, others who reject this (Dundas 2002).

3 As also happened with Buddhist monasteries and Hindu temples, costly buildings requiring patronage too.

4 Bathing image with milk and water; anointing it with sandalpaste; offering flowers; offering incense; offering a lamp; creating a rice diagram of the Jain universe; offering sweets on it; offering fruit on its crescent for liberation (Babb 1988, 1994: 18).

6 Teachers and their traditions

1 Although see Ballard (1996: 15–17) on the panthic dimension, and our Chapter 1.

2 'Guru' in Sanskrit means 'heavy'.

3 In Chapter 2 we saw that in Advaita Vedanta realization is of the identity of self and *brahman*. In yogic traditions, the realization is usually held to come from one's own efforts in meditation; in devotional traditions, it may also come through the Lord's grace. Other traditions may seek to merge the two approaches.

4 Here, '*avatar*' is not intended to imply 'partial', unlike with Anandamayi. Krishna devotional traditions had articulated the difference between so-called 'partial descents' of Vishnu, for example the boar avatāra (see Chapter 4), and the 'full descent' of Krishna. Modern gurus and their followers may use an established vocabulary to negotiate competitive status in quite different arenas.

5 You will find a very good description of Amritanandamayi's *bhava darshan* in Warrier (2005: 37–40).

6 We are grateful to Kiyokazu Okita for this reference (see Okita forthcoming).

7 Nanak himself seems to have reserved the term 'Guru' clearly for the inner voice of God (McLeod 1980: 252). In Chapter 9, we shall follow the development of Sikh traditions in more detail.

8 The collection of hymns brought together by the fifth Guru, Arjan, which the tenth Guru, Gobind Singh, declared to be the permanent Guru for all Sikhs, after his own death (see further Chapters 3 and 9). Note that '*sikh*' in Punjabi actually means 'disciple' from the Sanskrit '*shishya*'.

9 In the context of a religions model, such diversity is adduced as evidence for the particular tolerance of the Sikh community, one of two rather different ways of dealing with relations between the newly differentiating traditions in nineteenth-century Punjab (see McLeod 1980: 255, and Chapter 9).

10 The sound underlying all sounds.

11 Kaula sects, that is, Shaiva/Shakta Tantric lineages that want to associate themselves with the *Kula* path, will draw on this text in a variety of ways. The *kula* is the clan created by initiation into 'the essence of reality one takes to heart' (Brooks 2000: 348).

12 Hence Warrier's explanation of the 'avatar guru' claim earlier.

13 For a review and critique of the secularization thesis, see Casanova (1994: ch. 1).

14 For an interesting and quite fierce critique of this kind of exoticized tourism and associated cultural forms, see John Hutnyk's essay on the British band Kula Shaker, 'Magical Mystery Tourism', in Kaur and Hutnyk (1999).

7A Caste: social relations, cultural formations

1 For suggestions on possible ways in which social phenomena ordering society into hierarchies in early India may have been linked with the development of clan-based lineages, pastoral and urban organization, the emergence of segmented states and encounters with forest-clans, see Thapar (2002: 62–8). For an excellent study of the development of caste systems in the eighteenth century, see Bayly (1999).
2 We have italicized the names of the other *varna*s, but not 'brahmin'. There are two reasons why we do not italicize 'brahmin' (Sanskrit form *brāhmaṇa*): (1) it has become a term adopted into English; (2) this form and spelling conveniently distinguishes it from the following related terms: *brahman* (ultimate reality); Brahma (creator deity); *Brahmana*s (second layer of Vedic texts).
3 Translation: J. Suthren Hirst (cf. Johnson 1994: 20).
4 The term 'Scheduled Caste' was used in the 1935 Government of India Act to identify those that the colonial state had previously described as the 'Depressed Classes'. The castes included were identified in a list or schedule. The 1950 Indian Constitution retained 'Scheduled Castes' and 'Scheduled Tribes' as legal categories (Adeney and Wyatt 2010: 82).
5 As a general rule, *jati* is endogamous, whereas *got* is exogamous.
6 Some Tamil Mukkuvars are Muslim, also low-caste fishers. Some Sri Lankan Mukkuvars are wealthy and high status (see McGilvray 1995). Ram (1991) shows that Tamil Christian Mukkuvar fisherwomen have an ambiguous relationship to the Roman Catholic Church yet do not want to raise their caste status by change of occupation.
7 This revised Muluki Ain has recently been under major review (2010). In April 2011, the Nepali Supreme Court recommended legislation for a new Civil Code and Criminal Procedure Code be put to the Parliament, although the drafts of these are still a matter of controversy amongst the country's lawyers.
8 See Mayaram's (1997) study of the Meos.

7B The confluence of caste and religion

1 See, for example, the *Shorter Oxford English Dictionary*, in which a caste is defined as 'a Hindu hereditary class of socially equal persons, united in religion and usu. following similar occupations' (SOED 1993: 348).
2 See, for example, comments of devotees of Mata Amritanandamayi in Warrier (2005: 76–7).
3 This was Dayananda's view, and has since been pursued with varying degrees of enthusiasm by the organization he established, the Arya Samaj. See Zavos (2000: 46–8, 87–92).
4 An interesting exploration of this caste-based political dynamic is to be found in Ciotti (2010).
5 Other reformers since this period have also taken this view, including M.K. Gandhi. Frequently, these reformers have pointed to *Gita* 4.13 (see Chapter 7A) for textual affirmation of a model of four *varna*s, working in co-operation for the good of society as a whole, with *varna* status achieved (by developing appropriate actions and qualities) rather than ascribed (by birth).

6 For a comparison of the approaches of Gandhi and Ambedkar, see Zelliot (1996: 150–78). One notable difference was that Gandhi popularized the term 'Harijan', which translates as 'child of God', to refer to untouchables, claiming that this was a more respectful way of referring to these castes. Ambedkar rejected this as a cosmetic concession that would not change the predicament of untouchables.

8 Encounters with the West

1 Sometimes you will also see his name written as Syed Ahmed Khan.
2 As a Sayyid, Sayyid Ahmad could also claim descent direct from the Prophet Mohammed, through his grandsons Hasan ibn Ali and Husain ibn Ali.
3 Most Sunni scholars held that 'the door to *ijtihad* was closed' from around the eleventh or twelfth centuries. Whether the door is open or can be opened despite obstacles is still a matter of intense debate.
4 As one of the guiding principles of the school states:

> As long as the madrasa has no fixed sources of income, it will, God willing, operate as desired. And if it gain any fixed income . . . then the madrasa will lose the fear and hope which inspire submission to God and will lose His hidden help.
>
> (quoted in Metcalf 2004: 33)

5 These included two Muslims, a Jain, two Brahmo Samajis, two Christians, a Theosophist, the Buddhist Anagarika Dharmapala from Sri Lanka and Swami Vivekananda as a representative of Hinduism (see Chowdhury-Sengupta 1998: 22).

9 The construction of religious boundaries

1 Punjab was to become known in later years as the 'breadbasket of India', because of its intensive wheat production, and as early as 1920 it accounted for no less than one-third of wheat production in the whole of British India.
2 Although race theory has generally been discredited in contemporary social sciences, its legacies permeate contemporary societies (Mason 2000). In this case martial race theory is still evident in, for example, the continued recruitment of Nepali Gurkhas in the British army, and the continued over-representation of Sikhs and other Punjabis in the Indian army.
3 An extract from this tract is available in McLeod (1984).
4 A question on religion has been asked in Northern Ireland since 1861.
5 Cohn (1987: 248) also argues that the process of objectification is associated primarily with elite, urbanized Indians. Although undoubtedly it is the case that there is more evidence of reflection amongst this class, there is also evidence of non-elites engaged in this process. Indeed, Cohn himself presents a good example in his discussion of the Mahtons, a Punjabi lower caste group who aspired to be returned in the 1911 census as Rajputs (pp. 248–9).
6 The catalyst for the beginning of the rebellion is often cited as soldiers' objection to the use of pork and beef fat in the lubrication of cartridges used by the British Indian army, although it is clear that there were wider grievances and other sources of rebellion. See Bates (2007: 63–7).
7 'Memorial from the Chairman of a Public Meeting of the inhabitants of Nagpur and the adjoining Districts, praying that definite rules be framed for the guidance of District Officers in the matter of kine slaughter' – see Zavos (2000: 77).
8 *Mahratta*, 7 July 1889, quoted in Zavos (2000: 76).

9 *Kaliyug* refers to the age of darkness, one of four ages in Hindu cosmology. *Dharmaraj* refers to a vision of righteous rule on earth.

10 For a good account of Operation Bluestar, see Tully (1992: ch. 5, 153–80).

11 There is also a Maharashtrian Sant tradition that developed from about the thirteenth century, with slightly different characteristics – see Schomer (1987: 3).

10 Public and private space

1 O'Hanlon notes that these practices of seclusion were possibly quite newly enforced in families such as Tarabai's as part of a way of raising social aspirations. *Purdah* here, then, becomes an expression of gentility (O'Hanlon 1994: 5, 20–8).

2 As well as being scathing about men who use such passages, she is scathing against brahmin values. Note that her Mahratta family had connections with Phule's Satyashodak Samaj (see Chapter 7B) and shared its anti-brahminical stance.

3 There is also a compelling film of the book, made in 1984 by the famous Bengali director Satyajit Ray.

4 The Age of Consent Act, for example, only raised the age from 12 to 14 and is actually only a note to a Bill – both its actuality and the attention it has received have been gravely over-emphasized.

5 For a very clear restatement of this, see Nurullah and Naik (1951: 153).

6 Other groups were involved. One of the key campaigners for raising the Age of Consent was a Parsee, Behramji M. Malabari.

7 Whether of Muslim influence or of Hindu need for protection of their women against the threat of rape and violence. Although she is by no means a Hindu nationalist, this view was expressed by the then-President of India-elect Pratibha Patil in 2007. 'Women have always been respected in the Indian culture', she said. 'The purdah system was introduced to protect them from the Muslim invaders. However, times have changed. India is now independent and hence, the systems should also change' (quoted in Page 2007).

8 Although specific references are rarely given, it is the case that *Arthaśāstra* Book I, ch. 20, talks about the construction of the harem, including separate quarters for women, and the regulations on which women the king can see and when (largely to protect him against the danger of assassination).

9 For further reading on the way *purdah* is affected by region and social class, see in particular Agarwal (1994).

11 Conflicting paradigms

1 A significant development in the dispute occurred on 30 September 2010. A judgment of the Allahabad High Court on this date indicated that the site should be shared between three parties (including the UP Sunni Central Board of Waqfs). One member (Justice D.V. Sharma) of the three-judge bench of the High Court claimed categorically that 'the disputed site is the birthplace of Lord Ram' (Khan 2010). The judgment is currently subject to several appeals, and, as of May 2011, a Supreme Court ruling suspending the judgment.

2 You will be able to see some video footage of people lifting earth from this spot at Madhu Feast (2009).

3 The earth at the site is recognized as having special properties in this tradition, just as it does in the Catholic tradition. The 1911 census report notes that 'It is essentially a forest pilgrimage . . . the earth of Madu is considered to posses special medical properties, hence the sanctity, resulting in the reputation that

"Madhu Medicine" effects cures in cases of snake bite' (quoted in Gamage n.d.). Here, then, we can see the way in which the sacred power of the earth of the site is appropriated differently by different users, with traditions being interwoven and appropriated in different ways.

12 Twisting the kaleidoscope: reflections in conclusion

1 We prefer not to call them features, as this generates a model of a religion as an entity *having* these features, which is what we want to call into question.
2 Ballard (2011) has extended the number of dimensions to five in a subsequent article.
3 Even where theologies are clear that God transcends gender.
4 As covered in Mittal and Thursby (2006).

References

Adeney, K. and A. Wyatt (2010) *Contemporary India*, Basingstoke: Palgrave Macmillan.

Adiga, A. (2008) *The White Tiger*, London: Atlantic Books.

Agarwal, B. (1994) *A Field of One's Own: Gender and Land Rights in South Asia*, Cambridge: Cambridge University Press.

Ahmad, A. (1967) *Islamic Modernism in India and Pakistan 1857–1964*, Oxford: Oxford University Press.

Alam, A. (2008) 'The enemy within: madrasa and Muslim identity in North India', *Modern Asian Studies* 42 (2/3): 605–27.

Alam, F. (2007) 'Dhaka Diary: memories of Durga Puja', *Kitaab*, online posting in 'Features', 14 May 2009. Available: http://kitaabonline.wordpress.com/2009/05/14/dhaka-diary-memories-of-durga-puja/ (accessed 26 November 2010).

Ali, I (1994) 'Sikh settlers in the Western Punjab during British rule', Working Paper 94–04, Lahore: Lahore University of Management Sciences Centre for Management and Economic Research.

Ambedkar, B.R., 'What Gandhi and the Congress have done to the untouchables'. See Hay (1988).

Appadurai, A. (1986) 'Is homo hierarchicus?', *American Ethnologist* 13 (4): 745–61. Online. Available: http://www.jstor.org/stable/644464.

Appadurai, A. (1988) 'Putting hierarchy in its place', *Cultural Anthropology* 3 (1): 36–49. Online. Available: http://www.jstor.org/stable/656307.

Appadurai, A. (1996) *Modernity at Large: Cultural Dimensions of Globalization*, Minneapolis: University of Minnesota Press.

Asad, T. (1993) *Genealogies of Religion: Discipline and Reasons of Power in Christianity and Islam*, Baltimore: Johns Hopkins University Press.

ASI (2003) *Ayodhya: 2002–3, Excavations at the Disputed Site*, New Delhi: Archaeological Survey of India.

Assayag, J. (2004) *At the Confluence of Two Rivers: Muslims and Hindus in South India*, New Delhi: Manohar.

Aulia Allah (n.d.) 'Aulia Allah. In the name of Allah, introducing "Mazars of Pakistan" – all regions covered'. Online. Available: http://www.aulia-e-pakistan.com (accessed 30 December 2010).

Ayoub, M. (1999) 'Cult and culture: common saints and shrines in Middle Eastern popular piety', in R.G. Hovannisian and G. Sabagh (eds) *Religion and Culture in Medieval Islam*, Cambridge: Cambridge University Press.

Babb, L.A. (1987) *Redemptive Encounters: Three Modern Styles in the Hindu Tradition*, Delhi: Oxford University Press.

Babb, L.A. (1988) 'Giving and giving up: the eightfold worship among Śvetāmbar Mūrtipūjak Jains', *Journal of Anthropological Research* 44: 67–85.

Babb, L.A. (1994) 'The great choice: worldly values in a Jain ritual culture', *History of Religions* 34 (1): 15–38. Online. Available: http://www.jstor.org/stable/1062977.

Babb, L.A. and S.S. Wadley (eds) (1995) *Media and the Transformation of Religion in South Asia*, Philadelphia: University of Pennsylvania Press.

Ballantyne, T. (2006) *Between Colonialism and Diaspora: Sikh Cultural Formations in an Imperial World*, Durham: Duke University Press.

Ballard, R. (1996) 'Panth, kismet, dharm te qaum: four dimensions of Punjabi religion', in P. Singh (ed.) *Punjabi Identity in a Global Context*, Delhi: Oxford University Press.

Ballard, R. (2011) 'The re-establishment of meaning and purpose: *Mādri* and *Padre Muzhub* in the Punjabi diaspora', in K. Olwig (ed.) *Mobile Bodies, Mobile Cosmologies: Family, Religion, and Migration in a Global World?*, Aarhus: University of Aarhus Press.

Balzani, M. (2004) 'Pregnancy rituals among the Rajput elite in contemporary Rajasthan: anthropology and the world of women', in J. Suthren Hirst and L. Thomas (eds) *Playing for Real: Hindu Role Models, Religion and Gender*, Delhi: Oxford University Press.

Barrier, N.G. (1966) *The Punjab Alienation of Land Bill of 1900*, Durham: Duke University Press.

Basava, 'God, O God'. See Schouten (1991).

Basham, A.L. (1985) *The Wonder that Was India*, 3rd revised edn, London: Sidgwick & Jackson. First published 1967.

Bates, C. (2007) *Subalterns and the Raj: South Asia Since 1600*, London: Routledge.

Baumfield, V. (1991) 'Swami Vivekananda's Practical Vedānta', unpublished PhD thesis, University of Newcastle upon Tyne.

Bayly, C. (1990) *The Raj: India and the British 1600–1947*, London: National Portrait Gallery Publications.

Bayly, S. (1984) 'Hindu kingship and the origin of community: religion, state and society in Kerala, 1750–1850', *Modern Asian Studies* 18 (2): 177–213.

Bayly, S. (1999) *Caste, Society and Politics in India from the Eighteenth Century to the Modern Age*, The New Cambridge History of India IV.3, Cambridge: Cambridge University Press.

Behl, A. and S. Weightman (tr. and intro.) (2000) *Madhumālatī: An Indian Sufi Romance (Mīr Sayyid Manjhan Shaṭṭārī Rājgīrī)*, Oxford: Oxford University Press.

Bennett, L. (1983) *Dangerous Wives and Sacred Sisters: Social and Symbolic Roles of High-Caste Women in Nepal*, New York: Columbia University Press.

Bhagavad Gita 4: 6–8, 11: 10–12. See Johnson (1994).

Bhanot, D.K. (n.d.) 'Universal prayer: an original "translation"' [of Om Jai Jagdish Hare]. Online. Available: http://www.bhanot.net/bhaj21.html (accessed 29 December 2010).

Bharadwaja, C. (tr.) (1984) *Light of Truth or an English Translation of the Satyarth Prakash, the Well-known Work of Swami Dayanand Saraswati*, New Delhi: Sarvadeshik Arya Pratinidhi Sabha. Translation of the second revised edition of *Satyārth Prakāś*, first published in 1883; first edition 1875. 'A Statement of My Beliefs' comes right at the end of this book and actually uses Bawa Chhajju Singh's translation (see Bharadwaja 1984: 723).

Bhaskar, S. (2007) 'Guru Maharishi Yogi 2'. Online. Available: http://www.youtube. com/watch?v=yIbfhvjKq0o&NR=1 (accessed 21 December 2010).

Bhinmal Tragad Brahmin (n.d.a) 'How and why – Bhinmal Tragad Brahmin'. Online. Available: http://sites.google.com/site/bhinmaltragadbrahminsoni/history (accessed 20 December 2010).

Bhinmal Tragad Brahmin (n.d.b) 'Bhinmal Tragad Brahmin – welcome'. Online. Available: http://sites.google.com/site/bhinmaltragadbrahminsoni/home (accessed 20 December 2010).

Black, B. (2007) *The Character of the Self in Ancient India: Priests, Kings, and Women in the Early Upaniṣads*, Albany: State University of New York Press.

Bloch, M. (1992) *Prey into Hunter: The Politics of Religious Experience*, Cambridge: Cambridge University Press.

Bose, S. and A. Jalal (2004) *Modern South Asia: History, Culture, Political Economy*, 2nd edn, New York: Routledge.

Bowman, G. (1993) 'Nationalising the sacred: shrines and shifting identities in the Israeli-occupied territories', *Man: Journal of the Royal Anthropological Institute* 28 (3): 431–60.

Briggs, G.W. (1938 or reprints) *Gorakhnāth and the Kānphata Yogīs*, Calcutta: YMCA Publishing House.

Brihadaranyaka Upanishad 3.9.1. See Olivelle (1996).

Brockington, J.L. (1984) *Righteous Rāma: The Evolution of an Epic*, Delhi: Oxford University Press.

Brockington, J. and M. Brockington (intro. and tr.) (2006) *Rāma the Steadfast: An Early Form of the Rāmāyaṇa*, London: Penguin.

Brooks, D.R. (2000) 'The Ocean of the Heart: selections from the *Kulārṇava Tantra*', in D.G. White (ed.) *Tantra in Practice*, Princeton: Princeton University Press.

Brosius, C. (2010) *India's Middle Class: New Forms of Urban Leisure, Consumption and Prosperity*, New Delhi: Routledge.

Bryant, E. and L.L. Patton (eds) (2005) *The Indo-Aryan Controversy: Evidence and Inference in Indian History*, London: Routledge.

Butalia, U. (1998) *The Other Side of Silence: Voices from the Partition of India*, New Delhi: Penguin.

Caldwell, S. (1999) *O Terrifying Mother: Sexuality, Violence and Worship of the Goddess Kali*, New Delhi: Oxford University Press.

Casanova, J. (1994) *Public Religions in the Modern World*, Chicago: University of Chicago Press.

Chakrabarty, D. (2000) *Provincializing Europe: Postcolonial Thought and Historical Difference*, Princeton: Princeton University Press.

Chakravarti, U. (1989) 'Whatever happened to the Vedic *Dasi*? Orientalism, nationalism and a script for the past', in K. Sangari and S. Vaid (eds) *Recasting Women: Essays in Indian Colonial History*, New Delhi: Kali for Women.

Chāndogya Upaniṣad 6.14.1–6.14.2. See Roebuck (2003).

Chatterjee, P. (1993) *The Nation and its Fragments: Colonial and Postcolonial Histories,* Princeton: Princeton University Press.

Chattopadhyay, B. (1998) *Representing the Other? Sanskrit Sources and the Muslims (Eighth to Fourteenth Century)*, Delhi: Manohar.

Chaubey, B. (2006) 'BJP Poll Mantra: Vande Mataram', IBN Live. Online. Available: http://ibnlive.in.com/news/bjp-eyes-votes-through-vande-mataram/19986-4.html (accessed 25 October 2010).

Chopra, B.J. (producer) (1988–90) *Mahabharat* (TV series), Doordarshan. Online. Available: e.g. http://www.youtube.com/watch?v=ySSw8CdjIYk (accessed 28 December 2010).

Chowdhury-Sengupta, I. (1998) 'Reconstructing Hinduism on a world platform: the world's first parliament of religions, Chicago 1893', in W. Radice (ed.) *Swami Vivekananda and the Modernisation of Hinduism*, New Delhi: Oxford University Press.

Ciotti, M (2010) *Retro-Modern India. Forging the Low-Caste Self*, London: Routledge.

Coburn, T.B. (1995) 'Sita fights while Ram swoons: a Shakta version of the Ramayan', *Manushi* 90 (Sept–Oct): 5–16.

Cohn, B. (1987) *An Anthropologist among the Historians and Other Essays*, Oxford: Oxford University Press.

Cort, J. (2002) 'Bhakti in the early Jain tradition: understanding devotional religion in South Asia', *History of Religions* 42 (1): 59–86.

Csapo, E. (2005) *Theories of Mythology*, Oxford: Blackwell.

Dalit Freedom Network (n.d.) 'Quotes to remember'. Online. Available: http://www.dalitnetwork.org/go?/dfn/who_are_the_dalit/C157/ (accessed 12 December 2010).

Das, S. (n.d.) ' "Aartis" or hymns for Hindu gods and goddesses: Vishnu Aarti – Om Jay Jagdish Hare'. Online. Available: http://hinduism.about.com/od/prayersmantras/ss/aarti_hinduhymn.htm (accessed 29 December 2010).

Davis, R. (2005) 'The iconography of Rama's chariot', in D. Ludden (ed.) *Making India Hindu: Religion, Community and the Politics of Democracy in India*, 2nd edn, New Delhi: Oxford University Press.

Dawn (2010) 'Attack on Data Darbar condemned', 3 July. Online. Available: http://dawnnews.tv/wps/wcm/connect/dawn-content-library/dawn/the-newspaper/local/attack-on-data-darbar-condemned-370 (accessed 10 August 2010).

Dayanand Saraswati (1883) *Light of Truth*. See Bharadwaja (1984).

de Bruijn, T. (2005) 'Many roads lead to Lanka: the intercultural semantics of Rama's quest', *Contemporary South Asia*, special issue on 'Teaching across South Asian Religious Traditions', guest editors J. Suthren Hirst and J. Zavos, 14 (1): 39–52.

Dempsey, C. (1999) 'Lessons in miracles from Kerala, South India: stories of three "Christian" saints', *History of Religions* 39 (2): 150–76.

Devji, F.F. (1994) 'Gender and the politics of space: the movement for women's reform 1857–1900', in Z. Hasan (ed.) *Forging Identities: Gender, Communities and the State*, New Delhi: Kali for Women.

Dezső, C. (ed. and tr.) (2005) *Much Ado about Religion*, Clay Sanskrit Library, New York: New York University Press and JJC Foundation. Notes and a huge amount of background material (but not text) online. Available: http://www.claysanskritlibrary.org/volume.php?id=11 (accessed 15 September 2010).

Dirks, N. (2001) *Castes of Mind: Colonialism and the Making of Modern India*, Princeton: Princeton University Press.

Doniger, W. (1981) *The Rig Veda: An Anthology: One Hundred and Eight Hymns*, Harmondsworth: Penguin. Reprinted several times.

Doniger, W. (2009) *The Hindus: An Alternative History*, New York: Penguin.

Dumont, L. (1980) *Homo Hierarchicus: The Caste System and its Implications*, completely revised English edition, Chicago: Chicago University Press. First French edition Gallimard, 1966, 1979.

Dundas, P. (2000) 'The Jain monk Jinapati Sūri gets the better of a Nāth Yogī', in D.G. White (ed.) *Tantra in Practice*, Princeton: Princeton University Press.

Dundas, P. (2002) *The Jains*, 2nd edn, London: Routledge.

Dvaita home page (1995–2006) Created by Shrisha Rao, last updated 22 September 2009. Online. Available: http://www.dvaita.org (accessed 29 December 2010).

Dwyer, R. (2006) *Filming the Gods: Religion and Indian Cinema*, London: Routledge.

Dyczkowski, M.S.G. (2001) *The Cult of the Goddess Kubjika: A Preliminary Comparative Textual and Anthropological Survey of a Secret Newar Goddess*, Nepal Research Centre Publication no. 23, Stuttgart: Franz Steiner Verlag.

Eaton, R. (1987) 'Approaches to the study of conversion to Islam in India', in R.C. Martin (ed.) *Islam in Religious Studies*, New York: One World Press.

Eaton, R. (1996) *Sufis of Bijapur 1300–1700: Social Roles of Sufis in Medieval India*, Delhi: Munshiram Manoharlal. First edition 1978, Princeton: Princeton University Press.

Eaton, R. (2000) *Essays on Islam and Indian History*, New Delhi: Oxford University Press.

Eaton, R. (2004) *Temple Desecration and Muslim States in Medieval India*, Gurgaon: Hope India.

Eck, D. (1998) *Darśan: Seeing the Divine Image in India*, 3rd edn, New York: Columbia University Press.

Embree, A. (ed.) (1992) *Sources of Indian Tradition Volume 1: From the Beginning to 1800*, 2nd edn, Harmondsworth: Penguin.

Erndl, K. (1993) *Victory to the Mother*, Oxford: Oxford University Press.

Erndl, K. (2000) 'A trance healing session with Mataji', in D.G. White (ed). *Tantra in Practice*, Princeton: Princeton University Press.

Erndl, K. (2007) 'The play of the Mother: possession and power in Hindu women's goddess rituals', in T. Pintchman (ed.) *Women's Lives, Women's Rituals in the Hindu Tradition* Oxford: Oxford University Press.

Ernst, C.W. (1985) 'From hagiography to martyrology: conflicting testimonies to a Sufi martyr in the Delhi Sultanate', *History of Religions* 24 (4): 308–27. Online. Available: http://www.jstor.org/1062305.

Ernst, C.W. (2003) 'Muslim studies of Hinduism? A reconsideration of Arabic and Persian translations from Indian languages', *Iranian Studies* 36 (2): 173–95. Online. Available: http://dx.doi.org/10.1080/00210860305244 (accessed 18 October 2010).

Ewing, K. (1983) 'The politics of Sufism: redefining the saints of Pakistan', *Journal of Asian Studies* 42 (2): 251–68.

Fitzgerald, T. (1990) 'Hinduism and the "world religions" fallacy', *Religion* 20: 101–18.

Fitzgerald, T. (2000) *The Ideology of Religious Studies*, New York: Oxford University Press.

Flood, G.D. (2005) *The Tantric Body: The Secret Tradition of Hindu Religion*, London: I.B. Tauris.

Flueckiger, J.B. (2006) *In Amma's Healing Room: Gender and Vernacular Islam in South India*, Bloomington: Indiana Press.

Flügel, P. (1998) 'Review of L.A. Babb (1996) *Absent Lord: Ascetics and Kings in a Jain Ritual Culture*, Berkeley: University of California Press', *Journal of the Royal Anthropological Institute* 4 (1): 167–9. Online. Available: http://www.jstor.org/stable/3034476.

Flügel, P. (2005) 'The invention of Jainism: a short history of Jaina studies', *International Journal of Jain Studies* 1 (1): 1–14. Online. Available: http://eprints.

soas.ac.uk/98/1/The_Invention_of_Jainism_(without_photo).pdf   (accessed   27 December 2010).

Forbes, G. (1996) *Women in Modern India*, The New Cambridge History of India IV.2, Cambridge: Cambridge University Press.

Freeman, R. (2005) 'The Teyyam tradition of Kerala', in G. Flood (ed.) *The Blackwell Companion to Hinduism*, Oxford: Blackwell. First published 2003.

Frykenberg, R. (1989), 'The emergence of modern "Hinduism" as a concept and as an institution: a reappraisal with special reference to South India', in G. Sontheimer and H. Kulke (eds) *Hinduism Reconsidered*, New Delhi: Manohar.

Fuller, C. (1992) *The Camphor Flame: Popular Hinduism and Society in India*, Princeton: Princeton University Press.

Gamage, A. (n.d.) 'Attempt to make Madhu Church a "National Basilica" on false pretexts'. Online. Available: http://www.lankaweb.com/news/items02/190802–2. html (accessed 14 December 2010).

Gambhirananda (tr.) (1977) *Brahma-Sūtra Bhāṣya of Śaṅkarācārya*, 3rd edn, Calcutta: Advaita Ashrama.

Gandhi, L. (1998) *Postcolonial Theory: A Critical Introduction*, Edinburgh: University of Edinburgh Press.

Ganesh, D. (2011) 'Bhuvaneshwari arrives'. Email. 19 January 2011.

Gayatri Mantra (2010) Its meaning with audio. Online. Available: http://www.eagles-pace.com/spirit/gayatri.php (accessed 31 December 2010).

Gayatri Mantra – Enigma (n.d.) A melodic version posted by 1990ad. Online. Available: http://www.youtube.com/watch?v=nDnamSM3Z3s (accessed 31 December 2010).

Gayatri Mantra: the Mother of all Mantras (n.d.) Online. Available: http://www.gayatrimantra.net/ (accessed 31 December 2010).

Geertz, C. (1993) 'Religion as a cultural system', in Clifford Geertz (ed.) *The Interpretation of Cultures: Selected Essays*, London: Fontana Press. First published 1966.

Gerstenfeld, M. (2005) 'The Jews, Israel, and India: an interview with Nathan Katz', Jerusalem Center for Public Affairs, *Changing Jewish Communities* 2, 15 November. Online. Available: http://www.jcpa.org/cjc/cjc-katz-f05.htm (accessed 27 December 2010).

Ghose, J.C. (ed.) (1982) *The English Works of Raja Rammohun Roy*, New Delhi: Cosmo.

Ghose, J.C. and E.C. Bose (eds) (1906) *The English Works of Raja Rammohun Roy with an English Translation of 'Tuḥfatul Muwaḥḥidin'*, Allahabad: Panini Office. Reprint 1978, New York: AMS Press.

Gita Press (1968) *Śrī Rāmacaritamānasa or the Mānasa Lake Brimming Over with the Exploits of Śrī Rāma*, with Hindi text and English translation (a romanized edition) (no translator given), Gorakhpur: Gita Press. Online. Available: http://www.gitapress.org/BOOKS/1318/1318_Sri%20Ramchritmanas_Roman.pdf (accessed 22 December 2010).

Gladwin, F. (tr.) (1786) *Ayeen Akbery or the Institutes of the Emperor Akber*, translated from the original Persian, vol. III, Calcutta: printed by William Mackay.

Gold, D. (1987) *The Lord as Guru: Hindi Saints in North Indian Tradition*, Oxford: Oxford University Press.

Goldman, R.P. (intro. and tr.) (1984) *The Rāmāyaṇa of Vālmīki*, vol. I: *Bālakāṇḍa*, Princeton Library of Asian Translations, Princeton: Princeton University Press.

Gooptu, N. (2001) *The Politics of the Urban Poor in Early Twentieth-Century India*, Cambridge: Cambridge University Press.

Gottschalk, P. (2000) *Beyond Hindu and Muslim: Multiple Identity in Narratives from Village India*, New York: Oxford University Press.

Gould, W. (2004) *Hindu Nationalism and the Language of Politics in Late Colonial India*, Cambridge: Cambridge University Press.

Government of India (1909) Anand Marriage Act. Online. Available: http://www.lawyersclubindia.com/bare_acts/Anand-Marriage-Act-36.asp (accessed 10 December 2010).

Government of Oudh (1877) *Gazetteer of the Province of Oudh*, vol. 2, Lucknow: Oudh Government Press.

Granoff, P. (1988a) 'Jain biographies of Nagarjuna: notes on the composing of a bibliography in medieval India', in P. Granoff and K. Shinohara (eds) (1988) *Monks and Magicians: Religious Biographies in Asia*, Oakville, Ontario: Mosaic Press.

Granoff, P. (1988b) 'The biographies of Arya Khapatacarya: a preliminary investigation into the transmission and adaptation of biographical legends', in P. Granoff and K. Shinohara (eds) (1988) *Monks and Magicians: Religious Biographies in Asia*, Oakville, Ontario: Mosaic Press.

Green, N. (2004a) 'Oral competition narratives of Muslim and Hindu saints in the Deccan', *Asian Folklore Studies* 63 (2): 221–42.

Green, N. (2004b) 'Stories of saints and sultans: re-membering history at the Sufi shrines of Aurangabad', *Modern Asian Studies* 38 (2): 419–46. Online. Available: http://www.jstor.org/stable/3876520..

Green, N. (2006) *Indian Sufism since the Seventeenth Century: Saints, Books and Empires in the Muslim Deccan*, London: Routledge.

Green, N. (2010a) 'Sufi silsilas'. Email. 16 October 2010.

Green, N. (2010b) 'Consummating sainthood: death, desire and saintly power in the Indo-Muslim rituals of the spiritual wedding ('*urs*)', unpublished ethnography.

Green, N. and M. Searle-Chatterjee (eds) (2008) *Religion, Language and Power*, New York: Routledge.

Guneratne, A. (1998) 'Modernization, the state, and the construction of a Tharu identity in Nepal', *Journal of Asian Studies* 57 (3): 749–73. Online. Available: http://www.jstor.org/stable/2658740.

Guneratne, A. (2002) *Many Tongues, One People: The Making of Tharu Identity in Nepal*, Ithaca, NY: Cornell University Press.

Guneratne, A. (2003) 'Caste and state, India and Nepal', in M.A. Mills, P.J. Claus and S. Diamond (eds) *South Asian Folklore: An Encyclopedia*, London: Routledge.

Halbfass, W. (1988) *India and Europe: An Essay in Understanding*, revised and updated English translation, Albany: State University of New York Press. First German edition 1981, Basel: Schwabe.

Hall, S. (1992) 'The West and the rest: discourse and power', in S. Hall and B. Gieben (eds) *Formations of Modernity*, Cambridge: Polity.

Hall, S. (1997) 'The work of representation', in S. Hall (ed.) *Representation: Cultural Representations and Signifying Practices*, London: Sage.

Hallstrom, L.L. (1999) *Mother of Bliss: Anandamayi Ma (1896–1982)*, Oxford: Oxford University Press.

Hallstrom, L.L. (2004) 'Anandamayi Ma, the bliss-filled Divine Mother', in Karen Pechilis (ed.) *The Graceful Guru: Hindu Female Gurus in India and the United States*, Oxford: Oxford University Press.

Hann, M. (2005) 'Numbers in nirvana: how the 1872–1921 Indian censuses helped operationalise "Hinduism"', *Religion* 35 (1): 13–30.

Harappa (1995–2010) Producer Omar Khan. Online. Available: http://www.harappa. com (accessed 18 November 2010).

Hardiman, D. (1995) *The Coming of the Devi: Adivasi Assertion in Western India*, New Delhi: Oxford University Press.

Hasan, M. (ed.) (1993) *India's Partition: Process, Strategy and Mobilisation*, New Delhi: Oxford University Press.

Hawley, J.S. (1996) 'The goddess in India', in J.S. Hawley and D.M. Wulff (eds) *Devi: Goddesses of India*, Berkeley: University of California Press.

Hawley, J.S. (2006) 'Militant Hinduism: Ayodhya and the momentum of Hindu nationalism', in J.S. Hawley and V. Narayanan (eds) *The Life of Hinduism*, Berkeley: University of California Press.

Hay, Stephen (ed.) (1988) *Sources of Indian Tradition Volume 2: Modern India and Pakistan*, 2nd edn, New York: Columbia University Press.

Hefner, R. (1998) 'Multiple modernities: Christianity, Islam and Hinduism in a globalizing age', *Annual Review of Anthropology* 27: 83–104.

Henry, E.O. (1991) 'Jogīs and nirgun bhajans in Bhojpuri-speaking India: intra-genre heterogeneity, adaptation and functional shift', *Ethnomusicology* 35 (2): 221–42.

Hess, L. and S. Singh (trs) (1983) *The Bījak of Kabīr*, with notes and essays by Linda Hess, San Francisco: North Point Press. Also online (2002) *The Bijak of Kabir*, New York: Oxford, University Press. Available: http://www.oxfordscholarship.com/oso/public/content/religion/9780195148763/toc.html (accessed 23 December 2010).

Hewitt, V. (1997) *The New International Politics of South Asia*, Manchester: Manchester University Press.

H.H. Marthanda Varma (n.d.) 'Padmanabha', edited excerpts from *Ananda Varta* magazine. Online. Available: http://www.anandamayi.org/Padmanabha.htm (accessed 4 November 2009).

Hindu Council UK (n.d.) 'Hinduism: Hindu gods'. Online. Available: http://www. hinducounciluk.org/newsite/hindugods.asp (accessed 20 December 2010).

Hinduism Today (2003) 'Secrets from the *Kularnava Tantra*', July–Sept. Online. Available: http://www.hinduismtoday.com/modules/smartsection/item.php?-itemid=3785 (accessed 18 December 2010).

Hobsbawm, E. (1992) 'Introduction: inventing traditions', in E. Hobsbawm and T. Ranger (eds) *Invention of Tradition*, Cambridge: Cambridge University Press.

Hossain, R. S. (1931) *Abarodhbasini* [*The Secluded Ones*], in Abdul Quadir (ed.) (1999) *Rokeya Rachanabali*, 2nd edn, Dhaka: Bangla Academy.

Hossain, Y. (1992) 'The Begum's dream: Rokeya Sakhawat Hossain and the broadening of Muslim women's aspirations in Bengal', *South Asia Research* 12 (1): 1–19. Online. Available: http://sar.sagepub.com (accessed 31 March 2009).

Hutnyk, J. (1999) 'Magical mystery tourism', in R. Kaur and J. Hutnyk (eds) *Travel Worlds: Journeys in Contemporary Cultural Politics*, London: Zed.

Ibn 'Umar Mihrābī, *Hujjat ul-Hind*. See Embree (1992).

Inden, R. (1986) 'Orientalist constructions of India', *Modern Asian Studies* 20 (3): 401–46.

Jacobson, D. and S.S. Wadley (1997) *Women in India: Two Perspectives*, 3rd edn, Delhi: Manohar.

Jaffrelot, C. (2004) 'From Indian territory to Hindu Bhoomi: the ethnicization of nation-state mapping in India', in J. Zavos, A. Wyatt and V. Hewitt (eds) *Politics and Cultural Mobilization in India*, New Delhi: Oxford University Press.

Jahan, R. (ed. and tr.) (1988) *Sultana's Dream and Selections from the Secluded Ones*, by Rokeya Sakhawat Hossain, afterword by H. Papanek, New York: Feminist Press at the City University of New York.

Jai Bhim Network (n.d.) 'Ambedkar's 22 vows', Online. Available: http://www.jaibhim.hu/ambedkars-22-vows/ (accessed 30 December 2010).

Jaina Rāmāyaṇa (n.d.) 'Jaina Rāmāyaṇa (Sacitra) Muni Keśarāja kṛta' (by Muni Kesharaja). Online. Available: http://www.idjo.org/Manuscript.asp?id=17&i=2 (accessed 14 April 2010).

Jaiswal, J. (2000) 'Change and continuity in Brahmanical religion with particular reference to "Vaisnava Bhakti"', *Social Scientist* 28 (5/6): 3–23. Online. Available: http://www.jstor.org/stable/3518178.

Jaiswal, S. (2007) 'Review of K.M. Shrimali (2007) *The Age of Iron and the Religious Revolution, c.700–c.350BC*, New Delhi: Tulika Books', *Social Scientist* 35 (9/10): 88–91. Online. Available: http://www.jstor.org/stable/27644242.

Jalal, A. (2000) *Self and Sovereignty: Individual and Community in South Asian Islam since 1850*, London: Routledge.

Jamous, R. (2003) *Kinship and Rituals among the Meo of Northern India*, translated from the French by Nora Scott, New Delhi: Oxford University Press.

Jha, D.N. (2002) *The Myth of the Holy Cow*, London: Verso.

Jha, R. (2010) 'Tough life for Delhi Commonwealth Games workers', 9 September. Online. Available: http://www.bbc.co.uk/news/world-south-asia-11218833 (accessed 15 December 2010).

Johnson, W.J. (tr.) (1994) *The Bhagavad Gita: A New Translation by W.J. Johnson*, Oxford: Oxford University Press.

Johnson, W.J. (2003) 'The "Jina experience": a different approach to Jaina image worship', in O. Qvarnström (ed.) *Jainism and Early Buddhism: Essays in Honour of Padmanabh S. Jaini*, Fremont, CA: Asian Humanities Press.

Jones, K. (1976) *Arya Dharm: Hindu Consciousness in 19th-Century Punjab*, Berkeley: University of California Press.

Jones, K. (1989) *Socio-Religious Reform Movements in British India*, Cambridge: Cambridge University Press.

Jordens, J.T.F. (1978) *Dayānanda Sarasvatī: His Life and Ideas*, Delhi: Oxford University Press.

Juergensmeyer, M. (1982) *Religion as Social Vision*, Berkeley: University of California Press.

Juergensmeyer, M. (1996) *Radhasoami Reality: Logic of a Modern Faith*, new edn, Princeton: Princeton University Press.

Kabir, 'O servant'. See Tagore (1915).

Kabir, 'Saints'. See Hess and Singh (1983: 42–3).

Kakar, S. (1996) 'The construction of a new Hindu identity', in K. Basu and S. Subrahmanyam (eds) *Unravelling the Nation: Sectarian Conflict and India's Secular Identity*, New Delhi: Penguin.

Kapur, A. (1993) 'Deity to crusader: the changing iconography of Ram', in G. Pandey (ed.) *Hindus and Others: The Question of Identity in India Today*, New Delhi: Viking Penguin.

Katju, M. (2003) *Vishva Hindu Parishad and Indian Politics*, Hyderabad: Orient Longman.

Katz, N. (2000) 'The identity of a mystic: the case of Sa'id Sarmad, a Jewish-Yogi-Sufi courtier of the Mughals', *Numen* 47 (2): 142–60.

Katzew, A. (2004) *Casta Painting: Images of Race in Eighteenth-Century Mexico*, New Haven: Yale University Press.

Kauai's Hindu Monastery (2011) Website for the monastery, part of Saiva Siddhanta Church. Online. Available: http://www.himalayanacademy.com/ (accessed 1 January 2011).

Keith, A.B. (1909) *The Aitareya Āraṇyaka*, Oxford: Clarendon Press. Reprint 1969.

Kennedy, C.H. (1992) 'Repugnancy to Islam: who decides? Islam and legal reform in Pakistan', *The International and Comparative Law Quarterly* 41 (4): 769–87.

Ketelaar, J. (1993) 'The reconvening of Babel: Eastern Buddhism and the 1893 World's Parliament of Religions', in E. Ziolkowski (ed.) *A Museum of Faiths: Histories and Legacies of the 1893 World's Parliament of Religions*, Atlanta: Scholars Press.

Khan, A. (2010) 'High Court awards two-thirds of disputed Ayodhya site to Hindu parties, one-third to Sunni Waqf Board'. *The Hindu* 1 October. Online. Available: http://www.hindu.com/2010/10/01/stories/2010100165890100.htm (accessed 23 May 2011).

Khan, S. (1999) *A Glimpse through Purdah: Asian Women – the Myth and the Reality*, Stoke on Trent: Trentham Books.

Khan, Y. (2007) *The Great Partition: The Making of India and Pakistan*, New Haven: Yale University Press.

Killingley, D.K. (1993) *Rammohun Roy in Hindu and Christian Tradition: The Teape Lectures 1990*, Newcastle upon Tyne: Grevatt & Grevatt.

Killingley, D.K. (1998) 'Vivekananda's Western message from the East', in W. Radice (ed.) *Swami Vivekananda and the Modernisation of Hinduism*, Delhi: Oxford University Press.

King, C. (1989) 'Forging a new linguistic identity: the Hindi movement in Banaras, 1868–1914', in S. Freitag (ed.) *Culture and Power in Banaras: Community, Performance and Environment 1800–1980*, Berkeley: University of California Press.

King, R. (1999a) *Indian Philosophy: An Introduction to Hindu and Buddhist Thought*, Edinburgh: Edinburgh University Press.

King, R. (1999b) *Orientalism and Religion: Postcolonial Theory, India and the 'Mystic East'*, London: Routledge.

Kishwar, M. (1997) 'Yes to Sita, no to Ram: the continuing popularity of Sita in India', *Manushi* 98: 20–31.

Kishwar, M. (1998) 'Ways to combat communal violence: some thoughts on International Women's Day', in M. Kishwar (ed.) *Religion at the Service of Nationalism and Other Essays*, Delhi: Oxford University Press. First published 1991.

Kitagawa, J. (ed.) (2002) *The Religious Traditions of Asia: Religion, History and Culture*, London: Routledge.

Klostermaier, K. (1989) *A Survey of Hinduism*, Albany: State University of New York Press.

Klostermaier, K. (2007) *A Survey of Hinduism*, 3rd edn, Albany: State University of New York Press.

Knott, K. (2005) *The Location of Religion: A Spatial Analysis*, London: Equinox.

Kumar, N. (2000) *Lessons from Schools: The History of Education in Banaras*, New Delhi: Sage.

Kumar, R. (1993) *A History of Doing*, London: Verso.

Kurin, R. (1983) 'The structure of blessedness at a Muslim shrine in Pakistan', *Middle Eastern Studies* 19 (3): 312–25.

Laine, J. (1999) 'The *dharma* of Islam and the *dīn* of Hinduism: Hindus and Muslims in the age of Śivājī', *International Journal of Hindu Studies* 3 (3): 299–318.

Lambert-Hurley, S. (2007) *Muslim Women, Reform and Princely Patronage*, London: Routledge.

Lawrence, A. (2011) *The Lover and the Beloved: A Journey into Tantra*, produced, directed and filmed by Andy Lawrence, Blu-ray and DVD, 70 minutes, Asta Films with Granada Centre for Visual Anthropology, University of Manchester. Trailer online. Available: http://www.socialsciences.manchester.ac.uk/disciplines/social-anthropology/visualanthropology/archive/researchfilms/ (accessed 29 December 2010).

Lawrence, B.B. (tr.) (1992) *Nizam ad-din Awliya: Morals for the Heart: Conversations of Shaykh Nizam ad-din Awliya Recorded by Amir Hasan Sijzi*, New York: Paulist Press.

Lelyveld, D. (1978) *Aligarh's First Generation: Muslim Solidarity in British India*, Princeton: Princeton University Press.

Lelyveld, D. (1982) 'Disenchantment at Aligarh: Islam and the realm of the secular in late nineteenth century India', *Die Welt des Islams*, New Series, 22: 85–102.

Lincoln, B. (1999) *Theorizing Myth: Narrative, Ideology, and Scholarship*, Chicago: Chicago University Press.

Lipner, J. (1994) *Hindus: Their Religious Beliefs and Practices*, 1st edn, London: Routledge. Second enlarged edition 2010.

Lipner, J. (tr.) (2005) *Ānandamath, or the Sacred Brotherhood, by Bankimcandra Chatterji*, Oxford: Oxford University Press.

Llewellyn, J. (1993) *The Arya Samaj as a Fundamentalist Movement: A Study in Comparative Fundamentalism*, Delhi: Manohar.

Lochtefeld, J. (1996) 'New wine, old skins: the Sangh Parivar and the transformation of Hinduism', *Religion* 26: 101–18.

Lorenzen, D.N. (1976) 'The life of Śaṅkarācārya', in F.E. Reynolds and D. Capps (eds) *The Biographical Process: Studies in the History and Psychology of Religion*, The Hague: Mouton.

Lorenzen, D.N. (1987) 'The social ideologies of hagiography: Śaṅkara, Tukārām and Kabīr', in M. Israel and N.K. Wagle (eds) *Religion and Society in Maharashtra*, Toronto: Centre for South Asian Studies, University of Toronto.

Lorenzen, D.N. (1996) *Praises to a Formless God: Nirguṇī Texts from North India*, Albany: State University of New York Press.

Lorenzen, D.N. (2005) 'Who invented Hinduism?', in J.E. Llewellyn (ed.) *Defining Hinduism: A Reader*, London: Equinox.

Ludden, D. (2005) 'Introduction: Ayodhya: a window on the world', in D. Ludden (ed.) *Making India Hindu: Religion, Community and the Politics of Democracy in India*, 2nd edn, New Delhi: Oxford University Press.

Lutgendorf, P. (1991) *The Life of a Text: Performing the Rāmcaritmānas of Tulsīdās*, Berkeley: University of California Press.

Lutgendorf, P. (1995) 'All in the (Raghu) family: a video epic in cultural context', in L. Babb and S. Wadley (eds) *Media and the Transformation of Religion in South Asia*, New Delhi: Motilal Banarsidass.

Lutgendorf, P. (n.d.) *Philip's Fil-ums: Notes on Indian Popular Cinema: Jai Santoshi Maa*. Online. Available: http://www.uiowa.edu/~incinema/santoshimaa.html (accessed 21 December 2010).

McAlister, E. (2005) 'Globalization and the religious production of space', Division II Faculty Publications, Paper 39. Online. Available: http://wesscholar.wesleyan.edu/div2facpubs/39 (accessed 12 December 2010).

McDermott, R.F. (2008) 'The Pujas in historical and political controversy: colonial and post-colonial goddesses', *Religions of South Asia* 2 (2): 135–59.

McDermott, R.F. (2011) *Revelry, Rivalry, and Longing for the Goddesses of Bengal: The Fortunes of Hindu Festivals*, New York: Columbia University Press.

McGee, M. (1991) 'Desired fruits: motive and intention in the votive rites of Hindu women', in I.J. Leslie (ed.) *Roles and Rituals for Hindu women*, London: Pinter.

McGilvray, D.B. (1995) Review of Kalpana Ram (1991) *Mukkuvar Women: Gender, Hegemony and Capitalist Transformation in a South Indian Fishing Village*, London: Zed Books, *American Ethnologist* 22 (3): 643–4. Online. Available: http://www.jstor.org/stable/646006.

McKean, L. (1996) *Divine Enterprise: Gurus and the Hindu Nationalist Movement*, Chicago: University of Chicago Press.

McLaine, K. (forthcoming) 'Praying for peace and amity: the Shri Shirdi Sai Heritage Foundation Trust', in J. Zavos, P. Kanungo, D.S. Reddy, M. Warrier and R.B. Williams (eds) *Public Hinduisms*, New Delhi: Sage.

McLean, M. (1998) *Devoted to the Goddess: The Life and Work of Ramprasad*, Albany: State University of New York Press.

McLeod, W.H. (1980) *Early Sikh Tradition: A Study of the Janam-sākhis*, Oxford: Clarendon Press.

McLeod, W.H. (1984) *Textual Sources for the Study of Sikhism*, Manchester: Manchester University Press.

McLeod, W.H. (1987) 'The development of the Sikh panth', in K. Schomer and W.H. McLeod (eds) *The Sants: Studies in a Devotional Tradition of India*, Delhi: Motilal Banasidass.

McLeod, W.H. (1995) *Historical Dictionary of Sikhism*, Lanham, MD: Scarecrow Press.

Madhu Feast (2009) 'Madhu Feast August 2009'. Online. Available: http://www.youtube.com/watch?v=UXQVmIwlX7o (accessed 14 December 2010).

Mandal, D. (1993) *Ayodhya: Archaeology after Demolition*, New Delhi: Orient Longman.

Mani, L. (1998) *Contentious Traditions: The Debate on* Sati *in Colonial India*, Berkeley: University of California Press.

Mason, D. (2000) *Race and Ethnicity in Modern Britain*, 2nd edn, Oxford: Oxford University Press.

Masuzawa, T. (2005) *The Invention of World Religions*, Chicago: University of Chicago Press.

Maududi, S.A.A. (1987) *The Social System of Islam: Purdah and the Status of Women in Islam*, Lahore, Pakistan: Islamic Publications. First edition 1939, *Pardah*, Lahore, Pakistan. Chapter 12 edited by S.M. Ali as 'What is really behind the veil? A tantalizing look . . .'. Online. Available: http://imakuwait.org/downloads.asp (accessed 31 December 2010).

Mayaram, S. (1997) *Resisting Regimes: Myth, Memory and the Shaping of a Muslim Identity*, Delhi, Oxford University Press.

Mayaram, S. (n.d.) 'Beyond ethnicity? being Hindu *and* Muslim in South Asia', revised version of article published in I. Ahmad, H. Reifeld and M. Pernau (eds) (2003) *Lived Islam in South Asia: Adaptation, Accommodation and Conflict*, Delhi: South Asia Press. Online. Available: http://www.csds.in/pdfs_dataunit/ shail_mayaram/livedislam.pdf (accessed 22 September 2010).

Mehta, G. (1990) *Karma Cola*, London: Minerva.

Mendelsohn, O. and M. Vicziany (1998) *The Untouchables: Subordination, Poverty and the State in Modern India*, Cambridge: Cambridge University Press.

Meri, J.W. (2002) *The Cult of Saints among Muslims and Jews in Medieval Syria*, Oxford: Oxford University Press.

Mernissi, F. (1991) *The Veil and the Male Elite: A Feminist Interpretation of Women's Rights in Islam*, translated by Mary Jo Lakeland, New York: Basic Books. French edition first published 1987.

Metcalf, B. (1990) *Perfecting Women: Maulana Ashraf 'Ali Thanawi's Bihishti Zewar: A Partial Translation with Commentary*, Berkeley: University of California Press.

Metcalf, B. (2002) *Islamic Revival in British India: Deoband 1860–1900*, New Delhi: Oxford University Press.

Metcalf, B. (2004) *Islamic Contestations: Essays on Muslims in India and Pakistan*, New Delhi: Oxford University Press.

Mill, J. (1817) *The History of British India*, London: Baldwin, Craddock and Joy.

Miller, B.S. (ed. and tr.) (1977) *Love Song of the Dark Lord*, New York: Columbia University Press (Jayadeva's *Gītā Govinda*).

Miller, D. (1976–7) 'The guru as the centre of sacredness', *Sciences Religieuses/ Studies in Religion* 5/6: 527–33.

Mills, M.A., P.J. Claus and S. Diamond (eds) (2003) *South Asian Folklore: An Encyclopedia*, London: Routledge.

Mills, S.L. (1998) 'The hardware of sanctity: anthropomorphic objects in Bangladeshi Sufism', in P. Werbner and H. Basu (eds) *Embodying Charisma: Modernity, Locality and the Performance of Emotion in Sufi Cults*, London: Routledge.

Minault, G. (1998) *Secluded Scholars: Women's Education and Muslim Social Reform in Colonial India*, Oxford: Oxford University Press.

Mirza, S.T. (2010) 'Darbars bombed by Muslims, revered by Hindus', *Dawn*, 8 July. Online. Available: http://dawnnews.tv/wps/wcm/connect/dawn-content-library/ dawn/the-newspaper/local/lahore/darbars-bombed-by-muslims,-revered-by-hin- dus-870 (accessed 10 August 2010).

Mitchell, T. (1988) *Colonising Egypt*, Cambridge: Cambridge University Press.

Mittal, S. and G. Thursby (eds) (2006) *Religions of South Asia: An Introduction*, London: Routledge.

Mullatti, L. (1989) *The Bhakti Movement and the Status of Women: A Case Study of Vīraśaivism*, New Delhi: Abhinav Publications.

Nair, J. (1996) *Women and Law in Colonial India: A Social History*, New Delhi: Kali for Women.

Nammalvar, *Temple Tiruvāymoḻi* 10.9.11, translated by V. Narayanan, A.K. Ramanujan, F. Clooney and J. Carman. See Narayanan (1994).

Narayana Rao, V. (1991) 'A *Rāmāyaṇa* of their own: women's oral tradition in Telugu', in P. Richman (ed.) *Many Rāmāyaṇas: The Diversity of a Narrative Tradition in South Asia*, Berkeley: University of California Press.

Narayanan, V. (1994) *The Vernacular Veda: Revelation, Recitation and Ritual*, Columbia, SC: Carolina University Press.

Narayanan, V. (1996) 'Arcāvatāra: on Earth as He is in Heaven', in J.P. Waghorne and N. Cutler (eds) *Gods of Flesh, Gods of Stone: The Embodiment of Divinity in India*, New York: Columbia University Press.

Narayanan, V. (2001) 'The Ramayana and its Muslim interpreters', in P. Richman (2001) *Questioning Ramayanas: a South Asian Tradition*, Berkeley: University of California Press.

Narayanan, V. (2002) 'Casting light on the sounds of the Tamil Veda: Tirukkōnēri Dāsyai's "Garland of Words"', in L.L. Patton (ed.) *Jewels of Authority: Women and Textual Tradition in Hindu India*, Oxford: Oxford University Press.

Nilsson, U. (2001) '"Grinding millet but singing of Sita": power and domination in Awadhi and Bhojpui women's songs', in P. Richman (2001) *Questioning Ramayanas: a South Asian Tradition*, Berkeley: University of California Press.

Nirmal, A. (1994) 'Towards a Christian Dalit theology', in R. Sugirtharajah (ed.) *Frontiers in Asian Christian Theology: Emerging Trends*, New York: Orbis.

Nurullah, S. and J.P. Naik (1951) *A History of Education in India (during the British Period)*, Bombay: Macmillan.

Oberoi, H. (1990) 'From ritual to counter ritual: rethinking the Hindu-Sikh question, 1884–1915', in J. O'Connell, W. Oxtoby and M. Israel (eds) *Sikh History and Religion in the Twentieth Century*, Toronto: University of Toronto Press.

Oberoi, H. (1994) *Construction of Religious Boundaries: Culture, Identity and Diversity in the Sikh Tradition*, New Delhi: Oxford University Press.

Oddie, G. (ed.) (1991) *Religion in South Asia: Religious Conversion and Revival Movements in Medieval and Modern Times*, 2nd edn, New Delhi: Manohar.

Oddie, G. (2006) *Imagined Hinduisms: British Protestant Missionary Constructions of Hinduism, 1793–1900*, New Delhi: Sage.

O'Hanlon, R. (1985) *Caste, Conflict and Ideology: Mahatma Jotirao Phule and Low-caste Protest in Nineteenth Century Western India*, Cambridge: Cambridge University Press.

O'Hanlon, R. (tr. and intro.) (1994) *A Comparison between Women and Men: Tarabai Shinde and the Critique of Gender Relations in Colonial India*, Delhi: Oxford University Press.

Okita, K. (forthcoming) 'Who are the Mādhvas? A controversy over the public representation of the Mādhva *sampradāya*', in J. Zavos, P. Kanungo, D.S. Reddy, M. Warrier and R.B. Williams (eds) *Public Hinduisms*, New Delhi: Sage.

Olivelle, P. (1995) Review of J. Bronkhorst (1993) *The Two Sources of Indian Asceticism*, Bern: Peter Lang, in *Journal of the American Oriental Society* 115 (1): 162–4. Online. Available: http://www.jstor.org/stable/605355.

Olivelle, P. (tr.) (1996) *Upaniṣads Translated from the Original Sanskrit*, The World's Classics, Oxford: Oxford University Press.

Olivelle, P. (ed. and tr.) (2004) *Manu's Code of Law: A Critical Edition and Translation of the* Mānava-Dharmaśāstra, with the editorial assistance of Suman Olivelle, South Asia Research, New York: Oxford University Press.

Omvedt, G. (1995) *Dalit Visions*, Delhi: Orient Longman.

Oomen, G. (2010) 'The emerging Dalit theology: a historical appraisal', 27 June. Online. Available: http://roundtableindia.co.in/news/opinion/2120-the-emerging-dalit-theology-a-historical-appraisal.html (accessed 20 December 2010).

Openshaw, J. (2002) *Seeking Bāuls of Bengal*, Cambridge: Cambridge University Press.

Osella, F. and C. Osella (2003) ' "Ayyappan Saranam": masculinity and the Sabarimala pilgrimage in Kerala', *Journal of the Royal Anthropological Institute (N.S.)* 9: 729–53. Online. Available: http://eprints.soas.ac.uk/85/1/jrai6.pdf (accessed 9 August 2010).

Padoux, A. (1986) 'Tantrism', in M. Eliade (ed.) *Encyclopedia of Religions*, vol. 14, New York: Macmillan.

Page, J. (2007) 'Fury as presidential hopeful urges women to throw off "veil of invader" ', *The Times*, 20 June. Online. Available: http://www.timesonline.co.uk/tol/news/world/asia/article1957758.ece (accessed 3 January 2011).

Pandey, G. (1990) *The Construction of Communalism in Colonial India*, New Delhi: Oxford University Press.

Pandey, G. (2001) *Remembering Partition*, Cambridge: Cambridge University Press.

Panikkar, K.N. (1990) 'A historical overview', in S. Gopal (ed.) *Anatomy of a Confrontation: Ayodhya and the Rise of Communal Politics in India*, London: Zed.

Patton, L.L. (2009) 'Notes on women and Vedic learning in the 21st century', paper presented at the Sanskrit Tradition in the Modern World Symposium, University of Manchester, May 2009.

Pauwels, H. (2008) *The Goddess as Role Model: Sītā and Rādhā in Scripture and on Screen*, Oxford: Oxford University Press.

Penningtion, B. (2005) *Was Hinduism Invented? Britons, Indians and the Colonial Construction of Religion*, New York: Oxford University Press.

Perera, A. (2009) 'How the Virgin Mary survived Sri Lanka's civil war', *Time Magazine*, 17 August. Online. Available: http://www.time.com/time/world/article/0,8599,19168461,00.html (accessed 14 December 2010).

Philips, C.H. (1962) *The Evolution of India and Pakistan 1858–1947: Select Documents*, London: Oxford University Press.

Pinch, W.R. (2006) *Warrior Ascetics and Indian Empires*, Cambridge: Cambridge University Press.

Pinney, C. (2004) *'Photos of the Gods': The Printed Image and Political Struggle in India*, London: Reaktion.

Pocock, D. (1972) *Kanbi and Patidar: A Study of the Patidar Community of Gujarat*, Oxford: Clarendon Press.

Poitevin, G. and H. Rairkar (1993) *Indian Peasant Women Speak Up*, London: Sangam Books.

Pollock, S. (1996) 'The Sanskrit Cosmopolis, 300–1300 CE: transculturation, vernacularization, and the question of ideology', in J. Houben (ed.) *Ideology and Status of Sanskrit: Contributions to the History of the Sanskrit Language*, Leiden: E.J. Brill.

Poornaprajna Vidyapeetha (2006) 'ISKCON and Tattvavāda: some essential clarifications', Position paper on ISKCON, page created 2001, revised 2006. Online. Available: http://www.dvaita.org/shaastra/iskcon.shtml (accessed 29 December 2010).

Purushothama Naidu, B.R. (1965) *Acharya Hridayam with the Tamiḻākkam of the Commentary of Maṇavāla Māmunigaḷ*, Madras: Madras University.

Radha Soami Satsang Beas (2010) 'Radha Soami Satsang Beas: science of the soul'. Online. Available: http://www.rssb.org/ (accessed 30 December 2010).

Raheja, G. (1988) *The Poison in the Gift*, Chicago: University of Chicago Press.

Rai, L. (1915) *The Arya Samaj: An Account of its Origin, Doctrines, and Activities, with a Biographical Sketch of its Founder*, London: Longmans, Green and Co.

Rainbow Skills (n.d.) 'Kudal-Sangam'. Online. Available: http://www.rainbowskill. com/tour-to-india/karnataka-tour/kudal-sangam.php (accessed 26 January 2010).

Rajalakshmi, T.K. (2003) 'Ayodhya: a picture of diversity', *Frontline* 20 (22). Online. Available: http://www.frontlineonnet.com/fl2022/stories/20031107000207000. htm (accessed 14 December 2010).

Ram, K. (1991) *Mukkuvar Women: Gender, Hegemony and Capitalist Transformation in a South Indian Fishing Village*, London: Zed Books.

Ramanujan, A.K. (tr.) (1973) *Speaking of Śiva*, Harmondsworth: Penguin.

Ramanujan, A.K. (tr.) (1981) *Hymns for the Drowning: Poems for Viṣṇu by Nammālvār*, Princeton: Princeton University Press.

Ramanujan, A.K. (1991) 'Three Hundred *Rāmāyaṇas*: five examples and three thoughts on translation', in P. Richman (ed.) *Many Rāmāyaṇas: The Diversity of a Narrative Tradition in South Asia*, Berkeley: University of California Press.

Rāmāyaṇa of Vālmīki, vol. I: *Bālakāṇḍa*. See Goldman (1984).

Rammohun Roy. See Ghose and Bose (1906).

Rammohun Roy, 'A dialogue between a missionary and three Chinese converts'. See Ghose (1982).

Ramnad (c.1897) 'Address', in The Editor (1960) *The Complete Works of Swami Vivekananda*, vol. III, 8th enlarged edn, Calcutta: Advaita Ashrama.

Ramprasad, 'O mind'. See McLean (1998).

Randip-Singh (2007) 'Re: last name HEER', Jattworld.com. 18 October. Online. Available: http://www.jattworld.com/jattportal/modules/newbb/viewtopic.php? viewmode=compact&order=DESC&topic_id=5501&forum=14 (accessed 3 December 2010).

Raychaudhuri, T. (1998) 'Swami Vivekananda's construction of Hinduism', in W. Radice (ed.) *Swami Vivekananda and the Modernisation of Hinduism*, Delhi: Oxford University Press.

Richman, P. (ed.) (1991a) *Many Rāmāyaṇas: The Diversity of a Narrative Tradition in South Asia*, Berkeley: University of California Press.

Richman, P. (1991b) 'E.V. Ramasami's reading of the *Rāmāyaṇa*', in P. Richman (ed.) *Many Rāmāyaṇas: The Diversity of a Narrative Tradition in South Asia*, Berkeley: University of California Press.

Richman, P. (ed.) (2001) *Questioning Ramayanas: A South Asian Tradition*, Berkeley: University of California Press.

Rig Veda X.90.12. See Doniger (1981).

Rizvi, S.A.A. (1978–83) *A History of Sufism in India*, 2 vols, New Delhi: Munshiram Manoharlal.

Rizvi, S.A.A. (1980) *Shāh Walī-Allāh and His Times: A Study of Eighteenth Century Islam, Politics and Society in India*, Canberra: Ma'rifat Publishing House.

Roebuck, V. (ed. and tr.) (2003) *The Upaniṣads*, revised edn, London: Penguin.

Rokeya Sakhawat Hossain (1905) *Sultana's Dream*. See Jahan (1988).

Rosario, S. and G. Samuel (2010) 'Gender, religious change and sustainability in Bangladesh', *Women's Studies International Forum* 33 (4): 354–64.

Ruegg, D.S. (1999) 'A new publication on the date and historiography of the Buddha's decease ("nirvāṇa"): a review article', *Bulletin of the School of Oriental and African Studies* 62 (1): 82–7. Online. Available: http://www.jstor.org/stable/3107390.

Sabarimala Sree Dharmasastha Temple (2010) 'Mandala Pooja'. Online. Available: http://www.sabarimala.kerala.gov.in> > Videos > Mandala Pooja, 27.12.2010 (accessed 29 December 2010).

Sachau, E.C. (ed. and tr.) (1910) *Alberuni's India: An Account of the Religion, Philosophy, Literature, Geography, Chronology, Astronomy, Customs, Laws and Astrology of India about A.D. 1030*, vol. 1, London: Kegan Paul, Trench, Trübner. Reprinted 2000, London: Routledge.

Sagar, R. (producer) (1987–8) *Ramayan* (TV series), Doordarshan, India.

Sai Organization Sites (n.d.) Online. Available: http://www.sathyasai.org/organize/content.htm (accessed 30 December 2010).

Said, E. (1978) *Orientalism*, London: Routledge & Kegan Paul.

Sanford, A.W. (2002) 'Negotiating for Śrīnāthajī, Daūjī, and Jakhaiyā: narrative as arbiter of contested sites in Vraja', *International Journal of Hindu Studies* 6 (1): 19–45. Online. Available: http://www.jstor.org/stable/20106784.

Sanyal, U. (2010) *Devotional Islam and Politics in British India: Ahmad Riza Khan Barelwi and his Movement, 1870–1920*, new edition with new introduction, New Delhi: Yoda Press.

Sayyid Ahmad Khan, 'Letter to Mawlawi Tasadduq'. See Hay (1988).

Schomer, K. (1987) 'Introduction: the Sant tradition in perspective', in K. Schomer and W.H. McLeod (eds) *The Sants: Studies in a Devotional Tradition of India*, Delhi: Motilal Banasidass.

Schouten, J.P. (1991) *Revolution of the Mystics: On the Social Aspects of Vīraśaivism*, Kampen, the Netherlands: Kok Pharos.

Sébastia, B. (2002) 'Māriyamman – Mariyamman: pratiques catholiques et représentation de la Vierge à Velankanni (Tamil Nadu)'. Online. Available: http://hal.archives-ouvertes.fr/docs/00/27/82/91/PDF/PPSmariyamman.pdf (accessed 26 July 2010). English version (2002) 'Māriyamman – Mariyamman, Catholic practises: an image of Virgin in Velankanni (Tamil Nadu)', *Pondy Papers in Social Sciences* 27.

Searle-Chatterjee, M. (1993) 'Religious division and the mythology of the past', in B.R. Hertel and C.A Humes (eds) *Living Banaras*, Albany: State University of New York Press.

Shaffer, J.G. and D.A. Lichtenstein (2005) 'South Asian archaeology and the myth of Indo-Aryna invasions', in Bryant, E. and L.L. Patton (eds) (2005) *The Indo-Aryan Controversy: Evidence and Inference in Indian History*, London: Routledge.

Sharma, H.D. (2002) *Raja Rammohun Roy: The Renaissance Man*, New Delhi: Rupa.

Sharma, U. (1999) *Caste*, Buckingham: Open University Press.

Sharma, U. and M. Searle-Chatterjee (eds) (1994) *Conceptualising Caste: Post-Dumontian Approaches*, Oxford: Blackwell.

Shraddhananda (1926) *Hindu Sangathan – Saviour of the Dying Race*, Delhi: Arjun Press.

Shree Shree Anandamayee Sangha (2008) 'Official website of the Sangha', established 2008. Online. Available: http://shreeshreeanandamayeesangha.in/ (accessed 29 December 2010).

Shyam Lal (1952) *Shabdāmrit Dhārā*, Lashkar, Gwalior: Shabd Pratap Satsang, vol. 2, pp. 132–3. See Gold (1987).

Sikand, Y. (2002) *Sacred Spaces: Exploring Traditions of Shared Faith in India*, New Delhi: Penguin.

Smart, N. (1969) *The Religious Experience of Mankind*, London: Fontana.

Smart, N. (1998) *World's Religions*, 2nd edn, Cambridge: Cambridge University Press.

Smith, J.Z. (1982) 'Sacred persistence: toward a redescription of canon', in J.Z. Smith (ed.) *Imagining Religion from Babylon to Jonestown*, Chicago: University of Chicago Press.

SOED (1993) *New Shorter Oxford English Dictionary*, Oxford: Clarendon Press.

Spivak, G. (1988) 'Can the subaltern speak?', in C. Nelson and L. Grossberg (eds) *Marxism and the Interpretation of Culture*, Basingstoke: Macmillan.

Sreenivasan, R. (2007) *The Many Lives of a Rajput Queen: Heroic Pasts in India c.1500–1900*, Seattle: University of Washington Press.

Sri Guru Granth Sahib (n.d.) Khalsa Consensus English translation. Online. Available: http://www.sikhs.org/english/frame.html (accessed 30 December 2010).

Srivastava, P. (2010) 'VHP makes a new offer for Babri', *India Today*, 23 September. Online. Available: http://indiatoday.intoday.in/site/Story/113652/LATEST%20HEADLINES/vhp-makes-a-new-offer-for-babri.html (accessed 14 December 2010).

Stewart, T. (2001) 'In search of equivalence: conceiving Muslim–Hindu encounter through translation theory', *History of Religions* 40 (3): 260–87.

Stewart, T. and C.W Ernst (2003) 'Syncretism', in M. Mills, P. Claus and S. Diamond (eds) *South Asian Folklore: An Encyclopedia*, London: Routledge.

Sunder Rajan, R. (2000) 'Real and imagined goddesses: a debate', in A. Hiltebeitel and K.M. Erndl (eds) *Is the Goddess a Feminist? The Politics of South Asian Goddesses*, Sheffield: Sheffield Academic Press.

Suthren Hirst, J. (1997) *Sita's Story*, Calgary: Bayeux Arts.

Suthren Hirst, J. (1998) 'Myth and history', in P. Bowen (ed.) *Themes and Issues in Hinduism*, London: Cassell.

Suthren Hirst, J. (2005) *Śaṃkara's Advaita Vedānta: A Way of Teaching*, London: RoutledgeCurzon.

Suthren Hirst, J. (2008) 'Who are the Others? Three moments in Sanskrit-based practice', in N. Green and M. Searle-Chatterjee (eds) *Religion, Language and Power*, London: Routledge.

Suthren Hirst, J. and J. Zavos (2005) 'Riding a tiger? South Asia and the problem of "religion"', *Contemporary South Asia* 14 (1): 3–20.

Swami Vivekananda (1896a) 'My master', in The Editor (1962) *The Complete Works of Swami Vivekananda*, vol. IV, 8th edn, Calcutta: Advaita Ashrama. Amalgamation of two lectures given in New York and London, 1896.

Swami Vivekananda (1896b) 'The absolute and manifestation', in The Editor (1963) *The Complete Works of Swami Vivekananda*, vol. II, 10th enlarged edn, Calcutta: Advaita Ashrama.

Sweetman, W. (2003a) *Mapping Hinduism: 'Hinduism' and the study of Indian religions 1600–1776*, Neue Hallesche Berichte 4, Halle: Verlag der Franckeschen Stiftungen zu Halle.

Sweetman, W. (2003b) ' "Hinduism" and the history of "religion": Protestant presuppositions in the critique of the concept of Hinduism', *Method & Theory in the Study of Religion* 15 (4): 329–53.

Tagore, R. (tr.) (1915) *Songs of Kabîr*, with an introduction by Evelyn Underhill, New York: Macmillan. Online. Available: http://www.sacred-texts.com/hin/sok/index.htm (accessed 3 April 2009).

Tagore, R. (2005) *The Home and the World*, London: Penguin.

Tarabai Shinde. See O'Hanlon (1994).

Tarlo, E. (2007) 'Hijab in London: metamorphosis, resonance and effects', *Journal of Material Culture* 12 (2): 131–56.

Tarlo, E. (2010) *Visibly Muslim: Fashion, Politics, Faith*, Oxford: Berg.

Thapar, R. (1989) 'Epic and history: tradition, dissent and politics in India', *Past & Present* 125: 3–26. Online. Available: http://www.jstor.org/stable/650859.

Thapar, R. (1990) 'A historical perspective on the story of Rama', in Sarvepalli Gopal (ed.) *Anatomy of a Confrontation: Ayodhya and the Rise of Communal Politics in India*, Delhi: Penguin India.

Thapar, R. (2002) *Early India: From the Origins to AD 1300*, Berkeley: University of California Press.

Thapar, R. (2004) *Somanatha: The Many Voices of a History*, Delhi: Penguin India.

Tharu, S. (1989) 'Tracing Savitri's pedigree: Victorian racism and the image of women in Indo-Anglian literature', in K. Sangari and S. Vaid (eds) *Recasting Women: Essays in Colonial History*, New Delhi: Kali for Women.

The Holiday Spot (n.d.) 'National Song'. Online. Available: http://www.theholidayspot.com/indian_independence_day/national_song.htm (accessed 29 January 2010).

The Qur'an: A Modern English Version (1997) Translated by Majid Fakhry, Reading: Garnet Publishing Ltd.

Times Educational Supplement (2006) 'Hindus angry at distortion of faith', 5 May. Online. Available: http://www.tes.co.uk/article.aspx?storycode=2230834 (accessed 20 December 2010).

Trimingham, J.S. (1971) *The Sufi Orders in Islam*, Oxford: Clarendon Press.

Tuladhar-Douglas, W. (2005) 'On why it is good to have many names: the many identities of a Nepalese god', *Contemporary South Asia*, special issue on 'Teaching across South Asian Religious Traditions', 14 (1): 55–74.

Tull, H.W. (1991) 'F. Max Müller and A.B. Keith: "Twaddle", the "stupid myth", and the disease of Indology', *Numen* 30 (1): 27–58. Online. Available: http://www.jstor.org/stable/3270003.

Tully, M. (1992) *No Full Stops in India*, London: Penguin.

Tulsidas, *Śrī Rāmacaritamānasa*. See Gita Press (1968).

Union of Catholic Asian News (2009) 'More people flock to annual Saint Anthony celebration'. Online. Available: http://www.ucanews.com/story-archive/?post_name=/2009/02/12/more-people-flock-to-annual-saint-anthony-celebration&post_id=49914 (accessed 20 July 2010).

Usborne, C.F. (tr.) (1973) *The Adventures of Hir and Ranjha: Recounted by Waris Shah and Translated into English by Charles Frederick Usborne*, London: Owen. Also various previous prints.

US Department of State (2010) 'Annual Report to Congress on International Religious Freedom'. Online. Available: http://www.state.gov/g/drl/irf/rpt (accessed 3 January 2011).

Vachani, N. (1990) *Eyes of Stone*, 16mm 91-minute documentary, Mewari and Hindi, with English subtitles, A FilmSixteen production for Doordarshan India. Synopsis online. Available: http://www.nilitavachani.com/> Eyes of Stone > Synopsis (accessed 29 December 2010).

van Baaren, Th. P. (1984) 'The flexibility of myth', in A. Dundes (ed.) *Sacred Narrative: Readings in the Theory of Myth*, Berkeley: University of California Press.

van Buitenen, J.A.B. (ed. and tr.) (1973) *The Mahābhārata, Book 1, The Book of the Beginning*, Chicago: Chicago University Press.

van der Veer, P. (1987) ' "God must be liberated!" A Hindu liberation movement in Ayodhya', *Modern Asian Studies* 21 (2): 283–301.

van der Veer, P. (1989) *Gods on Earth; The Management of Religious Experience and Identity in a North Indian Pilgrimage Centre*, New Delhi: Oxford University Press.

van der Veer, P. (1992a) 'Playing or praying: a Sufi saint's day in Surat', *Journal of Asian Studies* 51 (3): 545–64.

van der Veer, P. (1992b) 'Ayodhya and Somnath: eternal shrines, contested histories', *Social Research* 59 (1): 85–109.

van der Veer, P. (1994) *Religious Nationalism: Hindus and Muslims in India*, Berkeley: University of California Press.

van der Veer, P. (2001) *Imperial Encounters: Religion and Modernity in India and Britain*, Princeton: Princeton University Press.

Varadarajan, M. (2010) 'Webpage for the Sri Vaishnava tradition of Ramanuja, Alvars, and rishis of the Upanishads and Vedas'. Available: http://www.ramanuja. org (accessed 26 January 2010) (later revised to 'Sri Vaishnava Home Page', accessed 23 December 2010).

Vaudeville, C. (1987) 'The Shaiva-Vaishnava synthesis in Maharashtrian Santism', in K. Schomer and W.H. McLeod (eds) *The Sants: Studies in a Devotional Tradition of India*, Delhi: Motilal Banarsidass.

Vedanta Center of Atlanta (n.d.) 'Swami Vivekananda at the Parliament of Religions'. Online. Available: http://www.vedanta-atlanta.org/articles/vivekananda/parliament.html (accessed 21 December 2010).

Vengara, S. (2010) Theyyam: an exclusive web scenario of Theyyam. Online. Available: http://www.vengara.com/theyyam/index.html (accessed 14 February 2011).

Viswanathan, G. (2003) 'Colonialism and the construction of Hinduism', in G. Flood (ed.) *Blackwell Companion to Hinduism*, Oxford: Blackwell.

Vivekananda. See Swami Vivekananda.

von Stietencron, H. (1989) 'Hinduism: on the proper use of a deceptive term', in G. Sontheimer and H. Kulke (eds) *Hinduism Reconsidered*, New Delhi: Manohar.

von Stietencron, H. (1995) 'Religious configurations in pre-modern India and the modern concept of Hinduism', in V. Dalmia and H. von Stietencron (eds) *Representing Hinduism: The Construction of Religious Traditions and National Identity*, New Delhi: Sage.

Walker, B. (1968) 'Historiography', in *Hindu World: An Encyclopedic Survey of Hinduism*, London: Allan and Unwin.

Warner, M. (1976) *Alone of All Her Sex: The Myth and Cult of the Virgin Mary*, London: Weidenfeld & Nicholson.

Warrier, M. (2003a) 'Guru choice and spiritual seeking in contemporary India', *International Journal of Hindu Studies* 7 (1/3): 31–54. Online. Available: http://www.jstor.org/stable/20106847.

Warrier, M. (2003b) 'Processes of secularization in contemporary India: guru faith in the Mata Amritanandamayi Mission', *Modern Asian Studies* 3: 213–53. Online. Available: http://www.jstor.org/stable/3876556.

Warrier, M. (2005) *Hindu Selves in a Modern World: Guru Faith in the Mata Amritanandamayi Mission*, London: RoutledgeCurzon.

Watson, H. (1994) 'Women and the veil: personal responses to global processes', in A. Ahmed and H. Donnan (eds) *Islam, Globalization and Postmodernity*, London: Routledge.

Werbner, P. (2010) 'Beyond division: women, pilgrimage and nation-building in South Asian Sufism', *Women's Studies International Forum* 33 (4): 374–82.

Whaling, F. (1980) *The Rise of the Religious Significance of Rāma*, Delhi: Motilal Banarsidass.

White, D.G. (2000) 'Introduction: Tantra in practice: mapping a tradition', in D.G. White (ed.) *Tantra in Practice*, Princeton: Princeton University Press.

Williams, R.G. (1996) 'The Holy Man as the abode of God in the Swaminarayan religion', in J.P. Waghorne and N. Cutler (eds) *Gods of Flesh, Gods of Stone: The Embodiment of Divinity in India*, New York: Columbia University Press.

World Bank (2011) *World Development Indicators 2011*, Washington: World Bank.

Zavos, J. (1999) 'The Arya Samaj and the antecedents of Hindu nationalism: an analysis with reference to the concept of reform in nineteenth century Hinduism', *International Journal of Hindu Studies* 3 (1): 57–81.

Zavos, J. (2000) *Emergence of Hindu Nationalism in India*, New Delhi: Oxford University Press.

Zavos, J. (2008) 'Bin Laden is one of us! Representations of religious identity at the Parliament of the World's Religions', *Culture and Religion* 9 (1): 45–61.

Zelliot, E. (1996) *From Untouchable to Dalit: Essays on the Ambedkar Movement*, New Delhi: Manohar.

Index

For simplicity, diacritical marks have not been used in the index (see Note on orthography, p. xv)